Imaging Russia 2000

Imaging Russia 2000
Film and Facts

Anna Lawton

 New Academia Publishing
Washington, DC

Copyright © 2004 by Anna Lawton
New Academia Publishing, 2004

All rights reserved. No part of this book may be reproduced or transmitted in any form or by any means, electronic or mechanical, including photocopying, recording, or by any information storage and retrieval system.

Printed in the United States of America

Library of Congress Control Number: 2004106654
ISBN 0-9744934-2-2 hardcover
ISBN 0-9744934-3-0 paperback

New Academia Publishing
P.O. Box 27420, Washington, DC 20038-7420
www.newacademia.com - info@newacademia.com

To my Russian friends

Contents

List of Illustrations   viii
List of Abbreviations and Acronyms   x

Introduction   1

1   **A Panoramic: Left to Right**   11

2   **History in the Making and on Screen**   39

3   **New Babylon**   101

4   **Faraway in Space and Time**   169

5   **Laughter through Tears**   241

Notes   293
Bibliography   324
Filmography   331
Index   334

Illustrations

1	Around the White House, August 1991	40
2	Around the White House, August 1991	42
3	Around the White House, August 1991	44
4	*Tale of the Unextinguished Moon* (1990) directed by Evgeny Tsymbal	58
5	*Gray Wolves* (1993) directed by Igor Gostev	63
6	Black stain, October 1993	72
7	*The Thief* (1997) directed by Pavel Chukhrai	80
8	*The Thief* (1997) directed by Pavel Chukhrai	81
9	*Khrustalyov, my car!* (1998) directed by Alexei Gherman	84
10	*Captain's Daughter* (1999) directed by Alexander Proshkin	87
11	*Captain's Daughter* (1999) directed by Alexander Proshkin	89
12	*The Barber of Siberia* (1998) directed by Nikita Mikhalkov	93
13	*The Romanovs: The Crowned Family* (2001) directed by Gleb Panfilov	97
14	*Moscow* (1999) directed by Alexander Zeldovich	113
15	*Moscow* (1999) directed by Alexander Zeldovich	115
16	*Limita* (1994) directed by Denis Evstigneev	119
17	*Luna Park* (1992) directed by Pavel Lungin	126
18	*Brother* (1997) directed by Alexei Balabanov	129
19	*Brother 2* (2000) directed by Alexei Balabanov	131
20	*The Voroshilov Marksman* (1999) directed by Stanislav Govorukhin	134
21	*Love* (1992) directed by Valery Todorovsky	149
22	*Non-love* (1992) directed by Valery Rubinchik	151
23	*Time of the Dancer* (1997), Abdrashitov (director) and Mindadze (screenwriter)	157
24	*Retro Triangle* (1998) directed by Pyotr Todorovsky	161

25	*The Muslim* (1995) directed by Vladimir Khotinenko	182
26	*American Daughter* (1995) directed by Karen Shakhnazarov	193
27	*Land of the Deaf* (1997) directed by Valery Todorovsky	195
28	*Humiliated and Insulted* (1991) directed by Andrei Eshpai	203
29	*Humiliated and Insulted* (1991) directed by Andrei Eshpai	204
30	*Moloch* (1999) directed by Alexander Sokurov	207
31	*Passions* (1994) directed by Kira Muratova	211
32	*Children of the Iron Gods* (1993) directed by Tomasz Tot	218
33	*Moscow Parade* (1992) directed by Ivan Dykhovichny	221
34	*Hammer and Sickle* (1994) directed by Sergei Livnev	223
35	*Prisoner of the Mountains* (1996) directed by Sergei Bodrov, Sr.	229
36	*Checkpoint* (1998) directed by Alexander Rogozhkin	237
37	*Old Nags* (1999) directed by Eldar Ryazanov	251
38	*Dreams of an Idiot* (1993) directed by Vasily Pichul	256
39	*Window on Paris* (1994) directed by Yuri Mamin	270
40	Red Square was the main marketplace from the Middle Ages until the GUM was completed in 1893	272
41	*Drum Roll* (1993) directed by Sergei Ovcharov	286

Cover: *Brother 2* (Balabanov, 2000)

Illustrations 1, 2, 3, 6: Anna Lawton. Illustration 4, courtesy of Evgeny Tsymbal. Illustration 7, courtesy of Stratosphere Entertainment. Illustration 22, courtesy of Valery Rubinchik. Illustrations 28, 29 courtesy of Andrei Eshpai. Illustration 35, courtesy of Sergei Bodrov, Sr. Illustration 40, courtesy of Helen Yakobson. All other illustrations are from the archive of the journal *Film Art*, reproduced with permission.

Abbreviations and Acronyms

IK	*Iskusstvo kino*
LG	*Literaturnaia gazeta*
TMG	*Moscow Guardian*
TMT	*Moscow Times*
NYT	*New York Times*
NG	*Nezavisimaia gazeta*
SE	*Sovetskii ekran*
VDNKh	Exhibition of Economic Achievements
VGIK	All-Union State Institute of Cinema
VNIIK	All-Union Scientific Research Institute of Film Art
WP	*Washington Post*

Introduction

The background

Early morning. December. The taxicab was rushing toward Sheremyetevo airport. I was leaving Moscow after a five-year stay and was not scheduled to come back for a while. The old Volga—still the staple model among Moscow cabs—was being passed by shiny Mercedes, Volvos, and BMWs, braving the inclement weather at a sustained pace. Large billboards appeared at equal intervals through the twirling snowflakes: Hyundai, Marlboro, Sony. . . . I was leaving behind a city greatly transformed, a world that did not exist when I landed there in early 1991.

I had been to the Soviet Union before—many times over a span of more than ten years. As a scholar sponsored by academic institutions, I had always had a precise project, a declared purpose, a mentor/facilitator, and designated housing in university hotels. Those U.S.-Soviet exchange channels made possible my previous publications, and I gave them full credit in the prefaces to my books.

But this time it was different. I went on my own. At the twilight of the Gorbachev years, as the Soviet Union was loosening up restrictions on private enterprises and individual ventures, I took up residence in Moscow. I had press credentials, which allowed me to move with considerable freedom over the territory of Russia and opened up many doors. Soon, I started working at the Press and Culture section of the American Embassy, as the Deputy Director of Public Information and Media Outreach and the editor of a magazine publicizing U.S. technical assistance to the new Russia. At the same time, I kept pursuing scholarly activities, recording the transformation of the film industry

2 Introduction

in the market economy and analyzing structural changes and new productions. My ongoing research appeared as a weekly column on Russian cinema in Moscow's largest English-language newspaper, *The Moscow Times*, and has now been incorporated in this book.

The collapse of the Soviet Union had the effect of making Russia even more of a riddle to the foreign observer than it had ever been. The Western powers and the political pundits who expected Russia to become a democracy overnight were disappointed. The general assumption was that once the Soviet institutions were removed, the democratic infrastructure would emerge naturally, sustained at the grassroots and sanctioned at the top—with financial help from abroad. Those expectations were based on the understanding of capitalist democracy as it applies to our Western civilization—the civilization that has its cultural roots in the Renaissance, the foundation of its political thought in the Age of Enlightenment, and the motor of its economic power in the "American dream." But for the Russians, capitalist democracy is not a "natural" condition. In its one thousand years of history, Russia has never been a democratic state. Rather, the population has been subjected to an uninterrupted series of authoritarian governments, from the yoke of Mongol khans to the rule of autocratic tsars to the dictatorship of Bolshevik commissars. Russia's borders were long sealed to the influence of the great cultural movements that in successive waves propelled Europe into the modern age.

But what about Russian ballet? The neo-classical architecture of St. Petersburg? Pushkin's exquisite iambic tetrameters? Malevich's conceptual art? True, these features are linked to European culture. They are the later result of the forced Europeanization the Russians underwent at the hands of Peter the Great in the eighteenth century. This was a most bizarre despotic act, the like of which has few parallels in the history of any other country. To achieve the emperor's goal—to catch up with Europe—the Russians were ordered to change their way of life and conceal their uncouth demeanor under a slick veneer of European civilization. This decree covered mainly fashion and etiquette. The idea of *"liberté-égalité-fraternité,"* which shook the Western world toward the end of the century, never figured in the imperial plan. It was actually banned by Peter's successors, and its sympathizers were sent to penal colonies in Siberia. Eventually, the European cultural implant grew and flourished, but never wholly supplanted Muscovy's native roots.[1]

This created a dilemma for generations of Russians, who saw themselves as having a dual nature, partly Asian and partly European. Central to Russian intellectual life was the quest for identity. This theme was played out in many ways in literature, the arts, and cinema, creating mythological oppositions such as East vs. West, Moscow vs. St. Petersburg, natural village vs. artificial city, soul vs. reason, and more. But under totalitarian rule, the quest for identity was merely an existential one. The state provided the citizens with an official identity, well encased within the parameters of established culture. When the totalitarian state collapsed, so did the cultural institutions. Identity became of paramount importance, because now it was going to affect not only a spiritual need but the political and economic setup of the country.[2]

The first reaction was to move sharply to the West. This direction was encouraged by the massive influx of financial aid from the United States and the European Union. During his first term, Yeltsin relied on Western economic advisors and gave Prime Minister Yegor Gaidar carte blanche in the implementation of the policy of shock-therapy reform, whose main pillars were price liberalization and privatization. This policy turned out to be a disaster. Deprived of the social safety net, a huge number of citizens plunged under the poverty level. Those were not just the traditional poor—rural area residents—but also the urban intelligentsia and the working class. Doctors, teachers, engineers, scientists, members of the creative unions, as well as the workers from giant Soviet enterprises, saw their salaries shrink to almost nothing as a result of the devaluation of the ruble and a galloping inflation that reached the triple-digit level in no time. I remember going shopping with a plastic bag full of ruble banknotes in denominations from 1 to 25. The twenty-five-ruble bill used to be the highest denomination normally used in daily transactions, when a loaf of bread cost a few kopeks. By 1992, the price of that loaf of bread had risen to 150 rubles. It took the government several months to print the new bills, in the hundred and thousand denominations. Until then, we carried two shopping bags, one for groceries and one for money.

But many citizens did not have the same resources. In the course of a few weeks, their life savings were wiped out. In addition, the government ran out of cash and deferred payment of salaries and pensions for months in a row. Citizens were left in limbo, without an income. This triggered the most amazing global performance in the art of survival. To make ends meet, factory workers resorted to barter exchanges—for example, textiles for fertilizer, glassware for sausages, and tractors for timber. Occasionally, imports were used to pay the workers instead of cash, as in the case of a factory that compensated its collective with a shipment of Tampax, causing the workers to line up along the main road to peddle the unseemly merchandise. White-collar workers and intellectuals reinvented themselves in all sorts of trades—from travel agent to graphic designer to breeder of Siamese cats. And the pensioners became street vendors, selling their heirlooms together with hand-knit socks and mittens. Moscow turned into a grand bazaar, with some points of intense concentration. The site of the largest open-air market was, ironically, the stadium proudly named after Lenin.

A few, however, struck gold. The oligarchs, a handful of men who emerged out of the Soviet structure, succeeded in appropriating the country's enormous natural capital, and to control finances, information, and politics. In the Yeltsin years, they became the real power behind the government.[3] On a much lower level, the embryo of a middle class began to emerge in Moscow (to a lesser extent in other cities), made of up and coming young executives hired by foreign corporations or operating in the various branches of the oligarchs' empire. Some small business entrepreneurs were also able to succeed, provided that they accepted racket protection. But to call this group a middle class is actually a misnomer, because their existence was extremely precarious. They had no solid economic foundation, or a bourgeois culture of work ethic and saving practices to rely on. Their good incomes allowed them to enjoy Moscow's new shopping malls and fancy nightclubs. But the income flow was volatile, and subject to be cut off at any time.[4]

The widening gap between the haves and the have-nots created resentment among the population, which eventually was vented out as an anti-Western, anti-capitalist attitude. The identity compass took a 180° turn and pointed to the East. The two extremist parties in the Duma that stirred nationalist feelings—the Communist Party under

Gennady Zyuganov on the left and the Liberal Democratic Party under Vladimir Zhirinovsky on the right—built substantial followings. The majority of the people began to blame "capitalism" and "democracy" for the bad economic turn in their lives.[5] Intellectuals and political commentators acknowledged that Russia should find its own unique way, rather than following the Western model. By the end of the century, with the election of Vladimir Putin as president, these sentiments materialized in a new policy that is generally characterized as "managed democracy." Even if the economic upturn was not immediately apparent, the new government satisfied the traditional Russian craving for the strong leader.

In the cultural field, after an initial wave of intoxication with Western products, there was a return to the domestic. Western labels were not rejected altogether, but Russian culture made a comeback. A renewed pride in being Russian resurfaced, which was lost after the country suffered the humiliation of falling from superpower status. This situation was reflected in the film world. While the screens at the beginning of the decade were flooded with Western imports, Russian productions emphasizing national traits gradually reappeared in the theaters. American films were still popular, but domestic films that criticized the U.S. and glorified a Russian hero, like *Brother 2*, were great box office successes. Such films, though, for all their Russianness, attempted to recreate the style of the American action movie. This is a good indication of what was the prevalent mood in the cultural arena, a pull toward the national roots to assert Russia's spiritual heritage together with a fascination for Western forms and products perceived to be technically superior. Most films present this dichotomy, expressed in different ways.

But it is futile to look for a trend or a movement in Russian cinema of the 1990s. The best way to deal with the productions of those years is to integrate film with life and provide a picture of Russia (with Moscow in the foreground) as the big stage on which the drama unfolded. For this book, I relied on my experience as well as on reports by other journalists and authors. I used archival materials and recent sources. I analyzed current politics and drew inspiration from the surrounding reality. I eye-witnessed the urban battles for the White House in 1991 and 1993, and attended the elite parties for the launching of the Russian *Cosmopolitan* and *Playboy*. I struggled to rent an apartment and buy a car, getting a taste of the shadow economy on the fringes of legality. I participated in film festivals and symposia. I talked to directors and producers, politicians, diplomats and journalists, as well as the emerging entrepreneurs rightly or wrongly surrounded with a mafioso aura. And I got to know the carpetbaggers from the West—the big corporate executive and the small con man—who by the thousands settled in that frontier town known to the expatriates as Moscowville.

Against this background, I discussed some eighty films made between 1990 and 2000. I sorted out the selected titles into four broad categories, each corresponding to a chapter. Chapter I covers the situation in the film industry and the many problems that threatened its survival in the market economy. It also deals with the changes in production and distribution and the reshuffling in the administration of the Filmmakers Union and Goskino (State Cinema Committee). Chapter II deals with history; the way history is recreated in film, and the way it is made in the street during extraordinary occurrences (the two uprisings of 1991 and 1993). Chapter III focuses on films that reflect urban violence and everyday life in the new Russia, with ordinary people struggling to survive in the highly criminalized environment of the big city. Chapter IV explores films that connote fantasy worlds. These may be idealized spaces such as the steppe, or demystified spaces such as the village; the myth of the West; nightmarish mental landscapes; Soviet dystopias; and war theaters. This chapter opens with the film festival circuit as a special fantasy world of its own. Chapter V discusses films that handle humor in a peculiar Russian way. This is the technique of "laughter through tears," the ability to discover the comic side of life even in tragedy.

The films selected in these five chapters may vary in technical quality and depth of thought; they may be mainstream pictures, or art films. But taken together, they provide an eloquent portrait of Russia, entering the new millennium still in search of its true identity.

The text

Several articles have been written on the cinema of this period, in Russian periodicals as well as in English-language publications. As for books in English, to my knowledge there are only two: one collection of essays, which covers a good part of the decade (up to 1998), and a general survey of Russian cinema focusing on genre, which includes some of the latest films.[6]

The present book takes a different approach from the typical scholarly publication. It incorporates into an organic whole the realities of film production, the films themselves, and the socio-political-cultural context, weaving these three threads into a narrative discourse. The result is an unfolding story, in which film and facts occupy the same space. Often, readers will have to step back and readjust the spectacles on their nose, in order to be able to switch the focus from film to fact and vice versa. To help along the way, I have provided plenty of notes—"Too many notes!" the general reader would complain. But my colleague-scholars may actually appreciate it.

This story is based on scholarship, even though the style may be unorthodox. The text combines different genres—chronicle, analysis, memoirs, scenarios, film criticism—all tied together in a rambling structure that allows for flashbacks, flash-forwards, fantasy flights, and jump-cut chronology. Facts are at times reported in the style of a film script. Some colleagues who have read the manuscript referred to it as postmodern scholarship. I think that what contributed to this characterization, more than the mixing of genres, was the persona of the "scholar *in fabula*."[7] The scholar in this book is endowed with a very obtrusive voice in her role as narrator. Like the "man with the movie camera," she roams through the *fabula*, opening fresh fields of vision, and building unexpected montage sequences. She invites the readers to follow her and engage in a challenging interactive game.

Thank you note

I want to thank the people who supported me during those difficult, yet wondrous, years in Moscow. I am grateful, first of all, to the "helpers" who made my life possible at the basic level—housekeepers, drivers, handymen, masseuses, seamstresses, finders, and buyers. This sounds like luxuries in our society, but in Russia, where basic services and consumer goods were lacking, these people provided the infrastructure that was essential for survival. While the Russians had a support network through their extended family, no foreigner could get around without the "helpers." These people were prodigious in their accomplishments, often producing results without resources, and absolutely loyal. They would take you under their wings as if you were their charge. And they would stick with you for months and years, until the very last day.

I am also very thankful to the numerous Russian colleagues and friends who facilitated my research, providing me with contacts, access to screenings and festivals, research materials, information, and fresh input. The input, in particular, was invaluable. There is no substitute for the broad, deep, passionate type of discussion that emerges naturally in Russia at any casual gathering. One would start talking about the latest film production and soon be dragged into a debate that includes universal history and cosmic mythology. This kind of interaction has been a tradition among the Russian cultural elite for two centuries, and is still one of its favorite pastimes. This group includes film critics, scholars, directors, screenwriters, producers, and administrators. Rather than naming each individual, I will extend my heartfelt thanks collectively to the colleagues from the following institutions: Filmmakers Union, Dom kino (Cinema House), Kinocenter, Museum of Cinema, Goskino, VGIK (State Film Institute), VNIIK (Research Institute of Film Art), Moscow Film Festival, *Iskusstvo kino* (*Film Art*), *Sovetsky ekran* (*Soviet Screen*), Mosfilm, and Fora Film.

In the expatriate camp, many people supported me with their friendship and expertise on various occasions. In particular, I want to thank the colleagues from the American Embassy who made my work at Press and Culture a most memorable experience. They not only contributed to a warm atmosphere of camaraderie, but provided me with their professional insight into many different aspects of the new Russian reality—politics, economics, commerce, education, defense conversion, and more—which afforded me a broad overview of the situation. My understanding of the evolving reality was also enhanced through my contacts with *The Moscow Times*, *The Moscow Tribune*, and the Russian and foreign press in general.

Here at home, I have a longstanding debt of gratitude to the National Gallery of Art in Washington, DC, and in particular to Peggy Parsons, Director of Film Programs, who over a period of fifteen years has supported public screenings of Russian films. As a member of the National Gallery Film Advisory Board, I had the pleasure to collaborate to the exhibition of a number of Russian film series. I am also deeply indebted to Georgetown University, which gave me the opportunity to introduce a course on Russian cinema in the curriculum of the School of Foreign Service. The contact with the students over the years has brought to my research fresh perspectives and new challenges, and the interaction with colleagues has kept my work on the cutting edge. Another institution that has supported my research since the time of perestroika is the Kennan Institute for Advanced Russian Studies (a branch of the Woodrow Wilson International Center for Scholars), to which I am very grateful.

Finally, I want to extend my heartfelt thanks to the following colleagues and friends, who read my manuscript: Boris Frumin, Louis Menashe, Robert Rosenstone, Blair Ruble, Richard Stites, and Denise Youngblood. They provided me with insightful suggestions, and alerted me to factual mistakes. This book benefited from their knowledge and experience, and I derived a great deal of strength from their generous support.

Technical note

For the transliteration of Russian names I used the generally accepted English spelling in the text and in the notes. I used the scientific Library of Congress system in the bibliography, the filmography, and in bibliographical references appearing in the notes. I also used it for titles of books and other works appearing in the text, as well as for quotations of speech. Abbreviations of journal and newspaper titles, which appear in the bibliography, are provided on the page preceding this Introduction. The filmography includes Russian films only; films from other countries occasionally mentioned in the text are not listed. To facilitate the reading, in the text I used film titles in their English translation; the reader will find the Russian original titles in the filmography.

Translations from Russian throughout the book are mine, if not otherwise indicated.

1
A Panoramic: Left to Right

Action!

It was the rumble of the tanks that woke me up on that late summer morning. For a long minute I was unable to make it out. I thought it was the thunder, perhaps, or the vibrations from the subway right under our building, or the permanent traffic jam that clogged the whole length of Leningradskoe Shosse, from the Ring Road to Red Square. But when I looked out the window I saw no traffic. That morning the six-lane thoroughfare was empty, as if a huge water hose had washed off all cars and people. It was empty, except for a column of tanks that moved at a slow, deliberate pace down toward the heart of the city, their caterpillar tread carving a white trail in the pavement.

The phone rang—"*Sniali Gorbacheva*! (They ousted Gorbachev!)" A colleague was calling to cancel a business meeting. "It's a coup. A self-appointed Extraordinary Committee has declared the state of emergency. There's no radio, no TV, no information. Let's go downtown and see if we can get any news."

On the metro the people were silent, their expressions concerned. They had a common destination, they wanted to know, and they wanted to act. Sokol-Aeroport-Dinamo-Belorusskaya-Mayakovskaya . . . the train would go no further. The line was cut off. Coming out of the subway, the people lingered on Mayakovsky Square, a favorite site for speech making. Some people were shouting from the monument steps, calling to action. They were waving the flag of the Russian Republic. Groups began to form. There, I met my friends. Soon the crowd started moving down Gorky Street toward Manezh Square, not as an organized demonstration but as a stream of individuals. We went along.

In the months and years after that day, I have been waiting for "the film" to be made. But, strangely enough, neither Russian nor foreign producers took up the subject. And yet, the events of those days were truly cinematic. With the addition of a love story, they could have turned into a blockbuster like, say, *Reds*, or *Doctor Zhivago*. Of course, the episode had to be put into perspective, given the grotesque reprise of two years later and its dismal aftermath throughout the decade. But the enthusiasm of the moment was genuine. I am going to place a few spotlights on those fateful days, and on other not so dramatic facts of everyday life, in order to provide a meaningful background to this book's main topic. But first I want to turn to the drama that has been unfolding within the film industry in the last decade of the twentieth century.

Woes of capitalism

The end of the Soviet era opened a decade of financial distress and artistic disorientation for the film industry. As a would-be democratic and capitalist Russia emerged from the ruins of the Soviet Union, film production decreased, quality deteriorated, and distribution relied mostly on American B-movies acquired for a fistful of dollars. In the new Russia of the 1990s, the economic climate did not favor the blossoming of a cinema new wave. The transition to the free market was too abrupt for many industries, including the film industry. Price liberalization, privatization, the collapse of the centralized system of production and distribution, the deterioration of the studios, inadequate law enforcement to guarantee copyright, rampant video piracy, and the general decline of disposable income among the population combined to push film production down to an alarming low. When the first phase of Yeltsin's democratization experiment ended, with the 1996 presidential election, the cinema industry was in critical condition. Production hit bottom, with only 21 feature films released. Never in the history of the Soviet Union had production been so low, except for the repressive twilight years of the Stalin regime. In normal times, the average annual figure was 150.[1]

One of the paradoxes emerging in the immediate post-perestroika period was that the arts did not benefit from the general process of liberalization. Rather, freedom of speech exploded with a vengeance including among its victims the intellectuals who once coveted it. There was a widespread sentiment among the intelligentsia that the artists lost their two-century old function as the conscience of the nation. Audiences no longer regarded them as beacons of enlightenment. With the disappearance of the tyrannical state, art works with underlying libertarian themes that conveyed clandestine information lost their *raison d'être*. People's lives and minds were now bombarded with messages from print and electronic media, billboard advertisements, and the Internet. In the cinema world, this situation resulted in cultural disorientation and loss of creativity. Many veteran filmmakers, who for decades had successfully sustained an intellectual struggle with the totalitarian government, were no longer sure of their role in society and had trouble finding themes and ideas relevant to the new situation. Some stopped making films altogether (such as Elem Klimov), while others continued to make pictures often with disappointing results (such as Eldar Ryazanov, Sergei Solovyov, Karen Shakhnazarov, and the pair Abdrashitov-Mindadze), or got bogged down in projects that dragged on for years (such as Alexei Gherman and Gleb Panfilov). Alexander Sokurov miraculously managed to produce art films on a consistent basis, notwithstanding financial difficulties. Among the younger generation, some directorial talent emerged but did not find a hospitable ground and their productions remained limited to one or two pictures of note (among them, Vasily Pichul, Evgeny Tsymbal, Andrei Eshpai, Ivan Dykhovichny, Tomasz Tot, and Pavel Chukhrai). A notable exception was Valery Todorovsky (son of renowned director Pyotr Todorovsky), who was able to produce box-office successes at a sustained pace.

In addition, cinema lost its commercial function, that of mass entertainment, which the Soviet state had consistently promoted. The liberalization of the studios, rather than creating new Drankovs and Khanzhonkovs, plunged the industry into a financial crisis.[2] Ten years into the age of reform, the Russian people were asking themselves whether they were currently better off. For a small minority, including the new rich and the emerging middle class of up and coming yuppies and small business entrepreneurs, the answer was: yes. For the masses scattered over the rural areas, the decaying mining towns, the polluted industrial regions, and the squalid tenements of the urban landscape the answer was: no. The populace was nostalgic for the "bad" old days when the state ruled their lives, but also provided them with a guaranteed income—no matter how meager—and a social safety net—no matter how thin. Those where the days when the movies were available and cheap. Now, most people could not afford the price of a ticket.[3]

With the inception of economic liberalization in 1992, and up to the monetary reform of 1998, ticket prices in Moscow went up from 50 kopecks to 7,000 rubles. At the end of the decade prices varied, from the equivalent of $4 to $25. Considering that the average salary in Russia was $50 a month, these figures were staggering to most Russians and simply put the movies out of reach.[4] In Soviet times, it was not unusual for a blockbuster to draw an audience of 100 million people, while post-Soviet distributors considered themselves lucky if a film attracted half a million viewers. Danil Dondurei, the editor-in-chief of the journal *Film Art* (*Iskusstvo kino*), offered a revealing commentary: "In Moscow, in 1995, only one ticket for every four people was sold (0.24 tickets per person), and in St. Petersburg, one ticket every three people (0.37 per person).... Nowadays in Russia, people go to the movies less often than in any European country, including Albania."[5] Official Soviet propaganda maintained that more than 50 percent of the total number of movie theaters in the world was located in the USSR. In post-Soviet Russia, the count may be different, as many theaters went out of business or turned over most of their space to fancy "auto salons" and nightclubs-cum-casino. The ones still in operation were overtaxed and lacked the modern facilities that would attract an audience. Only a few Moscow and St. Petersburg theaters were given a face-lift, starting in 1996, and were turned into high-tech cineplexes. But the ticket price there was for the money aristocracy.[6]

The picture looks even grimmer if we consider that the vast majority of the movies shown in Russian theaters were foreign productions, mostly cheaply priced American B-flicks. This trend was denounced by nationalist critics as another manifestation of the pernicious and pervasive Westernization of Russian culture. But the truth is that, after the collapse of the centralized distribution system, every theater had to fend for itself, and theater managers could only afford to buy low-cost movies if they wanted to make a profit. Russian movies were simply too expensive. With the liberalization of price controls in 1992, production costs skyrocketed from $50,000 to $500,000 for an average feature film—still a small figure by American standards, but big enough to make distribution unprofitable in Russia. Russian producers, who could not count on international releases, had to recover the money and generate revenues by local sales alone. As a result, they priced themselves out of the market. Alexander Golutva, head of Lenfilm studio at the time, said in an interview taken in 1993: "How are we going to sell our films? . . . Nobody wants to buy licenses; they buy prints because it is cheaper. Out of one print, they make a huge number of copies and distribute them. . . . [Also], how can we compete with American films? If our films were only 10 percent more expensive, they may appeal to the distributors' sense of patriotism; but when they are 10 times more expensive the patriotic appeal does not help."[7] The situation got only worse as time went by. Only a few years later, production costs for Nikita Mikhalkov's *The Barber of Siberia* (1998) amounted to $45 million—which made it the most expensive production ever in Russian history.

Still in the Soviet period, in the very last days of perestroika when the centralized distribution system fell apart, an aspiring movie tycoon made a splash and rapidly disappeared. His name, Izmail Suleimanovich Tagi-zade, made headlines in the foreign press, which reported the exotic extravagances of the Soviet millionaire at the 1991 Cannes festival. To introduce his latest production, *Tsar Ivan the Terrible*, to the international film market, Tagi-zade descended on the Côte d'Azur with a cohort of 637 people. With the largesse of an Oriental monarch, he treated his guests to champagne and caviar, deluxe suites, and a historical parade on La Croisette, complete with Cossacks on horseback, boyars in fur coats, Ivan on his throne, fair maids, black monks, and assorted icons. The French press reported expenses of 25 million francs, which sent shock waves through the filmmakers community back home. Coming from the party ranks and the government bureaucracy, where he was the deputy head of the Moscow Film Distribution Bureau, Tagi-zade began his ascent to the capitalist spheres with a co-op to sell carnations at metro stations. Rumor had it that, thanks to connections in his native Azerbaijan, Tagi-zade was gradually able to eliminate all competition in the flower business. With his first acquired capital, he bought a ranch for the breeding of Arab horses, a clothes factory, and other enterprises for the production of consumer goods. At that point he decided to go back to his first love, the movies, no longer sitting at the desk of a grayish state chancery, but basking in the glitz of the movie set.

His aggressive ways and financial capability stirred fears within the Filmmakers Union that he would monopolize the business. The fear became outcry when Tagi-zade went to Hollywood at the beginning of 1991, bought 158 fourth-rate adventure flicks, and dumped them on the Soviet market, notwithstanding his patriotic declarations. To strengthen his grip on distribution, Tagi-zade organized the Association of Film and Video Distributors (ASKIN), using connections in the Goskino network (State Cinema Committee), and giving a new veneer to the old bureaucratic system. In essence, this was a good idea, according to Alexander Golutva. He commented, in 1993, that ASKIN would have helped the film industry at the time of the disintegration of the state distribution system, but failed because of the opposition of the Filmmakers Union: "When Tagi-zade came up with his idea of the Association, everybody attacked him. And what did the Filmmakers Union do? The FU declared war on the distributors association and turned them into enemies. . . . And now that we're talking about friendly relationships with the distributors, they are afraid that we would deceive them."[8]

With a magnanimous gesture meant to improve his image within the cinema circles, Tagi-zade invited representatives of the Filmmakers Union to the Second ASKIN Congress (1991), supposedly to find a way toward cooperation. But the majority of the delegates received his speech as a challenge and a provocation. For the occasion, Tagi-zade rented the Palace of Congresses within the Kremlin walls, where sessions of the Supreme Soviet of the USSR usually took place. He paid 3,000,000 rubles ($100,000 ca.) for the rental and assembled 5,000 people. Those who expected concrete proposals were disappointed. Instead they got a lecture. "We must live like they do in the normal, civilized world," he said. "I am not talking about the fact that there they can buy forty different kinds of salami. I am talking about the way they deal on the film market. You like it, you buy it; you don't like it, you don't buy it."[9]

In fact, this is exactly what happened to Tagi-zade. His American movies sold millions of tickets, but the productions from his own studio, TISKINO, had practically no buyers. To follow up on the Cannes extravaganza, the munificent producer offered the Moscow audience a trumpeted premiere of *Tsar Ivan the Terrible* at the movie theater October. Numerous guests were invited to a sumptuous reception. "Among them," Tagi-zade boasted, "were our democrats, forty-one ambassadors, and almost all the cultural attachés of the Moscow embassies." Tagi-zade was seen in the cinema world as *l'enfant terrible* of those days, but his notoriety was short lived. He faded out together with the Soviet Union.[10]

The other obstacle to distribution was film piracy, which constituted 80-90 percent of the Russian video business.[11] Illegal printing, recording, exhibition, and sales of national and imported movies resulted in gross violations of copyrights as well as financial losses to the legitimate rights holders. The video business was a pirate's heaven. Stolen cassettes of foreign movies appeared on the market before their video release; they went directly from the big screen in the country of origin to Russian street kiosks in record time. Russian films were sold on video in Brighton Beach, NY, even before their official release on screen.

There was a huge marketplace for videos in the Moscow suburb of Fili, known as Gorbushka, where the cassettes were sold for $2 apiece, cheaper than the price of the cheapest movie ticket. On weekends hundreds of vendors set up stalls to trade the latest pirated movie hits, together with black-market copies of CDs and computer software. Accessible by metro, the market was the favorite destination of huge crowds of young buyers. When the Moscow city authorities made known their plan to close the Gorbushka market, in February 2001, demonstrators picketed City Hall. In addition to illegal markets, pirated films were shown throughout Russia on cable television stations that operated without a license from the broadcasting commission. These clandestine stations, besides violating copyrights, also cut into the turf of the licensed stations that dutifully paid the rights to the film's owners.

Legislative chaos and lack of law enforcement made it difficult to prosecute violators. The Soviet Union had neglected copyright laws within its territory, as it had all laws regarding private property, and had not signed the Bern Convention that guarantees the safeguard of copyrights among the nations. Eventually, the Russian Federation did sign it, on March 13, 1995. This was partly because, since 1991, the United States started applying pressure on the USSR through a boycott by the Motion Picture Export Association of America (MPEA). One year later, President

Bush, Sr. threatened to withdraw Russia's status as a Most Favored Nation if a law were not promptly passed. By the end of 1992, the Russian Intellectual Property Agency was established with the purpose of drafting a bill, and in 1993 the Russian parliament passed the new copyright legislation.[12] Armen Medvedev, the head of Goskino, commented on the law at a press conference: "This is not a return to censorship; this is a document that guarantees the property rights on films and provides ratings for audience guidance." He also cautioned that "this does not solve all problems . . . but it's a good start."[13] The MPEA boycott was officially lifted, but American major studios were still leery of the Russian market, because there were hardly any instruments for the implementation of the law. Only a few independent producers ventured to show their films there—the most notable being Spielberg's *Schindler's List*, in 1994—but in most cases they made sure one person accompanied the film all along the way and back to the United States, keeping an eye on the reels day and night.

The event that signaled a new willingness on the part of American producers to initiate a commercial dialog with Russia took place within the framework of the XX International Moscow Film Festival, in the summer of 1997. Jack Valenti, MPEA president, accepted an invitation to the festival, and brought up the issue of film piracy at the highest government level in a meeting with Prime Minister Viktor Chernomyrdin.[14] Notwithstanding this effort, *Star Wars: The Phantom Menace*, which was selected for presentation at the next International Moscow Film Festival in 1999, became available on pirated cassettes several months before the festival's inauguration. However, things looked better in the summer of 2000, judging by the marquee of a prominent film exhibition center, which was displaying the latest Western hits licensed for distribution.[15]

Concerned Russian filmmakers and distributors have routinely come up with initiatives aimed at containing, if not eradicating, the problem. In 1993, a group of respectable distribution companies—Initsiativa, Most-Media, Kredo-Aspek, Yekaterinburg-ART, Piramida, Tretyakovka, Fora, and Chance—formed an association with the main goal of fighting piracy. This and similar initiatives were announced with great fanfare, but had virtually zero impact. The president of the association, Oleg Chesnokov, who was also the president of Initsiativa, offered one example among many of how his company suffered at the hands of pirates.

Initsiativa bought the rights to *The Inner Circle* (1992), by Russian expatriate director Andrei Konchalovsky, but three days before the date of its release the film appeared on cable television nationwide. Another act of piracy became a joke. A copy of *Little Giant with a Big Sex Drive* (Dostal, 1992) was illegally shown in the city of Orenburg after being stolen from the library of Goskino, which, ironically, was in charge of film preservation and protection.

To help in the struggle, Kinocenter promoted the best of Russian movies, and offered programs of foreign films legitimately acquired.[16] This exhibition center became a joint-stock company in 1992. Previously the property of the Filmmakers Union, Kinocenter was privatized by a unilateral act of its administration over the opposition of the Union's board of directors, which resulted in bitter litigation in the courts. Eventually, Kinocenter won the fight due to the support of the vast majority of the Union's members who became the major stockholders. Later, in 1998, with the reorganization of the Filmmakers Union, an accommodation was found between Kinocenter and the new leadership. Among the many initiatives of Kinocenter was the festival of Non-Stolen Cinema, held in 1992-1993, and presided over by Andrei Konchalovsky. It featured high-quality American and French films, and offered round tables dedicated to issues concerning "stolen" films and ways of protecting them. One main goal of the festival was to find a new structure for the distribution network. Vyacheslav Shmyrov, Kinocenter director for cultural programs and the festival's initiator, claimed that the festival, together with pressure from the cinema lobby, prompted the Russian legislature to pass the copyright law that allowed for the prosecution of illegal video dealers. But, he complained: "What encourages piracy is the fact that there is no viable infrastructure for regular distribution of our own Russian films."[17] Consequently, Kinocenter also sponsored a festival called The Second Premiere, to rescue the best contemporary Russian productions from oblivion and launch them on the distribution circuit. The festival started in April 1993 and was repeated annually, but Russian films remained the great absentees from the national screens.

A legal company, ORT-Video, was established in 1996, as an offspring of the television network ORT. The company owned the rights to films from several foreign studios, as well as ORT productions. In the first year, it released sixteen titles, for a volume of 500,000 cassettes per month. Backed by tycoon Boris Berezovsky, ORT-Video aimed to dominate the video business nationally, and also film broadcasting by regional television stations. In order to succeed, ORT-Video openly declared war on video piracy, sponsoring a huge event within the frame of the XX International Moscow Film Festival (1997), titled "ORT Warns You: Video Is the Land of Law." But it was easier said than done. And the pirates continued to prosper. At that same time, a group of film enterprises and television companies formed still another association to fight piracy, the Russian Anti-Pirate organization. It included ORT, Mosfilm, various video distributors, the American MPEA, and others. Grigory Simanovich, a spokesman for ORT said: "The Russian government has taken virtually no steps against video piracy, and as a result it loses $250 million a year in tax revenues."[18]

To be in the film and video business it is not just a financial risk, it is a life risk. The statistics are appalling. Hundreds of victims in business, politics, and the media were assassinated throughout the decade by hit killers, and most of the cases remain unsolved. Some cases had an enormous impact on the collective imagination, like the murder of the popular TV host, Vladislav Listyev, who was gunned down on his doorstep in March 1995. He had been recently named general director of Russian Public Television, which was to run the Ostankino television station. One of his first plans was to stop the airing of commercials; a move, many speculated, which may have displeased criminal organizations connected with big business. Millions of viewers mourned for days the popular TV personality, who brought to Russia talk shows in the style of Phil Donahue and Larry King. Ten thousand people in Moscow alone gathered around the Vagankov cemetery during his funeral.[19] But the most devastating were the murders of the people we personally knew. When I first met Tomaz Topadze in the late perestroika days on the set of a Soviet-American documentary project, he was dreaming of setting up a legitimate video distribution company. He was an enthusiast, with the outgoing personality of a native Georgian. In 1994, he had realized his dream and was successfully running Varus Video, a joint venture that sold cassettes of foreign films under license. He was also an outspoken advocate for the enforcement of copyright laws. Obviously, the video underworld did not like this kind of competition. One evening in April, Tomaz got home from work unaware that the killer was waiting for him on the landing. The bullets hit him as he came out of the elevator. He fell against his apartment door, and was later found by his mother.[20]

It was not easy to be a producer in Russia. This was a brand new profession. Under the old structure, the officials from Goskino, who controlled all stages of production and distribution, acted as producers themselves and showed a good financial record thanks to their promotion of movies with mass appeal, and the fact that they had no competition.[21] With the transition to a market economy, many film directors reluctantly doubled as producers and had to struggle with the overwhelming task of raising money and accounting for production costs and box office revenues. "Before, the censor was Goskino. Now, we have a new censor that goes by the name of the dollar," complained Vladimir Naumov, director of Mosfilm's Soyuz division. "At least with the censor you could argue. But the dollar is cold and indifferent. No dollars, no film."[22]

In the initial phase of the reform, the new businessmen, in need of laundering capital poured money into film production. Soon, however, the Gaidar government under Yeltsin legalized private investments; big business stabilized and acquired a veneer of respectability, and money ceased to flow into the movie industry. Some producers were able to establish joint ventures with foreign partners; others, to find sponsors. Some joint ventures were quite successful, but in Russia such films were regarded by the critics as catering to Hollywood (for example, *Burnt by the Sun*, 1994, by Nikita Mikhalkov; or *Window on Paris*, 1994, by Yuri Mamin). A cherished dream of many Russian filmmakers kept eluding them: to make pictures, which expressed the Russian soul in esoteric images, financed with Western money. This did not happen, as the foreign producers kept an eye on revenues, rather than lofty aspirations. One way the big studios, such as Mosfilm and Lenfilm, financed their movies was by renting out the facilities to foreign filmmakers, who needed an authentic Russian background for their pictures. It was reported that Mosfilm covered the cost of two dozens of its own productions with the dollar rent it received from the producers of *The Inner Circle*, in 1992.[23]

However, the general picture was bleak, and the mood among filmmakers was one of frustration. In February 1994, the Moscow Directors Guild called a press conference to decry the current state of Russian film production. A despondent Savva Kulish, president of the Guild, addressed the journalists with a gloomy face. "We're not only standing at the edge of the abyss, we're already falling in," he told us. The Guild decided to send a resolution to the government that was tantamount to advocating the re-nationalization of the film industry. That was a rather desperate step, and probably became a factor in advancing the Federal Law for the Support of Cinema. The law was passed by the Duma in 1996, but remained inoperative for a long time. When it finally came into effect in January 1999, it became immediately clear that it would have no positive impact. The law granted the long-awaited privatization of the studios, as well as tax breaks to investors who would put money into film production and distribution, and the construction and refurbishing of movie theaters. But after the August 1998 economic crash no entrepreneurs had spare money to invest in the crumbling facilities of a glorious past.

Ultimately, what saved Russian cinema from extinction was, once again, the Russian government. The revamped Goskino agency provided funds for most of the films produced throughout the decade without exercising pressure on artistic decision-making.[24] The first head of post-Soviet Goskino, Armen Medvedev, was the former editor of the journal *Film Art*. He had joined the Goskino apparatus in 1984, but later sympathized with the Filmmakers Union's takeover in the perestroika days and embraced their cause. He was dedicated to helping Russian cinema out of the crisis, and played a big role in drafting the Law on Cinema. Funds, however, were limited, as only a small fraction of the federal budget was allocated for culture. In 1996 the allocation for all cultural activities was 0.84 percent of the federal budget. Out of its share, Goskino was able to fund 21 feature films and 12 documentaries. In 2000, it funded 65 feature films and 55 films for television.[25]

Ironically, it is an accepted concept that in the Soviet days the state subsidized the movies. Actually, those who were involved in the administration claim that the opposite is true. Allegedly, the film industry was so financially sound that it brought to the state treasury one third of its annual global revenues. Conversely, in the post-Soviet period there were no revenues from the film industry, and the filmmakers counted on government aid. The scarce resources available, however, were not put to good use. Most of the filmmakers who competed for state funds tended to make movies for festival programs, elite screens, and their own artistic prestige. Each year, a handful of films moved around the country from festival to festival—Sochi, Anapa, Podolsk, Artek, also subsidized by the government—mainly to allow the participants to indulge in self-congratulatory escapism, and to position the winners for a new round of subsidies. Russian cinema turned inward, losing creativity and vitality in the process.

Something began to change in the fall of 1996 when a new American movie theater, Kodak-Kinomir (Kodak-Cinema World), opened in Moscow. The theater offered Hollywood hits with Russian subtitles, and became a magnet for the young and affluent. The average ticket price was the equivalent of $25, but the price doubled when tickets were sold by scalpers for exceptional features, such as the international blockbuster *Titanic*. Kinomir was a joint enterprise of Eastman Kodak and the Russian company Golden Ring Entertainment, and the brainchild of two visionary entrepreneurs, Paul Heth and Raymond Markovich. Allegedly, it became the highest revenue-producing screen in the world, thanks to a revival of the movie theater culture. The Moscow facilities included a bar and a restaurant where moviegoers could socialize before or after the show.[26]

The financial success of the American theater, rather than driving Russian cinema out of business altogether, galvanized investment in domestic production. The first truly private film studio, NTV-Profit, was born under the aegis of the television network NTV (Independent Television) and in its first year of existence, under the guidance of general director Igor Tolstunov, produced the 1998 Oscar nominee *The Thief* (Pavel Chukhrai). This was followed by other successes such as *Captain's Daughter* (Proshkin, 1999) and *The Voroshilov Marksman* (Govorukhin, 1999). Both NTV and NTV-Profit were part of the large holding company, Media-MOST, owned at the time by tycoon Vladimir Gusinsky, who had more than one unpleasant brush with the Yeltsin administration. Another facility, the television network ORT, also started to produce films. This network, although nominally still the property of the Russian government was in fact part of the media empire of magnate Boris Berezovsky, Gusinsky's archrival. During the first half of Yeltsin's tenure, Berezovsky won the government's favor and enjoyed as many privileges as the other suffered attacks. But in 1996, for the presidential election, the two media tycoons joined forces and threw their massive support behind Boris Yeltsin, the only candidate that could defeat the Communist Party and ensure the survival of big capital. At the time of the electoral campaign, Gusinsky's Media-MOST included the newspaper *Segodnya*, the magazine *Itogi*, the radio station Echo of Moscow, and the television station NTV. Berezovsky's Logovaz held interest in the newspaper *Nezavisimaya gazeta*, the magazine *Ogonyok*, and the television stations ORT and TV 6. Both Berezovsky and Gusinsky had a free rein after the election, until Putin took over. Then, they fell under the axe, as a result of the campaign against the oligarchs launched by the new Russian president.[27]

Another successful independent producer was Sergei Selyanov, head of the St. Petersburg-based STV company. He started his producer career as a student of VGIK (State Film Institute) in 1980, still in pre-perestroika times. He was able to put together an association of students to produce the film *Angel Day*. [28] Eventually, in the 1990s, he established himself as the producer of a string of films of note, such as *The Time for Sadness Has not yet Come* (1995, also as director), *Peculiarities of the National Hunt in the Fall* (Rogozhkin, 1997), *Brother* (Balabanov, 1997), *Brother 2* (Balabanov, 2000), *Checkpoint* (Rogozhkin, 1999), and *Of Freaks and Men* (Balabanov, 1999). He also produced an excellent documentary directed by Evgeny Tsymbal, *Dziga and His Brothers* (2002), about the avant-garde filmmaker of the 1920s, Dziga Vertov. These achievements were partly the result of tax break expectations triggered by the Law on Cinema, which made private money for film production more readily available.

The government for its part took a more cost-effective approach to financing films through its major facilities, Mosfilm, Lenfilm, and Gorky Studio. While Mosfilm and Lenfilm supported a mainstream line of production, Gorky Studio promoted a trend of low-budget, dynamic, and provocative pictures by a new wave of directors that claimed to have learned their craft from David Lynch and Quentin Tarantino. The driving force behind this initiative was Gorky Studio's head, Sergei Livnev, who supported the idea of state subsidies on the European model, in the range of $300,000 per film. He also advocated the old Hollywood system of "vertically integrated" production, distribution and sales under studio control. The Gorky Studio produced a dozen features during Livnev's two-year tenure, but the program was terminated when Livnev resigned his post in October 1998. His decision was precipitated by the country's financial crash and the fact that the state had not yet made a decision in favor of the privatization of the studios. Another initiative that favored the young was the Studio of First and Experimental Films at Lenfilm, with Alexei Gherman as executive producer. This studio should be credited for a sustained output of quality first pictures.

At the beginning of 1998, the general situation looked promising. Medvedev had reasons for optimism:

> Today the situation is changing. Private companies begin to show an interest in cinema: in 1997 more than 50 pictures were produced, and only 20 of those were financed out of the government budget. And the role of the government is changing, too. Before, we considered it our task to subsidize the national filmmakers, in full or in part. Now our main goal is another: the government must create a favorable atmosphere for film production in order to attract private investment. Private capital will pour in if businessmen understand that they have government support. This is what happened this past year. Now, together with some large banks, we are elaborating a system of state-insured loans, whereby the film producers get a loan from a bank and the government guarantees the completion of the picture or the partial repayment of the loan. This system will force the producers to become more responsible.[29]

These plans and predictions were made before the economic meltdown of August 1998, which caused a temporary regression, as both government and private pockets suddenly became shallower. Nevertheless, the market seemed to be the direction of the future. The concept of "movies for the millions" was revived with the appropriate consumerist twist in lieu of ideological propaganda.[30] Some of the largest movie theaters in Moscow were restored to their original splendor and equipped with Cinerama screens and Dolby sound systems. The cost for the refurbishing of the theater Rossiia, renamed Pushkin, was estimated at $7 million.[31] Udarnik (Shock-worker) underwent a similar facelift. Khudozhestvenny (Art Theater) and Kinocenter were also transformed into modern facilities. In St. Petersburg the fancy Crystal Palace was modernized and outfitted for the screening of international hits. And a *kinodrom* (drive-in), opened in Moscow in 1999; this was an absolute novelty for Russia, because in the past there was no middle class who owned cars, and the concept of the drive-in would have been an oxymoron.

A few years before the restoration, Udarnik celebrated its sixtieth birthday with a special gala evening, packed with the movie stars of yesteryear. The facility originally opened in 1931 as a state-of-the-art theater to sustain the Stalinist policy of movie promotion. A milestone of Soviet cinema history, Udarnik was part of the infamous complex known as the "house on the embankment"—a building in the sleek functionalist style of the period, meant to provide deluxe apartments for the Soviet elite. The "house on the embankment," with the beginning of the purges, started to lose its tenants one by one, turning from a place of privilege into a symbol of terror.[32] Over the years, however, life in the building returned to normal; and nowadays, when a large number of the best apartments are rented out to foreign corporate executives for astronomical prices, the label "house on the embankment" has an ironical ring.

Udarnik, like the Variety Theater (*Teatr estrady*) on the other side of the complex, was meant to highlight Soviet popular culture and entertainment in a sophisticated environment. On opening night, it showed the film *Golden Mountains* (1931) by Sergei Yutkevich to an elite audience of invited guests. Yutkevich had worked in the theater with Eisenstein as production designer before turning to cinema. This was his first sound film, with a score by Dmitri Shostakovich. For the celebration of its sixtieth anniversary, the theater management retrieved the film from the archives and offered the audience a ten-minute clip, a taste of the "good old days." According to Udarnik's current manager, Ludwig Banyan, all the films that eventually became Soviet classics premiered in this theater, including the musicals of Grigory Alexandrov. This was also the first theater to offer live entertainment before the evening shows: a dance floor in the café, pop concerts, and art exhibits. Although dedicated to the promotion of national production, Udarnik hosted the first international film festival in 1935. One can only imagine, Banyan commented, what a memorable event it must have been to see foreign movies and movie stars in Moscow in that somber year.[33] To me, it was a memorable event to see the venerable stars of the Soviet screen parading on stage for the anniversary celebration, still beautiful, elegant, and spirited—a group of true survivors. The group included 83 year-old Marina Ladynina, the leading lady of Ivan Pyrev's village musicals.[34]

Popular culture and populist rhetoric

The revival of "the movies," as an outing, an event, a social experience, was part of a nostalgia wave colored with patriotic pride and a hopeful forecast. Its culmination was the restoration of the Soviet national anthem. The lyrics had to be replaced because they were too overtly ideological, but the search for the author of the new text ultimately favored Sergei Milkhalkov, the same author who wrote the old lyrics in 1944. The new anthem was officially approved by the newly appointed president, Vladimir Putin, on December 30, 1999, and sung out on New Year's Eve as part of the millennium celebration. One year later, in December 2000, the red banner was restored as the Russian Army's official flag. The cultural pendulum went full swing from the self-flagellation of the perestroika days to a Russia-forever attitude. Cultural icons from the communist past reappeared. Mosfilm's original logo—Vera Mukhina's sculpture of the worker and the collective farmer that towers at the entrance of the former VDNKh (Exhibition of Economic Achievements)—was reinstated and met with fond ovations from the audience.[35] The most popular movie magazine, *Soviet Screen* (*Sovetskii ekran*), having adopted the more neutral title, *Screen* (*Ekran*), for a few years, went back to the original name and to some of the features of the old days.[36] *Soviet Screen* made its comeback with the issue of January 1998, displaying the masthead in the original typefaces, together with the statement: "Published since 1925." The editorial reflected the current retro mood and rosy hopes: "We hope that the day is not far when our cinema will have in Russian society the same place that Hollywood has in American society, and that Soviet cinema had in the years 1930s and 1960s in our country."[37]

Not surprisingly, the wave of nostalgia in the film community included the wish for a strong leader who would take upon himself the task of imparting a new direction to the ailing cinema industry. The figure of the strong leader has been a central element of Russian mythology, adapting its form and function to specific historical circumstances. At the time, the leader's image was that of a patriot, a savvy businessman, and a renowned professional, possessing the required good measure of charisma. At the closing of the III Congress of the Filmmakers Union of Russia (December 1997), the participants elected such a leader in the person of Nikita Mikhalkov, until then considered by the majority to be too right wing.[38] The editor of *Soviet Screen*, reporting the event with a pinch of irony, stressed the cultural/psychological connotations of that choice: "The filmmakers found themselves sitting on the ruins of their disintegrating Union. Blaming the current secretariat for all their miseries, they felt a craving for the 'iron fist' and entrusted the reins of government to Nikita Mikhalkov, the strong and pragmatic leader."[39]

After his tempestuous parting with the "revolutionary" Union's leadership, at the historical V Congress in 1986,[40] Mikhalkov went his independent way—a way strewn with successes. He received an Oscar, served as the president of the Russian Culture Fund and revitalized its coffers, and founded the profitable studio TriTe. In his speech after the election, Mikhalkov castigated the Union's members and administrators for the mismanagement of the past twelve years. He said:

> I want to know why you're calling on me today, and I'm not sure I will accept because what I see here is horrifying. . . . In seven years, starting from scratch, we have established a studio with our labor, without producing a single sex and violence flick or a commercial spot. And our studio, TriTe, was rated by *Variety* ahead of Mosfilm. Talent is a gift from God, money can be made by gambling, esteem and respect are acquired through labor. Labor.[41]

Eventually, Mikhalkov accepted the post he was elected to. But only after running an audit of the Union's finances and drafting a concrete program. A few months later (May 1998), Mikhalkov called the Union's IV Extraordinary Congress, where he laid out a precise plan of action and asked for a vote of confidence. This move was controversial, like everything that concerns Mikhalkov. In assuming the Union's leadership, Mikhalkov had two priorities. One was to encourage the development of a cinema that would support the national identity and create a positive "myth," with heroes that stand for honor and dignity and serve as role models for the new generations—a truly national and popular cinema that would attract audiences and generate revenues. The other was to create a viable financial infrastructure based on private investment and favorable government policies. He argued that the Law on

Cinema existed only on the books. What he proposed was the creation of a Fund for the Development of Cinema, managed by Goskino, consisting of money collected from a tax on video sales and television broadcasting of films. He also proposed to give the Union's president the power to name a new secretariat made up of professional administrators rather than filmmakers.

His critics denounced this proposal as an attempt to subvert the Union's democratic setup and transform it into something close to a dictatorship, while his supporters saluted the opportunity to entrust a capable leader with the future of the Union. As it turned out, the latter were the majority. At the IV Congress, Mikhalkov reported a landslide victory. Whether sound or not, his plan was the only plan on the floor. And Mikhalkov presented it with irresistible passion. A master of the art of staging, he ensured his victory through a skillful choreography. Mikhalkov used a well-proven strategy, the direct appeal to the people over the bureaucratic structures, relying on populist rhetoric and personal charisma. The event was held within the Kremlin walls in the huge auditorium of the Palace of Congresses. All the Union members were invited, instead of the limited number of delegates that usually were selected to participate. Thousands came from all corners of Russia on a complimentary package that covered transportation and living expenses. Coming from the provinces, knowing next to nothing about the Union's politics and power games, they were genuinely delighted to be included in an important decision-making process and grateful to the new president. But this was not just a cheap stratagem on the part of Mikhalkov. He deeply believed in the agenda he put to a vote, based on the principles that have consistently informed his public life. A prominent film critic described this remarkable performance: "The IV Congress . . . was perceived as Mikhalkov's personal show. The entertainment effect given to the Congress by its main inspirer and organizer was so strong that its most fierce opponents unwittingly played their roles in the master's colossal, operatic staging. . . . At the IV Congress, even undemocratic issues passed by democratic means." And he concluded on a positive note: "Mikhalkov became the leader and, clearly, he is capable of being the leader."[42]

The Palace of Congresses was chosen for the event to emphasize a symbolic turning point. The only other congress of the Filmmakers Union to be held in that venue was the historical V Congress of 1986, which at the time was hailed as revolutionary because of its devastating challenge to Soviet ideology. It opened a new era in the relation between the Filmmakers Union and Goskino, which was expected to be the beginning of a true film renaissance. Later, however, that historical moment was perceived as the beginning of the decline for the Russian film industry. This latest Congress was meant to mark the end of the crisis. Mikhalkov made it clear in his speech:

> It seems symbolic to me that both the V Congress of the Filmmakers Union of the USSR that began this deadly movement of our cinema and the IV Congress of the Filmmakers Union of Russia that was called to consolidate our forces for the salvation of the field take place right here in the Kremlin. To me this event has a special significance because just like then, twelve years ago, my convictions remain unchanged. And all I said at the V Congress, I could repeat today. I regret one thing. If we did not succumb then to the seduction of destructive permissiveness, which we mistook for emerging democratic opportunities, today we would not have to wander like soldiers and generals of a defeated army among the ruins of a once great Soviet cinema, which we considered the most important of all the arts.[43]

The good intentions stated with great fanfare in 1986 in the "New Model" declaration—market reforms, financial independence, creative freedom—yielded mixed results. One major achievement has been the abolition of censorship and the elimination of production control on the part of Goskino. But the new freedom, instead of spurring truly creative endeavors, often exploited the previously forbidden subjects of sex and violence, and resulted in a long series of *chernukha* (dark and gloomy) and *pornukha* (pornography) movies. Financial independence was achieved through market reforms, but it did not bring profits; it only caused production money to disappear.

For sale

The Fund for the Development of Cinema promoted by Mikhalkov turned out to be impossible to realize, mainly because Goskino did not support the project. In January 1999, Armen Medvedev resigned his ministerial post as the head of the agency. Five months earlier, he had said that he was going to resign if the government did not take steps to halt the decline of the film industry.[44] His successor, Alexander Golutva, had been deputy minister for two years. Previous to moving to Goskino, Golutva was the director of Lenfilm studio, the moribund giant from the Soviet golden days. At the time of the debate on the Fund, Lenfilm's main source of income was from the rights it received from central and regional TV stations for the broadcasting of its archive films. Other studios were in the same situation. Opponents of the project argued that the realization of the Fund would deprive the studios of their sole means of survival, while its supporters argued that the money would be better managed by professional administrators, and the studios would get a larger share of it. Lenfilm's new director, Viktor Sergeev, was openly suspicious of the plan: "I talked to Mr. Piorunsky (first vice-president and manager of the Filmmakers Union), who tried to convince me that the professional top-managers can use our film's copyright better than we, that they can earn a great deal more and give us a better share. I don't believe this."[45]

It is short of a miracle that Lenfilm could survive at all. Interviewed in 1993, Golutva had this to say about the studio:

> Every night I dream that Lenfilm has declared bankruptcy. . . . Debts are piling up; whoever owes us money does not pay, but everybody else demands that we pay for everything in advance. Every day bills come in, and I look at them and must decide which ones we will pay off and which ones we can avoid paying without consequences. Here is a bill from the water company—they may shut off the water and the sewage service, which means we have to find the money and pay this bill. Every morning I pick up the telephone with a certain trepidation—there's the dial tone, it means the bill has been paid. But we do not pay those companies, which cannot retaliate. This is not good, this is shameful . . . but what can we do?[46]

Lenfilm's staff was cut from 2,000 in 1990 to about 800 in 1999, and its crumbling buildings were in a sorrowful state of neglect. The shoestring budget it received from Goskino was restricted to the production of new films and could not be used to cover the overhead. Lenfilm's strategy was to aim at production quality rather than quantity, and to make one film per year that would resonate widely. In 1999, it produced the prestige film, *Moloch*, by Alexander Sokurov, which was certainly prestigious, but hardly a box-office hit. Other meager sources of income for Lenfilm came from renting out space to banks and commercial firms, and providing services to foreign film producers. At one point, Lenfilm even considered going into the car wash business. The plan was to set up a network of German-made automated washing stations on the main access roads to St. Petersburg, using a city-council underwritten loan of $3 million. "The idea of getting into the car wash business for me is not exactly a pleasant one," said Sergeev. "But I have to do it. This is just one example of something that would have been absolutely unthinkable 10 years ago."[47]

These complaints were echoed by the other big studios, which, like Lenfilm, underwent a change of the guard at the top. Karen Shakhnazarov replaced Vladimir Dostal as Mosfilm's director, in 1998. That year, the studio was able to produce eight films thanks to a special grant from the city of Moscow, personally supported by Mayor Yuri Luzhkov. But in May 1999, Shakhnazarov complained that the studio did not have a single film in production. He explained:

> In the Soviet Union the studios were part of the cinema conveyor belt. Mosfilm, Lenfilm, Gorky Studio, Sverdlovsk Studio were huge film enterprises by European standards; they were designed to produce about one hundred films per year. At Mosfilm, in those days, there were about eighty films in production at any given time, and forty of them were released every year. These were colossal pictures with big budgets, gigantic mass scenes, and compelling decor. Russian cinema today is by necessity a chamber cinema on a small budget. And yet, cinema must be spectacular! Perhaps, the fact that our cinema today lacks the element of spectacle is the reason why the viewers prefer to watch old Soviet movies. Soviet cinema was a branch of industry, providing the ideological output commissioned

by the state. Therefore, in that system the big studios had a logical function. In the present situation, their structure does not fit the reality of the day.[48]

The Law on Cinema that finally came into effect in 1999 raised some hopes. But soon it became clear that it would not bring the financial relief many expected. The law granted the studios the 20 percent value-added tax exemption that normally is a big boost for businesses. But the filmmakers argued that they already enjoyed the exemption, if not by law, by an agreement with the State Revenue Service and by government decree.[49] Furthermore, they felt that the law could restrict freedom of expression. In order to qualify for tax exemption a film had to be certified by Goskino as a "national film." This meant that the film had to be produced and directed by a Russian company, have no more than 30 percent of the budget funded by foreign money, have the director and the screenwriter hold a Russian passport, and have a crew that included no more than 30 percent of foreigners. In addition, the law required that the film be in Russian or another language spoken in the Russian Federation, and that at least 50 percent of the budget be spent in Russia.[50]

Another provision of the law was the right to privatize the studios. This was too little, too late. After the crash of August '98, capital for this kind of investment evaporated. One observer of the situation commented: "Nobody today wants to buy the non-existent stocks of Lenfilm or of the Gorky Studio, unless they have second motives for the purchase--for example, to obtain a choice plot of land downtown, and turn the studio grounds into a Russian Disneyland."[51]

The Mosfilm privatization fiasco is a case in point. As early as 1997, the government placed Mosfilm on the list of enterprises to be privatized in order to breathe new life into the ailing film industry. The legendary film studio was scheduled to go on the block by the end of the year, together with rusty tractor plants and idle cotton mills. While some decried the decision as the loss of a symbol of the national cultural heritage, the Mosfilm leadership at first supported it. Vladimir Dostal, the studio director, had advocated privatization for many years. He himself eventually moved to the private sector in 1998, and became the head of Kino-MOST, an offspring of the Gusinsky holding for the production of TV programs and music videos--which was promptly nicknamed MOSTfilm. When Mosfilm was scheduled to be auctioneered, the studio management tried to dispel the idea that the glorious film facility would become a commodity. They reminded the plan's opponents that the recently passed Law on Cinema prevented film studios to be converted to other uses, such as hotels or office complexes. But fears were not unjustified, given the prevalent appetite for real estate development and the many ways law could be circumvented. Mosfilm occupies 15 acres of choice land on Sparrow Hills, an area that includes government mansions and foreign embassies. In those elegant surroundings, Mosfilm's decay had become more and more obvious since the money spigot from the government coffers dried out. The last time I visited the studio, on the occasion of a memorial for Sergei Bondarchuk, the sad state of the establishment reflected the passing of one of the pillars of its glorious days. Notwithstanding a valiant struggle for survival that included renting out space for offices and warehouses, the physical plant deteriorated beyond recognition, and needed an urgent injection of funds to repair leaking roofs, chipped walls, rusty pipes, and alleys overgrown with weeds. Maintenance personnel were decimated, as the studio staff dropped from 5,000 to 500.

By the summer of 1997, there were many pretenders to the ownership of Mosfilm. Among them were the major TV stations, which had an eye to the studio's film library believed to be holding more than 1,000 favorites of the Soviet era. Those films, which used to draw millions of viewers to the movie theaters, were still able to generate record-breaking ratings for television networks. Between 1994 and 1997, one hundred fifteen Soviet films were shown 10 times each. About 80 percent of those came from Mosfilm, which since 1990 had held exclusive broadcasting rights to its collection in both the former USSR and beyond its borders. The profits could be substantial. A one-minute commercial spot during prime time was priced up to $30,000. A Mosfilm movie, therefore, could potentially generate $180,000 for six minutes of advertising time.[52] Of all the pretenders, Gusinsky seemed to have the best chance to succeed. His Media-MOST group had offered $166 million in investment over six years to upgrade the studio, and a no-interest $15 million loan to finance film production. Media-MOST's plan also included the construction of several movie theaters to facilitate distribution, and broadcasting through its NTV channel. The money was supposed to buy a 49 percent stake in the film enterprise as soon as the government turned the studio into a joint-stock company, and the official bidding began.

However, at the end of the day it turned out that, contrary to their declarations, Mosfilm managers had preempted the government's move to privatize the studio. As early as February 1997, the studio leadership had set up a new, non-commercial association, also called Mosfilm, which replaced the government-owned Mosfilm concern. The new charter superseded Mosfilm's status as one of those enterprises that were born in the perestroika period, state-owned but managed on a self-financing basis. A battle in the courts ensued, with unclear results. But one result was clear: this imbroglio, together with the economic downturn of 1998 and Gusinsky's own troubles, made all the potential investors disappear.

Good-bye Goskino. Hello *"goszakaz"*

By the end of the 1990s, all the major film institutions had a new leadership--the Filmmakers Union, Goskino, Mosfilm, Lenfilm, and also the Gorky Studio with Vladimir Grammatikov at the helm.[53] Usually, a change in leadership brings about the expectation of a new beginning. But in this case, the Russian film industry was headed for another blow. In May 2000, Goskino became one of the victims of President Putin's restructuring of the federal government. The cinema agency was abolished and absorbed into the Ministry of Culture. The move was met with outrage by hundreds of members of the film community, who held a rally in central Moscow and sent an open letter to Putin, expressing their indignation. There is a bitter irony to the situation. Filmmakers, who for decades resented the heavy yoke of the agency under Soviet rule, were now rallying in its defense. The truth is that in the past ten years Goskino had turned into a structure capable of influencing decisions in favor of the studios. Goskino's head held the status of a minister and had access to the premier and the president. The filmmakers feared that they had lost a lobby. The government, eager to re-establish a good relationship with the Filmmakers Union, made concessions to resolve the conflict; among them, the creation of the Ministry of Culture Cinema Service, headed by

Alexander Golutva. Within the new structure, Golutva was named first deputy minister of culture. In August 2000, the Cinema Service submitted a five-year plan in support of the industry—"The Cinema of Russia"— as part of the federal program, "The Culture of Russia: 2001-2005." The initiative was taken without asking the filmmakers for their input, and the film community expressed concern that the 20 billion rubles allotted to the plan over five years may quickly be squandered for the realization of grandiose projects dear to a big bureaucracy's heart.

A Russian journalist described the document as being extremely vague and grandiloquent: "The basic theses of the program 'The Cinema of Russia' are written in the style of the Soviet socialist proclamations. The short-term goals are global and full of passion, as in Brezhnev's five-year plans—'steady cultivation of Russian cinema's creative potential,' 'stimulating the flow of new creative forces,' 'building a mighty Russian film industry,' 'improving the prestige of Russian films abroad,' and the like."[54] Mikhail Shvydkoi, the minister of culture, admitted openly that the entire five-year plan was reminiscent of the Soviet model: "Simply put," he said, "next year we will return to the *goszakaz* system (state-commission system) in the area of culture." He elaborated, saying that the federal budget will fund a small number of "socially significant works" that sustain the goals of the government's cultural policy. This policy raised the ghost of a re-ideologization of culture accompanied by favoritism and a nomenklatura-like elite.[55]

Subsequently, the 2003 draft budget for film production showed a 50 percent increase. Shvydkoy said on that occasion (September 2002) that by 2006 Russia should be producing up to 100 films per year, and that state funds would be used to finance films of "a patriotic, historical, or national" nature, as well as children's films.[56] And more recently, Putin reiterated the state's support for culture at a meeting of the Presidential Council for Culture and Art (February 2003). Putin declared that he supported calls for "reviving the so-called state-commission system for the creation of culture and works of art that have an indisputable social value."[57]

On the "right" side

The move from left to right was not good for Russian cinema in the short run. The filmmakers had to come to grips with a situation of great disorientation and instability. They did it individually, each following the course determined case by case by money availability and artistic inspiration, since there was no film industry as such that could set general trends, make policies, and provide the infrastructure. Neither was there an audience to make specific demands. Potentially good films could not be produced for lack of funds; others were not distributed because of the market dynamics. The ones that were produced and ended up on commercial screens were often the result of lucky circumstances, rather than a sustainable plan. The film market, offering a few national products and a lot of cheap imports, paralleled the free-trade form of the bazaar. Competition was shaped not so much by economic laws as it was by the laws of the jungle, from intellectual property piracy to murder.

The abrupt passage from socialism to capitalism (a regression in Marxist terms) produced a change of scene. New props were displayed. New actors entered, but without a coherent set of values. The Orthodox Church hastily repositioned itself as a conservative political force and reclaimed its role as the nation's official spiritual guide. Capitalism and democracy were concepts poorly understood in Russia, and in the current context they raised a fundamental question of identity. Placed between East and West, the Russians were unsure of which way was the Russian way--a question they have asked themselves for three centuries without ever coming to a comfortable conclusion. After the 1996 presidential election, the Yeltsin government assembled a commission to head the search for a "new Russian idea," an ideology appropriate to the new democratic era. But, despite many efforts, including a national contest to identify a set of principles, Yeltsin's tenure ended without producing the new idea.[58]

Amid the cultural breakdown, the filmmakers had great difficulties finding an adequate stance toward state and society. A successful producer, Andrei Razumovsky, founder of the studio Fora-Film, described this situation of moral confusion: "We have lost a large number of film artists—many of the older masters could not adapt to the new situation, or simply did not find any interesting subject for themselves or for the public. The absence of censorship turned out to be not a stimulus but an obstacle. Of course, it would be absurd to say that it was better before. But our people were used to living under the thumb. And in almost ten years, they had not learned how to use their freedom."[59]

And yet, regardless of the ongoing economic struggle, the political fights within the Filmmakers Union, frustrated hopes, and loss of prestige, the Russian film community was determined not to give up. It was this kind of determination, the will of many individuals, that allowed the cinema industry to survive throughout the decade and that, in the end, produced a considerable body of films. They will eventually become known as the "films of shock capitalism," or whatever labels the historians will think of. What characterizes them is diversity rather than similarity. The films of shock capitalism do not easily fall into a trend or a movement—unless we consider the prevalent anarchic cultural tendency itself as a movement. The general direction of the 1990s was a freewheeling, anything-goes philosophy resulting in a hodgepodge of genres and themes. Cinema offerings around Moscow reminded me of the selection of goods in the marketplace, in metro underpasses, and in the large bazaars—*babushki* peddling hand-knit socks and Marlboro cigarettes next to Daghestani rug sellers and dealers of Italian shoes, Korean computers, and Chinese parkas.

No more ideology, no more formal restrictions, no more thematic constraints. Many filmmakers rushed to realize whatever pet project had been waiting in the drawer for years. Others simply gave free rein to their imagination. Still others interpreted freedom as licentiousness and reproduced the basest aspects of imported capitalist cultures. It was an intoxicating celebration of freedom of expression, limited only by financial difficulties. Many of these films reassess the past, placing different spins on various epochs and figures according to the director's ideological orientation. Others reflect the reality of the present day, either in dramatic or grotesque form. Still others offer escapism into imaginary worlds. The films discussed in this book cover all of the above. They may vary in production values and intellectual level, but each is a document of the specific time and place in which it was produced. Each film, therefore, is relevant as a cultural product of this bizarre Russian *fin de siècle*.

2
History in the Making and on Screen

Forward to the past

The dramatic events that for three days shook the city of Moscow—if not the world—in August 1991 took place at the theater of another popular uprising. There, in the Krasnaya Presnya district, near the by now famous and infamous White House, every name commemorated the bloody repression of the 1905 workers' revolution—Ploshchad Vosstania (Uprising Square), Metro Barrikadnaya (Metro Barricade), Ulitsa 1905-go goda (1905 Street). The stage was set long ago, and the thousands that walked on it eighty-five years later gave a stupendous performance.

It started on Monday, at twelve noon. Not the coup itself, which took place in the wee hours, but the people's awakening, the first signs that a new spirit had taken hold of the citizens of Moscow. As the tanks converged downtown from three strategic directions, the Muscovites gathered on Manezh Square, where a rally had been called. Leaflets xeroxed in the thousands were circulated. They carried President Yeltsin's appeal "To the Citizens of Russia," denouncing the illegality of the self-proclaimed new government and calling for a general strike.[1]

I walked with the crowd down Gorky Street, which had been closed to traffic. Buses and trolleys had been placed at the crossing with Manezh Square to protect the rally. All other points of access to the square were also blocked. On the bus tops, clusters of citizens waved the tricolor flag of the Russian Republic, which had been adopted from the Netherlands by Peter the Great in the eighteenth century. On the square, speakers from a platform placed by the sidewall of the Hotel Moskva invited the crowd to calm. There was little information in those early hours. Mass

40 Imaging Russia 2000

1   Around the White House, August 1991

media were the first to be seized by the special forces in the morning. Only the decree of the State Extraordinary Committee (*Gosudarstvenny Komitet Chrezvychainogo Polozheniia, GKChP*) announcing the state of emergency was broadcast periodically on the radio. Most people stayed away from Red Square, where the plotters had hunkered down behind the Kremlin walls.

The mood was somber, but not passive. The comments were sad, and yet full of sardonic humor, describing the perpetrators of the coup as both a gang of criminals and a bunch of clowns. One thing was clear, the people were not afraid. Many were carrying signs, others had painted slogans on buildings and buses. The words were eloquent: "Fascism will not pass," "Down with the CPSU," "Yazov's gang, on trial." Notwithstanding the gravity of the situation, there was an atmosphere of excitement, a sort of euphoria bordering on carnival. On top of a bus, a group of punks with heavy-metal vests and Mohican haircuts displayed a black pirate flag with skull and bones.

Suddenly, the rumor spread over the square like a shock wave: the tanks are coming! The big green bugs were coming from the north, along Gorky Street, and from both the northeast and the southwest along Marx Prospect. The square had become a potential deadly trap. The crowd hesitated, swayed; then, decisively crossed the bus barriers to confront the tanks. It was the first victory. Solid matrons, mothers with children, workers, students, pensioners stopped three armed columns with the force of their presence. I was near a woman carrying two bags of groceries. She climbed on a tank and offered bread and milk to the soldiers. Another woman appealed to the feelings of the young recruits: "Sons," she said, "what are you doing? You can't shoot your own people. We are your parents, your brothers and sisters."

With hindsight, it all looks and sounds a bit melodramatic—like footage from *Battleship Potemkim* or similar epic dramatizations. But often life imitates art. That day the tanks stopped. The soldiers fraternized. Red carnations bloomed on guns.

At another location, by the white marble building on the bank of the Moscow River, Yeltsin was addressing the armed forces from atop a tank. His words, which were carried the next day by the press all over the world, seemed to belong in the same script:

2 Around the White House, August 1991

Soldiers and officers, at this tragic hour I call on you. Don't let yourselves be misled. Don't allow adventurers to use you as blind weapons. Soldiers, I call on you. Think about your loved ones, your friends and your people! . . . Remember that you have taken an oath to your people, and now your weapons may be turned against them. . . . Soldiers, I believe at this tragic hour you will make the right decision. The honor of Russian arms will not be covered with the blood of the people![2]

A crowd of supporters gathered around the leader. In the afternoon, the action concentrated around the White House. I lost my friends in the confusion and followed the people down to the embankment. At the time, the building was the seat of the Russian Republic's parliament, housing Yeltsin's headquarters. The White House was in danger of being stormed that very night. Barricades were hurriedly built all around it on the citizens' initiative. Again, buses were brought in, trolleys, heavy trucks, bulldozers, cranes, cement slabs, iron pipes, water mains, steel rods. At dusk, all strategic points were blocked. Behind the barricades the vigil began. People gathered around bonfires. There was trepidation and hope. Guitars appeared out of nowhere and the music helped keep the spirit high.

Hope turned into elation, when later in the night it became clear that the expected confrontation would not take place. The Ryazan Division paratroops, under General Pavel Grachev, had crossed over to the side of the citizens of Moscow. Support also came from a still unknown major general from Tula, who was dispatched to Moscow with his 106th Guards Airborne Division. As soon as the troops entered the city, he ordered them to defect to Yeltsin's camp and take up defensive positions around the Russian parliament building. The general's name was Alexander Lebed.[3]

Around the White House and on the Kalininsky Bridge, a number of stray tanks were "adopted" by the people, and, like pet dinosaurs, were adorned with flags and flowers, patted, pampered, and fed until the end of the ordeal. But fearing a second attack, the people kept the vigil, shivering through the cold rainy night, with little water and food. The next day, citizen defense committees were organized and collected provisions, money, blankets, tents, and wood for the bonfires. I kept running into

44 Imaging Russia 2000

3 Around the White House, August 1991

colleagues and friends—journalists, filmmakers, artists, scholars—all moved by a spirit of solidarity, and anxious to witness that extraordinary piece of history. When I left, around 2:00 a.m., I walked against a human stream, rushing down to the embankment in defiance of the curfew.

On Tuesday, there was a widespread feeling that the State Extraordinary Committee was not in control. The defense around the Russian parliament got more organized. The volunteers were grouped in detachments of 1,500 men each, including many of the renegade paratroopers. At noon, a large rally took place by the White House. One hundred fifty thousand people gathered in the park behind the building to listen to political leaders and cultural figures. The crowd was even bolder now, as if charged with the strength that radiated from the second floor balcony. They chanted: "Down with the junta," "Dictatorship will not pass," "We will win." And more often, "Russia, Russia," "Yeltsin, Yeltsin." From the balcony, the speakers avoided the usual form of address, "comrades," and called the people "friends," "citizens," "Muscovites."[4]

Fiery words resonated. "We were held down on our knees for seventy years," said Yuri Vlasov, a member of the Supreme Soviet of the Russian Republic and a weight-lifting Olympic champion, "that gang counted on that, they counted on our meekness. They were wrong." The people responded: "Down with the CPSU!" Vlasov continued: "This is not a coup, this is an acknowledgment of their bankruptcy. They are the cowards, not we." The people chanted: "Down with the reactionaries!"

The rally turned into spectacle as a number of popular figures alternated at the microphone. Father Gleb Yakunin blessed the crowd. He had served five years in Soviet jails and internal exile for human rights activities, and later became a radical leader of the reform movement.[5] The poet Evgeny Yevtushenko showed up, as he has since the 1960s at all historical turning points, and offered a newly composed poem. Sakharov's widow, Elena Bonner, struck a dramatic figure in a black dress and red scarf. Her pale face and lapidary words brought to mind the image of Inessa Armand ("La Pasionaria"), the Spanish revolutionary who spent most of her life in Russia. Bonner's speech was forceful and emotional, and at one point she was moved to tears. General Oleg Kalugin, former deputy head of the KGB's foreign intelligence service, received a roaring ovation when he came out to declare that many of the security forces were siding with the Russian government.[6] Actor Gennadi

Khazanov, a member of the Supreme Soviet of the Russian Republic, offered some comic relief. "Dear friends," he said in Gorbachev's southern accent, "I want to let you know that I am well, and that now I think that clean politics cannot be done by dirty, shaky hands." The crowd burst out laughing. The reference was to the junta chief, Gennady Yanaev, whom Gorbachev had chosen as his vice president in November 1990. When Yanaev appeared on TV after the coup, as the acting president of the Soviet Union with the other members of the putsch to explain the action of the committee, his hands were shaking with the tremor of advanced alcoholism.[7] A highlight of the rally was the appearance of Eduard Shevardnadze, who had warned about the coming of dictatorship less than a year earlier, when he resigned as Foreign Minister of the USSR. He had not been in the public eye for some time, but he came to the rally because, as he said, "true political actions are where the people are."

Another compelling moment was the appearance of the representative of the Donbas miners' strike committee, Malygin. Referring to the desperate action taken by the miners in defiance of the government the previous year, he said that the miners were ready to go on strike again. "But," he added, "don't let us down as you did before. Alone, we cannot succeed." The people shouted: "We are with you!" A nation-wide miner's strike of 500,000 people had occurred in the summer of 1989. This was the first massive strike recorded in Soviet times, and the beginning of a spontaneous labor movement. The miners of the Donbas took the lead and put forward a package of economic demands. On July 1990, the miners went on strike for the second time, now with political demands, asking for the resignation of Prime Minister Ryzhkov and his government. The miners' mood in the aftermath of the struggle was captured on film by TV journalist Vladimir Molchanov, in the documentary *Coal Miners*, which was aired on national television on June 29, just two months before the coup. About the film, Molchanov said prophetically: "We see our film as an obituary to what is called a 'socialist choice.' An obituary to the system which, from generation to generation, was churning out obedient slaves."[8] Down in the mine pit, microphone in hand, Molchanov is surrounded by the restive "slaves," their headlamps shedding a dim light around the cramped space. The eyes are like sparkling diamonds on the blackened faces when, in answer to Molchanov's questions, they refer to themselves as "former Communists," and claim that their greatest moment of happiness occurred "when we announced the strike." The film had a tragic coda. On the night it was aired, an explosion in one of the mines took the lives of thirty-two men.[9]

At the rally the enthusiasm reached its peak when Yeltsin himself came out on the balcony, his silver hair shining in the sun that had just come out from behind the clouds. He charmed the crowd. His speech was direct and captivating. "This is the first time our government talks to us in a human voice," my neighbor marveled. At that moment I saw Yeltsin with the thousands of eyes that surrounded me. He stood there, solid as a rock, unshakable, the last bastion for the defense of democracy and the people's hopes.

The "Yeltsin film" should have ended with that shot, an image of the leader forever charismatic and inspiring. Unfortunately, history's script is out of control, and the sequels that followed—Yeltsin 2, Yeltsin 3, etc.—did not measure up to the original.

On Tuesday night, the uprising claimed its victims. Three young men were killed in a skirmish with heavy military personnel transport. It was a freak accident. They got crushed while trying to stop the armored vehicles. Nevertheless, it ennobled the insurrection with the blood of martyrdom. The accident occurred in the underpass at the crossing of Kalinin Prospect and the Garden Ring. I arrived at the scene, by chance, minutes after the episode occurred. Pools of blood were still on the pavement. Paramedics had just removed the bodies. Two armored carriers were burning, as the result of Molotov cocktails. All around the entrance to the underpass people were standing shoulder-to-shoulder, leaning on the railing like spectators on a theater balcony. Many were weeping—and not because of the smoke.

On Wednesday, the mood wavered between mourning and a hardly contained exuberance. Victory was near. Radio Russia was operating from an improvised station inside the White House. The first independent radio, Echo of Moscow, had also miraculously resumed broadcasting. The station had been in operation for exactly one year, and had acquired a reputation for accuracy of information and a refreshing viewpoint. During those fateful days, it became a popular hero.

I was able to attend the extraordinary session of the Supreme Soviet of the Russian Republic that took place that morning. Security was haphazard outside and inside the White House, notwithstanding the great display of force and the fierce stance of the voluntary militia that provided a human shield all around the building. I only had to show my press credentials to get through the cordons. Actually, two militiamen literally lifted me up and over a barricade to facilitate access to the steps that lead to the upper esplanade from the riverside. The guards at the door did not even check my bag.

From the press box up on the balcony, I saw how the discussions were constantly interrupted by deputies and aides delivering urgent dispatches to the podium. The dispatches were immediately read aloud and subsequently broadcast over the airwaves. The news from the White House bombarded the radio audience every half hour: the junta has fled, some members have been arrested, Gorbachev has been rescued, he is on his way back to Moscow. In the early afternoon, General Gromov and the commander of Soviet ground forces, General Varennikov, overturned the order issued by Defense Minister Dmitri Yazov and recalled the troops. At dusk, a three-mile-long column of tanks and trucks was retreating from Moscow, flying the tricolor of Russia.

Thursday was a celebration day. The Russian colors flew on the pinnacle of the White House. Even on the Kremlin dome, red-white-and-blue waved side by side with the Soviet flag. The pre-revolutionary Cross of St. George was reinstated as a military decoration for the troops that sided with the Russian Republic. V-signs in the crowd replaced clenched fists.

But with all revolutions, the romantic élan is just a flash. What follows is never as stirring or as inspiring. In the following days, a vengeful atmosphere set in. The prevalent mood was for squaring accounts with the Soviet regime. The headquarters of the Central Committee of the Communist Party were sealed and the Party disbanded. The monument to Felix Dzerzhinsky, the first head of the Cheka (secret police), which towered in front of the Lubyanka, was torn down by the junior staff of the Russian Commodities Exchange—which had just been inaugurated three weeks before, on August 1. The founder and CEO of the Commodities Exchange, Konstantin Borovoy, at a reception bragged that his guys were the ones that took the initiative and replaced the monument to "iron

Felix" with the Russian flag--a flag, he added, that will soon cover the whole map. These words fueled fears among some observers of a resurgence of Russian nationalism. And they had not seen anything yet, as Vladimir Zhirinovsky was still in the wings.

Other bronze idols fell—Sverdlov, Kalinin. They were taken to a peculiar site by the Central House of Artists, a sculpture cemetery of sort that eventually became a tourist attraction. Marx's statue in front of the Bolshoi Theater was splotched with paint and graffiti. Only Lenin's monument on the October Square esplanade did not suffer any indignities. Neither was Lenin himself kicked out of his Mausoleum, as it had been rumored and threatened for some time. Eventually, his guard of honor was removed (in October1993, after the second insurrection). This was a pity, because the change of the guard under the Kremlin chimes was a significant aesthetic component of the Red Square setting. But at that historical juncture, Soviet kitsch was about to be replaced by "restoration" kitsch à la Luzhkov.[10]

As the lights went out on the stage of the dramatic struggle, a brief period of hopes and expectations began. Boris Yeltsin was the embodiment of those feelings. However, throughout Russian history the need to rely on a new leader has always been as strong as it has been short-lived, and Tsar Boris' popularity lasted no more then a couple of years.

But the first to fall was Gorbachev. The other major protagonist in the August '91 drama was forced off screen throughout the entire action by the perpetrators of the putsch. Consequently, he was eclipsed by Yeltsin's burly figure, and demoted to a secondary role. There was already a black cloud over Gorbachev's head when the coup occurred. For more than a year, Gorbachev's political allies had been greatly concerned with his shift toward the party's conservative wing. The people were disappointed with Gorbachev's economic performance and blamed him for the slow pace of perestroika. During the ordeal, popular resentment changed to sympathy for the president and his family held under house arrest in the Crimea—but no more than that. Upon Gorbachev's return, uneasy questions were raised, which were not satisfactorily answered. Why did Gorbachev support the hard-liners who eventually betrayed him? Why did he still support the Communist Party? The cool reception Gorbachev got in the capital was an indication that he had lost the popular power base.

Only a few recognized that it was thanks to glasnost and the democratic reforms introduced by Gorbachev that the people were able to take the situation in their own hands. Six years of open debate and freedom of expression had changed the people's psychology and behavior beyond recognition. This was not only a Moscow phenomenon. Many came from Leningrad, the Russian provinces, and the Baltic republics to mix with the Muscovites in the defense of democracy. But even among the intelligentsia the general feeling was that Gorbachev did a good deed, and it was now time for him to step down graciously and take his place in history. It did not happen that way. Gorbachev was forced to step down, and most Russians saw his exit, sad to say, as less than honorable. Public opinion turned against him in the newly born Russian Federation, and history was rewritten in the people's mind. The prevalent belief—still well alive in the year 2000 and beyond—was that "Gorbachev dissolved the Soviet Union," "destroyed the economy," and "sold the country to the Americans." The facts were ignored.

It was conveniently forgotten that Gorbachev was the author of the Novo-Ogarevo treaty, designed to save the Soviet Union by ceding more power to the republics without relinquishing Moscow's central role. The coup prevented the signing of the treaty that was scheduled to take place on August 20, and afterwards Gorbachev lost the support he needed to revive the project. But until the end, as one after another the republics declared their sovereignty, Gorbachev struggled to keep together at least a semblance of the Soviet Union, convinced that its disintegration would mean an economic catastrophe. As late as November, in a meeting with the presidents of the republics, Gorbachev showed his frustration in no uncertain terms: "You know, when you set up your shantytown instead of a united state you will put your people to torture. We are drowning in the shit as it is! . . . If you reject the confederate state version, then just go on without me!"[11] On December 7, Yeltsin, Kravchuk, and Shushkevich did exactly that. The presidents of Russia, Ukraine and Belorussia met in Belovezhskaya Pushcha, near the Polish border and erased the Soviet Union from the world map with a stroke of the pen.

The irony is that in those early days, the populace looked at Yeltsin as the savior of the motherland. They ignored Yeltsin's personal animosity toward Gorbachev for forcing him out of the Politburo, and his desire to get even—factors that heavily influenced his actions. But as the country's prestige dwindled and the economic situation worsened, the mood began to change. Yeltsin eventually joined the villain camp; yet, that did not exonerate Gorbachev in the public's eye.

Screenwriter Rustam Ibragimbekov, looking back to that fateful turning point from an eight-year perspective, gave the following assessment of the post-Gorbachev period:

> The intelligentsia sincerely believed in the banners and the slogans of the new people in power, as if they themselves had acquired the power—the democrats, the liberals, the reformers. There was no doubt, everybody was to help and sustain the new power.
>
> The front of the new power took shape rather quickly and the intelligentsia was part of it. With the best of intentions the intelligentsia began to help building a new society. Exactly as in the 1920s, when the average intellectual believed that a cook could become the head of government overnight, and served the communist ideals without understanding that those in power would exploit him for their interests.
>
> But very soon everything changed, even faster than after the Bolshevik revolution. . . . The media fell into the hands of those who were interested in maintaining a pseudo-democracy and a pseudo-market. . . . We do not have democracy, and never did, and never had a free market either. It's all a lie. As a result, something terrible happened: the people's disillusionment with democracy as such.[12]

History lessons and tales

History is a difficult subject for cinema, especially in Russia, where it has been distorted by seventy years of Soviet propaganda. Several history pages were deleted altogether. But even in democratic countries, where people tend to trust history books, institutional and personal interpretations remain an issue. There are many theories of "what" history is, and no general consensus among historians. Is history a science, and therefore quantifiable and objective? Or, is history a narrative, and therefore a literary genre, subjective by nature? Or, as Michel Foucault postulated, there is no history, only a series of "epistemes" (systems of discourse), which came to dominate each historical era. In cinema, both the concept of narrative (artistically created) and the concept of "episteme" (power generated) seem to apply. Both *Battleship Potemkin* and *Saving Private Ryan*—just to name two examples—are pieces of fiction. Certainly, they show realistic details and build the action around historical facts. But those facts do not come down from the screen in a pristine form. They are mediated by the authors' sensibility, values, experiences, and ideology, which comprise the power/knowledge environment at the time of production. And most of all, assuming that records and documents are not falsified and the authors maintain an honest point of view vis-à-vis history, visual representation is in itself an altering factor. Cinematic representation involves selection and organization of images and sound track, and the final outcome is determined by how each element is chosen and combined in an overall meaningful configuration. The final product is, therefore, a cultural object whose mode of representation reflects the contemporary sensibility, and the way this sensibility interprets the past.[13]

If we look mostly for factual materials in a historical film, we are missing the point. We might as well get the information from *Encyclopedia Britannica*. The value of a historical film lies elsewhere. It consists of two factors. One is a record, not of the period depicted, but of the period when the story was conceived and given an aesthetic form. To stick with our examples, *Battleship Potemkin* is a document of the USSR of 1925, and *Saving Private Ryan* reflects the psychological and political setup of the United States in 2000. This is true of pure fictional narratives as well, and when the film is an adaptation from a literary original the issue is doubly compounded. The other factor is the condensation of history in a cluster of images that emotionally convey a concept or a message. Eisenstein conceived *Battleship Potemkin* as a visual distillation of all revolutions--"Revolution" as an idea. This is the real truth of the film.

While the first factor is a matter of fact, the second one requires talent and skills, and only a few films achieve that artistic level. But with those that do, an interesting phenomenon occurs. Fiction turns into history. The cinematic image impacts the human psyche in such a way that it is perceived as real. Eisenstein reported that an actual sailor from the Potemkin, after seeing the film, wrote him a letter complimenting the director for the accuracy of the historical details, and saying that he was among those sailors who were to be executed under the tarpaulin before the mutiny. The truth was, Eisenstein confessed, that that scene in the film was entirely made up.[14] Thus, context at the time of production and visual impact will be the predominant criteria in the discussion of Russian historical films of the end of the twentieth century.

In the last years of the Soviet regime, the film industry enjoyed an unprecedented situation. Still fully funded by the government, it was free from censorship and party directives. Gorbachev's policy of glasnost encouraged film production and the pursuit of previously forbidden topics. The rediscovery of the past became an obsession with both the suppliers and the consumers of information. The filmmakers turned out dozens of films meant to "fill in the blanks in the history books." This tendency continued into the 1990s, but with less of a sense of urgency. The new films focused more intimately on the protagonists of the historical events; they turned to the individual's inner world, to personal dramas and feelings against the background of Russia's tragic destiny. While some films portray historical figures, others use historical settings as a backdrop for fictional characters. They reveal not so much a quest for historical truth as a need to understand the relation of the individual to history and assess his/her responsibility. The question of individual responsibility is then transferred to the present time.

The Assassin of the Tsar (1991) is an Anglo-Soviet co-production directed by Karen Shakhnazarov. The film revolves around the execution of Nicholas II and his family. However, as the title suggests, the focus is on the killer who masterminded the execution, Yakov Yurovsky. He had been a Bolshevik in the underground for several years, a jeweler, a photographer, and a medic. After the October revolution he became a member of the Cheka in Ekaterinburg, and eventually was put in charge of the guard at the imperial family's exile home.

The subject of the last Russian tsar and the cruel fate that befell his family was banned under Soviet rule. Only two films were produced previous to this one—*The Fall of the Romanov Dinasty* (1927), a documentary by Esther Shub, which reflected the Bolshevik position, and *Rasputin* (1975) by Elem Klimov, which represented the view of the liberal intelligentsia in the Brezhnev years and, therefore, was banned. Another film was produced at the end of the century, *The Romanovs: The Crowned Fam-*

ily (2000) by Gleb Panfilov, which turned the tables on the image of the tsar fostered by Soviet propaganda, and rehabilitated the man.

The Assassin is concerned with the murderer's psychology more than the factual event, although the scenes of the family's last days are depicted in detail, with emotional participation. The main action takes place in the 1980s in a Soviet mental institution, where a schizophrenic patient (Malcolm McDowell) fancies that he is the man who killed the tsar. The doctor in charge of the case (Oleg Yankovsky) gets so involved with the patient's neurosis that he himself falls victim to the same pathology. In an effort to confront the ghostly assassin directly, the doctor assumes the tsar's personality, and eventually dies of a heart attack. Flashes from the tsar's family life in the exile town of Ekaterinburg alternate with the drab environment of the psychiatric ward, weaving a web that connects four individual personalities across time and space. Motifs from Chekhov's story, "Ward Number Six," are obvious, as well as echoes of Dostoevsky's tormented doubles.

Dostoevsky's position on ethics and politics is in fact one of the main underlying elements. The mental patient during a therapy session explains his motivation for killing the tsar. If there is no God, he argues, there is no limit to free will; if one asserts his free will and kills a monarch, then he will cease to be a nonentity and his name will go down in history. He mouths the well-known superman theory that was espoused by Raskolnikov in *Crime and Punishment*, as well as by Ivan Karamazov and the unsavory characters from *The Possessed*. But the film is larger than a single individual's case; in fact, it broadens the philosophical discourse to the very concept of regicide, commenting on history's inevitable dynamics between state and revolution. In the prologue, we hear the tale of Balthazar, the last king of Babylon, who was killed by his servants; the tale is later repeated by Voikov, one of the Bolsheviks involved in Nicholas's execution. The assassination of Alexander II is also part of the patient's delusional universe. The doctor, talking as Nicholas, says that when his grandfather, and later his father, were murdered at the hand of the revolutionaries he knew that he would be next, that "they'll kill us all"—and adds: "Perhaps, Russia would be better and happier for that." Therefore, the film does not resolve the philosophical opposition between tyranny and liberation violence on the rational level, leaving the regicide dynamics in a state of tension. However, it does resolve it on the visual/emotional level.

In the case of Nicholas and his family, the viewer's emotions are stirred toward the perception of the episode as the slaughter of innocent victims. In the flashbacks, which are part of the patient's account, Yurovsky is often seen riding a bicycle, clad in black from hat to boots; the ends of his coat flapping in the air like the wings of a raven, a bearer of death. He moves in circles on the muddy streets of Ekaterinburg, waiting for its prey. Around the house, separating elements such as doors and windows keep him apart from the family, creating two distinct worlds—the world of sacrificial lambs and the world of murderous plotters. One is connoted by beauty, dignity, devotion, and courage. The other, by secrecy, isolation, and fear. The fear is palpable in Yurovsky's nervous behavior; everything suggests that he is frightened by the task but determined to carry it out. In order to sustain his will, he relies on official words and slogans—a coded telegram signed by Sverdlov, authorizing the execution, and an official sentencing by the Ural Executive Committee. After the fact, he justifies the murder repeating a line from the revolutionary catechism: "I fulfilled the will of the revolution."

The film was likely inspired by a document that appeared in 1989 in the journal *Ogonyok*, having been dug out from the Central Archive of the October Revolution as soon as the policy of glasnost opened it up to scholars. This was the legendary "Yurovsky Note"—the shocking report by the executioner of the night of July 16–17, 1918—which until then nobody had seen, although there were rumors about its existence.[15] Yurovsky, who in the Note refers to himself as "the commandant" left a chilling account of the massacre, which presumably served as a base for the cinematic reconstruction of the scene. Here are a few fragments:

> I suggested everyone dress right away.... When they were dressed I myself led them down the inner staircase to the cellar room. Downstairs a room had been chosen with a plastered wooden partition [to avoid ricochets] from which all the furniture had been removed. The detachment was at the ready in the next room. The R[omanov]s had no inkling.... Nich[olas] was carrying Alexei in his arms, the rest were carrying small pillows and various little items. Entering the empty room, A[lexandra] F[yodorovna] asked: "What, no chairs? May we not sit?" The com[mandant] ordered two chairs brought in.

Nich[olas] put A[lexei] in one and A. F. sat in the other. The rest the commandant ordered stay in a row. . . . When they were all standing, the detachment was called in. . . . When the detachment com[mandant] walked in, he told the R[omanov]s: "In view of the fact that your relatives are continuing their attack on Sov[iet] Russia, the Ural Executive Committee has decided to execute you." Nicholas turned his back to the detachment, his face to the family, then sort of came to and turned around to face the com[mandant] and asked: "What? What?" . . . Nich[olas] was killed by the commandant, point blank. Then A[lexandra] F[yodorovna] died immediately. . . . A[lexe]i, three of his sisters, the lady-in-waiting [Demidova], and Dr. Botkin were still alive. They had to be finished off. This amazed the com[mandant] since we had aimed straight for the heart. It was also surprising that the bullets from the revolvers bounced off for some reason and ricocheted, jumping around the room like hail. . . . The remaining bullets . . . went to finish off Nicholas's daughters and the strange vitality of the heir. . . . The whole procedure . . . took about twenty minutes.[16]

As it turned out from other eyewitness accounts, the daughters had the family jewels sewn up in their corsets, which created a sort of armor and prolonged their agony, and the heir had not yet been fatally hit because of the nervousness of the shooting squad. On screen, this scene becomes a devastating indictment of the execution. The sequence of the burial of the bodies is lengthy and sinister, and for Yurovsky it is clearly a rite of closure. His fear of transgression (*prestuplenie*, to use Dostoevsky's term) is being buried deep into his subconscious. When he meets with Lenin briefly three years later, the two of them talk about using the Romanovs' jewels to buy grain abroad, like two business partners discussing a commercial transaction. The only thing that upsets Yurovsky at that meeting is the fact that Lenin does not recognize him as the tsar's executioner. "He knew I did it and I waited for some kind of acknowledgment, but he did not say anything. Not a word, not a sign. And yet, we did it together, he and I," Yurovsky says in the film. His pride is hurt, but his conscience does not bother him.[17]

The guilt buried in Yurovsky's subconscious resurfaced seventy years later in the mind of the schizophrenic patient, who adds a contemporary dimension to the psychology of the killer. Talking as Yurovsky, he confesses that when he saw Nicholas as a family man concerned with the health of his son, he had doubts about his mission— "How does this relate to the guillotine?" he asked himself. But the doubts were suppressed. Another flicker of consciousness was stirred by a young peasant mother, whose girl had disappeared, probably murdered. Yurovsky was disturbed by that death; subconsciously he made the connection between the murder of the peasant girl and that of the imperial girls. They were mirror images, and no amount of ideology could change that. The patient seems to be quite distressed by the role he played as a killer. His emotions are obviously encroaching on the facts, expressing feelings that are appropriate to the political context of the late 1980s. At that time, history was being revised and guilt reassessed. Terms such as "execution" and "revolutionary duty" were often recognized as euphemisms for murder. The patient could be seen as a metaphor for the collective consciousness of the nation coming to terms with its past. But in the realistic framework of the narrative, the resurfacing of guilt lacks a clinical explanation. The viewer has to accept the observation of the old ward director, now retired, that science cannot explain all phenomena: "We're not supposed to understand everything, and we should not even try to."

The other film that deals with the assassination of a prominent leader is *Tale of the Unextinguished Moon* (1990) by Evgeny Tsymbal. It is adapted for the screen from a short story by Boris Pilnyak, which had been banned until the era of glasnost. When it was originally published in the journal *New World*, in 1926, all copies were confiscated on Stalin's orders and the subscribers had to sign a statement promising never to reveal the existence or the contents of that issue. Pilnyak was eventually arrested in a subsequent wave of purges and executed. Tsymbal recalled how, as a student in 1970, he received the story in great secrecy from one of his professors, who had preserved a copy of the journal for forty-four years at the risk of his own life.[18]

The novella dealt with the alleged murder of War Commissar Mikhail Frunze (slightly disguised under a different name), which occurred in 1925 while he was undergoing surgery for a stomach ulcer. Rumors had it that the surgical team was ordered from above to recommend an unnecessary operation, and to quietly liquidate the patient. That was Stalin's

4 *Tale of the Unextinguished Moon* (1990) directed by Evgeny Tsymbal

way of getting rid of a potential challenger at the beginning of his ascent to power. Pilnyak, already in those early days, understood very well the nature of the tyrant and the psychology of the victim. In the novella, as in the film, Stalin remains behind the scenes, while the victim submits willingly to the macabre game. The same game was repeated in the course of the next two decades, during several rounds of show trials, where hundreds of top political and military leaders falsely incriminated themselves. Tsymbal, in his previous film, *Defense Counsel Sedov* (1989), conveyed the chilling atmosphere of the tragicomedy of errors unfolding in the Stalin courts against "the enemies of the people."[19]

In *The Tale*, Tsymbal follows the spirit of Pilnyak's text as well as the style. Pilnyak's avant-garde prose is close to a movie script, and its dynamic pace, fragmented time, and haunting rhythm are well suited to the film. But besides the aesthetic appeal, it is obvious that the story held a human interest for the director. War Commissar Frunze, in the interpretation of Vladimir Steklov, comes across as a dramatic figure, a man caught in a tragic predicament. A hero of the Civil War, privileged, popular, and charismatic, he becomes suddenly aware of being vulnerable and defenseless against the monstrous political machinery that he helped to build. It is a case of the Revolution devouring her own children. As the Commissar's end approaches, the action is intercut with documentary footage of his bloody deeds on the battlefield. In particular, he is haunted by the memory of an action in which he had 350 cadets of the White Army drowned. He submits to his own death with a sense of frustration, the sad realization of being just another link in the chain of destruction. Previous images of the Commissar surrounded by his loving family in their sumptuous villa in the Crimea, give the character a human dimension that contrasts with the figure of Stalin. The dictator is portrayed as a sinister demon sitting by the fire, in the dark, within the Kremlin walls, from where he weaves a network of terror.

Director Andrei Konchalovsky, after spending ten years in Hollywood with varying fortunes, brought his latest film to Moscow in 1993.[20] *The Inner Circle* (1992), another film in the long series of works on the Stalin era, is an American-Italian-Russian co-production released in the West by Columbia Pictures. As in other co-productions, foreign actors were a requirement. Luckily, Tom Hulce and Lolita Davidovich turned out to be good fits for their roles, and the film had a moderate success in the director's homeland.

Hulce plays Ivan, a skilled movie projectionist who has the good fortune of getting a job at the Kremlin, showing movies for Stalin himself. It is a well-known fact that Stalin loved the movies and was a big fan of Chaplin's comedies. Ivan's job comes with a good salary, a food basket, and a uniform of the NKVD. Ivan is a true believer in the magnificence of the Soviet empire and the greatness of its leader. When his wife Nastya asks him whom he loves the most, he answers automatically: "Comrade Stalin!" To which Nastya replies: "And I love you most of everything in the world." Ivan is puzzled by the irreconcilable dilemma. Only many years later, after Stalin's death, does Ivan realize that he has been both the victim and the accomplice of a murderous system that destroyed millions of people, including his Jewish neighbors and his loving wife. In a compelling scene, an old professor, emaciated and frail, looks at the well-fed young simpleton in the uniform of the secret police and says: "If it weren't for those naive, honest Ivans like you, there would be no tyrants in this world." This is the pivotal idea of the film. The "Ivan syndrome" is emphasized in the final sequence, where on the occasion of Stalin's funeral 1,500 people were crushed to death in the crowd that wanted to get a last glimpse of their beloved idol.

Some Russian critics found fault with Konchalovsky's film for being too "Americanized." The picture, certainly, has a sleek veneer, facts and characters are simplified, the metaphors are transparent, and the ending is a sentimental soup meant to be appeasing and uplifting. On the other hand, there are touching moments, which allow the audience to identify emotionally with the characters. One of these is Nastya's visit to the orphanage for children of the "enemies of the people." The film also captures the terror that alienated husband from wife, children from parents, human being from human being. And it convincingly reiterates the paradox that evil holds a morbid fascination to its victims and thrives on their willingness to submit.

A director of proven fame, Pyotr Todorovsky, returned to the screen with a film whose title suggests enthusiastic approval by cheering audiences, *Encore, Once More, Encore!* (1992). To a Russian, however, the title also suggests a grimmer picture—the well-known painting by Pavel Fedotov (1815-1852) of the same title. The painting shows an army officer lying on a sofa in a drab garrison room, having a small dog perform a trick over and over by giving him the "encore" command--a picture of pettiness and entrapment. Todorovsky's previous film, *Intergirl* (1989), was a blockbuster. The story of a hard-currency prostitute, who marries a Swedish businessman and is then consumed by nostalgia for her Russian motherland while living in the lap of luxury, was not critical of the prostitute but of the Soviet system.[21] The same critique of a system that breeds moral prostitution underlies Todorovsky's *Encore*. The film's symbolism is often too obvious, and sometimes annoying. But, taken as a well-crafted period soap opera, it shows Todorovsky's professional handling of the genre. Like another of his previous pictures, *Wartime Romance* (1984), *Encore* deals with the post-World War II period, an epoch that Todorovsky knew first as a young man on the front line, and later as a career officer in a dull, provincial town.

Encore is set in a garrison enclave on the Soviet border with Eastern Europe. In this isolated microcosm, the elation of victory is short-lived. Soon the atmosphere is poisoned with the nightmare of totalitarian rule, party regulations, repression, and denunciations. Lies penetrate all layers of social and private life, betrayal becomes a means of survival, and fear conditions everybody and everything. The characters moving on this shady background are well suited for the unfolding melodrama. The garrison commander (renowned stage actor Valentin Gaft), a war hero legendary for his courage, is now morally paralyzed, and finally commits suicide. The commander's lover, Lyuba (Irina Rozanova), tired of his wavering, finds herself a young lieutenant (Evgeny Mironov). But he, too, has no will of his own. He has been turned into a slave by an elusive despot, and prefers to take a hardship post in Siberia rather than getting involved in a steady relationship with Lyuba, which may put him at risk politically. Although for many there is no way out of this kingdom of darkness, Lyuba in the end finds her path to salvation. Leaving behind the hellish enclave of the garrison, she sets out on a long road that cuts straight through a clean, vast, snowy plain.

Focusing on more recent history, director Igor Gostev made the docudrama *Gray Wolves* (1993), which deals with Nikita Khrushchev's last days in power. When Khrushchev's memoirs appeared in the West, the

Soviet archives were still under seal. Although interesting as the subjective account of one of the protagonists of world history, the book lacked documentary evidence. Only after the events of August 1991, were researchers able to crack top secret archival materials. Gostev said that his film is based on documents, including KGB recordings of bugged conversations between Politburo members, interviews with Khrushchev's staff, and unpublished parts of Khrushchev's memoirs provided by his son, Sergei, who worked on the film as a consultant. Nevertheless, Gostev added, the film reflects the authors' point of view and, therefore, artistic interpretation blends with facts.[22]

Indeed, an enticing docudrama must have some zest to it. Here, the zest is provided by the adventure/romantic thread that hinges on the figure of estranged KGB captain Sorokin. This hero defies the establishment single-handedly, informing Khrushchev of the imminent 1964 coup, using high-tech intelligence devices, performing stunts, and romancing a girlfriend on an exotic beach by the Black Sea. Gostev said that the captain character was based on a real figure, although "things did not happen exactly that way." Alexander Mokhov, who plays the role of the hero with an appealing matter-of-fact sense of justice, said that he felt close to the character because he shared the same moral values.

A superb cast of actors brings to life a gallery of political figures from the Khrushchev entourage, which to younger generations had been nothing more than inane-looking portraits on official billboards. The plotters and their associates—V. Semichastny, KGB Chairman; N. Ignatov, President of the Supreme Soviet; L. Brezhnev, Party's Second Secretary; K. Malinovsky, Defense Minister; and Politburo members, M. Suslov, N. Podgorny, and A. Mikoyan—all project their ambitions, ruthlessness, treachery, as well as fears and human weaknesses. "Just like gray wolves," said Gostev, "they are strong in a pack, but vulnerable when alone." Alexander Belyavsky is especially effective in the role of Brezhnev, imparting to the character a substandard mannerism of speech without turning it into a caricature.

But the show is stolen by Russia's great actor Rolan Bykov (who passed away in 1999, at the age of 70) in the leading role. Having started his acting career in the Khrushchev days, he belonged to the generation of the 1960s, the *"shestidesiatniki,"* who fondly remember the thawing of

5   *Gray Wolves* (1993) directed by Igor Gostev

the cultural ice prompted by Khrushchev's policies. Bykov gained international recognition at the time, playing the buffoon in Andrei Tarkovsky's controversial film *Andrei Rublev* (1965). About his role as Khrushchev, Bykov said: "I tried to make Bykov-the-actor disappear, in order to convey the most intimate shades of Khrushchev's personality as I understand it." He succeeded only partially in his intent. The leader's personality comes across in a lively and convincing way, but the viewer is constantly aware of Bykov's superior craft. While empathizing with the character, one is forced to admire the performer.

   Khrushchev's image in the film stresses the populist, wise, and good-hearted reformer, an image that by analogy with Gorbachev fits the end of the perestroika period. Any reference to Khrushchev's Stalinist past is absent. The film covers the last two months of the Khrushchev administration. The plot thickens and the dramatic tension mounts with the approaching coup. The suspense is peppered with clichés from the gangster genre, including the blowing up of a woman in a car, accompanied by a Godfather-like musical score. The villain here is not the Sicilian mafia, but the Soviet KGB. The real drama, however, is a psychological one. As Bykov put it, "it is the drama of a man who suffers the defeat of an idea and of his faith in it." Twice in the course of the film, Khrushchev sadly acknowledges: "In Sweden they have socialism, not here." In the end, he realizes that the new top party echelons are remote from the revolutionary ideals of his youth, and are interested only in lining their pockets with fat accounts in foreign banks. "The timing of this film is ironical," said Gostev, "because of the analogy with the August 1991 putsch, and today's political rift between the branches of power." Khrushchev describes this situation best in the movie, when he reminds his son: "You see, sonny, as my dad used to say: What was will be, and what will be already was."

What was, what is, and what will be is the subject of Stanislav Govorukhin's portrayals of Russia. Govorukhin first shocked the audience with images of the contemporary society on the brink of spiritual and material collapse in the film *This is No Way To Live* (1990), where he lamented the degradation of life brought about by seventy years of Communist rule. It was a poignant denunciation and offered no solution.[23] The solution came two years later with the documentary *The Russia We Lost* (1992). This is the way to live, the film tells the viewer, placing all hopes for salvation on the recovery of pre-Revolutionary values. Govorukhin's critics were quick to label the film an opinionated statement, biased by nationalism and monarchist nostalgia. But moviegoers, who flocked to the theaters in unusually large numbers, showed their appreciation for Govorukhin's "history lesson." This is what the film was meant to be, a survey of the history of Russia from the turn of the century to our day. "The history of Russia has been written by her murderers," Govorukhin says in his commentary. "We must know Russia, we must know who our fathers were, in order to be able to build our future."[24] The director concedes that the account is not objective. Indeed, the facts presented are carefully selected to express the point of view of a conservative intellectual, and are dealt with rather superficially, although supported by archival materials and illustrated with rare photographs and documentary footage.

While the subject matter is familiar, the visual materials, freshly re-

History in the Making and on Screen 65

trieved from state archives, are fascinating to watch. The prosperous society of 1913, supported by a solid middle class of entrepreneurs, is revived on screen through family pictures, individual portraits, scenes of leisure in urban parks and suburban resorts, busy trade, and industrial labor. A photo album of Nicholas II, and film clips from his personal collection, present the profile of a family man in love with his wife and devoted to his children, while glossing over the shortcomings of his performance as the country's ruler. His prime minister, Pyotr Stolypin, infamous in Soviet times for his ruthless repression of revolutionary terrorism, is praised here for that very reason as well as for his policy of land reform.

The negative counterpoint is provided by the life story of Vladimir Ulyanov, alias Lenin. A measured dose of irony belittles the figure of the leader, reducing him to the status of a petty demon. Petty, but pernicious, since he started "a domestic war against his own people," in which 66 million died over the years. The images of how they died, either by execution or famine, are shocking even to a sophisticated audience. And yet, as petty a man as he was, Govorukhin tells the viewer, "Lenin was a Leonardo da Vinci in comparison to the leaders that followed." In the director's view, the present leaders of the new Russia are of the same breed. They, too, he maintains, betrayed the Russian people by turning the tables and depriving the older generations of their dreams, dignity, and basic means of subsistence—a view which created a stir among Russia's current democrats, and gained Govorukhin an opposition seat in the Duma. The director's disillusionment with the democratic leadership gradually grew larger. While the first film was, in his words, "a letter to the Supreme Soviet," the second one was addressed to the people. It was a subjective history lesson, one-sided but not demagogic, redeemed by irony and tragic humor.

In Govorukhin's third film of the series, *The Great Criminal Revolution* (1994), the tone is decisively tragic. The title refers to the current "revolution." "Since the elections last December (1993), they refuse to tell the truth about Russia," said the director at the presentation of the film—a statement that revealed his hardening position on the parties in power.[25]

The film is divided into three parts, "The Robbing of Russia," "Criminal Russia," and "Does Russia Have a Future?" The director is at his best when he refrains from passionate commentary and lets the images speak for themselves. The viewer sees Russia being robbed through images that have the impact of live TV reportage. Illegal traffic at the Russian-Chinese border proceeds undisturbed, while a continuous flow of trucks deliver precious iron and granite to prosperous Chinese towns and come back empty to miserable Russian villages. The profits, the movie shows, are converted into sumptuous country mansions for mafia bosses. Govorukhin has a knack for interviewing people, and especially children. Street kids aged 9 to 12 talk about a life of crime at the periphery of an organized ring—the only life they know—with an openness bordering on indifference. Since these are the only images the film offers about young people and the future, the answer to the question raised in the third part is sadly obvious.[26] Govorukhin's unrelieved pessimism is often colored with xenophobia. He sees Russia squeezed between two menacing perils: a new Yellow Horde from the East, and West-supported criminal capitalism of the "generation that chose Pepsi."

Govorukhin's position was shared to a greater or lesser degree by an impressive number of Russians. Dissatisfaction, disaffection, distrust, and finally disgust with the government inefficiency and corruption started to crystallize back in October 1993, around the image of the blackened White House. A symbol of idealism betrayed.

The day the White House turned black

It was sunny and warm on that Sunday in early October, a bright *babye leto* day (Indian summer). I was to meet two artist friends, Masha and Maxim, at the Central House of Artists across from Gorky Park. The House of Artists hosts painting and sculpture exhibitions as well as film programs, but that morning our destination was the open-air arts and crafts market on the surrounding grounds.

As I was walking on the Krimsky Bridge, coming down from Metro Park Kultury, I noticed a thick row of special police in riot gear, extending across the street from the House of Artists to Gorky Park's gates. I saw them from behind, as they were facing in the direction of October Square. Masha and Max were already there, in a small group of onlookers that was rapidly growing. I walked around the police line and joined my friends. "*Buntuiut anpilovtsy* (Anpilov's thugs are on the rampage)," said Masha, referring to the members of Viktor Anpilov's Workers Party, an extremist left-wing group that disrupted the May Day parade early that year, causing the death of a policeman. "They're expecting trouble," she said pointing to the OMON (special forces) troops. Masha quickly filled me in, "Anpilov and his gang are rallying at the Lenin monument on October Square. We heard that they would soon be here and try to break through the cordon. They want to march on to the White House." I looked back. The OMON range was impressive from a frontal view. Four rows deep, behind a shiny wall of aluminum shields, it looked like a monolith, a Roman legion.

Clashes between OMON and pro-parliament demonstrators have occurred throughout the week. On Thursday, about 1,000 protestors tried to force the cordon at Metro Barrikadnaya, which blocked off reinforcements and supplies to the rebels in the White House. The OMON beat them back into the subway. The most violent among them resurfaced on Pushkin Square and were met by 400 riot police that attacked with shields and truncheons. Bloody-faced and dazed, the demonstrators dispersed, and some were chased down the metro steps where the beating continued.

The relationship between President Yeltsin and the Congress of People's Deputies had been deteriorating for more than a year, since the time the government adopted Yegor Gaidar's economic shock reform. The tension mounted, and reached a turning point when Yeltsin declared the parliament dissolved on September 21, 1993. This was a daring decision. The president appeared on TV that evening with a solemn countenance: "In accordance with the presidential decree, which I have signed, the exercise of legislative, administrative, and supervisory functions of the Congress of People's Deputies and the Supreme Soviet of the Russian Federation are suspended. The Congress shall no longer convene," he said in a grave voice.

Yeltsin's opponents claimed that he had violated the Constitution. Even among his supporters, some felt that Yeltsin might have destroyed democracy in order to save it. But the majority of Russians, according to the polls, recognized that the situation was extremely serious and demanded drastic measures from the government. International support for Yeltsin was also quick to come and it was unconditional. The dissolution of the parliament triggered open rebellion in the White House, the seat of the Congress of People's Deputies. The two rebel leaders and former Yeltsin allies, Vice President Alexander Rutskoi and Speaker of the Congress Ruslan Khasbulatov, declared the current government unconstitutional and proceeded to name a new one, with Rutskoi as interim president. The White House was put under siege by Interior Ministry forces. Six hundred Congress deputies as well as political leaders, staff, journalists, and hard-liner activists were all trapped inside the rebels' den without water or electricity.

A crowd of White House defenders gathered around the building, their numbers ranging from a few thousands during the first days to a few hundreds as the stalemate dragged on. There was an irony to the situation. Two years earlier, the defenders of the White House were the pro-Yeltsin democrats, fighting against the attack by a moribund communist system; now, it was a mob of anti-Yeltsin activists, including the diehard representatives of that dead system, who gathered to defend the White House. And what a mob it was. There were large groups of older people, pensioners nostalgic for the social safety net, together with opposition forces of all kinds, from monarchist slavophiles to teenage boys with red swastika signs on their armbands. There was also a detachment of Cossacks, in uniforms that seemed to come from Mosfilm's costume department. The most militant groups were paramilitary contingents assembled by such figures as Albert Makashov, a retired general of Stalinist persuasion; Aleksandr Barkashov, specialized in the recruiting and training of young neo-Nazis; Stanislav Terekhov, leader of the extremist Union of Officers Party; general Vladislav Achalov, the defense minister of Rutskoi's "provisional government"; and Viktor Anpilov, founder of the Workers Party and notorious provocateur. The stand-off reached its peak the first week of October when, on Saturday, Yeltsin issued the ultimatum to vacate the White House within forty-eight hours.

"They're coming," said Max. The front line of the marchers appeared. They were about half a mile away, moving toward us in compact ranks. As they approached, their figures acquired more definition. It was a motley crowd, almost surreal in its configuration. Tsarist uniforms and communist red scarves; Stalin placards and portraits of Nicholas II; religious icons and anti-Yeltsin cartoons. They sang patriotic tunes, ranging from the hymn, "God Save the Tsar," to World War II Red Army songs.

We were mesmerized, too fascinated to be scared. People were standing on the sidelines, as if they were watching the recreation of a historical battle. The choreography was so perfect that every sense of reality was lost. Then the demonstrators were within talking distance of the OMON. One of the leaders asked the commander to let the column through. The request was denied. The marchers linked arms and moved forward toward the OMON wall. The clash was bloody but short. After a few minutes the battle was over. The OMON ranks, inexplicably, evaporated and an angry crowd emboldened by the action launched ahead on a path of violence and destruction.

In the aftermath, nobody was able to explain why the OMON offered no resistance to the mob, and why the same happened a few hours later around the White House, when that same mob broke the government blockade of the parliament building. Together with the sparse defense forces on the ground, the attackers went on to storm the Moscow mayor's office in a nearby high-rise, while the police fled the scene. Some critics offered the view that non-resistance on the government part had been arranged to encourage violence, in order to provide Yeltsin with a pretext to later storm the White House. Whether framed or not, the anti-Yeltsin forces that night regrouped, and under the command of General Makashov boarded stolen armed personnel carriers and trucks and triumphantly rushed across town to seize the main television station, Ostankino.

The demonstrators were not the only ones to believe that victory was within reach. The leaders, too, were convinced that the ordeal was finally over. As soon as the siege was lifted, around 3:00 p.m., Rutskoi himself came out on the balcony dressed in fatigues, wearing a bulletproof vest, with an automatic rifle dangling from his shoulder. His looks and posturing stressed his status as a veteran hero of the Afghan war. He called on the parliament supporters to storm the mayor's headquarters and proceed to the Ostankino television station. Around 6:00, Khasbulatov told a cheering session of the Congress of People's Deputies that he was sure the next day pro-parliament forces would seize the government headquarters.

Those optimistic statements were prompted by rumors that the Taman and Kantemirov army motorized divisions, which were dispatched earlier in the day to crush the rebellion, had so far refused to move. Defense

Minister Pavel Grachev, as soon as the demonstrators broke through the siege barrier around the White House, received an order from Yeltsin to bring troops into the capital. But the idea of using the army against the population was so repugnant to the generals that they stalled and wavered well into the wee hours. Nevertheless, motorized divisions and tanks had started moving and were waiting for orders within a short distance from the city.

After the skirmish at Krimsky Val, we woke up to the danger of the situation. Leaving the city behind, we spent the rest of the day on more idyllic pastures, at Masha's and Max's dacha, where the local folks had little or no notion of what was happening in Moscow. Then we decided to go back and have dinner at my place. It was past 8:00 when we got home that night— in time for the evening news. No broadcast from Ostankino, obviously. But the Russian station, ORT, was operating from a makeshift studio. Throughout the night, broadcasters loyal to Yeltsin kept us informed of the unfolding events.

The battle for Ostankino started at 7:00 p.m. Parliament supporters crashed a military truck through the glass entrance door to the TV station building. Someone from the Cossack detachment under the orders of General Makashov launched a shoulder-fired grenade into the breach. Interior Ministry forces and OMON special police, already positioned within the building responded to the fire. The crowd outside had swelled to 10,000 people. Many died among the attackers as well as the bystanders attracted by the battle scene. Journalists were in the forefront, and a British colleague lost his life. Anpilov instructed his militia on how to use Molotov cocktails and several fires broke out. The battleground was mayhem. It was already past 9:00, when a column of six government armed personnel carriers broke through the attackers' lines and engaged the insurgents. The battle continued until 5:00 a.m., when the uprising was finally crushed.

We forgot about dinner and stayed glued to the screen, grateful to the brave journalists—Svetlana Sorokina, Nikolai Svanidze, and others—who would hang on in those trying moments. Government figures, Moscow Mayor Yuri Luzhkov, and various celebrities would alternate on camera to offer comments and encouragement. But we had the uneasy feeling that nobody in the Kremlin was in charge and the situation was getting out of hand. Around 10:30 p.m., an announcer read Yeltsin's declaration of the state of emergency for Moscow, but still no word of which concrete measures were being taken to protect the city. Where is the army?—everybody was asking.

The uneasiness was reinforced, rather than alleviated, by the intermittent appearances of Yegor Gaidar, the only top government official that spoke to us that night (he had recently been reinstated as First Deputy Prime Minister). He looked overwhelmed and powerless as he pleaded to the people to come out in the street to defend democracy. It was a pathetic plea. And yet the people responded to it, and began to rally in front of City Hall. Thousands of candles lit up the faces in the crowd. But there was no excitement this time; only anxiety and trepidation, a sense of impending danger and abandonment.

Where was Yeltsin? Chernomyrdin? As it turned out later, they had left the Kremlin to attend a meeting of Russia's leading generals at the Defense Ministry. Grachev and the generals were paralyzed with the enormity of the responsibility placed on them. It took Tsar Boris' presence to finally break the impasse. Grachev gave in to Yeltsin's plan to take the parliament by force, and by 4:00 a.m. two special army divisions from Tula and Ryazan arrived in Moscow and joined the Taman 2nd Motorized Rifle Division that had arrived two hours earlier.

Moscow did not sleep that night. At 7:00 a.m. on Monday, after hours of exhausting negotiations, the Kremlin issued the ultimatum to the White House rebels to lay down arms and vacate the building. Soon after, a column of T-80 tanks from the Kantemirov Division appeared on Kutuzovsky Prospect, coming from the south-west—the same way they had rolled in two years before, the same *"smolenskaya doroga"* that saw both the arrival and the retreat of Napoleon's army in 1812. They must have looked ominous from the windows of the White House. According to reports, panic broke out within the building. The sense of doom intensified when Yeltsin appeared on TV to address the nation on the imminent action. "Only bandits are in the White House," he said, implying that the military attack was justified. Actually, inside there were also journalists and service personnel.

CNN provided us with a front-row view of the show through its cameras placed on the roof of the Kutuzovsky Prospect building, where the

72   Imaging Russia 2000

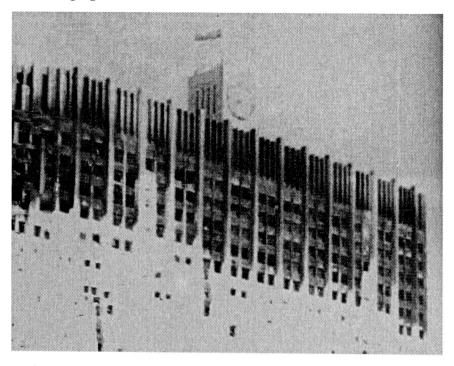

6   Black stain, October 1993

studio was located. The cameras were facing the White House from across the river, enjoying an unobstructed view of the Novy Arbat Bridge (formerly Kalininsky Bridge), where the tanks had positioned themselves within fire range from the target.

At 8:50, one tank aimed its cannon and fired the first shot. It hit the higher floors, right in the middle of the facade. The smoke that came out of the window produced the first black stain. The fusillade continued for two hours. Then, Rutskoi announced that he was ready to discuss the terms of surrender. White flags blossomed on the stained wall. At 11:00, Chernomyrdin ordered the ceasefire. At 2:30, crack Alpha units of the Interior Ministry and government negotiators entered the building. By then, a huge black band of soot, six floors high, ran all around the top of the White House.

We left my apartment around 12:00 noon. We wanted to join a group of friends who were gathering at the Cinema Café in the Kinocenter building, a few yards from the White House. This Italian café had been opened for less than one year, providing hard-currency cappuccino and tiramisu cake to moneyed moviegoers. In the days of the uprising, the café became a field news bureau for dozens of foreign correspondents reporting from behind the barricades and sustaining themselves with double shots of espresso coffee. As we walked through the park across from Kinocenter, I realized that we were in a war zone. People were running in all directions. Fire was being exchanged. Bullets were flying over our heads. The friends who were already there warned us: "*Snaipery povsiudu. Streliaiut s krysh, s okon. Bandity!*" (There are snipers everywhere. They're shooting from the roofs, the windows. Bandits!)." Eventually the fire subsided and we moved down toward the embankment. We saw people wounded. Among the hundred and fifty killed and the many hundreds injured during those days, the majority were onlookers, people who lingered along streets, alleys, and the bridge to get a glimpse of the action as if it were a staged pageant. Many of the casualties were teenagers who mistook the deadly confrontation for an exciting game and jumped right into it. A colleague who was browsing all by himself described this same scene:

> On the embankment, people were everywhere, lots of foreign tourists among them. The locals also behaved like tourists. There was no great excitement, there were no banners or slogans, no singing, jokes, or other forms of camaraderie, no sense of commitment, no passion—the things that made the August '91 scene so unforgettable. . . . The nice-looking snow-white building, beautifully lit by the sun, was being shelled by tank cannons and machine guns. . . . After every good shot the public applauded. Some direct hits were really spectacular. In one case, a whole cloud of papers flew in the air from the crushed window—Hollywood special effects masters could do no better. . . . There were quite a few curious civilians displaying suicidal tendencies: dozens of school kids with sacks on their backs running everywhere, apparently playing war games, amateur photographers taking pictures, smartly dressed young women walking their fancy dogs. It all looked totally surreal, considering the flying bullets.[27]

Many lives were saved by the heroic efforts of hospital doctors and nurses who worked for three days straight. But many others were lost because ambulances could not get through the ring of security forces and parliament barricades. Suddenly, we realized how idiotic it was to put ourselves at risk and left the battlefield behind to watch the final surrender on TV.

The parade of some 200 White House defenders emerging from the building with hands on their heads started around 5:00 p.m. Khasbulatov and Rutskoi came out last. Close ups of their faces filled the TV screens. Khasbulatov had a ghostly look, he was pale, gaunt, with deep black circles under the eyes, and his expression betrayed the terror of someone who expected to be put to death on the spot. Rutskoi concealed his fear under the bravado posture of a war hero, but behind his mustache à la Chapayev I could sense a desperation bordering on madness.[28] They were taken away and history ran its course. As it turned out, it was a very easy course for the rebels, who after a few months were back into politics.[29]

For the second time in two years, the curtain came down on the White House stage. It had been an odd remake of the first show. The set was the same—scenery, barricades, tanks. And the characters were the same, except that they, and the thousands of extras, had switched sides. They had also changed personality, as if they were wearing a different make up. The rules of the comedy of errors seemed to apply. But, alas, it was not a comedy; if anything, it was theater of the absurd.[30] In 1991, Yeltsin defended Russia and the democratic principle against the Soviet plotters. Rutskoi and Khasbulatov had been at his side when he climbed on top of a tank and symbolically stopped the military attack. The White House shone like a beacon in the background. In the end, Yeltsin exited the stage as the victorious hero of an epic drama. In 1993, Yeltsin acted again in defense of democracy. He was right to crush the rebellion by force. But the images carried by the airwaves and reaching millions of households throughout Russia were grim and sinister. They showed the heavy hand of the Kremlin firing cannon shots at the White House. And no matter how justified those shots may have been, the visual impact made many hearts sink. It was a Pyrrhic victory for Yeltsin. And the ending of the drama had none of the heroics. In the folks' imagination, the good tsar turned into Boris the Terrible.

The government was quick to erase all memories of the event. The White House facade was patched, painted, and restored to its immaculate splendor in no time. But the black stain on Yeltsin's image remained, and marked the end of his honeymoon with the Russian people. The parliamentary election of December 1993, meant to give Russia a new legislative system—and to provide Yeltsin with a friendlier parliament—confirmed that the popular mood had moved away from the camp of Yeltsin's democracy. The results, giving a substantial victory to the party of nationalist extremist maverick Vladimir Zhirinovsky, struck the democrats-reformists like a thunderbolt.

In the power struggle that followed, through a presidential election in 1996, up to the end of the decade, Yeltsin and his entourage became progressively more concerned with their personal interest and political future. The country sank into a deep crisis and more than once was on the brink of collapse. The film industry followed the general trend of decline.

The search for Russia

There were a few notable exceptions to the disappointing performance of the film industry. Toward the middle of the decade, Russian cinema scored high points abroad with Nikita Mikhalkov's portrait of the Stalinist era, *Burnt by the Sun* (1994). First the co-winner of the Grand Prix de Jury at the 1994 Cannes Film Festival, then the Oscar recipient for Best Foreign Film, *Burnt by the Sun* confirmed that Mikhalkov's star was still in the ascendant. With this film, the director returned to the ambiance and themes that he had treated successfully in previous works. The historical time varies in each of his films, but it always involves a moment of impending change, the eve of a major turning point bound to sweep away an epoch and a way of life.[31]

In *Burnt by the Sun*, Mikhalkov reconstructs the atmosphere of a summer day at the dacha of a family of the old intelligentsia, in the mid 1930s. The first round of the purges is about to begin, and the apparent calm is a foreboding of the great terror to come. Superficially, life could not be more attractive: sipping tea on the verandah, playing the piano, swimming, boating, and making love. All these activities, however, are burdened by a sense of anxiety, an ominous premonition that gets on people's nerves and affects their relations. This is the twilight malaise that Chekhov had captured so masterfully in his plays and that became a leit-motif in Mikhalkov's works. But apart from literary suggestions, the nostalgic attachment to genteel country life is a result of Mikhalkov's own upbringing; raised in the bohemian-chic family of a well-established Soviet writer, he enjoyed the privileges accorded to the high echelons of the nomenklatura as well as the cultural heritage of his mother's aristocratic background. She was the daughter of artist Pyotr Konchalovsky. Nikita's father, Sergei Mikhalkov, made a political career in the Soviet cultural establishment as a poet/writer, and capped it during WW II by writing the lyrics to the national anthem. He actually capped it twice. As it happened, he was commissioned to write the lyrics for the national anthem a second time in 2000, when the old Soviet tune was restored and the original words were no longer suitable to the new times.[32]

In the film, however, Mikhalkov plays the role of the outsider, the hero of peasant stock who rose through the ranks in the Red Army to a top commander grade and married into an upper class family that needed his protection. The situation allows for dramatic conflicts both on the personal and the political planes. Central to plot development is the confrontation between General Kotov (Mikhalkov) and Mitya (Oleg Menshikov), an old-time friend of the family and the former lover of Kotov's wife. Mitya returns to the scene of his youth as an agent of the NKVD to orchestrate Kotov's arrest. In the end, both men fall victim to the terror machine, but the confrontation between the two brings to the fore their different attitudes toward the official ideology. While Kotov is an idealist who believes in the fundamental humanitarian goals of communism and acts out of allegiance to the cause, Mitya is the self-loathing, decadent son of a defeated class, motivated by vengeful feelings. The dichotomy, however, allows for character nuances and, therefore, for realistic human personalities. It becomes clear in the course of the film that Kotov had once pushed Mitya into the ranks of the NKVD, and assigned him to a mission in Paris, in order to remove him from the scene. That episode reveals that Kotov too, at least once, used the system for his own interest. But basically, Kotov believes in the system as an expression of the state. And his belief is highlighted by the naive fascination his six-year-old daughter feels for the trappings of the regime: the pioneers' parade with smart uniforms and fanfare, civil defense games on the beach, and the shiny limousine that comes to take away her father (Mikhalkov's own daughter, Nastya, is captivating in the role). Kotov's awakening is brutal. It is realistically portrayed by the savage beating he suffers at the hand of NKVD thugs, and symbolically conveyed by the parallel image of a gigantic head of Stalin on a dirigible rising above the fields—a red rising "sun" that burns equally friends and foes.

For all its success abroad, the film did not get a good press at home. Judging the man, Russian critics showed a grudge against Mikhalkov's nationalist views and his alleged political ambitions. Judging the film, they objected to the fact that it was too slick, "too commercial," and designed to be distributed in the West. It was criticized for not being "serious," which in the parlance of the Russian press means not ponderous and philosophical enough. What the critics perceived as a flaw, however, accounted for the film's box office success. The film cost of 3.6 million dollars, with one third of the budget being subsidized by Goskino, was very high for a Russian production. In order to recover the money, Mikhalkov decided not to rely on distributors, but to peddle the film himself with the mayors of major cities and provincial towns, controlling showings and ticket prices. The strategy, apparently, paid off, and also prevented pirating to a considerable extent by having the prints watched by guards at all times.[33]

Discussing the success of his film, Mikhalkov bragged about the fact that *Burnt by the Sun* stood out from the general trend of period pictures about the Stalin years: "My intention was to oppose all the recent movies set during the Stalinist era which simply reverse the familiar heroes and villains of Soviet cinema. Over the past ten to fifteen years, the Reds have been inevitably portrayed as villains as previously they were heroes."[34] Actually, Mikhalkov is not correct. The film that first approached, with courage and sadness, the issue of the self-destructive idealism of those who believed in the Soviet state and were crushed by it was *My Friend Ivan Lapshin* (1985), by Alexei Gherman. This was the first swallow of glasnost and remains the best film of the 1980s.[35] After that, many films followed that dwelled on the same theme, including several discussed here. The truth is that this approach was unusual for Mikhalkov. Red Army commander Kotov was a novelty in Mikhalkov's gallery of characters.[36] In his previous films the director kept a sharper divide between the ideological camps, associating the Bolshevik element with the forces that eroded the national cultural heritage (e.g., industrialization, Westernization, urbanization, and feminism). But, to Mikhalkov's credit, ideology never suffocated creativity, and every one of his works, up to and including *Burnt by the Sun*, is an excellent piece of film craft.

Another film that portrays daily family life, but avoids the tragic element, is *The Iron Curtain* (1997) by Savva Kulish. It is a domestic chronicle unfolding on the background of events of national resonance in the late Stalin years and their aftermath. The focus is on Kostya, the main hero who grows from age 8 to 18 in the course of the three-hour long movie. The post-war period, the twilight of Stalin's rule, and the beginning of the thaw are a backdrop to the little big things that occur day after day in Kostya's life. Government policies, terror trials, executions are just a whispered topic of conversation around the dinner table, or at most a brush with reality when one of the neighbors is arrested for being of noble descent. Although fear among the adults is an ever-present feeling, Kostya's life unfolds relatively smoothly in the warm nest of a middle-class family that surrounds him with love and care. He moves from soccer games to school pranks, from street fights to rendezvous with his girl friend in the elite apartments of the nomenklatura, and from a sing-along around the bonfire with wanted criminals to a New Year's gala ball at the Kremlin. Only once is Kostya in danger of being hurt by the power of the state bureaucracy that remained alive well after Stalin's death. Because of an unfortunate incident, his name is struck from the list of students admitted to the State Film Institute. But Kostya's firm position in defense of his rights eventually prevails—those were the Khrushchev days—and he is quickly reinstated.

The film was in the making for some fifteen years. Originally the script ended with the 1957 International Youth Festival, the huge pageant that first lifted a corner of the iron curtain and brought to Moscow groups of young people (rather, young Communists) from around the world. The Festival was highly promoted by the state as an expression of Khrushchev's new policy of cultural liberalization. As such it was a PRs tool, both for internal and external consumption. Nevertheless, it did indeed mark the beginning of contacts with the outside world. Later, Kulish, who also wrote the script, added a short coda to include footage from the events of 1991 that tore down the iron curtain for good. At the same time, the last sequence is a reminder that things did not turn out as expected, and an encouragement to keep up the guard.

The reconstruction of the Stalinist period continued to haunt Russian directors throughout the decade. *The Thief* (1997), by Pavel Chukhrai, offers another glimpse of those years from the point of view of a child. The film is complex in its apparent simplicity. On the surface it is a melodrama laced with adventure. But the deeper structure reveals a psychological conflict of personalities and a symbolic level of historical interpretation.

Katya (Ekaterina Rednikova), a young war widow, and her six-year old son Sanya (Misha Filipchuk) meet a handsome Red Army officer on the train in their aimless journey across Russia. The time is 1952. The country has yet to recover from the shock of WW II that disintegrated the social fabric, and people live precariously, day by day. The theme of instability and casual crossing of human destinies is conveyed by the leitmotif of the train throughout the film. That chance encounter with the stranger, Tolyan (Vladimir Mashkov), will turn out to be fatal to Katya and will deeply affect the course of Sanya's life. Katya falls instantly for the man's good looks and brute magnetism, and agrees to join him in his wanderings. The threesome settle down as a family in a desolate provincial town and rent a room in a communal apartment. They do not have to provide papers thanks to the mystique of Tolyan's uniform that opens all the doors. Soon, however, Tolyan reveals his true self. One night, after having taken the neighbors to the circus, he robs the communal apartment and hops on the next train with the loot. Reluctantly, Katya follows him with little Sanya. They move from town to town and from robbery to robbery for a few months, enjoying the modest affluence Tolyan's activity affords them. But Katya, wearied of dodging the police and living as an outlaw, decides to leave Tolyan. That very night Tolyan is arrested and later sentenced to seven years in a labor camp.

Pavel Chukhrai was about Sanya's age in those years, and the period reconstruction is inspired by his childhood memories. Far from being autobiographical or sentimental, the film nevertheless reveals the director's fascination with the time. The perfect blend of settings, decor, types, and situations creates a peculiar atmosphere, tangible and yet remote behind a sepia-colored patina. The viewer is guided throughout the

7   *The Thief* (1997) directed by Pavel Chukhrai

story by Sanya's point of view. Now in his fifties, the protagonist recounts his childhood experience, and it is clear that for him the emotional wounds of those faraway days are still raw and throbbing. The human drama that binds together the three main characters is so powerfully conveyed that no distancing device can prevent the viewer from being sucked in and becoming a virtual participant.

Sanya is fascinated with the father figure Tolyan projects, and at the same time repelled by the man's callousness. He is also terrified by what he perceives as Tolyan's absolute power over his and his mother's lives. Sanya sees Tolyan as a usurper of Katya's attentions and occasionally stands up to him, only to be crushed and humiliated in the uneven match. Eventually Tolyan realizes that Sanya can be a valuable accomplice, and begins to teach him how to get tough of body and soul. A male bonding process takes place, which involves Sanya emotionally, and which Tolyan exploits for his own purposes. Tolyan shows off his killer's instinct in a fistfight with neighbor thugs and impresses the kid with macho tricks, such as twirling a razor blade around his mouth with the tongue. Sanya is particularly mesmerized by Tolyan's tattoos, a leopard's

8   *The Thief* (1997) directed by Pavel Chukhrai

head on the shoulder ("To scare people off," Tolyan explains), and Stalin's head on the chest. "Stalin is my father," Tolyan tells the child, "but this must remain a secret between the two of us."

Vladimir Mashkov endows the character of Tolyan with the exotic looks of an Antonio Banderas and the rough edge of a young Anthony Quinn, while Misha Filipchuk in the role of Sanya joins that gallery of little heroes from Italian Neorealism that occupy a special place in the viewer's heart.[37] Ekaterina Rednikova gives a touching performance as Katya, but hers is a supporting role. Dominated by Tolyan, Katya is a commodity for the man to acquire respectability in society and to enjoy a warm body in bed.

The film would stand in force of the dramatics of the plot alone. But given Russia's recent changes, the historical perspective is inevitable. The director stated: "I made a film about the childhood of the generation that is today shaping the life of our country. It was important for me to understand and to be able to convey to the viewer how and why the post-war generation grew up to be what it is and not something else."[38] Thus, the viewer can engage in the game of interpretation with relish, because all the elements are in place. Here is Tolyan who stands for Stalin, father and predator, charmer and despot; here is Katya, nurturing mother, Russia herself, abused and exploited, and still devoted; and here is Sanya, Stalin's progeny, not by blood but by bent, having been robbed of his innocence. In one gripping scene, the little kid in tears runs after the van that takes the convicts to the Gulag, and calls out desperately to Tolyan. The scene is significant because it marks a transition. Sanya calls Tolyan "father," transferring his love from the image of the war hero he used to fancy in his daydreams to the figure of the thief. "That day," Sanya recalls later, "I betrayed my true father, and his image disappeared forever." When Sanya and Tolyan meet again some ten years later, the boy performs an extreme rite of passage by shooting Tolyan with the gun that once belonged to the thief. "After the first time it got easier," says fifty-year old Sanya. He is now an army colonel in a war zone, bringing death and destruction to the occupied land. His heart has hardened, as well as his features. Like Tolyan, he sports a leopard's head tattoo on the shoulder "to scare people off." But deep down, Sanya himself is scared and lonely, and the little boy inside him still craves the father that he never had.[39]

The film was shown abroad with a different ending. The epilog, showing fifty-year-old Sanya in the war zone is missing. The revised version ends with the shooting of Tolyan and the boy's comment that he will bury the memory of the thief. Which is exactly the opposite of the original version. There, what gives the film a historical perspective is the heritage issue—the implication being that Stalin is not really dead, and his spirit lingers in the conscience of the generation that he has affected as children. It is not known for sure why the change was made. Perhaps, it was just a foreign distributor's requirement. Or, perhaps there was another reason. The Russian producers may have felt that the heritage issue was a "Russian" issue, for discussion on national soil, and that foreign audiences would not able to address it with the kind of sympathy and compassion it requires.

As the century drew to a close, one more major film on the Stalinist years appeared, *Khrustalyov, my car!* (1998) by Alexei Gherman. Those who were familiar with the director's previous works expected another masterpiece, like *My Friend Ivan Lapshin* (1985) that marked the beginning of the perestroika period; but the film was received at first with mixed reactions. *Khrustalyov* had been in production for ten years, which is revealing of the complexities Gherman faced in the realization of his artistic idea, and the difficulties of the economic realities. The film shares some features with *Ivan Lapshin*, but brings them to a paroxysm in which reality dissolves into nightmarish visions. Like the previous film, *Khrustalyov* looks back to the Stalinist society, its way of life, inhibitions, and neuroses, but rather than portraying the beginning of the terror period, it focuses on its end. *Khrustalyov*'s time is the winter of 1953, a few days before the death of the tyrant, and the action revolves around the infamous "doctors' affair," used to justify the planning for the deportation of thousands of Jews.

Khrustalyov's narrator relates the events he lived through as an adolescent, coloring his memories with a subjective point of view. Gherman used this strategy in *Ivan Lapshin* to build an original narrative structure, informed by postmodernism but still realistic enough to command the attention of the general audience. Conversely, *Khrustalyov* is structure, informed by postmodernism but still realistic enough to command the attention of the general audience. Conversely, *Khrustalyov* is narrated in a sustained grotesque style—a style in which Russian literature excelled with Gogol, Bely and, to a certain extent, Dostoevsky. The literary style was based on hyperbole, saturation of details, displacement, and shifting of planes. In the film, shot in black and white, the viewer is visually assaulted by images that create a physical malaise and convey a sense of the absurd in a world outside of conventional logic. Spectral landscapes inhabited by snowy ghosts alternate with cluttered interiors where the individual comes face to face with his double.

In those labyrinthine apartments, human speech has turned into an unintelligible mixage of growls, grunts, snorts, sniffs, shrieks, and squalls. Language has dissolved, leaving a void in human relationships that has been filled with the corporeal mass of bodies and things. The images convey the smell of that mass, thick and nauseating, a smell that penetrates the nostrils like a virus, and sticks.

84 **Imaging Russia 2000**

9 *Khrustalyov, my car!* (1998) directed by Alexei Gherman

History in the Making and on Screen 85

Outside, in the land of ice and darkness, the automobile is king. A fantastic, overbearing array of trucks, sedans, vans, and limos rule over the frozen earth. At the top of this cohort of mechanical demons are the ZIS (*Zavod imeni Stalina*) from the Kremlin stables. Mighty symbols of power, they suddenly materialize out of a vortex of snowflakes, jumping to the fore like primordial beasts. Or, they wind away in a column, like a black snake on the snowy ground. Human beings are defined by their relationship to the car: either behind the wheel, or under the wheels. Either empowered, or crushed. This is the logic that prompts Lavrenti Beria, the secret police chief, soon after having verified that Stalin is dead, to call out to his driver, Khrustalyov. He hurriedly gets in the car, the protective shell of his authority. This is the symbolism that has the hero of the story, General Klensky (Yuri Tsurilo), pompously ride his government limo at the beginning, and later being bestially sodomized in a convict transport van.

The story is sketchy, but the main outline is clear. Klensky, a prominent and privileged physician of the regime, who runs a psychiatric institution, is arrested in the latest round up of the "enemies of the people," and his family is evicted from their stately apartment. He is thrown in a van with a bunch of hardened criminals who promptly proceed to rape him. Soon after, Klensky is rescued on Beria's orders and summoned to Stalin's deathbed, in an effort to save the dictator's life. But it is too late for Stalin. Klensky eventually ends up in the Gulag, and is released a few years later as a result of Khrushchev's general amnesty. But he is no longer fit for normal life. Actually, he never was. The assumption is that he has always lived in an absurd universe—the psychiatric ward, the grotesque family environment, the spectral cityscape, the Gulag—which has become his natural habitat. The only way opened to him in the end is to join a group of vagrants engaged in a sort of banquet of the fools on a train rolling out to nowhere.

The narrator, Klensky's son, in relating the story reveals an Oedipus complex. The theme emerges in the love-hate relation with the father. At one point, the boy picks up the phone to report on Klensky to the secret police, but is stopped before he can carry out his intention. The recognition that the father's perceived superiority and his overwhelming charismatic power can be conquered only by destroying him is echoed in the two master scenes: the scene in which the general is raped (symbolically killed), and the scene where Stalin, the surrogate father, turns into a rotten corpse whose fetid gases saturate the room. Realistically, the narrator had no knowledge of these two episodes; as a kid, he could not have witnessed them. But the poetic license gives those scenes an even greater symbolic charge.

For all its visual sophistication and psychological significance, the film bombed at the Cannes Festival in 1998, when half the audience walked out. Gherman was so crushed that he withdrew it from circulation for more than a year. When it was eventually released in St. Petersburg, Gherman told the audience: "You all go ahead and watch the movie, and I'll run away, because I'll be scared of answering your questions afterwards." This time, the invitation-only audience was impressed, and the film was highly praised by the Russian critics. It received five Nika awards in 2000—for best film, best director, cinematography, costumes, and design. The film also enjoyed a certain success with the public in St. Petersburg, where allegedly it played five times a day to a full house. In France, after the unfortunate premiere at Cannes, it became a cult movie. Yet, it was not distributed widely, either at home or abroad.[40]

Director Alexander Proshkin went back to a more remote historical period for his film, *Russian Uprising* (1999), distributed abroad with the title *Captain's Daughter*. The film is based on the short novel *Captain's Daughter* (1836) by Alexander Pushkin, and was made in the framework of the festivities for the bicentenary of the poet's birth. The action takes place under the rule of Catherine the Great, in the 1770s, and revolves around the love story of two teenagers on the background of a bloody peasant uprising.

The charismatic peasant rebel, Emelyan Pugachev (Vladimir Mashkov), claimed to be Tsar Peter III, assassinated during the coup that put his wife, Catherine, on the throne. As the pretender to the throne, Pugachev moved toward the capital with an army of Cossacks, reinforced by a troop of thieves and thugs gathered along the way. The love story, interwoven with gory scenes of violence, follows the adventures of a young army officer, Pyotr Grinyov, and Masha, the sweet but intrepid daughter of the commander of the Belogorsky fortress, an outpost in the Orenburg region that happened to be on Pugachev's devastation path. The two youths get caught in the turmoil of a major historical event that

History in the Making and on Screen 87

10   *Captain's Daughter* (1999) directed by Alexander Proshkin

threatens to destroy their happiness.
"God save us from a Russian uprising, senseless and merciless," Pushkin wrote in a chapter of the novel, later omitted, and these lines resound in the film over scenes of brutal assaults and bloody battles. Pushkin's

words seem to suggest that a "Russian uprising" is something peculiar, like no other uprising. Indeed, those words point to the fundamental dichotomy of the Russian soul, which, real or perceived, is one of the most consistent motifs both of popular and high-end culture. Supposedly, the Russian folk are meek and enduring, and rely on authority. But once in a while something snaps, and an irrational upsurge of violence takes the upper hand, resulting in a savage bloodbath, only to return to the previous order. Actor Pyotr Zaichenko, who plays a role in the film, characterized the uprising as "an emotional concept, an outburst due to pain, when one reaches the point where it is no longer possible to endure; yet, endurance is a Russian national trait."[41]

The film is spectacular, although made on a shoestring budget of merely $6,000,000 — which was provided partly by NTV, partly by Goskino, and partly by the Orenburg region where the film was shot. The region's administration funded the construction of the set, recreating the Belogorsky fortress from illustrations and documents of the period with meticulous accuracy. The film crew used the set as their quarters during the filming, and afterwards the whole site was turned into a museum. The same high degree of attention to historical details throughout — in costumes, locales, and ethnic types — gives the film a look of authenticity. Proshkin said that he hired hundreds of extras from the region to recreate the Pugachev army, because those were the true descendants of the rebels.[42]

But realism does not exclude poetry. Camera work and editing often elevate the action to the metaphorical level. The camera establishes itself as a presence from the opening shot. At first, the camera seems to float on a river, pulling the viewer along into a rapid in-depth movement; then, abruptly, it veers to the left and is now on the bank, on solid ground, speeding on with the same disorienting floating movement. Moments later, it becomes clear that the camera was not floating but flying, tracking the point of view of a raven.[43] Cinematography is an integral part of the aesthetic experience that ultimately gives meaning to the action. Extreme long shots of Grinyov's sleigh, a mere speck in the vastness of the steppe, evoke a sense of inadequacy and vulnerability. The well-appointed transport, with its master and servants, is reduced to a minuscule bug, toiling wearily against the snowstorm. The image suggests that in a country so vast and mighty, civilization has not been able

11 *Captain's Daughter* (1999) directed by Alexander Proshkin

to tame nature. And on this background, the uprising acquires striking connotations, being perceived as a force of nature itself. In its first attack the army of peasant insurgents blends with the overpowering blizzard; horses and riders seem to be made of twirling snow, and to be carried away by sweeping winds. The thumping of the hooves becomes a rumbling thunder, adding an aural dimension to the terrifying image of an unleashed elemental force. From that moment, it is clear that the steppe is going to reclaim its territory, and that the pitiful fort with its imperial garrison trained in inane military maneuvers will not be able to sustain the impact of the Pugachev storm.

As in the novel, a core of characters becomes the victim caught between the two warring sides. On one side is the corrupt and autocratic imperial court, and on the other, an impostor with his band of cutthroats. The historical setting is used as a mirror to comment on the contemporary situation. The director commented: "In the 200 years since Pushkin was born much has changed, but in essence things are the same. We see this eighteenth-century Russian drama repeated over and over. Today, there is a war going on in Chechnya, and every night there is blood on our TV screens. The whole of our twentieth century was a permanent civil war." Significantly, one of the co-screenwriters is Stanislav Govorukhin, who has been a vocal critic of the current government. Parallel to his contribution to this film, he developed the theme of the "people's uprising" in a different context and in a different form (see *The Voroshilov Marksman*, 1999).

Proshkin indicated that the two young lovers have the same uplifting role they had in the novel, as the repositories of high moral values, which are the ultimate hope for the future. They stand out even more brightly in opposition to the villain, the Russian officer who betrays the motherland and kidnaps the girl (Sergei Makovetsky). Therefore, some critics were disappointed that in a cast of excellent Russian actors the two young leads were Polish (Mateus Damiecki and Karolina Gruszka), and wondered about the significance of the director's choice. Proshkin had to explain repeatedly that his casting choice was prompted by purely aesthetic reasons. "I was looking for two people who would fit the typology of the period," he said. "And I could not find those types in Russia, where our youth look very much like American teenagers nowadays. I could cast them in a contemporary action movie, but not in the role of two eighteenth-century aristocrats. They simply do not have those features. Furthermore, those characters must convey a sense of absolute purity of soul, and I could not find such teenagers in an unhealthy society like ours."

The film that caused the most controversy in Russia at the end of the century was Nikita Mikhalkov's *The Barber of Siberia* (1998). Most Russian critics had a problem either with the film's aesthetics or the director's ideology, or both. Let us first listen to what they had to say:

> One cannot talk about the substance of the picture, because there is no substance. There is only a series of gags such as the floor polishing and the dance on the slippery parquet, carnival merrymaking, the fight on the ice, and the generals' drinking bout (Viktor Matizen).
>
> It seems that Mikhalkov was able to do what Govorukhin had tried to do before: bring back the "Russia we lost." Virtually—like they say nowadays. Here you have the cadet pack, epic drinking fits, bloody fist-fights as popular entertainment, and the Asian fascina-

tion with military culture—and this is filmed in such a way that we all moan from nostalgia (Lev Anninsky).

This Russia reminds us of the Austro-Hungarian empire of the Hollywood operettas filmed in the 1920s-30s by European emigres: wanton buffoon-generals who swallow their glasses together with the vodka, idiotic pranks and carousals, and bearded anarchists with bombs in candy boxes (Mikhail Trofimenko).

Everything sparkles like champagne--it's hard not to get drunk. But when the fireworks go out and the hangover is gone, one feels puzzled and asks himself: What was that noise all about? (Alexander Troshin).

My main impression of the film is of a sidewalk puppet theater with 5,000 puppets (Irina Pavlova).

There is no doubt that the image the film conveys is kitsch (Viktoria Belopolskaya).

Very, very Mikhalkov-like. It's the first blockbuster of the Russian empire. It's a Russian specimen of top-quality Hollywood production (Yuri Gladilshchikov).

It's mindless nonsense, absolutely harmless and, in the final analysis, useless. Nobody needs it, neither the people, nor the intelligentsia, and least of all, the European distributors (Dilyara Tasbulatova).

Even the few voices that wanted to stress something positive about the film did not come across as enthusiastic:

Notwithstanding the unfortunate casting, the failure of the script, and the poor musical score, *The Barber of Siberia* holds the viewer's attention for the good part of three hours (Karina Dobrotvorskaya).

The American model of mass culture pictures seems to have succeeded because the people are actually going to see the film (Yuri Bogomolov).

Mikhalkov's movie is an ointment on the wounds of national pride, and has a very therapeutic function. For that, many thanks (Natalya Sirivlya).[44]

Attacks by the press are nothing new when it comes to Mikhalkov, except that this time even the director was stunned by their volume and intensity. "Why do you dislike me so much?" he hypothetically asked the critics. "Four hundred and twenty articles in two months. . . . At first I was shocked. . . . Then I thought: what's going on? What did I do to you, guys, to have you squawk that way? . . . Look, write whatever you want. . . . You cannot imagine what joy it is when they say all these things about you and you know that it's all a lie."[45]

What the critics did not like besides the picture itself was the surrounding atmosphere of political ambitions and commercialism. The film came out one year before the 2000 scheduled presidential election, and rumor had it that Mikhalkov was positioning himself to run as a candidate for the presidential post. He had been active in the political arena for some time, promoting his conservative-monarchist views as a member of the party led by Viktor Chernomyrdin, Our Home Is Russia. He was even elected to the Duma on the party list in 1995, but he declined the office. Whenever asked, he denied any plan to run for president, although he admitted that if the people called he would be ready to serve. As late as the middle of November 1999, when he brought the film to Washington for private screenings, he reiterated once more at a private reception that he had no intention to pursue the presidential candidacy.[46]

Nevertheless, the promotion of the film was mixed with politics. The premiere took place with much fanfare in the Palace of Congresses inside the Kremlin, a six-thousand-seat auditorium that used to host the congresses of the Communist Party, and also served as the second stage for the Bolshoi Theater. The official reason was that such a film needed a Panavision screen and Dolby sound system, facilities that are hard to come by in Moscow. But the location stressed the special importance of the event. The gilded crowd included invitees from the international entertainment scene—Julia Ormond, Richard Harris, Shirley MacLaine, Steven Spielberg—together with representatives of the Russian political world—Prime Minister Yevgeny Primakov, former Prime Minister Viktor Chernomyrdin, Communist Party chief Gennady Zyuganov, last Soviet leader Mikhail Gorbachev, and the Patriarch of the Orthodox Church, Alexi II.

No aspect of commercial promotion was neglected. The event took place with fireworks outside the theater and young couples dancing to

12 *The Barber of Siberia* (1998) directed by Nikita Mikhalkov

nineteenth-century waltz tunes in the lobby. Ushers wore period servant costumes. Young men in the imperial cadet uniform greeted the guests, and samples of products wearing the *Barber* logo where on display everywhere—Hermès silk scarves, fancy-packaged cigars, and a men's cologne called "Yunkersky," a Russian borrowing from the German, *"junker"* (cadet).

One specific point of criticism was the fact that Mikhalkov cast himself in the role of Tsar Alexander III in a cameo appearance set in the very middle of the narrative, like a gemstone centerpiece. This added more fuel to speculations of his aspiration to rule. Which Mikhalkov dismissed: "Yes, I wanted to play the emperor," he said, "and I wanted it for two reasons. First, I love him. Second, it was my duty to think about the safety of the boy with whom Alexander rides out onto the square. Today, not so many actors my age can go horse riding with a child on the saddle. You must agree to that."[47]

That scene is remarkable, but not because of Mikhalkov's physical fitness—although that, too, is relevant. It is remarkable primarily because of the ambiguity Mikhalkov imparts to it—an ambiguity that runs throughout the film and peaks at that very moment. Notwithstanding his physicality, the tsar projects the image of a puppet theater stock character. The gala uniform seems to be painted on him. The rider and his son seem to be glued to the horse. The horse is so white and perfectly shaped that it seems to come from a merry-go-round. The riders' posture is wooden, their movements are spare and jerky. The child is a clone of the tsar. The tsar's salute to the cadets who graduated to officers is a cliché, promptly echoed by the boy. The setting is so stylized that the real Kremlin location is perceived as an artificial stage surrounded by pretty churches of *papier-maché* with golden aluminum foil domes. The reality of the location and the physical presence of the emperor are disguised under a colorful, folksy makeup. Why?

Is this Russia or Disneyland? The question is actually legitimate, given the "American perspective" embedded in the film. The story is narrated by an American woman, who relates the Russian experience of her youth, complete with adventure, intrigue, and a fateful love affair. The narrator, back home in the USA, tells the story in a letter to her twenty-year old son. It is the turn of the twentieth century, but the main action takes place twenty years earlier, when Jane (Julia Ormond) went to Russia as a young prostitute on a mission. Her patron and exploiter, the ruthless McCracken (Richard Harris) wanted Jane to help him to find a Russian investor to finance a devilish contraption, the Barber of Siberia, a tree-felling machine that would allow the American entrepreneur to harvest timber throughout the Siberian forest. Eventually, Jane fell in love with a Russian cadet (Oleg Menshikov) and the plan fell through. The cadet got involved in an intrigue, was arrested and exiled to Siberia. And Jane, back on American soil, gave birth to a Russian son.

The narrative strategy explains the stylized image of Russia that the film conveys. Jane's memoirs allow the film director to present a peculiar Russia that exists mainly in the memory of a Western visitor—a woman in love, for good measure. The images are selected and distilled, filtered through the rosy lens of romance and reflecting the folksy stereotypes foreigners often take for reality. At the same time, these same images exist in the collective consciousness of the Russian people—the good tsar on the white horse, streams of vodka, mountains of caviar, saccharine balalaika songs, fair maids, mighty warriors, and holy fools. This is the stuff of fairy tales, folk legends and cheap popular prints—the *lubok*. These are images both devoid of historical realism and endowed with the spirit of history.[48]

This is perhaps the "national idea" behind the film, which Mikhalkov referred to on numerous occasions—an idea of patriotism, spiritual values, and political stability that was paramount to the reign of Alexander III. The idea was to have a physical and emotional impact, as Mikhalkov explains: "I did not put Russian history on the screen, and I did not want to teach anything to anyone. I only wanted the rhythm and pulse of the film to convey the measured and grand rumbling of the earth. . . . A mighty, powerful energy fuels the picture."[49]

There is no denial that often the mighty energy that drives Russia and her people emanates from the screen. But there are moments where the energy is lacking. And these are the moments when it is most needed—namely, in the love story. Menshikov's character lacks the animal magnetism that would have made the story compelling. Instead, he comes across as inept, weak, and what is worst, clownish—a cross between Ivan-*durachok* (the folk tale village idiot) and Dostoevsky's Idiot. No doubt, this is the director's choice. But, while it may work intellectually, it does not work at the gut level. The same can be said for the two "American" characters played by British actors. Like Menshikov, they are seasoned professionals and give the best of themselves in their performances; and yet, they are misfits.

Since the film has no pretense to realism, ideology is conveyed symbolically through folk motifs. The opposition East-West, which Mikhalkov used in many of his previous films, is here mediated by Jane and her Russian-American son—perhaps, as critics said, a ticket to Western markets. Still, evil forces from the West are present in the film and take the form of a mechanical destroyer—the Barber of Siberia. This ravenous contraption violates the Russian land and the Russian soul, which in the Slavic mythology resides in the woods. Mechanization as a symbol of progress detrimental to the Russian spirit here takes up the form of a mythical monster. Ideology dissolves into popular culture. Distant relatives of this mechanical nightmare are the terrifying horned helmets of the Teutonic Knights in *Alexander Nevsky*.[50] Notwithstanding the film's nationalistic slant, Mikhalkov's critics pointed out that the "national idea" was not reflected in the commercial makeup of the film, which is a French-Russian co-production. Furthermore, they remarked that seventy percent of the dialogue is in English, an indication that the film was meant for the foreign market with an eye to dollar revenues and, perhaps, an Oscar. Ironically, though, the film did not have any resonance abroad. It was not well received at international festivals, and foreign distributors did not pick it up. Conversely, the Russian people loved it. They were willing to put up with voice over translation in order to lose themselves in the make-believe world of their national past. Here, at least, Mikhalkov hit the mark.

The search for Russia through the revival of her past will continue to be a subject of interest to filmmakers until a new identity is established. Gleb Panfilov's, *The Romanovs: The Crowned Family* was finally released in 2001, after it premiered at the XXII Moscow International Film Festival (2000). The project started twelve years ago, and the whole film was shot in 1997 in only four months. But a few years were wasted in the post-production stage. Panfilov wrote the script together with his wife, actress Inna Churikova, and their son, Ivan Panfilov. Nicholas is played by Alexander Galibin, usually a film director rather than an actor. English actress Lynda Bellingham plays Alexandra, reflecting the fact that the empress was a foreigner and received a British upbringing. Young actor Vladimir Grachev gives the character of tsarevich Alexei a truly tragic demeanor. Each one of the four young actresses who play the grand

History in the Making and on Screen   97

13   *The Romanov: The Crowned Family* (2001) directed by Gleb Panfilov

duchesses endows her character with grace, beauty, and intelligence. With this film, Panfilov wanted to rehabilitate the figure of Nicholas II, who was called inept and naive, at best, and blood-thirsty, at worst. *The Romanovs* covers the last year in the life of the family after their arrest, first in the residence of Tobolsk and later in Ekaterinburg. The history pages of the country in the convulsion of the revolution are left off screen, except for a gory sequence that marks the beginning of the February Revolution. The director focuses on the family that became the victim to those fateful events. The film is based on diaries, letters, eyewitness memoirs, and photographic materials, with the addition of the authors' subjective interpretation. The main idea of the film is that in Russia only truly tyrannical leaders can succeed. The populace longs for the "iron fist," and mistakes tolerance for weakness. Nicholas is portrayed as a decent man, a doomed Chekhovian anti-hero, who lacked the ruthlessness necessary to control the impetus of the revolution.

The Chekhovian motif of people left behind in the inexorable progression of history, and finally lost like an extinguished species, is conveyed in the scene of the family's departure from their residence of Tsarskoe Selo. The mise-en-scène is reminiscent of many a staging of *Cherry Orchard*. The curtains are lowered over the panoramic windows overlooking the park; heavy covers are thrown over the graceful sculptures decorating the atrium. As the family walks out, the camera remains inside, framing from a distance the suite of doors, which close up one after the other, until the place is left empty and dark.

Sets and decor stress the portrait of the tsar as a private person and a family man. There are no images of the sumptuous Winter Palace. The family is first seen in their suburban palace at Tsarskoe Selo, tastefully decorated in the simple style they favored: Russian *moderne*. The same decor is replicated in the exile residences; although in Ekaterinburg they were deprived of many comforts—most notable is the tin dinnerware assigned to the family, the kind found in workers' *stolovye* (cafeterias). The mise-en-scène is exquisitely crafted and conveys a loving atmosphere among the characters. The harmony between husband and wife, parents and children, and among the children themselves at times seems too perfect—and yet, not farfetched. It is one of Panfilov's main achievements that the film never slips into sugary melodrama; its realism maintains a poignant grip on the viewer throughout. Because of this skillful buildup, the ending is even more tragic. The provincial house that nurtured the family's life becomes their tomb.[51]

Until the 1960s, the place where the Ipatyev house stood in Ekaterinburg (renamed Sverdlovsk) was called People's Vengeance Square. The name was changed in the Khrushchev years to Komsomol Square. Eventually, when Yeltsin was party boss in the region the house was torn down, and the events surrounding the massacre of the imperial family remained a forbidden topic until the era of glasnost. The place is now called Square of the Ascension, its original name. In 2000 the political pendulum swung all the way to the other extreme. The Orthodox Church's Council of Bishops voted unanimously to canonize Nicholas II, his wife, and their children because they "tried to carry out the commandments of the Gospels in their lives" and "underwent their incarceration with gentleness, patience, and humbleness."[52] These are virtues highly valued in Russian culture since the time they were celebrated in the medieval tale of Boris and Gleb, the first Russian saints. Previous to the Council's decision, the Church made it clear that the tsar would be canonized for how he faced his fate rather than how he ruled Russia.

The 1990s ended as they started, with a film commemorating the last Russian tsar. The decade is symbolically framed by two films that revive a fateful turning point in Russian history, when a political order and a way of life disappeared together with the imperial dynasty. Both films aim at recovering the spiritual values that were lost and, therefore, tend to idealize the old regime, leaving off screen the great failures of the tsarist administration, and of Nicholas himself, which led to the Bolshevik revolution. The overall message in Panfilov's film is one of love and reconciliation. And, perhaps, this is what Russia needs at the beginning of a new chapter of her tormented history.

3
New Babylon

A hit

The large square in front of the Kievsky train station was dark and wet. The humidity rising from the river covered it with a damp coat. The sidewalks were slippery, as the grime turned to slush. The winter was late to come. It was November already, and no sign of snow. An oppressive cap hung over the city.

A streak of neon lights suggested a row of vendors' kiosks through the mist. They were lined up along the edge of the small park that runs parallel to the side of the station. From the station's ornate façade a faint circle of light spread to the surrounding area—porter carts, a taxi stand, the steps to the metro underpass. The big clock on the tower looked like a yellow moon with a fuzzy halo. The clock said 4:50. In contrast to the rest of the square, there was some animation around the station. But it was nothing in comparison with the hustling and bustling of a normal weekday, when people come from the South by the thousands with bundles of goods to trade on the market. On that Sunday night, only a few passengers were hurrying along, some homeless people were lingering on the sidewalk, last-minute buyers were getting a bottle of vodka or a pack of Marlboro from the kiosks before rushing to a party.

One man did not seem to be in a hurry. He moved slowly from kiosk to kiosk, as if inspecting the merchandise. But he would not engage in conversation with the vendors and would not buy anything. He carried a shopping bag that looked heavy, holding it close to his chest to ensure that it would not accidentally drop. The man looked at the clock—4:55. He looked around—a quick but careful look to make sure that everything was OK. Then, he crossed the street and stopped by the parapet around the steps that led down to the subway.

On the other side of the station, a short distance away, three men emerged from the glass doors of the Radisson-Slavyanskaya Hotel. The hotel was aglow with hundreds of brightly lit windows—a luring attraction, an island of luxury surrounded by a tall iron fence. The men walked across the parking lot, reached the gate, and stepped out of the compound into the foggy night. Two of them were tall and brawny, obviously bodyguards. They kept at a few feet distance from the third man, one in front and one in the rear. The threesome skirted the station building, headed for the metro entrance. The man with the shopping bag saw them coming. His body tensed. He looked at the tower—5:00 o'clock. Then, he focused on the three men that were approaching. They were now hurrying down the steps. The first bodyguard got to the bottom and disappeared in the underpass, the second hulk was behind, half a way from the top. In between, the man they were protecting was reaching the last few steps. The killer got a Kalashnikov assault rifle out of the shopping bag, leaned over the parapet, and took aim. The victim was hit with eleven bullets.

Moscowville

The assassination of Paul Tatum, an American entrepreneur and a highly visible figure in the expatriate circles, sent a chill through the corporate suites of Moscowville.[1] It happened on November 3, 1996. I have drawn on reports from the local newspapers to recreate the scene of the murder. I also used a bit of imagination to add emotional emphasis to the scenario, but the basic facts are accurate. Nobody could identify the murderer, who after the shooting discarded the weapon and fled in a getaway car. Even the bodyguards were unable to provide a description of the killer, because the man stood above them in the dark. They were not targeted and remained unharmed. After the shooting, one of them rushed to Tatum's aid, and the other ran off to raise the alarm. By that time, the killer had disappeared into the night. The getaway car, a model-9 Zhiguli, was recovered on the same day on Rostovskaya Naberezhnaya, but it provided no leads. The documents were in the name of the previous owner, who said he had sold the car five days earlier at a market to an unknown buyer.

"It was dark," said a vendor who had a kiosk a few yards from the scene of the murder. "I heard a long burst of machine gun fire, but all I could see was a muzzle flash."[2] This is about all the police were able to collect from eyewitnesses. From the beginning of the investigation, most people believed that the case would never be solved. There were many reasons for pessimism, judging by the statistics. In 1995 there had been 560 registered cases of suspected contract killings in Russia. Of those cases only 60 had been solved, and two thirds of the solved ones turned out to have been committed by the victims' bodyguards.[3] Many unanswered questions remained lingering over Tatum's case. His bodyguards were routinely investigated and exonerated. The police looked for leads in his telephone logs. One of his associates said that Tatum left the hotel after having received a phone call from an English-speaking caller, and speculated that someone knew he was on his way.[4] A question that troubled Tatum's friends was why was he using metro at all. The police believed that Tatum thought it was safer—more people, fewer chances of an attack than in a car or a taxi. According to people close to him, in the weeks before the murder Tatum regularly traveled on public transport, arguing that "they would have done it a long time ago; they're not going to do it now."[5]

Why would someone want to kill Paul Tatum? The deputy prosecutor appointed to the case said that "Tatum was mixed up in a great number of conflicts which had arisen on the Russian market, and in many situations he would resort to straightforward solutions with a certain stubbornness, which meant he didn't opt for possible compromises."[6] Many expatriate businessmen said more bluntly that Tatum paid the price for taking on the mafia single-handedly. One of Tatum's closest friends mourned the passing of a hero: "Paul did in real life those things that American legends and stories talk about. . . . He believed in the movies that spoke about truth, justice and the American way. . . . Was Paul a cowboy? He sure was, and damned proud of it."[7]

A native of Oklahoma, Tatum was president and chairman of Americom Business Centers. In 1990, he became a founding partner in a $50 million Moscow-based joint venture formed by Americom Business Centers (40 percent stake), the Radisson Hotels International (10 percent) and the Soviet agency Intourist (50 percent). Those were the late days of perestroika, when the recent transformation in the Soviet Union held a promise of lucrative opportunities for the free market pioneers. Only a handful of Western businesses had set up shop in Moscow, but many were sniffing the air, waiting for the right moment to jump in and share a piece of the pie. The Soviet housing and service infrastructure was dismal, and office buildings for rent were nonexistent. Tatum saw the need for new hotels with modern business centers, and Radisson seized the opportunity to get a foothold in a market that had just begun to open up. Americom was to provide business suites and communication services adjoining the Radisson hotel. On the Soviet side, Intourist saw a chance to turn one of its stalled projects—the half-built Slavyanskaya Hotel contracted out to a Yugoslav construction firm—into a hard-currency money machine.

But soon after the signing of the agreement Americom began to experience financial difficulties and its relationship with the joint venture's Russian management steadily deteriorated. Part of the problem was that, with the disintegration of the Soviet Union, the Russian partner changed four times—Intourist gave way to the Russian Property Committee, followed by the Moscow tourist agency MosIntour, and finally Moscow City Property Committee under the jurisdiction of Mayor Yuri Luzhkov. Many foreign partners in those years found themselves in the same disorienting situation, where the Russian side kept changing its identity every other week, and signed agreements or real estate deeds evaporated as if they had been written on the sand.

By 1994 it was war. The Russian management deployed armed agents at the entrance to bar Tatum from the hotel, but the American forced his way in with a host of bodyguards and barricaded himself in his suite. He lived there, practically under siege, for the next two years, protected by a small army of nineteen men. In the meantime, Mayor Luzhkov threatened to liquidate the joint venture, and Radisson sought to distance itself from Americom. In 1995, a Minnesota court granted the dissolution of Radisson's partnership with Americom. Soon after, Tatum received an eviction note from the hotel management, citing that he owed the hotel $300,000 in unpaid rent. This triggered a string of lawsuits on Tatum's part against both his former partners. He continued to wage his war from the hotel suite, maintaining that as long as the lawsuits were in process nobody had the right to evict him. The stakes were high. For the first half of 1994, the hotel generated $16.5 million in sales and earned $8.5 million in operating profits. According to Tatum himself, the venture "grew from $200,000 in 1991 to $17 million in 1994."[8] To finance his legal battles Tatum issued six-month "Freedom Bonds" securities at a 100 percent return, and advertised the offer in *The Moscow Times*. He also began to borrow large sums from shady lenders. Moscow struck back. The venture's founding documents were declared not valid because of a technicality, and in the summer of 1996 the city announced that it was about to sell the hotel to a foreign investor.

At the time of Tatum's assassination, an arbitration court in Stockholm was deciding the case of the hotel's ownership in a lawsuit filed by Americom. In January 1997, the arbitration court's decision dealt a hard blow to Tatum's heirs and to his hero image. The tribunal ruled that Americom improperly diverted funds offshore and, as a consequence, owed the joint venture about $2.6 million in damages. It also ruled that Americom's management contract over the hotel's business center was to be terminated. While the ruling closed this chapter of the ongoing saga, Tatum's family continued to fight in both the Swedish and the U.S. courts in order to reach an acceptable settlement and to vindicate the victim's reputation. As befits the image of a pioneer, Tatum never made the trip back home. One year after his death, his ashes were buried in Moscow's Kuntsevo cemetery in compliance with his wish. To detractors, Tatum was a carpetbagger with a dubious business past. To friends and admirers he was a lone cowboy, fighting for investors' rights in a lawless business environment. The latter is the image his brother-in-law intended to preserve in words and images, when he announced that he was writing a book on Paul Tatum and that copyrights were being discussed for a television movie to be broadcast in the USA.[9]

Actually, Tatum's connection with cinema was more direct. It had been part of his business venture all along. He was the first entrepreneur to provide the Moscow expatriate community with English-language films. The venue was the Americom House of Cinema, a 550-seat theater within the posh Radisson-Slavyanskaya—not to be confused with the Cinema House (*Dom kino*), which is located in the headquarters of the Filmmakers Union. The House of Cinema was one among the many amenities that turned the hotel into a magnetic center for hundreds of

Moscowvillians. The hotel was popular especially among Americans, who felt at home there. Between 1991 and 1996, it was practically our club. We would get a snack at Café Mozart, or dine in the upper-crust Exchange Steak House, or have a drink at the bar, set up as an island under a white canopy and surrounded by soft couches and chairs. The bar occupied a corner of the huge lobby, where the crystal chandeliers were reflected in the marble floor, and a sparkling fountain stood at the bottom of a double staircase leading up to the mezzanine balcony. At night, romantic melodies came from a white grand piano, and blended with the soft-spoken voices in the background—business talk, love chat, gossip, breaking news. This was the place where we were sure to find people we wanted to see, and could not avoid those we did not want to.

On the mezzanine, the Americom Moscow Art Gallery offered a new exhibit every month; among the most memorable pieces that had been on display were two original sculptures, August Rodin's Eternal Spring and Camille Claudel's The Waltz, brought to Moscow by the Belgian Dieleman Gallery. They were for sale, and there were speculations that some Russian collectors had outbid competitors from Australia, Japan, and Europe.

Walking down the hall from the lobby, we could go window shopping as if we were strolling along Rodeo Drive—Chanel, Gucci, Hermès. To buy anything was unthinkable, though. Only the diamond-studded-mink-coated girlfriends of the Russian moneyed elite could afford those prices. At the other end of the arcade, a state-of-the-art fitness center with pool and sauna offered much sought after relief to our sore joints and muscles, strained by the rough urban environment out there, in the real world. The fitness facility adjoined the International Press Center and Club that catered to foreign correspondents in particular, but not exclusively. Big and small executives, local journalists, embassy personnel, entrepreneurs, and fortune seekers made up the eclectic membership that every night crowded the IPCC's cozy bar/dining room. The center had both a business and a social calendar, from press conferences by government officials (Russian as well as American) to tennis tournaments at the refurbished Luzhniki courts, to Super Bowl parties with food, beer, and the game on a giant screen. The IPCC had an important function. Established as a Russian non-profit organization, it provided a unique independent forum for press conferences, and stimulated the development of a free press by awarding two annual prizes, Freedom of the Press Award and Excellence on Reporting on Russia Award. But it was short-lived. Because of financial difficulties due to a sharp rent increase, it had to fold up in June 1996. Subsequently, with the takeover of the joint venture by the Russian management, the space was turned into a casino.

Another journalist venture, *The Moscow Times*, took up residence at the Radisson-Slavyanskaya in 1992. The newspaper started as a twice-weekly publication, and after a few months expanded to become a daily. It grew at a galloping pace together with the foreign community, and became the true Moscowville's voice. It catered mostly to foreigners—but also to a growing readership of English-speaking Russians—bringing them investigative reports, business news, political analysis, cultural features, art, entertainment, sports, and community news. In one-year time, the hotel suite that hosted it was no longer sufficient to contain the expanding editorial offices. *The Moscow Times*, the first independent Western daily to be published on Russian soil, ironically moved to the *Pravda* headquarters. The old communist paper, now in need of funds, agreed to rent out the best part of its facilities. But this takeover was not the ultimate humiliation for the once proud organ of the Communist Party. Independent Media, the parent company of *The Moscow Times*, was quick to exploit the new Russian market, and by 1994 had established in the *Pravda* building the editorial headquarters of the Russian-language *Cosmopolitan* and *Playboy*. *Cosmo*'s American editor Helen Gurley Brown launched the Russian edition at a gala reception for hundreds of VIP guests at the Radisson-Slavyanskaya, maintaining that the magazine's philosophy about women's independent choices and independence was timely in the changing Russian society.

Behind the fancy social façade, Moscow foreign residents had always had the impression of living in a thriller. This was true in Soviet times, when we felt the presence of the KGB as close as our own shadow, as well as in the post-Soviet period, when political surveillance gave way to criminal activities. The patrons of the Radisson had a taste of it one day, when masked security forces raided the hotel and rounded up a dozen suspected mobsters. The Interior Ministry troops burst into the bar in camouflage gear, with deployed machine guns. They snatched the suspects from their stools and forced them to the floor. Some guests fled in panic; most watched the scene in bewilderment, holding their Martini glasses in midair, while enjoying the frisson of a gangster movie sequence come to life.

But the hotel had its moments of glory when members of the U.S. Congress and the executive branch checked in on their official visits. The highlights were the visits of President Clinton and Vice President Gore on different occasions. The Clinton-Yeltsin summit of January 1994 marked the first time a U.S. president chose to occupy a suite in a public facility, rather than the gilded master bedroom at the U.S. ambassador's residence. This was a bold decision, given the obvious security risks. It was also a calculated PR move meant to stress the end of the cold war. It was designed to emphasizes the fact that in the new times an American president felt comfortable sleeping on Russian territory rather than on embassy grounds, legally considered U.S. soil. Another reason was to show visible support for the hotel joint venture as a paramount example of American-Russian cooperation, and to promote the concept of private enterprise. Too bad it turned out to be the wrong example.

Security was tightened. The secret service blocked off the hallways leading to the presidential suite, and handpicked maids and other hotel personnel. Concerned about potential spying on documents, they also secured access to the White House delegation's working rooms. Signs all over the hotel warned that the place was unsafe for discussion and storage of classified documents. Most of the hotel's 400 rooms were booked by members of the delegation and the press, which considerably cut down the number of tourists. Other than that, the hotel remained open for normal operations—the guests continued their dining-shopping-swimming-movie-going activities, and the corporate suites in the Americom wing kept doing business as usual. There was, however, an extra charge of excitement in the air.

In those days, I worked in the Press and Culture section of the U.S. Embassy, and for two Clinton visits and two Gore visits I was part of the support team staffing the huge press center set up on each occasion at the Radisson for the American media. Three enormous banquet rooms on the mezzanine were packed with endless rows of tables and chairs, hundreds of yards of cable, cameras, monitors, computers, communication equipment of all kinds; there, a human tide of reporters, correspondents, spokespersons, TV anchors, cameramen, and helpers rose and fell according to the time of the next briefing or the latest press release. Media celebrities hurriedly crisscrossed the floor to and from their respective network desks. There was an almost surreal element to it. First of all, it was bizarre to see those talking heads moving around on actual human legs. Secondly, it was odd to see them all together in the same space, when we were used to see them as the occupants of neatly separate niches on TV screens. And here they were—Ted Koppel, Tom Brokaw, Peter Jennings, Dan Rather, Claire Shipman. It was as if characters from different soap operas were suddenly thrown into the same play. The time-space dimension of television was disrupted, and its inhabitants looked like fragments of a world topsy-turvy.

At the time of Clinton's second visit, in May 1995, the dispute over the ownership of the Americom business center had reached dramatic proportions. Tatum was already living under siege in his suite, and made a theatrical gesture to draw attention to his predicament. He flooded the press center with flyers, inviting the entire press corps to a party in his quarters. I could not attend, but I was told the party was packed and afterward Tatum's plea resonated in various forums. Nothing, however, helped him to avoid his fate.

But we have to backtrack. I was leading the reader to the House of Cinema along the shopping arcade and past the IPCC, before getting detoured by vignettes of mafia warfare and presidential visits; just as if walking down a virtual hallway, I clicked on this sideway icon, and then on that one, and each time found myself on a new page—a new branching out space. Something similar happened to Alice, when she kept opening those Wonderland doors, one after another. But now we are back to the original menu—let's click on the House of Cinema.

The House of Cinema was inaugurated in September 1993, with the Russian premiere of *Much Ado about Nothing,* co-produced and directed by Kenneth Branagh. It was not exactly an international blockbuster, but in those early days Russia was still the target of the Hollywood boycott and only independent studios had agreed to supply the theater, provided that the films would not circulate outside of Americom's premises. The studios were going to get a percentage of ticket sales with a minimum guarantee. And the prospects were good. Americom marketing experts estimated the expatriate population in Moscow at 80,000 and growing, and the local middle class at 100,000—a sizable audience willing to pay $10 for a ticket. The House of Cinema, however, had a rocky beginning. The titles were not appealing enough, the prints did not arrive in time, and the audience did not turn out in mass. Nevertheless, the movie-starved hard-core Moscowvillians were grateful for anything they could get—even bad movies, when shown in a state-of-the-art theater and accompanied with popcorn and Pepsi. This deprived audience did not speak Russian for the most part, and was missing out on the latest Russian releases beyond Moscowville's borders. But things were actually improving on all fronts. Starting in 1994, the U.S. boycott was lifted and a new Russian distribution company, Gemini Film, began to release Hollywood features with Russian dubbing throughout Russia. Gemini Film enjoyed the luxury of solid financial backing from its German mother-company and Western-style advertising skills and means.[10] In those days, many Russian movie theaters still displayed hand-painted advertising posters.

In the end, competition turned out to be good for the cinema business in general, creating a favorable cultural climate. Americom House of Cinema acquired a partner, Golden Ring Entertainment, which managed the theater efficiently for about a year, improving the repertoire as well as attendance. Golden Ring was eventually fired in the summer of 1995, when the joint venture was dissolved and Americom fell under the management of the Russian partner. Many charges were leveled against Golden Ring, but it was abundantly clear that this was just one more episode in the whole imbroglio directed at getting rid of Paul Tatum. One additional twist in this intricate story is that Golden Ring president, Ray Markovich, was also Tatum's attorney and represented him in the lawsuits against the Russian management.

This was not the end of Golden Ring Entertainment, however. Rather, it was just the beginning. Ray Markovich and his partner Paul Heth three months later opened a second English-language cinema in a similar venue, the Penta Renaissance Hotel, and called it the Dome Cinema. But the big breakthrough that made them rich and famous occurred one year later, when they struck a deal with Eastman Kodak and together opened the Kodak-Kinomir theater on Pushkin Square. Kinomir was an immediate financial success and became one of the main attractions on the Moscow scene.

The Radisson-Slavyanskaya was not the only hotel in the early 1990s that catered to both a resident and a transient upper-scale clientele. The legendary Metropol had been meticulously restored in all its art nouveau details by a Finnish company and, under the management of the Intercontinental group, hosted an ongoing flow of international VIPs from government, business, and the entertainment world. Another landmark of pre-revolutionary glamour, the Hotel National, was given a new lease on life by the French chain Le Meridien/Forte, and re-established itself as the premier Metropol's competitor. The Baltschug-Kempinsky also offered the same ritzy atmosphere, and the revived Savoy Hotel lulled its patrons in intimate elegance. The Mezhdunarodnaya Hotel (International Hotel), which was the only Western-style complex favored by foreign businessmen in Soviet times, experienced a decline as a result of competition from the newer, more luxurious hotels. It was built by Armand Hammer in the 1970s, thanks to his special relation with the Soviet leadership—a relation that dated back to his friendship with Lenin, whom he met in Moscow the early 1920s as a young entrepreneur. Other less glamorous hotels, remnants of the Soviet era, were eventually refurbished by foreign partners and managed by international chains. By 1998, there were ten four- and five-star hotels in Moscow. And in the previous two years, four high-profile executives in the hotel business were murdered.[11] The Radisson-Slavyanskaya was not unique, but it was the one that I knew best, and that possessed all the connotations of the grand-hotel culture in the frontier town known as Moscowville.

MOSKVA

In 1929, film directors Grigori Kozintsev and Leonid Trauberg made a film called *New Babylon*. The title referred to the name of an exclusive department store in Paris, in 1870, which was a metaphor for the whole of the Parisian decadent upper class lost in an orgy of materialistic pleasures. Because of the requirements of Soviet culture, the plot had an ideological counterpoint, the Paris Commune fighting for high ideals of freedom and equality. Who would have thought that some seventy years after the film was made Moscow would have become the *new* New Babylon, minus the idealistic Communards?

Many films of the 1990s portray Moscow as the dehumanizing big city *par excellence,* with its deluxe shopping malls, wondrous monuments, international restaurants, and alluring night clubs-cum-casino, all controlled to various degrees and in various forms by organized crime rings. In the film *Moscow* (1999) by Alexander Zeldovich, the subtext suggests that the "three sisters" of Chekhovian memory have fulfilled their dream and come back to the capital. But what they found does not belong in a Chekhov play.[12]

I have a vivid memory of one night in the early 1980s at the Taganka Theater, watching an unorthodox version of *Three Sisters,* staged by the controversial, legendary director, Yuri Lyubimov. Those were the dark days of the interim regime before Gorbachev, which, although brief, dimmed the hopes of the intelligentsia. At the end of the play, when the garrison departs leaving the sisters trapped in the despair of a no-way-out predicament, the young playwright who was my escort that night had tears running down his cheeks. "*Bednaia, nasha strana . . .* (Our poor country . . .)," he whispered. And all I could do was hold his hand and cry with him, out of solidarity and contagious melancholy.

Moscow shows that the situation has changed, but not improved. Irina, Masha and Olga have changed, too. And, the story is a different story; only the women's names evoke the classical play. There is still a family nucleus, but here there are only two sisters, while Irina is their mother—still young enough to rival them in the seduction game. There is also a threesome of men to balance the picture. The relations among these characters are more slippery than in a Shakespeare play. I quote from the film's press release:

> Irina (Natalya Kolyakanova) is a socialite, a latent alcoholic, a bohemian of the 1970s. In the 1990s she has become the owner of a night club, and is deeply in debt. Since the age of sixteen she has been sleeping with Mark, and now occasionally she is having sex with Mike. Masha (Ingeborga Dapkunaite) is Irina's older daughter. She studies international law. She is engaged to Mike. She betrays Mike with Lev. Olga (Tatyana Drubich) is Irina's younger daughter. She suffers from autism. She sings in the night club. She is emotionally dependent on Mark, but loses her innocence to Lev. Mark (Viktor Gvozditsky) is a psychiatrist who represents the golden generation of the 1970s.

14   *Moscow* (1999) directed by Alexander Zeldovich

He sleeps with Irina and is Olga's therapist. He is secretely in love with Olga, and commits suicide when Olga loses her innocence. Lev (Stas Pavlov) used to be a cellist, and is now an international cash courier. He works for Mike. Back from his latest trip, he delivers a sum a hundred times less than the expected $300,000. He endures torture and waits until his turn comes. He seduces Masha and, later, Olga. In the end, he becomes rich and marries both of them. Mike (Alexander Baluev) is a new businessman, sponsor of the arts and a ballet lover. He plans to marry Masha but sleeps with Irina. He dies at the hand of a hit-man at his own wedding.

This synopsis may sound like a parody, but the film's tone is serious. The idea is that Soviet power has created a culture of brutish violence and cynicism which, rather than disappearing, is gradually metamorphosing into the new capitalist structure based on crime and big money. The new money power is seen as an offspring of the totalitarian system, generating the same nightmarish atmosphere. The cinematography provides the nightmarish effect from the very first shots, while the credits roll, by dissolving the cityscape into an abstract canvas of dribbling colors—the opening sequence is filmed through a windshield covered with streaks of heavy rain, which reflect the kaleidoscopic lights of advertisements and shop windows as the car speeds through the streets of Moscow.

The soundtrack supports the disintegration of the image, as patriotic songs of the Stalinist era pop up in incongruous contexts. The abstract cityscape sequence is intercut with Olga's performance in the nightclub, where she renders the heroic Soviet songs of old as syncopated tunes, feeble and pitiful. She highlights a disconnect between the text and the music—a cultural language that has shifted. Later, the "Song of the Motherland," the leit-motif from the most popular film of the 1930s, *Circus*,[13] is revived in a mock-performance at the same grand piano in an identical elite apartment, but the Soviet positive hero of the original film is here replaced with the money trafficker, Lev. The linguistic shift shows its most tragic consequences in everyday speech, where human communication has become impossible. The characters utter empty sentences that do not find a receiver. It is Antonioni *à la russe*, or, in the national model, dysfunctional Chekhovian dialogue. The compulsive promiscuity of the six protagonists is a frenetic search for a way of communication through sex. Physical contact is used to replace the breakdown of the verbal communication system.

Sex is also associated with violence—the two are graphically connected in several notable scenes. When Mike suspects Lev of having embezzled the money, he subjects him to a form of torture that connotes rape: a tire pump is inserted in Lev's anus and air is forced into his intestines until they burst. Lev survives, and in turn rapes Masha, while she is too drunk to react. Lev leads Masha into a game, where he covers her body with a big map of Russia, after having carved a hole right in the spot where Moscow is; then, he proceeds to fuck both motherland and girl in one shot. A livid, bluish light gives a sinister connotation to this scene. Lev's figure is rendered in a very dark shade, creating the image of a demon.

Lev is the embodiment of the hybrid monster begotten by the merging of the old and new cultures (the fact that the character is coded as a Jew seems to be an instance of political incorrectness, to which the Russians are not so sensitive). Unlike the other characters, who are conditioned by

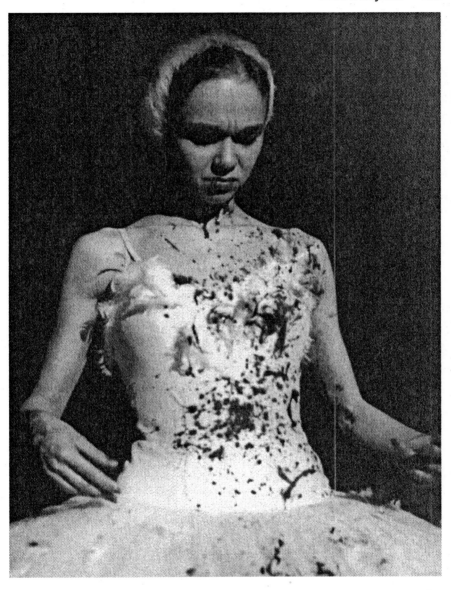

15   *Moscow* (1999) directed by Alexander Zeldovich

their past and restrained within the parameters of their predicaments, Lev has a chameleon personality, able to adapt to all circumstances and to fill empty spaces like an expanding amoeba. It is because of the ability to fill the cultural void with his insidious presence that he wins in the end, causing the death of the other two men, retrieving the cache, and getting the three women. These three achievements are conveyed by kitschy metaphors—the kitsch is, obviously, deliberate and the images are skillfully constructed.

Mark stages his spectacular suicide on the ski jump on Sparrow Hills. The sightseeing from the top terrace had become a mandatory ritual for all newlyweds in Soviet times. Mark takes his life there after having lost Olga to Lev, by sliding downhill headlong on a suitcase filled with his favorite books and portraits of his beloved. When he hits the ground, the suitcase breaks open, scattering around the symbols of Mark's lost world.

Mike ends up the victim of a hit murder. His "new rich" life style displayed a core of ruthless cynicism coupled with a gusto for grandiose gestures. He was the patron of a ballet company--partly because he liked that art form, but mostly for prestige. The night of his murder, the prima ballerina had just completed the swan's death scene, which was part of the festivities at Mike's and Masha's wedding. Mike climbs on stage to present her with a bouquet of flowers. His back is shown in the killer's viewfinder, filling the frame and blocking the view of the stage. After the shot is fired, Mike's body falls forward, revealing the ballerina who watches in horror, her white swan feathers spattered with Mike's blood.

In the meantime, Lev implements phase two of his plan. Under the cover of dark, he climbs up the huge iron sign that spells the name of Moscow (MOSKVA) on a main access road and pulls the cache out of the letter O. Blood money emerges from the very heart of the city. "Where were you hiding the money?" Masha asks Lev at the end. "In Moscow," he answers.

With the money in his pocket and no more rivals around, Lev moves in to fill the void in the women's lives. In a bizarre, and totally unrealistic, ceremony, he marries both Olga and Masha in the old Soviet marriage bureau (ZAGS). Irina is also present, strongly suggesting that she is a member of the female threesome, rather than the mother of the brides. The surrealist mode continues in the next scene, as the wedding party, in jeans and T-shirts, proceeds to the Tomb of the Unknown Soldier on Manezh Square. That was another mandatory ritual for newlyweds in Soviet times. Olga asks, "What's the Unknown Soldier?" Lev replies, "The soldier that did not exist." Olga, "How can there be a monument to someone who did not exist?" Lev, "Those who did not exist also have the right to a monument. Maybe, more than the ones who did exist."

It is twilight. The characters stand in a sort of stupor by the perennial flame which gleams in the dark and casts ambiguous shadows on their faces, underlying the incongruity of sacred Soviet icons and Russia's new lifestyle. The women cut a pathetic figure as symbols of a genteel world coopted by the Babylon Moloch.

"*Bednaia, nasha strana* . . . ," would again whisper my sweet friend of old. This time without tears, but with a sad, ironic grin.

"What is to be done?" The Russian intelligentsia has asked itself this question for more than a century, without ever finding a practical answer.[14] The film's director, Alexander Zeldovich, raises the question again in a contemporary setting, focusing on the problems rather than on the solution. He said that the film is rooted in the cultural tradition, but the inspiration came from everyday reality:

> The immediate inspiration for this film came from various impressions I had gathered. In Moscow, in the Hermitage Gardens, was the club "Hermitage," located in a huge shed and belonging to a friend of mine, Svetlana. Once, I came into the club at around 7:00 p.m.; there were no visitors; Svetlana and her daughter, aged around 19 or 20, were sitting in the bar in luxurious fur coats. Both of them had just split up with their boyfriends, and both looked toward the door as if they were waiting for some prince to come into their lives. Another impression: sitting in their kitchen they were watching television, drinking tequila instead of tea, and having Chekhovian conversations . . . all this was nice and quite lyrical. But something else was far from lyrical: Svetlana asked me whether I had not seen so-and-so . . . who had disappeared several days ago. . . . The harsh and gruesome features of this decade turned into everyday reality: people disappeared in fact quite frequently in Moscow. Apparently, they were killed. . . . From time to time I returned to Moscow in the 1990s,

and I got the impression of a growing vacuum, some kind of emptiness that surrounded me. Life was bubbling, people were making money and building their careers. Every time I returned, I felt like I was falling into a city where the gaping void was growing, and a city that became more and more cruel.[15]

The Hermitage Gardens, on Karetny Ryad, was a green oasis in an otherwise congested urban area where I used to pause and rest between errands. The Gardens hosted the cozy Hermitage Theater, nestled among flowerbeds and stone sculptures—until 1993. At that time, the organization that owned the place turned it over to some entrepreneurs who opened a night club, and the gardens were soon flooded with laser lights, giant TV screens, rock bands, disk jockeys, and hip party goers. It was about that time that Moscow began to grow "more and more cruel."[16]

One of the first films that raised the issue of Moscow as a heartless city, and that became a great success, was *Limita* (1994), by Denis Evstigneev. He made his debut as a director with this film, after distinguishing himself as a cinematographer.[17] The title is better left in the original, as it denotes those vagrant laborers (*limitchiki*) who in the old days came to the urban centers for seasonal work, and were housed in barracks beyond the city limits. Today, the term has the special flavor of a time past. The protagonists of the story, Ivan (Vladimir Mashkov) and Misha (Evgeny Mironov), arrived in Moscow in the late 1970s from Pyatigorsk. They managed to survive through the loopholes of the system, and then got well established in the computer business as soon as the new wave of opportunities made it possible. Now, thirty-something, they are riding the high tide. Ivan is an independent code-breaker, Misha is a program specialist with a financial institution. Together with their female companion (Kristina Orbakayte),[18] they live the privileged life of the high-tech elite. But in the big city, big money means big trouble. Ivan gets a lucrative order from a client associated with the mob: he must crack a disk that Misha has encoded for his company. When Ivan realizes the nature of the job and tries to back out and save himself and his friend, he is already enmeshed in a thriller in which ultimately Misha comes to his death.

16   *Limita* (1994) directed by Denis Evstigneev

Black and white clips from the *limita* times contrast with the slick interiors of Ivan's apartment, the high-tech décor, his designer clothes and stylish clients. The question in the end seems to be whether the new wealth is worth the loss of innocence—and of lives. Evstigneev has a practical answer. Talking about the new Russians, he said: "Civilized or uncivilized, they are the first people in the country who are making decisions about their life for themselves. They may be egotistical, concerned only about themselves or those close to them, but for me that is better than what we had before, when people talked about the 'happiness of millions'."[19] Notwithstanding the underlying cynicism, or just because of it, the movie was very popular.

The death of utopia, and the consequent loss of faith in a bright future, has been expressed most poignantly in films about youth. Valery Premykhov added one more picture, *Migrants* (1992), to his bleak portrait gallery of a doomed generation.[20] This is a *film d'auteur*, in which Premykhov has the triple function of screenwriter, director, and actor. But it is not a film for an intellectual elite. Rather, it is meant for a mass audience, with its American-style action scenes, dynamic montage, a tragic love story, and the jungle-of-asphalt dehumanizing setting. It's a pity that the film disappeared from circulation soon after its premiere. In *Migrants*, Premykhov plays the role of a road construction worker—a background observer who senses his own tragic end and the unhappy outcome of the lives of two young lovers, Pavel and Polina. Moscow is presented as a powerful city-monster, hostile to the human being. Premykhov and his cameraman, Boris Brozhovsky, convey a compelling image of the contemporary megalopolis, seething under the scorching sun. In this big city, people are "migrants," uprooted, unprotected, deprived of their existential anchor.

Pavel, who came to Moscow from his village, drives a steamroller, and considers himself lucky to have an underpaid job and a bed in a workers' dorm. Polina, too, came from the provinces, but with a different goal: to marry a rich foreigner and leave behind the misery of Russia. However, fate decides otherwise. After a casual meeting, the two teenagers fall in love. It is a harsh street romance on the melting asphalt, in empty buses, and overcrowded communal quarters. To escape those surroundings, the couple decides to retreat into the depths of rural Russia. In Pavel's native village, they think, they could make a home for themselves, have children, and live a normal life. But there, they find only dilapidated shacks, mephitic marshes, hungry women, and drunken men. They come back to the big city, where the pace of the action picks up speed and precipitates a dramatic outcome. To defend Polina from a street gang, Pavel gets into a fight and is falsely accused of killing one of the attackers. As a result, he is charged with murder and sent to jail. Youth problems have been a central theme to other Premykhov's films, but in *Migrants* they have become more extreme and complex. They have reached a crisis point that reflects the crisis of a whole society.

Urban wolves

The phenomenon of alienated youth burst to the surface in the late 1980s. Documentaries such as *Is It Easy to Be Young?* (1986) created a sensation by bringing this social problem to the public's attention.[21] Fringe groups and paramilitary associations started to organize in those days, but they emerged in full force in the early 1990s, after the fall of the Soviet Union. In the last decade there were basically two camps that attracted thousands of alienated teenagers looking for group support and a cause: politicized right-wing nationalists and hate-driven skinheads.

The largest neo-Nazi movement, Russian National Unity (*Russkoe Natsional'noe Edinstvo*, RNE), was founded and headed by Alexander Barkashov.[22] The RNE registered with the Moscow authorities in 1993 as a club for military training and patriotic education, but in their daily practice they openly professed Hitler's ideology of genetic purity, nationalism, anti-Semitism, and totalitarian rule. They called themselves national socialists and adopted the symbols of the Nazi regime: black uniforms and swastika signs on red armbands. The group first gained notoriety during the uprising of October 1993 when, together with other anti-Yeltsin forces, they participated in the storming of the Ostankino television station. Since then, they kept aloof from the opposition parties officially represented on the left by Zyuganov's Communist Party, and on the right by Zhirinovsky's Liberal Democratic Party. They also shunned the other unofficial extremist movements. In 1998, the Moscow Anti-Fascist Center estimated that there were approximately a hundred Fascist organizations in the country, although many were very small. RNE soon spread to the provinces, where in the course of a few years it grew into an organization of 33 regional branches duly registered. The federal umbrella group, though, was denied registration. The existing laws prohibiting the use of Nazi and Fascist symbols were not enforced; the members were rarely prosecuted; and, when it happened, they were easily acquitted. In 1999, the Moscow authorities moved in to disband the local organization, after a court ordered the withdrawal of RNE's Moscow branch registration and the banning of its newspaper, *Russian Order* (*Russkii poriadok*). The charge was that the group had violated several laws governing political activities, but many believed that the real reason was a clash between Barkashov and Mayor Yuri Luzhkov, after six years of mutual support. At that time, the RNE claimed 300,000 members around the country—a figure that was believed to be somewhat inflated, but still substantial. One element that attracted the young was the conspiratorial aura surrounding the organization. RNE prided itself on being a political party; in fact, its practices recalled a brotherhood with secret society initiation rituals and periodical ceremonies.

Barkashov was a child of Pamyat, the right-wing movement that came into being in the mid-eighties, as soon as Gorbachev's glasnost policy made it possible. But Pamyat was not aggressive enough for Barkashov, who in the early nineties left it to found his own movement. As a working class man, he despised intellectual activities and believed in the enforcement of law and order. From the very beginning, RNE dedicated itself to practical action, rather then theory. Behind the legal facade of a youth club, the Viktoria Club, RNE had the setup of a voluntary militia with headquarters in Terletsky Park. There they practiced vigilante skills by cleaning up the park of the homeless, the drunkards, and vagrants of all kinds. Later, they joined the police in the campaign to drive illegal immigrants from the Caucasus and Central Asia out of Moscow, raided the markets, and rounded up the undesirables. RNE financed its activities primarily with money earned in the security service business, but it was rumored that they also enjoyed the patronage of some sympathizers in the armed forces and the police, who regarded the movement as a good recruiting ground. Barkashov was in his mid-forties, while most of the members were disaffected young people. Some had been in combat in Chechnya, and a few older ones were Afghan veterans. Others came from former Soviet republics, where the Russians felt part of a persecuted minority. Most of them were just teenagers, mesmerized by a flamboyant ideology and self-important war games.

As early as 1994 the organization split and a number of teenage members broke away to form the Werewolf Legion, under the leadership of Igor Pirozhok. Horror stories were associated with the Werewolves, who conducted a hate campaign against Jews, democrats, communists, hoboes, and renegade members. They allegedly tortured homeless people and used them as slaves. One particularly gruesome episode involved Pirozhok's appearance on Swiss television, holding a jar that contained the ear of a murder victim. The victim in question was a group member who had been entrusted with blowing up Moscow's Olympic Stadium during a congress of the Jews for Jesus organization--and failed. But the Werewolves' targets were not just live enemies; celluloid characters aroused their hatred as well. At the time of the release in Moscow of Spielberg's *Schindler's List*, they had a plan to set fire to the theaters showing the film. The plan was eventually averted, thanks to the intervention of the police who made several arrests. In the final analysis, the difference between the RNE and groups such as the Werewolves was only a pretension. All of them were violence-driven thugs. But, while RNE clad itself in the mantle of a popular militia inspired by a political ideology, the Werewolves and other extremist groups, generically known as the skinheads, seemed to go on a violence spree just for the heck of it. The occasion would be a rock concert, a soccer game, or Hitler's birthday celebration.

The skinheads' favorite victims in the late nineties were African and Asian people, who in those years became more conspicuous in the Moscow population tapestry. Students from those regions were often attacked in metro stations and underpasses and severely beaten. Occasionally, the skinheads would swarm on campuses and attack minority students in the dorms. Hate crimes against foreign students were not unheard of in Soviet times. The Patrice Lumumba University that was established in Moscow in 1960 to host students from "friendly countries" had been promptly renamed "the zoo," and the people's attitude towards its guests was certainly less than friendly. Ugly incidents were often sparked by minority students dating Russian women. The difference was that in those days the police strictly enforced the laws regulating hate crimes and hooliganism, while in the post-Soviet period the authorities were more inclined to tacitly accept racial intolerance. In fact, they even encouraged it when it was politically expedient, as in the hate campaign against the Chechens and other minorities from the Caucasus known in Russia as the "black-asses" (*chernozhopye*).

However, some cases were prosecuted more vigorously than others. One incident made headlines in 1998, when an African-American Marine was beaten at the Gorbushka video market on a crowded weekend. He was attacked by four skinheads, who punched him in the mouth, knocking out two teeth. One of the assailants, the head of the gang, was promptly arrested the next day and charged with inciting racial hatred.

The mantra that sustained skinhead violence was "genetic socialism," the urge to preserve the purity of the Russian blood from interracial mixing. Typically, these teenagers came from working class suburbs, where unemployment was high and life was dull, to look for excitement and action in the heart of the big city. Racial hatred was mostly an excuse to give vent to a more general deep-set resentment. The skinheads' rage hit whomever happened to be in their way.[23]

At times, people disappeared with a motive; at times, without. The day Katya came to the apartment in a state of agitation and told me about her brother's disappearance, I thought she was being overly emotional about nothing. The guy will certainly show up the next day. Katya was my landlady and became my friend. For four years I lived in her beautiful apartment, and for four years she came over twice a week to clean and cook for me. She was slightly younger than I, but from the onset she took up the mother role, or more appropriately, the role of the traditional Russian nanny. She pampered or scolded me, as the case would be, and she was always there for me, bending backwards to make my life easier. Her features matched her personality. She was rounded all over; a gentle round face, blue round eyes, and a plump figure that she carried around with extraordinary agility. She was constantly worried that I was too thin and did not get enough to eat. Routinely, she would check the refrigerator only to discover that I had left over most of the food. "*Nu, chto takoe?* (Well, what's that?)," she would say with a hurt face. "*Vy nichego ne kushali. Tak nel'zia. Ya bol'she ne budu vam gotovit'* (You did not eat anything. That's not good. I'm not gonna cook for you anymore)." And I would have to mollify her with promises to amend my eating habits. Soon we began to rely on each other for emotional support. She would make tea and bring it to me to the kitchen table, then stand by, her hands joined on the apron, telling me about her life, the good and the bad of it. It took me more than a year to bring her to sit down with me.

It happened that day, when her brother disappeared. Now, we were facing each other across the table, and we were drinking vodka, not tea. She told me that she learned from his wife how he went out that morning to go walk the dog in the park. And did not come back. They had notified the police, and feared the worst. Unfortunately, it turned out that they had the right premonition. The next day, the police found the body in a pond. The autopsy revealed that the man had been clubbed to death and dumped. The dog, too. The case was closed rather quickly, since there were no suspects and no motive. He was an ordinary citizen, living a tranquil life, with no connections other than work and family. Katya and I spent long hours at the kitchen table making up our own scenario about the incident; in order to understand, and in order to heal.

Early morning in the park. Summertime. The sun is already high, filtered down through the thick foliage like thousands of luminous dancing dots. The man walks along the alley, stopping frequently to pick up a stick and throw it in the bushes for the dog to retrieve it. He gets to the pond; here, the alley ends and gives way to a trail that skirts the water. A few yards ahead there are three young men in fatigues, with high boots and colored bandanas around their shaved heads. Two are sitting on a bench, involved in some sort of transaction. Drugs, perhaps. The other is standing, on the lookout. The dog darts off toward the group, in a playful mood, to make new friends. "*Laika! Laechka, stoi!* (Layka! Layechka, stop!)." The man recalls the dog. He senses the danger. "*Siuda, Laechka!* (Come here, Layechka!)." Too late. The guy who was standing kicks her in the head with his metal-studded boot, and she is now on the ground, a thin stream of blood flowing out of her ear. The man rushes to her. As he leans over the dog, the three guys attack him with truncheons; the blows fall on the head, the shoulders, the back; then, they turn him over and kick him in the face, the stomach, the abdomen. The man is reduced to pulp.

The skinheads pick up the body by arms and feet, sway it back and forth a couple of times, and throw it out in the middle of the pond. They do the same with the dog. Both lives have the same value to them. They sweep the trail with a green branch, covering up the signs of the crime with fresh dirt. They pause, exhausted. It's hot in the sun. They dampen their bandanas in the water and wipe off the sweat from the brow. They wash off whatever blood remains on their hands and boots—the camouflage suits conveniently conceal all other traces. Then, they walk back up the alley, regaining the gates just as the usual stream of grandmothers and children enters the park for the daily outing.

The skinheads were variously portrayed in film, but their activities have hardly been the focus of the narrative. They provided a backdrop element to the general atmosphere of crime and lawlessness, as in Pavel Lungin's film *Luna Park* (1992). Two years after having achieved international fame with the Cannes Festival winner, *Taxi Blues* (1990), Lungin

17   *Luna Park* (1992) directed by Pavel Lungin

released another Russian-French production. As in the first film, *Luna Park*'s urban setting generates alienation and violence, and an ironical overtone undermines the story's lyrical accents and high drama. The subtitle, "contemporary fairy tale," refers to social types and events of today's Moscow life as well as to imagined relations and situations. The story pits against each other two generations, two worldviews, and two lifestyles in the figures of Andrei and his alleged father.

Young and handsome, Andrei (Andrei Gutin) is the leader of a gang devoted to the destruction of "Jews, homosexuals, vagrants, and Coca-Cola drinkers." Its members wear black uniforms and practice martial arts and bodybuilding in their headquarters situated in a Luna Park underground. The Luna Park's visual leit-motif is a gigantic roller coaster, divested of any connotations of fun and romance. The ominous structure of steel and neon lights is reinforced by the parallel image of a Ferris wheel. Both are heightened by Denis Evstigneev's cinematography, and look sinister and deadly.[24] Against this hellish background stands a demonic female figure, the statuesque Luna Park performer, Alyona (Natalya Egorova), who masterminds the gang's political program and holds Andrei in her sexual grip. Her ferocity is eventually sublimated in a spectacular fire, which engulfs the roller coaster together with Alyona on the wave of Wagnerian melodies.

All this would be macabre indeed if it were not treated tongue-in-cheek and redeemed by the sparkling performance of Oleg Borisov in the role of Andrei's estranged father.[25] This character, emeritus composer Naum Kheifitz, is a fussy, funny man with an intriguing personality, incorporating generosity and pettiness, kindness and cynicism, passion and selfishness, and a lighthearted acceptance of life's vagaries. He can, with equal ease, cheer up a party of nostalgic workers with patriotic songs, captivate an audience of schoolchildren, and perform in the celebration of an Uzbek national holiday. When Andrei learns that his father is a Jew, he resolves to kill him. But, in the process, he is charmed by the man, and gradually hatred becomes love. The two men, who turn out not to be related after all, develop a human bond which takes them to the pure expanses of the Russian Far East in search of a new life.

The non-professional actor, Andrei Gutin, had a difficult task working with a seasoned performer such as Oleg Borisov, but what he lacked in experience he made up for in good looks. Natalya Egorova, too, displays more looks than feelings, but this was a script requirement. One must also note the fine performance of Nonna Mordyukova in the role of Andrei's aunt, a staunch believer in the Communist myth.

Duba-duba (1993) is the first film of director Alexander Khvan.[26] The playfulness of the title, which is the verbal rendering of a saxophone tune, hints at the tricks the director plays on the viewer, disrupting the narrative flow, mixing up time and space, and juxtaposing non-sequential events. All this is handled with a certain skill, and sustained by the uncommon talent of Oleg Menshikov in the role of the protagonist.[27] To a Western eye, though, it has a quality of déjà vu.

The movie's hero, Andrei, a screenwriting student at the State Cinema Institute, organizes a jail escape for his girlfriend, Tanya, who got involved with a narcotics ring. To get the money necessary to bribe a guard, Andrei decides to rob one of the millionaires who populate the new Moscow high-rises of glass and steel. The plan succeeds, but the dramatic climax is soon deflated. Andrei and Tanya are no longer in love. She moves in with the gang's leader, Nikolay, and is again arrested and jailed. The next scene, where Andrei confronts Nikolay, is not for the faint-hearted. With a knife stuck in his heart, and vomit dribbling down his chin, Andrei finds the strength to set off a hand grenade and blow himself up together with his nemesis. Andrei's agony is conveyed by a very long take, where violence is treated with aesthetic enjoyment. The same sadistic refinement is displayed in the scene of the robbing of the millionaire, which is a reference to Stanley Kubrick's young thugs in *Clockwork Orange*. Here, Andrei wears a grotesque mask and submits his victim to physical and psychological torture.

But Andrei's death is not the end of the film. The director has another card up his sleeve. The film hero shows up in the U.S.A., his nightmare having been nothing more than a film script he wrote.

Judging by theater attendance, the audiences did not favor these kinds of intellectual games. They preferred the hero's treatment on a more realistic plane, as in the film *Brother* (1997) by Alexei Balabanov. This has been a great box-office hit, notwithstanding, or perhaps because of, the predictable plot and the sex-and-violence clichés borrowed from the American B-movies that had saturated the Russian screens in the past ten years. The authors counted on the viewers' expectation to see the same cheap formula duplicated on native soil and spruced up with a good dose of chauvinism. Independent producer Sergei Selyanov, head of the St. Petersburg-based STV company, scraped together a budget, and produced a film that soon became a cult movie.

The young hero, Danila Bagrov (Sergei Bodrov, Jr.), after having been hardened in military operations in the Caucasus, comes home to his brother who lives in St. Petersburg and works as a contract killer for the mafia. Danila gets involved in a dirty deal, shoots a dozen people that happen to be in his way, defeats the mafia boss, rescues the older brother, gets a bag of money, and leaves the scene unscathed, like a lone knight errant. In his spare time he sympathizes with the city's homeless, and enjoys the favors of a loving woman who offers him shelter. However, the potential excitement the script promises is not translated into action. Actually, the action looks slow and dull to a Western viewer—as dull as the hero himself, whose violence is neither morally nor emotionally motivated, but is triggered by an automatic reflex acquired in

18   *Brother* (1997) directed by Alexei Balabanov

combat. As a result, there is no drama; just a series of mechanical actions.

This would not be a flaw in itself if the film had been constructed with a degree of distancing allowing for stylization of the genre. In fact, this may have been the intention of the director. Balabanov, previous to this film, was known as an *auteur* filmmaker, adapting Kafka and Beckett to the screen for an elite audience. But *Brother* lacks both the self-reflexive second layer of discourse as well as the dynamism of an action movie.[28] Moreover, the problems are not only aesthetic. Ideologically, the film abounds in racist slurs and nationalistic one-liners, and tramples on all traditional values. Balabanov declared that his interpretation of the moral standard responded to the demand of the younger generation, and Bodrov, Jr. qualified the film's criminal values as "strange," "new," "absolutely accurate in sociological terms."²⁹ The public response, especially among the young, seemed to support these claims. The younger generation longed for a hero with whom they could identify. So, what if his values were not those of the archetypal hero? What if they were closer to those of a skinhead gang chief? What if the hero displayed zero values? No problem. The moral vacuum gives Danila unlimited freedom and superhuman power. The film exalts that power and caters to the aspirations of the young viewers.³⁰

This successful story called for a sequel, and *Brother 2*, was released three years later, in 2000. Here, Balabanov plays a more obvious game, relying on the previous film and turning it into a parody of itself. The same hero makes a comeback, resurfacing in Moscow. He displays the same philosophy and the same inclination to get into tough action, but this time he has money and connections. Instead of being a lone wolf roaming St. Petersburg's desolate cityscape of dilapidated tenements and dirty alleys, he is the chief of a brotherhood and the leader of the pack. This group resides in a different habitat, the glittery apartments and nightclubs of the new Babylon. To stress Moscow's connotation as a criminalized city, the authors create a cinematic space that includes Moscow itself, New York, and Chicago. They send the hero on a trip across the ocean to the mythical land of opulence and crime, showcasing him on the set that once saw the deeds of Al Capone and other venerable godfathers. But, to maintain the Russian connection visually, the props are from stereotypical immigration enclaves such as Brighton Beach-- colorful signs in Cyrillic characters on shop and restaurant doors, colorful imported hookers and bullies, colorful street crowd whose only spoken language is the mother tongue. There, the Russian superman performs his deeds as swiftly and efficiently as he did at home. This time, his mission is to rescue a hockey player who has been lured to the land of plenty under a bad contract. On the side, he also defeats a powerful Russian crime ring, has a brief affair with a Chicago TV news anchor, saves a Russian prostitute, and exits the American scene with a million dollar in his bag.

And yet, *Brother 2* suffers from the same problems as its predecessor. The action never picks up speed. The hero remains as dull as before. And sex is only suggested, not shown. One can appreciate the effort on the part of the director to approximate the garish color scheme and flashy

19 *Brother 2* (2000) directed by Alexei Balabanov

editing of the Hollywood adventure movies. But these efforts fall short of the target. The effect achieved in *Mission Impossible 2* and other similar cartoonish flicks is to transpose the image from the realistic mode to a virtual dimension, where hyperbolic action and superhuman features are the norm. This super-reality is laid bare and presented as entertainment. Conversely, *Brother 2* lacks the fantastic dynamism that would propel it beyond the boundaries of realistic representation.[31] Therefore, the young audiences identify with the hero and admire his nationalistic ideology—here enhanced by an anti-American bias—instead of seeing him as a cinematic creature. Allowing for emotional participation, both *Brothers* offer a role model that reinforces negative social trends.

The people strike back

Another popular hero, this one appealing to an older, working-class audience, is the protagonist of *The Voroshilov Marksman* (1999) by Stanislav Govorukhin. The film is based on the novel, *The Wednesday Women*

(*Zhenshchiny po sredam*) by Viktor Pronin, and, like most of Govorukhin's films, displays a conservative ideology. Govorukhin has been a member of the opposition in the Duma since 1993. He also ran for president in 2000 on a nationalistic platform. Over the last decade, his films have become progressively more reactionary and critical of the current government, which he openly labeled as "criminal" in his 1994 documentary triptych. In an interview, Govorukhin stated his position:

> Q. You have repeatedly called yourself a 'reactionary.' Are you proud of this title?
> A. Of course. I'm a traditionalist and a reactionary.
> Q. Excuse me, but the two aren't quite the same.
> A. Really? I'm still not sure what precisely the word 'reactionary' means. . . . But, come to think of it, yes, I'm an enemy of progress. Because in terms of morality, progress hasn't brought about anything good.[32]

In *Marksman*, the director sets up a paradigmatic opposition of "establishment" versus "people." The "establishment" is presented as an extension of the old nomenklatura in collusion with its allies—the new Russians—and is connoted by greed and corruption. The "people" are portrayed as the ordinary folk, connoted by moral values, such as honor and patriotism. The ideological framework is unambiguous and sustained by a savvy combination of narrative and visual codes, designed to elicit the appropriate emotions of revulsion or compassion. The realistic style allows for a total suspension of disbelief and commands participation from the point of view of the leading character. While the main action itself may seem out of the ordinary, the general socio-political setup faithfully mirrors the reality of the day. Most of all, the feeling of authenticity comes from the filming on location—a tenement courtyard, cramped apartments, a vulgar pied-à-terre, a sumptuous banker's office, a shady marketplace, a dull police station—and also from a cross section of types (even stereotypes) populating those spaces, accurately portrayed down to the minute details: mimicry, postures, clothes, and speech nuances. The casting is flawless. But the glue that keeps all these elements together is the outstanding performance of Mikhail Ulyanov as the hero. A most beloved interpreter of many old favorites, he reinforces the viewers' nostalgia for the past and their resentment of the present.

The film hit a raw nerve among the disgruntled masses of workers and pensioners who saw their life savings evaporate and their wages disappear, while a class of unscrupulous dealers lined their pockets by stealing the national wealth. The class of the new Russians, with their top elite of oligarchs, is a complex phenomenon that deserves a serious discourse in another venue.[33] In the film, the popular resentment toward the new capitalist class is stirred by a threesome of young bullies, who rent a pied-à-terre in a suburban tenement and impose their ostentatious lifestyle on the workers community, still living under communist egalitarian values. These youngsters are small fry; nevertheless they have enough money for sport cars, booze, and loud parties with call girls. Every Wednesday, the quiet life of decent, law-abiding citizens, struggling to put a bowl of soup on the table, is being violated by the crass sound and look of money. From the second floor balcony, blaring rock music pours down into the courtyard, where elderly men are clustered around the chessboards. They raise their eyes for a minute to stare at the window with a frown, then look at each other, shake their heads, sigh deeply, and resume their games. One of them is the retired railroad worker and decorated WW II veteran Ivan Fyodorovich (Mikhail Ulyanov), who will be forced into action by a terrible occurrence and, in the eyes of the viewer, will become the "people's avenger."

On that Wednesday, Fyodorovich's eighteen-year old granddaughter falls victim of multiple rape at the hands of the three bullies. Fair, blue-eyed, trustful, and fragile like a field flower, Katya (Anna Sinyakina) is the embodiment of the Russian peasant girl—a conventional victim of the urban male in much of popular fiction, since Nikolay Karamzin established the archetype two-hundred years ago in his novella, *Poor Liza* (1792). Here, Katya is also a symbol of Russia herself, being raped by the brute force of capitalist expansion. The grossest of the three studs— ironically identified as "a hero of capitalist labor"[34] —says of Katya: "*Ne dast? Otnimem.* (She won't give it to us? We'll take it.)" The rape scene that follows is detailed and jarring; the fast-paced, jumping montage, together with the pulsating rhythm on the sound track, reinforces the affect of violence. In fact, the brutality is directed at Katya as well as at the viewer, and is absolutely necessary as a prologue to set the stage for the main act.

Tough cops, who grew up in the neighborhood with a sense of honor

134 **Imaging Russia 2000**

20 *The Voroshilov Marksman* (1999) directed by Stanislav Govorukhin

and justice, know how to rough up the thugs and extract a confession;but the case stops at the desk of the chief, who happens to be the father of one of the suspects. The populist note is played insistently throughout the film, underlining the divide between the privileged who are in power and the underprivileged who are exploited and humiliated. After the system fails him, Fyodorovich feels that he has no choice but to take justice into his own hands. What follows is a meticulously planned and executed action. The former sniper in the end succeeds in hitting his targets one by one, with precision and in cold blood. This action occupies a good three quarters of the narrative, and is built in such a way as to have the viewers painstakingly follow the hero through every step of the ordeal and give him their unconditional sympathy. In fact, there were reports that in some locations the audience cheered after each hit.

Within the film, too, the character has his sympathizers. He finds solidarity in an unlikely circle—a den of arms traffickers. The scene that depicts Fyodorovich's purchasing of the rifle adds one more connotation to the "people" paradigm. The arms dealers conduct a lucrative underground business, which according to the logic of the film should automatically place them in the capitalist camp. But, some of them are young veterans of the Chechnya war, physically and spiritually scarred, and as such, victims of the establishment. They are foils for the daddy's boys charged with rape. Their arms business is seen as a protest against the established order, motivated as much by anger as it is by money. They, instinctively, recognize the old man as one of their own, and address him respectfully as "*batya*" (father). Moreover, they are filled with admiration for the Red Army comrade's shooting skill and tough stance. "Wow! He's a true Voroshilov marksman!," says one of the bunch.[35] At the end of the transaction, Fyodorovich leaves with a state-of-the-art rifle, equipped with telescope and silencer. Of course, he had to pay for it. And in order to get the money, $5,000, Fyodorovich had to sell the rural cottage where he was born to a banker/developer. This scene stands in contrast to the camaraderie displayed by the arms merchants. The banker, a prosperous twenty-something with a fortune offshore, happens to be Fyodorovich's distant nephew. He treats his old uncle with condescension, while trying to cheat him on the deal—an instance of the rip-off of the land from the legitimate owner, the "people."

Now, with rifle in hands, the sniper is on his own. From his vantage point in an empty neighbor's apartment, facing the infamous balcony across the courtyard, he waits for the right time to strike. The scoundrel who masterminded the rape is the first to be whacked; he has his balls taken out by a precision shot. The second one gets his butt and genitals severely burnt in a fire that engulfs his newly acquired BMW, when the sniper's bullet hits the gas tank. The third guy is set up so that he accidentally shoots and kills his own father, the police chief, and is taken to jail. The "avenger" has carried out his mission, stealthily and unfailingly like a wild cat, leaving no evidence behind. The "people" win, the audience cheers.

And yet, what is the ultimate moral of the story? This issue was heatedly debated in the Russian press, with the liberal critics expressing dismay at a film that upholds unlawful violence, no matter how justified it may be by circumstances. They argued that vigilante tactics, such as those adopted by Ivan Fyodorovich, bring the hero down to the level of a criminal, no different from the three rogues who had offended him. "The 'Voroshilov marksmen' can always find a common language with the new Russians, the businessmen, the bandits and their like. They will also find a common ground with the bureaucrats—they are all of the same stock," said one voice. And another, "The viewer can draw only one lesson from the film: the only way to defend oneself is to become one of the scum . . . to accept their morals as a guide in practical life."[36] Even worse, they said, the film rejects the concept of the rule of law, recently introduced into the infant democratic state, bringing the country back to an ideology typical of the Soviet system. "In the film, the irony is effaced by the lofty idea of social retribution and undeclared class warfare. This brings us back to the time of the 'Voroshilov marksmen,' the time of an inflexible class ethic, when metaphysics were automatically eliminated."[37]

The counter-argument to the film critics figures prominently on the jacket of the video release: "*Ne radi mesti, a vo imia spravedlivosti* (Not for revenge, but in the name of justice)." The slogan resonates with revolutionary pathos, and switches the discourse from the concept of law to the concept of ethics. Popular uprisings by definition occur outside the law; they are meant to subvert an unjust order and restore the people's rights. This is implied in the film, but it is not the only justification that is offered. There is a deeper level of cleansing that the film also suggests.

In fact, Ivan Fyodorovich comes across not as a cold assassin, but as a man of feelings. His relationship with Katya is truly moving for the tenderness, concern, and despair the old man projects. The film exonerates Ivan of all criminal charges, as well as any moral taint. In the end, he is "acquitted" by a friendly cop, who disposes of the rifle—literally, destroys the smoking gun—and simply tells him, "You are free." Ivan is confused and deeply troubled; his previous determination now gone, he does not know what to make of all that happened and how to deal with his conscience. He replies, "How am I going to live?" and receives the same answer again, "You are free." Ivan answers: "Thank you, Alyosha." These last lines sound like an absolution. On the practical level, Ivan has been set free by the "people's tribunal"; and in a higher spiritual sense, he has been relieved of a moral burden and is now free to choose his future path.

Govorukhin's reference to the "humiliated and insulted," in an interview, indicated that he had in mind a kind of Dostoevskian morality: "My heart always goes out to the 'humiliated,' whether they are right or wrong. Today, when people are being robbed and lied to, my heart is with them. . . . My heart is on the side of this 'humiliated and insulted' generation."[38]

Outside and inside

While moviegoers applauded episodes of individual rebellion on the screen, in real life most of the population focused on the everyday struggle for survival. Alienation intensified in the reform years, when well-tested strategies meant to shield the citizen from the abuses, or inadequacies, of the Soviet system, suddenly lost their viability. Before, it was the intellectual elite that felt estranged from the state, while ordinary citizens were generally proud of their country and accepted the well-publicized sacrifice-today-for-a-better-tomorrow formula with resignation, as long as they had a roof over their heads and vodka on the table. But with the reform, the familiar world burst like a soap bubble. The Soviet state, despot and patron, was no longer around. The void was filled with a government oblivious of the population's needs, a mob on the rampage, triple-digit inflation, the shut down of state enterprises, the collapse of the social safety net, and lack of law enforcement. The more resourceful among the urban folks figured out how to navigate the new map, but many never adjusted to the changes and fell through the cracks.

It was late in the afternoon and I was hurrying home. It was terribly cold. The car had not started in the morning, as often happened in sub-zero temperatures. The old BMW which I bought the previous summer from a second-, perhaps third- or fourth-hand dealer, had seen better days in its native country. I emerged from the metro station in a cluster of passengers that slowly pushed its way upstairs like a blob, contracting and expanding. As the cluster dissolved in the street, a sheet of cold air clung to my body, sending a shiver down the spine. I tried to walk fast, but I had to negotiate the icy sidewalk and the heaps of snow along the curb. It was a short walk, less than a block. Soon I turned into the porte-cochere to our stately building.

When I reached the courtyard, I tripped and almost fell over something that lay on the alley leading to my wing. The lamp by the entrance shed a dim light on the surrounding area. I had some trouble seeing what it was. Then, I saw it. It was a corpse. Someone had covered it with a tarp that was too short, reaching down only to the hips. The legs were sticking out, naked, bluish, frozen. They looked nonhuman, two dead twigs. It was hard to imagine that attached to those sticks there were a torso, a head, a "thing" that once was a human being. A couple hurriedly stepped around it, hardly acknowledging its presence.

Having lived in Washington for many years, I got used to seeing the homeless in the street, those pitiful rag piles on park benches, in doorways, in metro entrances, and I had tried to assume the prevalent attitude of considering them as part of the cityscape—"they have a survival technique," "they do not really want your help," "there is no way you can help them." But I could never get over a feeling of guilt and inadequacy for not getting involved.

Now, I stood and looked at the "thing" under the tarp, hesitating. This one, really, did not need my help any more. Or, perhaps, it did; more than the living ones, because it could not get up and move itself to a more dignified place. I saw a neighbor coming my way. "Marina Aleksanna," I called her. *"Kto eto? Chto sluchilos'?* (Who's this? What happened?)," I asked. She was one of the old dwellers; she had lived in the building for fifty years, since the time it was built. She wore the kind of footwear that had almost disappeared in the cities, felt boots and galoshes, and her head was bundled up in several layers of woolen scarves. "*Bog znaet. Malo li chto byvaet segodnia!* (God only knows. The things that happen nowadays!)," she said and crossed herself. She explained that they found the man in the morning; he was already dead. He probably took shelter under the archway last night. When he froze to death, whoever was with him, perhaps another homeless, took his clothes and ran. I realized that I went out through the small door in the morning, on the other side of the courtyard, and I could not have seen it. "Well, we have to call an ambulance," I said. "What d'you think, we didn't? Of course, we did," she replied. "We called the hospital, the militia, the morgue, City Hall. Nobody's rushing to pick up a dead body. They cannot even service the living. *Gospodi pomilui. Eto ne po-chelovecheski* (Lord, have mercy. This is inhuman)." She crossed herself again and moved on.

I reached my apartment on the fifth floor. As always, I felt blessed. Every time I got home and shut the door behind me, I entered another world—a world of comfort, elegance, and privacy. I went straight to the living room window and lifted the lace curtain. The corpse was still there, a gray dot on the snowy ground. The courtyard was deserted, except for a dog that came out of the dark to sniff at the frozen feet. I felt terribly uneasy, unsure of what to do. There was no phone book in the apartment; it does not come automatically with the service, and I had forgot to buy the directory of public phone numbers the telephone company sold to its customers. Besides, according to Marina Aleksanna, the authorities had already been notified.

I went to the kitchen to make tea. From the fridge I got some cheese, and the potato salad Katya had prepared for me; I put it all on a tray and went back to the living room. 7:00 p.m. I slouched down in an armchair and turned on the TV. The news was awful; partly because bad news was considered an attribute of the new freedom of speech, and partly because there was nothing good to report. Destruction and casualties in Chechnya, a car bomb killing a prominent businessman, galloping inflation, workers not getting their wages for the fourth month in a row, and, to top it all off, bad weather keeping Moscow in its icy grip for the foreseeable future. I turned it off.

Once again I looked around at my beautiful place and felt privileged. The living room alone was the size of the diminutive apartments the Soviet state mass-produced for its citizens since the 1960s. In addition, I had a bedroom so large that my queen-size bed seemed to disappear in a corner. There were also a second bedroom that I used as a study, a foyer with French doors to the living room, and a big kitchen. The bathroom, too, was spacious, with decent fixtures and tiles—although not the latest deluxe Italian imports that became a staple in all remodeled dwellings for new Russians and corporate foreigners.

But its best feature was the plumbing, efficient, forever unclogged, happily gargling waste waters away. "Of course. It's German!" the Russians would say. The joke referred back to the post-war period, when the Soviet state used German POWs as construction workers. They built many of the stately tenements and baroque skyscrapers in the ornate style that is now known as "Stalinist." The underlying irony has to do with the perceived dichotomy in Russian culture between the native tendency to daydreaming and philosophizing and the German propensity for efficient action and practical results. This theme has been played out in many films in different periods, and possibly never better than in Mikhalkov's *Oblomov*.[39] Whether the theme has any roots in reality, or it is just a cultural myth, one thing is certain: bad plumbing has been plaguing the dwellers of cheap Soviet-built "*khrushchoby*" for forty years.[40]

It had not been easy to find this apartment. When I was looking for housing, in the summer of 1991, there were very few offers on the market; and those were not systematically advertised. One would learn of an opportunity by word of mouth, or by sheer luck. The whole concept of rental and real estate had just begun to emerge, together with the policy of privatization. As part of Gorbachev's perestroika reform, the Soviet state had decided to renounce its property rights on apartment buildings, and to transfer the titles to the dwellers that wished to claim them. Used to a state that for seventy years took citizens' rights away, many had a hard time believing in the change and, rather than rejoicing of this reversal of fortune, remained suspicious. After all, that was still the Soviet Union, where only the day before it was a crime for a private citizen to engage in commercial transactions. Some thought the law would change back again in a few months, and they would be arrested. Others did not trust the state on economic grounds. They realized that, once they became owners, the cost of maintenance and utilities would fall on them, and they were not ready to take up such a responsibility. Up to this day, there are still apartments in Russia that have not been privatized by their occupants. Worse, there are citizens who, having privatized their apartments, changed their mind and wanted to give them back to the state.[41]

But the vast majority eventually saw the benefits of privatization and went along with the reform. After the collapse of the Soviet state, the process accelerated and millions of Russian citizens became legal owners for the first time in their life. This was actually the only privatization program that worked out with a high degree of success. To us, Westerners, the deal looked surreal. As it happened, many citizens acquired not one, but two, even three or more apartments: the apartment they lived in, the apartment of the aunt who moved to the country home, the one they inherited from the grandfather, and so on. We were envious. Imagine, all of a sudden someone knocks on your door and tells you that you have been given a piece of real estate for free. No down payment, no closing costs, no mortgage. Please, sign this paper; here, it's yours. But our Russian friends argued that for generations the state had not given them the opportunity to save or make money, and this was some sort of compensation. Fair enough. However, the pie was not shared in equal measure, because those who enjoyed a privileged position under the Soviet regime got to privatize the choice apartments their families had been assigned over the years—the ones built by the Germans, or the refined dwellings of the pre-revolutionary bourgeoisie which were at first confiscated and turned into communal apartments—while the others ended up with a pitiful piece of *"khrushchoby."*

Privatization also led to the crudest real estate speculation and the wildest price inflation. Shady enterprises would buy an entire building, or an entire block, from the owners, piece by piece, in order to tear it down or refurbish it, and rent out the new apartments and offices to the expats at over inflated rates. Most citizens did not realize that even the shabbiest apartments in downtown Moscow had a market price of $30,000 to $50,000, and the better ones would command $500,000 or more. The dealers would acquire properties in prime locations for a fraction of their price, and relocate the occupants in inferior quality buildings on the outskirts. Eldar Ryazanov portrayed one similar case in his comedy *Old Nags* (1999), where a victim of the real estate scam is relocated to a shack on the cemetery grounds. Here the tragic situation blends with comic elements, but in the real world there was no humor. A scam that targeted the elderly turned into a macabre affair. The dealers would offer senior citizens a substantial monthly payment—many times their pensions—for the rest of their life, if they agreed to sign the apartment title over to them. In a few weeks, the senior citizen would mysteriously die or disappear, and the dealer would take possession of the property. By 1995, twenty-two thousand Muscovites had sold or exchanged their apartments, but only five thousand had been registered at new addresses. The others were missing, and quite a few were eventually found murdered.[42]

The criminal element was not the only one to profit from the real estate boom. Legitimate enterprises sprung up all over the city. Every district was dotted with hundreds of construction cranes, foundation pits, scaffoldings, and wooden fences. Moscow City Hall, during the Luzhkov administration, became a major enterprise, sharing in the profit of dozens of businesses. *Rossiiskaia gazeta* pointed out the growing personal power of Luzhkov, who had "unchecked control over the land, buildings, property, budget, and tax services of a city of 9 million."[43] The mechanism was simple. The city government would give a piece of its vast property to a company to house a business, provided that the company would restore or rebuild it at its expense. At completion, the city government would keep for itself 50 percent of the renovated building and, in addition, acquire shares of the newly-formed joint venture—such as 51 percent of Moskva-McDonald's and Pizza Hut, 30 percent of Hotel Metropole, 100 percent of Hotel National, 100 percent of the Moscow Central Market, 30 percent of the All-Russian Exhibition Center, 100 percent of the sumptuous shopping center at Manezh Square, and so on. The Russian developers usually relied on foreign contractors for construction projects and materials. The Italians were the first to enter the market successfully. For them it was nothing new; they were just keeping with a practice established in the 15th century by architect Aristotele Fioravanti, who was commissioned to build the Kremlin. But soon they were challenged by the Turks, who were able to offer fairly good quality at a lower price. All other international bidders lagged very much behind.

The system seemed to please everybody involved, the Moscow bureaucrats as well as their partners, whose businesses got substantial benefits from City Hall in terms of land rental, allocation of premises, and credits. Criticism came from those outside the inner circle, who argued that a public institution, such as the city government, was not supposed to own any business; that the present situation was rife with corruption, and the public coffers had become a trough for the city bureaucracy.[44]

But Mayor Luzhkov had a vision. He set out to create an image of the city that would show its centuries-old path toward its manifest destiny. By the time of Moscow's 850th birthday, in 1997, this vision was largely realized. Old monuments, embedding the "Russian idea" of Moscow as the world's spiritual guide, had been brought back to life; first among them, the Cathedral of Christ the Savior, a massive marble construction with five golden domes that was built in the nineteenth century under the rule of three successive tsars, and was then blown up in the 1930s by Stalin. Other grandiose plans, still at the project stage, looked at the future, perhaps at the "new Russian idea," Moscow as the world's financial and economic guide. One such project was Moscow City, a 40,000 sq. meter expanse of gold and glass towers, aerial bridges and gleaming fountains on the Krasnopresnenskaya Embankment—a cross between Wall Street and the Stalinist VDNKh (Exhibition of Economic Achievements).

I found the apartment through an agency; one of the many makeshift agencies that in those days mushroomed overnight and disappeared the next day. Actually, an agent found me; she said she heard I was looking for housing. She was a young woman, obviously improvising in her new job. I must have been her first client. The first stop was the agency office—a hole of a place in the back of a courtyard and up a flight of dark, narrow stairs. She rang the doorbell, and a hulk in fatigues, conspicuously dangling a heavy truncheon, let us in. In the small room, a guy was sitting at a desk. He was all in black from head to toe—black suit, black shirt, and dark glasses. I had been informed that a "rental fee" was required in advance: $200 cash, non-refundable. That was a huge sum at the time; the ruble was 30 to $1 and the prices still controlled; it was the equivalent of a worker's yearly salary. Besides, all transactions in foreign currency were illegal. I put the envelope on the table. "What if I don't like the apartment you find me?," I asked. "We'll find you one you like," Mr. Black said with absolute finality. I parted with my money with some apprehension. But, as it turned out, Mr. Black kept his promise. A few days later, the agent called me and said that we had an appointment with the landlady.

That day I met Katya. We met at the metro station, and she escorted us to the apartment. Later, she told me that she wanted to see and evaluate the prospective tenant before letting us in. The fact that I was wearing a jogging suit and sneakers told her that I was an unpretentious person. She liked that, and I passed the glance test; still, Katya remained suspicious and extremely reserved. We signed a protocol of intent that day. Katya was hesitant, and did it only because the agent twisted her arm. We were to meet again and sign the contract in a couple of days. But when the time came, Katya did not show up. I was crushed; I fell in love with the apartment at first sight, after having seen a dozen of absolutely unsuitable mouse holes. I asked the agent to be persistent. But, of course, they had already collected the fee; what would she care? She gave me Katya's phone number only because I begged her on the verge of tears. And that was the last time I heard from her. When I called Katya she was taken aback and upset that I had been able to track her down. It took me a good fifteen minutes to convince her to meet one more time, without the agent. She agreed to meet me at the apartment. I rang the bell and waited for a couple of minutes. I felt she was looking through the peephole to see whether I was alone. Finally, she opened the door just enough to let me in and quickly shut it back, locking it on three heavy bolts. Then, she smiled at me and said: "Nowadays you must have a safety door, and keep it on all locks all the time. And you should let in only the people you know and trust." Wonderful, I thought, I've been accepted.

In the course of our conversation that day, I learned that she had been introduced to the agency by some friends of friends, who were renting out their apartment at a good profit. But after her first contact with the agency, she got cold feet. For one, her apartment had not yet been privatized, although the paperwork was in the pipeline. She was scared at the idea of breaking the law. And even more terrifying to her was the fact of dealing with foreigners. She wanted to make sure that I would rent the apartment as an individual and not as the representative of a firm—"All these rooms just for one person?"—and that I would not set up an "export-import business." At the end of the day, we reached an agreement. There will be no written contract—no paper trail—I will pay her cash at the beginning of each month; and we will give each other one-month notice. The price we negotiated, 2,500 rubles, was very high—five times the monthly salary of a university professor. Still, to me it was a mere $85. And it included Katya's services. Our agreement was sealed by a handshake and a glass of vodka, and lasted for nearly five years.

The rent rose dramatically with each political change, and each new monetary policy. In the new Russia the ruble exchange and the transactions in foreign currency became legal. All of a sudden, the color of money changed to green. Nobody would accept anything but dollars—the *greeny*, as they had been known for ages on the black market. Only the bare necessities and staple food could still be obtained in rubles from state-owned stores. But even these relics of the Soviet past were gradually being privatized and turned into Western-looking currency shops. The ruble fell precipitously and, in the course of two to three years, the official exchange rate plunged to 6,000 to $1. My rent, too, turned green, and rose to $400 by 1993; it kept going up, and when I left the apartment in 1995 it had reached the $800 mark. Even so, it was still four to five times below market value. The international organizations, the big corporations, the law firms, and the U.S. and European government contractors were willing to pay hyperbolic prices for their executives' housing—from $3,000 to $6,000 per month. This created a fantastic superstructure, disproportionate with the real country's economy. The bubble eventually burst, in 1998, and everything was resized down to more realistic proportions, including real estate prices. The ruble reacquired its status and pricing in foreign currency was banned. But before that, the ordinary Russian thought that prices would go up indefinitely—"This is capitalism, isn't it?"—and everybody, at every level, tried to squeeze as much as possible out of whatever they had, prompted by fear to miss out on the opportunity. Katya's family and friends urged her repeatedly in the course of those years to charge me more. "*Ved' u tebia zhe inostranka* (After all, you're renting to a foreigner)," they would say. "*Da, no u menia bednaia inostranka* (Yes, but mine is a poor foreigner)," Katya would reply in a protective way. And, no matter what, she would stick to the course of action that she considered right and fair. For reasons that I did not care to clarify, Katya was the only heir to her father's apartment. She was very proud of her property and exercised total control over it. Neither her husband, nor her brother, nor her son, were allowed to interfere in the least in her decisions. Perhaps, together with the apartment, she inherited some of her father's commanding attitude. She painted a fond portrait of the handsome army colonel who both ruled her life and brightened her days until the time she got married.

She was in grade school when the family moved to the newly built complex assigned to high-ranking officers of the armed forces and the KGB. "Things were different then," she would say, starting off on a wave of nostalgia that often colored her long tales with a rosy tint.

> I am for the reform and the opportunities that this government offers to the young, but life was better in those days. The building was well kept, spotless. We even had a concierge. There was a great sense of community, we knew all our neighbors, and every Sunday the recreational committee organized movie screenings or dance parties in the huge hall down in the basement. My father was the best dancer, and all the ladies wanted to dance with him. I was very proud of him, and so was mama, who sat at a table with her girlfriends eating chocolates and patiently awaiting her turn. Now that hall has been rented out to some *kommersanty* (business people) who use it as a storage space. And the common areas are nobody's land. Chipped walls and trash all over.

This was unfortunately true. In order to get to the elevator, we had to get through a disaster zone, where the mosaic floor showed large bare spots, the walls were covered with graffiti, several windowpanes were broken, and many light bulbs were dead. Katya would go on spinning her tale:

> We had a happy childhood . . . and even later, when we were teenagers. Every night, we would gather around the dining table, here in the living room—the children, mama, papa, and Marina Aleksanna. She came to Moscow from her village as the young bride of an army

officer, and later lost her husband who had been badly wounded in the war. She was very lonely, and practically spent the whole day with us, helping mama around the house. Mama would serve us tea with jam and a delicious poppy seed cake that was Marina Aleksanna's specialty. After tea, papa would sit at the piano and play old romances. He sang in a nice baritone voice, and we all sang along.

It was a nice tale I liked to listen to. But, a few times, I tried to bring up the "other" reality of those years, the reality outside the privileged apartment complex, the reality of a brutal regime that certainly the colonel knew well. Katya would simply retreat, like a turtle in her shell, and repeat: "Things were different then, but we had a very good life." Undoubtedly, this had been a happy home. I could feel the positive aura left behind by Katya's sweet mama and her flamboyant husband. The colonel's piano was still there, in a corner, as well as his massive desk, on which now my computer sat, incongruously.

The upholstered furniture, however, was mine. I insisted in getting a new set, and embarked in a hunting expedition, exhausting and hopeless, because those were the days when furniture stores were rare and generally empty. But those were also the days when anything under the sun could be obtained *po blatu* (through connections). And so it happened that, at the end of a long chain of acquaintances, I acquired a sofa and soft chairs of the highest Soviet quality directly from the factory. Not a furniture factory, though, but the gigantic metallurgic plant, *Serp i molot* (Hammer and Sickle), a Soviet heavy industry old glory. This may sound absurd, but in Russia absurdity is the norm; and in this case, there is actually an explanation. When the plant was built, the planners included a furniture workshop on its grounds, as an added bonus to the *Serp i molot* workers. As the industrial giant started to slow down, the workshop broke away and found new life. A brand new sign over the door, in the corner of a huge courtyard, advertised to the prospective customers that a furniture-trading cooperative had just opened.

8:00 p.m. I took another look out the window. They had removed the body. A brown van, unidentified, had just shut its doors and was getting ready to take off, leaving behind no trace or memory of the dead man. I wondered how many rounds the little brown van did that day, collecting frozen bodies from under the bridges, from parks and marketplaces, in its anonymous way, making itself no more conspicuous than the garbage collection truck.

Life goes on

Several films of the decade present personal stories that highlight the difficulty of coping with everyday reality. The private sphere, which was the subject of popular sitcoms of the 1970s and 1980s, takes on a neurotic coloration. The characters' alienation translates into difficult relationships, troubled psychological conditions, and survival struggles. Many of these films provide flashbacks of past episodes that give a historical perspective to the present condition and the characters' lives.

The true blockbuster of the early 1990s was *Love* (1992), by Valery Todorovsky.[45] This film is as much about hatred as it is about love, one being the complementary side of the other, and both being inescapable elements in the dynamics of opposite forces which constitute life itself. *Love* moved audiences to tears with the unhappy story of a young couple, and elevated the young protagonist, Evgeny Mironov, to the status of a movie star. Valery Todorovsky, the son of a director of the old guard (Pyotr Todorovsky) well known for his successful sentimental comedies, got inspiration from the stockpile of Soviet popular movies that offered the audience stirring melodramas, compelling characters, a blend of humor and passion, and a selection of realistic details. He enlivened this proven recipe with new features, rejecting the prudishness characteristic of the old days, and peppering the film with colorful teenage slang and sex. The film, however, has deeper implications than a simple love story, because of the racial issue it presents.

Sasha, a student from a working class family, meets Masha and falls in love with her. Their idyll is suddenly shattered by the arrival of the official papers Masha's family had requested to emigrate to Israel. Suddenly a barrier comes between the two lovers: Masha is a Jew, while Sasha is a Russian. The Romeo and Juliet motif here acquires an anti-Semitic coloration. A few years earlier, Masha had been the victim of a collective rape by a gang of Russian teenagers, but when her mother pressed charges the judge dismissed the case and Masha's assailants went

21   *Love* (1992) directed by Valery Todorovsky

unpunished. The shock from that episode makes it difficult for Masha to accept Sasha's love at the beginning of their romance and, although later she overcomes the mental block, the idea of her identity as a Jew remains connected to the memory of the violence she suffered. At the end of the film, the ancient wound prompts her decision to leave for her "historical motherland." But it is clear from the context that for Masha this is a rhetorical notion, and that she sees Israel as a never-never land rather than the crisis-ridden place it really is. After the first glasnost movies on the subject, which supported the plight of the Soviet Jews, this film treats the Jewish theme with a deeper awareness that reflects the attitude of the younger generation. The film undermines both Russian nationalism and Jewish fundamentalism, suggesting that polarization of ideological positions leads to an unhappy ending.[46]

A title counterpoint, *Non-love* (1992) by Valery Rubinchik, was released at the same time and could not have been more different. According to the director, "Non-love is not hatred, it is the absence of feelings and the longing for them. It is the state of mind of Chekhov's heroines, or the psychological space of Gabriel García Márquez's *One Hundred Years of Solitude*. This corresponds to today's inner void, while everything around is driven to a frenzy."[47] Shot in soft black and white, the film conveys that twilight atmosphere of the spirit, which is typical of a decadent mode. Existential anguish is elegantly brought to the fore by the acting, the framing, and the mise-en-scène. Rubinchik began working in cinema in the 1960's, when the poetic trend was in fashion, and he retains a taste for that early style. The director's stylistic finesse is remarkable, and so is the performance of the young actress who plays the leading role, Ksenia Kachalina. She had just enrolled at the State Cinema Institute (VGIK) when Rubinchik, her teacher, chose her for the part of Rita. The screenwriter, Renata Litvinova, was also a young graduate from VGIK, who later wrote the script for the avant-garde film *Tractor Drivers 2* (Aleinikov brothers, 1994), and eventually became famous for her cooperation with Kira Muratova.

The film narrative is built like diary entries in Rita's imaginary journal, which is meant to convey truthfulness and immediacy. In her notes, she makes references to the two men in her life, while wavering from one to the other without ever finding what she seeks. Rita thinks at first she will find elation in her liaison with a middle-aged photographer, a gray-haired kid who stubbornly refuses to grow old. Stanislav Lyubshin is perfect in the role of the old hippie who on the surface approaches life with the same vitality of his roaring youth, but who in reality is a disillusioned man, whose life is already spent. In a scene, where he lies in bed with Rita, he is like a corpse in a white shroud. At the opposite end of the spectrum, Rita's boyfriend Roman is loving and patient, putting up with her oddities. But there is no passion in their relation; he is apathetic and capable of adapting to anything, even to sharing Rita with the photographer. Throughout the film, clips from Marilyn Monroe's pictures, and newsreel footage of the actress, underline the motif of burned lives. It also opens a discourse on the representation of women in media such as photography and cinema, and the use of women images as sex objects. By focusing on the Monroe myth, Rubinchik breaks with the prevailing norm, which so far has remained hostile to feminist concerns. But the Monroe motif came from Litvinova's script; she later used it again in Kira Muratova's *Passions* (1994).

22 *Non-love* (1992) directed by Valery Rubinchik

St. Petersburg, or rather, Leningrad of the 1960s, is the setting of Alexander Proshkin's *See Paris and Die* (1993). For generations of Russians, the West held an exotic fascination. Restrictions on crossing the border were not introduced with the Bolshevik regime, although they became much harsher from the 1930s onward; traveling abroad has always been state-controlled and the privilege of a few. Of the film title, the director said: "It is a saying I used to hear in my childhood. It referred to an impossible dream, a myth."[48] Proshkin gained international recognition in the early days of perestroika with *The Cold Summer of '53* (1988), which was one of the first film to deal openly with the consequences of Stalinism.[49] *See Paris and Die* is a film in a different key, "a chamber drama, an intimate family tragedy," in the words of the director. Nevertheless, there is a continuity line between the two films; the second one could conceivably be called "the hot summer of '63."

Ten years have gone by since the death of the tyrant and society no longer lives under a regime of terror. The younger generation seeks normal human relations and looks at the future with hope, but the parents are still enmeshed in a psychological trap of fear, suspicion, and racial prejudices. A communal apartment provides the background for a cross section of society, where the conflict between the two protagonists, mother and son, acquires vast cultural and historical resonance. "Every new generation judges the older one, as in Turgenev's *Fathers and Sons*," said Proshkin. "The film portrays the time of my youth, the sixties, after the Twentieth Congress, when the children judged their parents for the genocide perpetrated against the country in the 30s and 40s. This was the ultimate blow to a generation that survived only because they loved their children and wanted to protect them." The mother figure is an overwhelming presence in the life of Yura, a talented pianist in love with a conservatory schoolmate who happens to be Jewish. Obsessed with erasing the past and building a future for Yura, the mother conceals the fact that Yura's father was also a Jew and died in the Gulag, and fiercely opposes her son's relation with the girl. Her dream is to send Yura to Paris in pursuit of a brilliant career. To this end she sacrifices her personal life, developing a relationship with her son, which acquires morbid connotations. Eventually, her dream comes true, but it is too late for her. Tatyana Vasileva gives a powerful performance in the role of the mother. Dmitri Malikov, in real life a top pop singer, creates a sensitive Yura, who in the end is capable of overcoming his Oedipus complex and develop an independent life.

The bitter end to the dreams of the 1960's generation, the *shestidesiat-*

niki, is the subject of *Old Young People* (1992), based on a screenplay by Anatoly Grebnev and directed by Oleg Shukher. The film deals with the hopes, struggles, and disillusionments of that segment of the intelligentsia who became marginalized during the perestroika years. The action moves back and forth in time from the period of the first "cultural thaw" under Khrushchev to the democratization process under Gorbachev—which was the ultimate goal of those who first dreamed of "socialism with a human face." The ambiance of the period is effectively conveyed by the reconstruction of the circle of friends striving toward "the truth," in unhealthy basements where underground artists lived and died, and in crowded kitchens where the most secret and sacred debates took place.

After Khrushchev, when the government eventually cracked down on the dissidents, many among the best exponents of the intelligentsia left the country by any means available to them, or were expelled. The feeling of solidarity that sustained the intellectual community gave way to anguish and frustration, as everyone had to make an individual choice on how to cope with the regime. Among the close circle of friends, Felix Poznyansky (Vladimir Rozhin), a writer, after being fired from his job and banned from the profession because of a controversial article he wrote, took a job as a janitor; Dmitry, a sculptor, managed to emigrate; a third friend, Konstantin, cautiously but steadily moved up in the party hierarchy. The film adds the irony of the present to the bitter experience of the past. Now, in the new Russia, the same people who blossomed in the years of party rule have moved easily into key positions within the new structure and are once again calling the shots. The film has merit as a reminder that today's democratic rights have been partly paid for by the experiences of the dreamers of the 1960s. However, the treatment of the issue is lacking in finesse and is flawed by historical inaccuracies.

For decades, the comedies of Eldar Ryazanov have figured in the top range of popular ratings. But in the film *The Foretelling* (1993), he abandoned the comedy genre to move into unknown territory. The director described this picture as a story "about two beautiful, pure people, about love, and the time in which we live."[50] The problem is that the story of the two lovers is so encumbered with spurious elements that it is often lost in the background. It is as if narrative threads from different movies converged into one, and did not quite blend. Ryazanov explained that the film was based on a short story that he had written. "This is not a comedy," he said, "rather, a detective story with mystical elements and social analysis. It is an undefined genre I cannot explain, but it's not a comedy."[51]

The film starts off with a touch of mystery, the foretelling by a Gypsy woman that spells love and imminent death for the hero, writer Oleg Goryunov (Oleg Basilashvili). It continues with the appearance of a "double," who invades Oleg's privacy and takes charge of his life. The double (Andrei Sokolov) turns out to be a reincarnation of Oleg as a youth, which helps him to come to grips with several unresolved conflicts buried in the subconscious and, finally, with life itself.[52] To heighten the suspense, ingredients from the spy-gangster-detective genre are inserted ad lib. The selection includes assassinations of political enemies on the Moscow-Leningrad night express (in the old times), and street shootouts between mob families (in the new times). In the midst of all this, Oleg's beautiful lady, who is the wife of "a very rich man, owner of joint ventures and a new BMW,"[53] walks unscathed, radiating that peculiar brand of self-abnegating love that many Russian authors consider to be quintessentially feminine. She is the hero's salvation, his life giver. Notwithstanding the shortcomings of the script, one can appreciate Irene Jacob's performance in that role. The film being a Russian-French production required one of the protagonists to be French, and Ryazanov had the good fortune of signing her up. Unfortunately, a few good actors and an optimistic ending as to the future of Russia cannot save the movie. For all its mixed ingredients, *The Foretelling* does not even make it as a postmodernist text, lacking self-irony and a sense of playfulness.

The "double," though of an unusual kind, is also the leit-motif of the film *Makarov* (1993), directed by Vladimir Khotinenko with a screenplay by Valery Zolotukha. Alexander Makarov (Sergei Makovetsky) is a respected poet in a provincial town, equally popular among literature students and police recruits. He has a comfortable life, a good apartment, a devoted wife, and a lovely child. All of a sudden, this serene life is shattered by an intruder, a Makarov pistol, which the poet buys, allegedly for self-defense but actually because he is attracted to the object as such. Gradually, the pistol becomes an obsession with him; it affects his whole life, getting him involved with shady entrepreneurs and mafia bosses, and destroying his relationship with friends and family. The Makarov pistol takes charge of Makarov the poet, surfacing from the dark folds of the subconscious as the materialization of his id. At the bottom of the downward spiral, the poet realizes that he has betrayed everybody and everything that was dear to him, including poetry. In an ironical twist, his wife walks out on him, leaving a note: "I can forgive you your affair with that woman, but I cannot forgive you the poem about the Makarov."[54] In reality, what she believed to be an avant-garde poem, was an application to register the Makarov with the police.

Makarov the man, in the end, is alone with his double. Once he was told that "a Makarov is only good to commit suicide," but the poet cuddles the pistol, calling it "old man." The identification of the two personalities is then completed by a leap into the magic of cinema. The poet is seen as a bullet in the pistol chamber, slowly advancing towards the barrel. Finally, the pistol fulfills its function and shoots. The man Makarov becomes at once the weapon and its victim. A shot is heard, but physical death is not shown, and self-destruction remains an abstract concept. Khotinenko handles the dramatic subject in a deceivingly light-hearted manner, mixing all the ingredients with the precision of a savvy chemist—human passions and distancing irony, tragedy and humor, word games, cinematic metaphors, and literary references in funny contexts. All this, plus a touch of fantasy, makes up the texture of a well thought out and thought-provoking film, which won the Nika award in 1993.

By the end of the 1980s, the team Abdrashitov and Mindadze could proudly point to a series of veritable milestones in the development of Soviet cinema, which went back fifteen years. Their films were rooted in everyday reality and raised questions of ethics. In the perestroika period, they continued to produce films of moral concern, while developing surrealist features that connoted alienation from the Soviet system.[55] In their first picture of the post-Soviet era, *Armavir* (1991), alienation deepened as a human condition and intensified as an aesthetic form, but this approach did not produce good results. The opening shots, showing the cruise liner Armavir proudly parting the ocean waves, bring to mind Fellinian memories—*And the Ship Sails* (1983) and *Amarcord* (1973)—and with them great promises. But what follows is lengthy and redundant. The allegory is clear: the sinking ship, the passengers scattered on unknown beaches, the loss of connections, the search for relations and roots in an alienating landscape are a reflection of the current situation of a country in turmoil. But the treatment of the subject is heavy-handed and does not soar above the level of obvious symbolism. Their next film, *Play for a Passenger* (1995), confirmed that the authors were still struggling to find the right approach to the new times. This film came out on the twentieth anniversary of the authors' collaboration as a team. Their first film in 1975, *The Train Stopped*, created a sensation because of the bold way it addressed the issue of individual responsibility vs. official regulations. In *Play for a Passenger* there are echoes of that first film, twisted to suit the current reality. Here, too, the train is a recurrent setting and the question of ethics vs. duty is central to the plot. But, while the first film was firmly placed within the parameters of Soviet reality, the recent one reflects a society that lacks a defining framework. In the contemporary reality, "right" and "wrong" as absolute values are lost, and the two categories keep switching back and forth between the protagonist and the antagonist (Sergei Makovetsky and Igor Livanov). The film is meant to convey a situation of moral confusion. But to do so in a meaningful way, the film itself should possess inner clarity.

Abdrashitov and Mindadze scored better with their next film, *Time of the Dancer* (1997). In many ways this film is a continuation of issues and concerns that the authors treated in the course of their career. The overarching theme of individual choices within the constraints of the sociopolitical order is placed in sharp focus by the narrative's time/space setup. The time is a post-war period, the space is a post-war zone—and both are left unidentified. Anachronisms prevent the viewer from enjoying a complete suspension of disbelief. Locations and characters in the film's first part have the flavor of Soviet bygone days after WW II; while in the second part, they connote post-conflict Chechnya. The vagueness of the settings accounts for a universal discourse on the condition of displacement—spiritual and material—and expands the scope of the narrative to an existential dimension.

A philosophical underpinning has been the authors' hallmark from the very beginning. And yet, their films were very popular in the Soviet Union, attracting millions of viewers. Commenting on *Time of the Dancer* before the film's release, Abdrashitov said:

23 *Time of the Dancer* (1997), Abdrashitov (director) and Mindadze (screenwriter)

I am absolutely convinced that if there were a normal distribution system this film would beat all records. This is strong melodramatic material, with plenty of stories about friendship, love, rivalry, betrayal, loyalty, and jealousy, mixed with things that the viewer can relate to and that have a general meaning, such as war, the destiny of this country, and the loss of home as an existential category. Moreover, the film displays that humane trait which is typical of the Russian mentality, and of Russian literature. And finally, it's full of young, beautiful people, music, horses, dances, and merrymaking.[56]

Indeed, the film includes all of the above. But it is more than a melodrama. While employing melodramatic materials, the film debunks them through a stylization of the genre. Perhaps the image that had the strongest impact on the viewers' imagination was the one that recurs a couple of times in the course of the narrative, and that was used to advertise the film: two figures on a white horse, a Cossack and a beautiful woman, both wrapped in his black cape, galloping toward the unknown. These romantic figures stand out from the everyday background that anchors the narrative, and seem to provide the viewer with an escape from life's irreconcilable contradictions. But this is actually an illusion, as the handsome riders are characters with no inner life, "playing" the role of the romantic outcasts. In fact, the whole story is presented as fiction, with frequent allusions to stage performance, and self-referential stylistic elements borrowed from the repertoire of Soviet war movies.

The horseman is one of a threesome of comrades in arms who are reunited after the war in a small town by the Black Sea. They represent three psychological types, three life choices, but a common destiny. Valery is the most pragmatic of the three, to the point of being cynical and opportunistic. Married with two children, he enjoys an extra-marital affair, but is careful not to let it disrupt his comfortable middle-class life. In the end he becomes a businessman and falls back into the family fold. Fyodor has been spiritually burnt in the war, and looks for a source of soul rejuvenation. He finds it in a rural retreat at the foot of the mountains, and in the care of a loving woman. But ghosts from the past come back to haunt him, and he is accidentally killed. Andrei is an estranged character, who remains an outsider even among his comrades. His life aspirations are never articulated, but it is clear that he is not after money, or power. Not even love, because his relationships with women are devoid of emotional involvement. Actually, he does not have a personality, only a persona. He lives in the artificial dimension of "representation," performing as a dancer in a Cossack costume and riding a white horse.

The only person who seems to relate to Andrei is Katya, a free spirit devoid of inhibitions and not conditioned by society's rules. This character does not have an active role in the narrative, but appears out of nowhere at strategic moments as a dramatic catalyst. Katya engages in sex freely—with Valery as well as Andrei—underscoring the theme that true relations are not possible in this crippled world. While for Valery sex involves guilt, jealousy, and violence (he rapes her in an ugly scene), for Katya it is a form of provocation. Her challenge to society, however, is not sustained by purpose or cause like in the real melodrama, and is therefore meaningless. She sexually provokes Andrei to arouse his interest and calls him: *"Vashe blagorodie"* ("Your Excellency"—literally, "Your Nobleness"), making fun of his "noble" detachment from world's passions. The viewer is tempted to read this relationship between the "spiritual outsider" and the "fallen woman" as a parodic allusion to Dostoevsky's *Idiot*.

In this picture of a society deeply scarred by the war experience, there is also another important set of characters: the couple Tamara and Timur. As in most of the film's situations, their life background is only sketched rather than related in detail. The spare information tells the viewer that they are Southerners (the viewer would read: Chechens), and that because of the war they have been displaced from their home. They have also grown apart. Their paths cross again, when each on his/her own intrude into the lives of Andrei and Fyodor who now live in the couple's former house, with tragic consequences. All are victims: those who had to leave their homes and those who now live in those homes.

In the end, no closure is possible. The theme of displacement is not resolved. The loss of the self as a consequence of the war precludes the possibility of the return to normal life. Fyodor is killed, Valery is crippled and walks with a cane, and Andrei mechanically performs his Cossack dance act in a restaurant. In the last scene, Katya comes to his rescue, and the two depart in a fantasy flight on the white horse. However, as noted before, this is not a signifier for the they-lived-happily-ever-after motif. Rather, it is an aesthetic image that belongs in the "dancer" paradigm—the concept that informs the film. Abdrashitov defined the "time of the dancer" as a masquerade:

> The present time is the time of the dancer. Everyone sings, dances, plays the bayan . . . life is being transformed in a variety show. It's the time of the dancer. . . . There are people who wear tails, a bowtie,

pretend to be noblemen. . . . A new class has appeared: the servants of the people—Duma deputies, senators, governors. . . . Others dress up as Cossacks. They have no Cossack roots—they just put on a uniform and began to prance and jump. And one of them began to dance. It's the time of the dancer.[57]

In 1927 a controversial film appeared on the Soviet screens, *Love Triangle*, directed by Abram Room with a script by Viktor Shklovsky.[58] In 1998, *Retro Triangle* by Pyotr Todorovsky revived and updated that story. *Love Triangle* (known in the West as *Bed and Sofa*) presented the reality of life in unvarnished images. Its naturalism and the issues it raised were considered offensive at the time. The film focused on the interrelation of three individuals rather than the collective, and on "bourgeois" concerns such as adultery and its consequences. The situation in *Retro Triangle* is similar, although the ideology, or the lack thereof, is contemporary and so is the outcome. In the older film a man invites an old buddy to share his tiny apartment with him and his wife because of the chronic housing shortage. The inevitable happens and the friend has an affair with the wife when the husband is on a work assignment. The husband, upon his return, accepts the situation. Soon the wife announces that she is pregnant and does not know who the father is. The two men decide for her that she must have an abortion. She refuses. Having realized that she has been used as an object for the men's pleasure, she walks out on the two buddies, leaving them trapped in the tiny apartment and in their petty concerns. The last sequence shows the woman, emancipated heroine, crossing a bridge on the train that takes her toward a bright future.

Love Triangle is now regarded as a classic and Room is rightly held in high esteem. Todorovsky in the new film pays homage to the master with numerous references to the original picture—the title itself, intertitles as narrative transitions, sparse verbal language, and a fast-motion fistfight scene in the style of a silent comedy. But the overall atmosphere reflects today's ordinary life with its lack of heroines and passions. In both films the woman is the key character, although in a very different way. While in the old film, Lyuda (Ludmila Semenova) was presented as an oppressed woman, a spoil of war for the conqueror of the bed, the new protagonist, Rita (Elena Yakovleva), is totally in charge of the situation. Todorovsky reconstructs the original mise-en-scène on a number of

24 *Retro Triangle* (1998) directed by Pyotr Todorovsky

occasions to stress this difference.

The significant checkers game scene in Room's picture was a metaphor for the men's power struggle. The framing isolated them from Lyuda, showing the two rivals at the checkerboard, confronting each other. While Lyuda resentfully sat in a corner all by herself, the cute kitty that connoted the woman throughout the film sat right under the checkerboard, reinforcing the perception of the males' competition over their object of desire. Conversely, Todorovsky places Rita at the table with the men, in the central position, somehow controlling and directing the game (this time, it is chess). Later, the chessboard reappears with the three characters lying in the same bed. Popular actors play the male pair in both films: Nikolay Batalov and Vladimir Fogel in 1927, and Evgeny Sidikhin and Sergei Makovetsky in 1998.

Another reversal of the mise-en-scène occurs in the sequence on the roof. In the old film, the outdoors was presented as the men's domain, while the indoors suggested Lyuda's entrapment. The epitome of the husband's privileged position was a scene on the roof of the Bolshoi

Theater, where he spent the day as a construction worker. During his lunch break, he would take in the panoramic view of the city from that vantage point with a self-congratulatory sense of superiority. In Todorovsky's picture, the husband owns a business for the installation of satellite dishes. While he is working on the roof of a building, Rita hangs out on that same roof, having fun and flirting with the other man in the triangle. To stress the self-reflexiveness of the mise-en-scène, the TV set used to test the dish shows the Bolshoi Theater roof scene from Room's film.

Similarly, the indoor space connotes the different status of the two women. While Lyuda was confined in a basement apartment that physically underscored the psychological oppressive atmosphere, Rita lives in a loft apartment on the top floor of an elegant building. And, furthermore, she is the apartment owner, having inherited it from her father. In short, while Lyuda was an exploited housewife, Rita is an art photographer and the men's partner.

Therefore, the film's big issues such as adultery, abortion and, above all, women's emancipation, which in 1927 carried the ideological message, lost their political relevance in the new version. The general similarity between the two historical periods makes the ideological difference stand out even more sharply. In 1927, the Soviet Union was approaching the end of the NEP policy, which had created a certain degree of affluence in the urban centers thanks to the establishment of small private enterprises. The relaxation of revolutionary austerity also generated a return to the bourgeois mentality. *Love Triangle* criticized the petty bourgeois values that had infiltrated the working class, and celebrated the reaction of the woman who was able to extricate herself from that milieu.

In *Retro Triangle*, the economic situation is similar—emerging capitalism with all the marks of a bourgeois society. But the ideological underpinning is missing. There is no criticism of this life style, only an acknowledgement of it, without commentary. If anything, the point of view is sympathetic. Furthermore, in the new film the focus is not on the working class, but on the intelligentsia—and, therefore, on a more "natural" middle class environment. Both the director and the producer, Pyotr and Mira Todorovsky—a married couple—said in an interview that their film is about love, not ideology, and that they chose to give the old story a different twist to stress the fact that nowadays in Russia ideology is dead, and the heroine of their film is just a woman who honestly loves two men and wants to share her life with them both. "These characters are pure and innocent," said Mira, "it is a real love triangle, where they share genuine feelings. . . . This is the twist Pyotr gave to the story."[59] Torn between her two loves, Rita wants to deconstruct them and rebuild the ideal man, combining the domestic husband with the imaginative lover. And, being a photographer, she shows us graphically, in the dark room, how to put together key features of the two men. However, what comes easy through the magic of editing often creates a dilemma in life. The threesome struggle with the dilemma, but the situation never rises to the level of drama, and all conflicts dissolve into comedy.

In fact, there is even a tinge of Eccentrism[60] in the texture of the film. Yakovleva, with her mimicry and gesturing, brings to mind the performance style of Alexandra Khokhlova; Makovetsky's character, being a clown by profession, fits the image of the "eccentric actor"; and Sidikhin, who was associated with hulk figures in thrillers and adventure movies, looks a bit odd in this role. Even supporting characters, such as Rita's neighbor who is a midget, reinforce the eccentric mode. Although Eccentrism was a trend in the Soviet cinema of the 1920s, *Love Triangle* had none of its playful features. That film belonged to a different genre. It was a parody of the bourgeois melodrama that enjoyed a revival during the NEP period. It substituted middle class cliché types and ambiance with proletarian characters and locale—an infusion of realism and ideology into the soap opera. This generated a hybrid text, much appreciated by the intellectuals and much criticized by the authorities.

Conversely, *Retro Triangle* is a straightforward, well-crafted sentimental comedy with clever references to the original story. The film's concerns are individualistic and private. The many problems that plague Russia and hinder the country's economic development are only hinted at, often with humor: a war zone in the South, unemployment (for a circus performer, of all things), crime, new money, and the like. All this provides a blurred backdrop to the personal life of the threesome. Most of the time, they interact inside the cozy apartment. And when they go out, they are able to recreate around themselves the same private space, an extension of the indoors, and to see the surrounding reality through a rosy filter.

The generation of those who were born after the Twentieth Party

Congress (1956) is "evasive and languid, cynical and estranged" and has "none of the unselfish devotion to an ideal" that characterized the previous generations, in the words of one of its representatives, film critic Alexander Timofeevsky.[61] *Retro Triangle* is a denial of the collective and the heroic in favor of the private and the ordinary. The three protagonists represent ordinary people who care for each other, take life as it comes, and try to cope the best they can. The end is anticlimactic; the threesome becomes a quartet when the baby is born, and they simply stick together as life goes on.

A flashback

Timofeevsky was himself a "languid" adolescent when I met him, in the early 1980s. At that time, the portly gentleman who is now one of the most notable film critics was sort of a groupie. Thin and tall, with velvety eyes under a bang of dark hair, he hung out with the "independent" cultural elite. The term *nezavisimye* (independents) referred specifically to a group of painters who established an alternative space, non-state-controlled, to exhibit their works. But it extended to all those writers, poets, theater and film artists, composers, critics and exponents of culture who considered themselves independent-minded, and walked a fine line between the marginal ground of legality and the dangerous zone of dissidence. They carried on the tradition that sustained the Russian intelligentsia since the time of the Decembrists—to oppose the tyrannical state. But it was mostly a passive resistance, where the frustration of the powerless manifested itself in a mocking attitude, cynical laughter, and aesthetic refinement. The atmosphere was decadent, foreboding the end of the empire. They regarded themselves as the children of the Bronze Age (*Bronzovyi vek*), an ironical reference to the previous two periods in which Russian culture flourished—the Golden Age (early nineteenth century) and the Silver Age (early twentieth century). The exponents of the Bronze Age lived in comfortable urban apartments and country dachas; applied their creative energies to artistic pursuits that were alternately ignored or crushed by the KGB for no apparent reason; received an income, either by affiliation with an artistic Union, or through a nominal job with a state institution; and spent the best part of the night partying away their frustrations.

A typical night, one of the many I shared with them, would start at the theater At the Nikitin Gates, headed by Mark Razovsky; would move on to the studio of an "independent" artist for viewing and buying, or to a poet's apartment for verse reading and literary debate; and would proceed to the Cinema House restaurant for a late dinner with the "who's who" in the film world. Occasionally, the evening would reach its climax at a Gypsy establishment, where caviar and vodka were cheap and plentiful, and the frenzied rhythm of the violins was the prelude to passionate one-night romances.

The theater At the Nikitin Gates was a typical phenomenon of those twilight years. It existed in a state of suspension between the official institution and the unofficial enterprise. The theatre was a recreational facility, which belonged to a club of medical workers. They hired Razovsky as the art director, and he managed to turn the modest stage into a locus of experimental ferment and avant-garde performance. Every premiere was an event in the cultural circles and in the foreign community, which in those days comprised only a handful of diplomats, journalists, and academics. Razovsky never got into serious trouble with the KGB, although he walked on the edge of the danger zone all the time. The medical workers club and its theatre eventually became a metaphor for innovation and vital energy in a film of the perestroika years, *Forgotten Melody for Flute* (Ryazanov, 1988), which opposed amateur avant-garde performances to the stiff official culture supported by the bureaucrats.

In those days there was a close symbiosis between the liberal intelligentsia and the foreign community. They needed each other. The few foreigners admitted behind the iron curtain were constantly under the watchful eye of the Soviet organs. We lived in guarded compounds; had to be seen at our workplace every day; were assigned undercover handlers in various guises—a guide, a colleague, a housekeeper—who reported on our moves and acquaintances; could not spend the night at a place that was not our residence; and could not travel beyond the city limits without a special permit. The housing compound that hosted the foreign press corps was nicknamed "Sad Sam"—shorthand for the street address, Sadovaya-Samotechnaya—which placed an ironical emphasis on the sad atmosphere of those enclaves. The intoxicating world of underground culture and the extravagant genius of its exponents offered us an escape from the confines of officialdom. It was like a drug, combining a heightening of the senses with an element of risk. On their part, our Russian friends clung to us because we represented a link with the Western world. A psychological link, first of all, which would reconnect them with the civilization that influenced Russia's development since the time of Peter the Great. And a material link as well, because paintings were bought, manuscripts were smuggled, and censored films were privately shown. We became the ambassadors of Russian unofficial culture in our respective countries.

But it was risky. The circles of the liberal intelligentsia were infiltrated by informers, disdainfully known as *stukachi*. These unsavory types have caused many a foreigner to be expelled from the USSR and permanently blacklisted. There were some exemplary cases, such as the highly publicized episode involving Nicholas Daniloff, the American correspondent for *U.S. News & World Report*, who was arrested in 1986 on a fabricated espionage charge. He was released after a few days thanks to diplomatic intervention and deported to the U.S.A. More often, the charges revolved around the laws regulating contacts between foreigners and Soviet citizens and the smuggling in and out of censored materials. For the Soviet citizens the risk was much higher, they could lose their jobs and privileges, and end up in jail without due process. Our Russian friends considered socializing with foreigners as a double-edged weapon. Contacts with the foreign community were regarded with suspicion by neighbors and colleagues, and made the individual involved vulnerable to harassment on the part of the authorities. On the other hand, those same contacts afforded the individual a certain amount of protection, because the Soviet organs did not want to publicize abroad the brutal handling of their own citizens. This was especially true with those who were invited to attend cultural events at foreign embassies.

The foreign embassies in Soviet times were divided into two ranks, the *kapstrany* embassies (capitalist countries) and the *sotsstrany* embassies (socialist countries, i.e. the clients of the USSR). The most sought after invitations were those from *kapstrany* embassies, and first among them the U.S. Embassy. The Russians who made the guest list were closely monitored and placed under permanent police surveillance. Nevertheless, our friends displayed a fearless attitude and used those events as a defiant gesture. The KGB played cat and mouse, giving them a rather long leash, while standing ready to rein them in at any moment.

During his tenure, Ambassador Arthur Hartman hosted screenings of American films at his residence. The charming nineteenth-century mansion, known as Spaso House (from its location on Spasopeskovsky pereulok), every Saturday afternoon opened its doors to a stream of Russian guests. This was an instance of the cold war being waged on the cultural battlefield. Some bureaucrats considered it a political provocation, exposing Soviet citizens to Hollywood pictures, which they regarded as subversive and "decadent." For the Russian guests, the challenge was to make it past the Soviet guards at the gate, who were posted there supposedly to protect the American territory from intrusions. In effect, the guards screened every citizen and filed the information with the KGB. Occasionally, they denied access to someone whose name was on the black list, for whatever reason—it could be simply because the person had been offered to collaborate with the organs and he/she refused. To provide a certain measure of protection, we would escort our Russian friends in small groups through the gate, and monitor the inspection. Once inside, it was like stepping into another dimension. The world that looked so shabby and hostile in the street was suddenly filled with color, light, and laughter. The atmosphere was informal; to the credit of Arthur and Donna Hartman there was none of the stiffness that usually accompanies such events in official government venues. It was a real party among friends. One of the splendid halls on the ground floor doubled as a screening room, where old classics and new releases filled the screen and the eyes with the magic of their images.

Eventually, the KGB adapted to this extravagance of the American ambassador and the weekly screenings proceeded without major disruptions. Except for one instance. One Saturday, the program featured *Ninotcha* (Lubitsch, 1939), a light comedy with Greta Garbo in the role of a Soviet agent on a mission to Paris, who in the end is lured by the Western way of life and switches sides. This was too much for the guardians of public safety. All Soviet guests were stopped at the gate and turned away. We left with them, and the show was cancelled.

Twenty years later, Russia is a different country. Civil rights, human rights, economic freedom, freedom of expression, freedom of movement have catapulted the citizens into the reality of the Western world they used to dream about. With these liberties also came the problems of democracy, which did not always figure in the dream. Nowadays, there is no need for underground culture, everything is on display; no need for "independent" artists, everyone is on his own; no need for the Spaso House showings, American films have flooded the Russian screens; no need to seek out "the foreigner," the number of expatriates in Moscow alone is in the tens of thousands; no need to defy law enforcement agencies, the cops have more pressing problems to address than harassing maverick intellectuals. The tight-knit artistic community of old has disintegrated. The special feeling of being bonded by a common predicament, fraught with danger but dignified by the struggle, is gone. Social life has caught up with the West, has become "normal." And, therefore, less romantic.

4
Faraway in Space and Time

Lukomore

"By the bay a green oak tree stands . . ." Since the appearance of Pushkin's poem,[1] the common word *lukomore* (bay) has been used by children and adults as the name of a never-never land. Lukomore with a capital "L" is a realm of the imagination that provides an escape into fabricated dreams—fairy tales and, more recently, the movies. In contemporary Russia, filmmakers have offered the viewers only a very few movies capable of carrying them away from the dreary reality. They have, however, created a special dream world for themselves in the form of film festivals.

In the Soviet heyday of heavy state subsidies and ideological control, one major biennial film festival was all it took to highlight the achievements from the fifteen republics of the USSR and to announce the award winners—always the most grandiose and politically correct. That was a propaganda showcase for the national film industry, meant to keep Soviet cinema on the international map. Starting in the early 1990s, while the prestigious Moscow International Film Festival lost its glitz together with a large part of the government's financial support, minor festivals of all kinds mushroomed. They had different sponsors and different targets, but one thing in common: they were meant to gratify the ego of those filmmakers who managed to complete their films but failed to get an audience. "[Today] nobody wants to shake up the world," wrote film scholar Nina Tsyrkun. "Instead of creating a message for mankind, participation in international festivals is their [the filmmakers'] main concern."[2] The fanciest and most exclusive festivals took place somewhere on the balmy Black Sea coast, such as the Kinotavr festival in Sochi, the

Kinoshock festival in Anapa, and the Kinoforum in Yalta, to name only a few. There, by the bay, the embattled representatives of the film industry would find their Lukomore, recovering the past splendor of those resorts that have lulled the pre-revolutionary upper classes first, and the Soviet elite later.[3]

Every summer, the Sochi seaside hotel Zhemchuzhina (Pearl) opened its doors to thousands of Kinotavr participants, who would spend the next ten days in a whirlwind of festivities. The hotel's name evokes a mythical marine landscape. In effect, it is a misnomer because the building displays the functionalist architecture of the 1960s, boxlike and uninspiring. But this is more than compensated by the lush surroundings. The most grandiose constructions are the ones built in the 1930s in the ornate Stalinist style, like the colossal Winter Theatre that was the focal point of the festival. There, a mile-long red carpet greeted the star-studded audience to award ceremonies and nonstop celebrations. Such princely buildings can be found all along the coast and around the Crimean peninsula—sanatoriums, grand hotels, spas, and private residences of government top officials and the new rich. They are surrounded by exotic gardens, where the luxuriant vegetation competes with the architectural frills. Graceful pavilions, Greek colonnades, and curved balustrades looking out to the sea emerge from the foliage as a white dot constellation. In the botanical garden Dendraria, on the hillside not far from the Kinotavr festival site, cypresses, eucalypti, and rhododendrons fill the air with a fragrant bouquet. Majestic peacocks display their vibrant palette. The ruins of an abandoned palace and the occasional hooting of an owl add a note of mystery to the place. But the festival guests for the most part did not seek out those romantic hermitages. They navigated between sparkling banquet halls and palm tree-lined promenades, where they could see and be seen.

Kinotavr was born in 1990 at the hands of an energetic entrepreneur, Mark Rudinstein, who made cinema his business. The original idea was to provide a forum for native cinema, in order to promote the national industry. Later, Kinotavr expanded to include an international competition. In 1993 the festival was divided into two categories, Open Russian Film Festival and Sochi International Festival, but the main focus remained on Russian films. The festival proved to be sustainable throughout the decade thanks to Rudinstein's indefatigable dedication to his brainchild. Seen by many as a wheeler-dealer, poorly educated and lacking class, Rudinstein became the target of attacks in the media. His critics would say that his attraction to the movie world was prompted by a desire to boost his ego and line his pockets. But in the film community, the majority was willing to recognize his merits. Konstantin Ernst, ORT general director, expressed eloquently a widely shared opinion:

> What is the motivation behind Rudinstein's business? To make money, to be able to pat on the head the most prominent film masters, or something else—this is not important. As a result, thanks to his drive, or in spite of it, he created the only full-fledged annual Russian film festival—notwithstanding his weird and gross demeanor. I'm not a fan of Rudinstein's, but I admire him because he did it. He has no manners, and does not know how to be nice to the press. This, unfortunately, reflects on the festival, which lacks class. But I think there is some logic to it. We live in the chaos zone, and a well organized and perfectly shaped festival—like the Cannes festival—here would be incompatible with the films presented. . . . The festival is a mirror that reflects the life process. . . . When the country becomes more logical, sated, and stable, everything will be normal in cinema as well. . . . And Kinotavr, in its tenth or twentieth anniversary, will become stylish and classy. There cannot be an accomplished festival in a country where distribution is in shambles, films are made against all odds, and everything floats in the air. That's why I tell Rudinstein: Bravo![4]

Financed by a combination of private and public funds, Kinotavr acquired a certain status among the new festivals and gained the appellation of Russia's Cannes. But the name was somehow ironical, because Kinotavr amounted to a celebration of films that would hardly find their way to the theatres. While restaurants and beaches were full of guests, the booths at the festival's film market were empty, testifying to the fact that the Russian films that were considered the cream of the industry were unable to attract the interest of distributors. At the 1995 Kinotavr, a producer bluntly put it: "This festival is a *tusovka* (hangout). We can do what we like here but our films aren't reaching the public."[5] Some directors with an international reputation snubbed the festival. The distributors, on their part blamed the filmmakers. According to a distributor, "today the dream of filmmakers is not to create something saleable, but to find a sponsor and sweet talk him. . . . Sometimes they produce such nonsense that it's dull even for intellectual viewers."[6]

All the films shown at Kinotavr received full or partial financial support from Goskino, which decreased the incentive for commercial success. While the filmmakers indulged in their tendency to put aesthetics ahead of entertainment, they alienated the mass audience. Danil Dondurei lashed out, "Nothing compels [filmmakers] to somehow morally support the so-called ordinary people—to console them, and with the help of unforgettable stories give them a chance to forget about [the difficulties of life today]. Under the motto of servicing real art, a cult of unprecedented hopelessness is being financed. . . . No one specifically—from producer to bank executive, from director to the spot man—bears any real, that is, economic responsibility for the results of his work."[7] That year—1995—Kinotavr was dedicated to the one-hundredth anniversary of the birth of cinema; "One Hundred Years of Cinema" was the proud festival logo. Ironically, Russian cinema showed all the ailments of a centenarian.

There are many smaller, specialized festivals which are of interest to film amateurs. One of those is Faces of Love, which has been in existence since the mid-1990s. This festival is dedicated to old and new films about love, and has scored high marks with the audience group nostalgic for the romances of yesteryear. In 2000, the festival's theme was less sentimental and more provocative, "The History of Sin." Among the many pictures about fall and retribution, which in today's society are as relevant as the Blue Fairy's admonitions to Pinocchio, there were some really historical pieces. These were the pre-sexual revolution pictures meant to stir the revolution itself, which were banned in most Western democracies, not to speak of the Soviet Union. Among them was the Danish film *Quiet Days in Clichy* (Jens Torsen, 1970; from a novel by Henry Miller), which had the distinction of being impounded by the U.S. customs and not admitted into the country for two years, and of being prohibited in England and Italy until 1979. Another sexual revolution old glory shown at the festival was *Private Vices, Public Virtues* (Miklos Jancso, 1975). Although these films generated a great deal of curiosity as sociological documents, it was clear that they had lost their shock value. The young spectators, mostly VGIK students, watched them with a blasé attitude.[8]

Besides the many festivals that punctuate the current cinema scene, there is an award winning ceremony, the Nika Award, which was established in 1988. The Nika is the equivalent of the American Academy Award; in fact, it is called the Russian Oscar. This is an official affair that takes place with much pomp at prestigious venues in Moscow and is attended by film administrators, politicians, government officials, and businessmen, in addition to Russian film celebrities. The tone is that of a serious pageant, with an elaborate choreography, including speeches, musical performances, and dance. On one occasion, when the Nika was held at the Cinema House in the middle of the winter, sparkling ice sculptures of international cinema prizes dazzled the guests outside the main entrance—Oscar was there, too, in a ghostly version divested of his golden coat. Notwithstanding the official recognition, though, the films that won the Nika award in the early years had a hard time finding their audience. They came from the select group that had already made the round of the other festivals and gathered prizes, only to disappear from circulation. Toward the end of the decade, however, there were a number of winners that became box-office successes.[9]

But the true barometer of the Russian film industry on an international scale is still the old-time Moscow International Film Festival.[10] First organized in 1959, the Moscow Festival was perceived as a sign of new openness toward the outside world. Within the framework of the cultural revival that the Soviet Union enjoyed in the Khrushchev years, the festival brought to Moscow hundreds of foreign guests and dozens of films. For many, the event marked the first contacts with the West, although the festival was rigidly structured and closely monitored by the security organs. Legendary encounters between the celebrities of the day, such as cosmonaut Yuri Gagarin and Italian movie star Gina Lollobrigida, delighted millions of fans, who could only glimpse at them on the pages of illustrated magazines.[11]

In 1963, Federico Fellini's *8 and 1/2* was awarded the first prize, which alone indicates a measure of ideological relaxation. The president of the jury that year was Grigory Chukhrai, whose 1959 film, *Ballad of a Soldier*, had been recognized internationally as a masterpiece of the Soviet new wave. Chukhrai's third film, *Clear Sky*, won the Moscow Festival first prize in 1961 and galvanized the audience with a hint of criticism of Stalin's policies. However, those were exceptions. None of the best works of the Russian film artists of the period—for example Andrei Tarkovsky's *Ivan's Childhood* and *Andrei Rublev*—ever succeeded in winning a prize in Moscow. *Andrei Rublev* was accused of disrespect to Russian history. In reality, the artistic formalism of Tarkovsky's films made many administrators uncomfortable, especially after the ousting of Khrushchev and the return to a more conservative and duller party leadership under Brezhnev.

Working under the cumbersome slogan of the regime, "For the Humanism of Film Art, for Peace and Friendship Among the People," the festival continued to be held every two years over the next three decades. The choices of the selection committee, and the jury awards, reflected the phony wording, and the Moscow Festival gradually lost its prestige in the eyes of the Western film community. At the beginning of the 1980s, the guests consisted mostly of filmmakers from Third World countries. But in the late 1980s, the perestroika cultural revolution, which swept away the old cadres together with the old slogans, turned the 1987 Moscow Festival into a major international event in the spheres of both film and politics. As in the old times, world-renowned stars came to Moscow to express their support for Mikhail Gorbachev and their solidarity with fellow artists—the ageing Fellini and Mastroianni, Robert De Niro, Nastassia Kinski, Milos Forman, and Gérard Depardieu, to name a few. The Moscow Festival that year became a celebration of glasnost and democracy. But in order to sustain its status as a first-class international competitor, the Moscow Festival needed more than artistic creativity and freedom from ideological constraints. It needed firm business contacts and a solid material base. Instead, the festival organizers, as well as the film industry as a whole, started experiencing the pain of the transition to the free market economy. No longer able to treat the festival guests to sumptuous banquets and lavish boat cruises on government money, the organizers had to cut corners and find resourceful ways to raise funds.

The last Moscow Festival of the old era took place in 1989. I was among the guests invited to the banquet that followed the closing ceremony. The stage was set in St. George's Hall within the Kremlin, a venue that spoke of the grandeur of Russia's past. Walking through twenty-foot tall mirror doors, from a foyer painted in an intense aqua color, I entered a bath of golden light. The white walls of the immense hall reflected the glitter from the suite of bronze chandeliers hanging along the central nave. The architecture recalled the interior of a cathedral with its elongated vertical lines. A series of pillars encased in the walls on each side sustained the arched ceiling that seemed to be as high as the celestial vault. This was food for the soul. As for the other kind of food, two rows of tables, running through the entire length of the hall, were covered with the best of Russian cuisine. And the vodka was not just ordinary vodka; it came in different flavors, including the rare amber-colored "Starka," which in subsequent years disappeared completely. The whole ensemble was a fantastic scene, the like of which are only seen in the movies. And then, the feast was over.

Serious signs of decay were evident at the XVIII Moscow Festival (1993), sponsored by Goskino, the Filmmakers Union, and various private enterprises. Until the last minute, though, the festival organizing committee was not sure whether the sponsors would participate. There were rumors in the Russian press that the festival might have to be canceled due to financial difficulties. When the festival finally did open, there was a noticeable lack of famous names on the competition program, as well as on the guest lists. There was no "revolutionary" atmosphere like in the late 1980s to attract film stars; it cost the festival almost $1 million to get Claude Lelouche to head the jury that year. Another factor that aggravated the situation was the boycott of the Russian market by the major American studios because of rampant violations of copyrights by video-pirates. The only American film in competition was the independently produced *Fathers and Sons* by Paul Mores. But amidst cancellations, disorganization, and the absence of major American productions, there was also an impressive display of talent. Among the films in competition, two Russian films stood out, *Children of the Iron Gods* and *Drum Roll*. Those that were not in competition included Wim Wenders' *Far Away, So Close*, which in addition to its artistic merits regaled the public with a cameo appearance by Mikhail Gorbachev.

The situation did not brighten up with the next festival, in 1995, although the organizers were able to raise sufficient funds this time, thanks to the personal involvement of Prime Minister Viktor Chernomyrdin and Moscow Mayor Yuri Luzhkov (chairman of the organizing committee), and also to the collaboration of Resurs Bank that opened a line of credit for the festival. Federal and municipal funds, along with private sponsors' contributions, provided more than $10 million to finance the event. Prizes carried a monetary value: Grand Prize, $50,000 for the director and the producer of best film; the other major prizes, $20,000 each. But in the end, the international jury headed by Richard Gere, after six hours of deliberation, failed to award the Grand Prize. They cited a lack of quality among the twenty-two competition entries. The festival slogan that year was a quotation from Dostoevsky, "Beauty will save the world." The jury's decision made it clear that, for the time being, the world would have to look for beauty somewhere else.

The loss of prestige of Russian cinema around the world became even more obvious in the summer of 1997, at the XX Moscow Festival, although first-rank stars were in attendance—Robert de Niro, Sophia Loren, Jacqueline Bisset, and Catherine Deneuve. The festival organizers were painfully aware that international studios were not eager to submit their latest productions, even after the official lifting of the American boycott. They had to make do with second run films already shown at other world festivals. One commentator made a sarcastic remark on the selection criteria: "The festival president [Sergei Solovyov] formulated the principle for the film's selection as follows: 'Let's take whatever we can get, and be thankful for that.'"[12] The Grand Prize went to the U.S. with *Marvin's Room* (Jerry Zaks, 1996), hardly a novelty by that time.

Solovyov, understandably had a different view. Although he, too, talked about a *bol'shaia tusovka* (great hangout), he saw it as a positive feature, and went on stressing the festival's *bol'shaia udacha* (great success).[13] Solovyov's statement may have served a political purpose, because a battle of words and deeds had been waged for a while between the Solovyov camp and rival camps for the control of the Filmmakers Union and other major organizations, including the Moscow Festival. Soon after the historical V Congress of the FU (1986), Solovyov and his clan gained the upper hand in the nerve centers of the business. Although he never succeeded in obtaining the chairmanship of the national Filmmakers Union, he headed the Moscow branch, and that became his power center. The publisher of the journal *Kinoatele* assessed Solovyov's role in 1997: "One cannot judge Sergei Alexandrovich from just one angle. It's true that he killed our Soviet cinema, and destroyed the film distribution network, and managed to monopolize every single thing one can imagine. He also grabbed the festival. And yet, he has a right to do this. Objectively, we have to recognize that . . . except for Solovyov no one else realistically and consistently is putting forward proposals for the development of the industry."[14]

This was soon to change, as Nikita Mikhalkov was elected president of the Filmmakers Union in 1998 and replaced Solovyov as the president of the Moscow Festival the following year. The 1999 event was the last festival of the century, and Mikhalkov was determined to boost its international profile. Indeed, the festival showed some signs of revival. With the full support of the Filmmakers Union and the official sponsorship of the government, the Moscow Festival seemed to recover some of its past glory. Prime Minister Sergei Stepashin became the head of the organizing committee and 63 million rubles ($2.6 million) were allocated to help the festival recover from a deep crisis. Over 300 films were shown at 10 venues around town. Many international stars from the old guard made the trip to Moscow—Michael York, Vanessa Redgrave, Pierre Richard, Alain Delon, 87-year old Kaneto Shindo, and Italian neo-realist Mario Monicelli. Mikhalkov said that the festival managed to "reemerge from the ashes."[15] It remains to be seen whether this phoenix can indeed fly into this century successfully, or whether it will migrate south to join the Lukomore movieland.

Paradise lost

The Russian Far East, the wilderness, the village.
Whether it is the Russian Far East, the wilderness, or the rural village, faraway space and time dimensions were used by a number of filmmakers to deal with reality on a poetic level, and to address questions of identity in relation to the self and the environment.

A good example of the "paradise lost" theme is Nikita Mikhalkov's *Urga, Land of Love*, which in the West was aptly titled *Close to Eden* (1991, Grand Prix at the Venice Film Festival). Mikhalkov takes the viewer away from the contemporary urban world into the wilderness of the Siberian steppe, and develops one of his favorite themes, the search for the natural roots, lost in the technological process of civilization. A Russian truck driver (Pyotr Zaychenko) comes by chance to a remote area East of the Urals and makes the acquaintance of a Mongol family that lives in the vastness of the plain, where land and sky meet. He is invited to spend a few days in their tent, and develops a fascination for these people who have preserved a primordial purity in their human relations. Everything is simple there, like the pulsing of life and the breathing of the steppe. After the first moment of disorientation, the Russian begins to feel comfortable in that environment, as if his ancient Slavic roots, which extended far to the East and were nurtured in the course of history with Mongolian blood, surfaced in his consciousness. But the idyll is spoiled. The germs of progress have already infiltrated the pristine environment in the form of a TV set that causes both pride and turmoil in the household. The chronicle merges with the emotional representation of the events. Mikhalkov, supported by the expert hand of cinematographer Vilen Kalyuta, while recording everyday reality, turns the ordinary into a poetic experience.

The same theme is at the core of *A Piebald Dog Running Along the Sea Shore* (1991), based on a story by Chingiz Aitmatov. Director Karen Gevorkian transposed Aitmatov's prose into suggestive images of pristine nature and primitive life. The film, shot on location in a remote area on the Arctic Ocean coast, records the life of a small tribe, the Nikhvs. Unvarnished scenes of the natives struggling for survival against the natural elements connect the crudeness of the daily routine with an overwhelming sense of participation in the eternal cycle of life. Gruesome images are offset by an overall soothing effect, as the film reestablishes the link between humans and nature.

A less romantic environment, the Russian countryside, provides the setting for *Oh, You Geese!* (Lidya Bobrova, 1992), which delighted Moscow critics and film connoisseurs when it came out. When dealing with the Russian village, the "paradise lost" theme switches from the plane of being to that of representation. In fact, the village has been a paradise only in the films of the 1930s and 1940s, dictated by socialist realism and modeled on Hollywood musicals. The representation of the Russian provinces has always been a problem for filmmakers and writers in the Soviet period, since it was not possible to denounce their state of economic and social abjection. Pictures produced under Stalin were expected to idealize the village, and therefore resulted in rural operettas. In more recent times there were a few attempts to present a truer portrayal of the countryside, but they were usually thwarted by censorship; for example, Andrei Konchalovsky's *Asya's Happiness*, made in 1967. Konchalovsky shot the film in a documentary style, bringing the camera to a collective farm and using the farmers to play themselves. For that he was penalized and the film was not released until the mid eighties.[16] With the exception of Vasily Shukshin, who was able to introduce some realism in his pictures, the filmmakers for three decades chose to ignore country life.[17]

Lidya Bobrova wrote the script of *Oh, You Geese!* in 1981, when she was a third-year student at the State Cinema Institute, but was unable to get it approved. After censorship was abolished in the glasnost period, Bobrova could not find a sponsor, and finally decided to produce the film independently. She started production at the Studio of First and Experimental Films in St. Petersburg with a meager budget. Then, she moved to her native Stavropol region, where the whole film was shot on location taking advantage of the natural sets and real-life interiors. The original intention was to make a short, but the result was a full-length feature, which eventually received an array of prizes.[18]

Notwithstanding the realism of the sets, the black-and-white film stock, and the use of direct sound, the film displays motifs typical of folk tales. The title itself is a line from a folk song. The narrative follows the destiny of three brothers whose life paths now meet, now part, each time confronting the heroes with a new turn. But the tone is tragic. Living in an environment where cynicism and indifference were raised to the status of life principles, the three brothers became alcoholics and social outcasts. The three female characters that share their lives, weave a recurrent elegy about unfulfilled destinies, wasted dreams, and doomed efforts to escape their misery. A vignette of the brothers' childhood is placed at the beginning of the film as an epigraph. Three cute, fair-haired boys are singing accompanied by their father on the accordion. They are happy and filled with hope. The scene is then repeated at the end, where it acquires a bitter meaning underlining the human potential that was not realized.

The main action is set in the early 1980's. Brother Dmitry and his daughter Natasha watch a newsreel of the Moscow Olympic Games that shows the lovable mascot, Misha, and the lavish tables set for the guests. The hungry girl looks at the screen with wistful eyes—she will never have a taste of it. Dmitry is an invalid who cannot find a job and lives on the money his sick wife makes sewing clothes. Brother Pyotr is victimized by a dictatorial wife, who is in love with the older brother, Alexander. This brother is serving time for murdering a fellow during a drunken fight. When Alexander returns, it is clear that there is no place for him at home. In fact, there is no home as such because family ties and brotherly love have been crushed by a life of spiritual isolation.

Bobrova conveys all this in a detached, unsentimental style, interspersed with touches of bitter humor. But she also shows flickers of light in the darkness. They occur when Dmitry and his wife find a rare moment of intimacy; or when Pyotr is able to move in tune with his wife in an impromptu folk dance; or when Alexander, himself destitute and homeless, extends a helping hand to a vagrant alcoholic woman. Toward the end, the action moves up to the present day. The new times, requiring a pragmatic frame of mind and calculating self-interest, have not brought any improvements in the lives of the three brothers. They will continue to be victims, but with a function: to nurture the flickering light, which alone may be able to save the individual and the whole country.

In her next film, *In That Land* (1997), Bobrova recounts the same kind of story, casting it in an even gloomier mold. Once again the style is documentary-like, the actors are non-professionals (her brother plays one of the three leading men), and the setting is the natural countryside, this time in Northern Russia. But, more obviously than in the previous film, the realism of the style embodies an abstract concept—the concept of "villageness," which carries in itself the germs of its own degradation. The reference to "that land" may suggest a link with the village of the previous film. But it may also be broader, including all of Russia's villages—and possibly, the whole country. The film is an adaptation of short stories by Boris Ekimov and depicts a patriarchal society headed for extinction. The physical decay of the men is contrasted with the vigor of their women, who often boss them around with a firm disciplinary hand. But the film does not foresee a change of the guard, where genders will eventually switch roles. Although weak and degraded, the village males maintain their dominance in society, with the complicity of their wives. This is the kind of symbiosis that worked for centuries in "that land," and has now reached its last stage. The film does not suggest what will come next.[19]

Andrei Konchalovsky returned to the theme of the village that he treated at the beginning of his career in *Asya's Happiness*. In his new film, *Ryaba My Chicken* (1994), Asya (Inna Churikova) is struggling with the realities of the market economy superimposed on the communal way of life of the farmers. The film starts with Asya's monologue addressed to the audience on the negative effects of capitalism. She is coming home from the marketplace, where a bullish dealer, obviously from the south, interfered with her business of selling eggs. She complains: "They call it free market. We had free market under Brezhnev. Then, we could set our prices, and there was order, and it was clean." She goes on saying that democracy is only good when order is enforced, otherwise it is not democracy, "it is a bordello." Back in the village, many share Asya's views and the film treats their attitude as a parody of the revolutionary struggle against the kulaks. The peasants organize a demonstration against the "capitalist" among them, who has set up a sawmill in the village and has built himself a new cottage with a refrigerator and a dishwasher. They carry red banners and signs saying: "Against capitalism" and "For our way of life," but ironically they also carry a portrait of Gorbachev. "Why him?" Asya asks with indignation; "We didn't have another one," they answer.

Gorbachev is the target of Asya's discontent. In a conversation with her chicken, Ryaba, she blames perestroika for the current state of the village. The portrait she paints--of failed reforms, decaying life quality, and deterioration of human relations--intercuts with clips from *Asya's Happiness*. The black and white images of the harvest, which were considered crudely realistic at the time, look almost idyllic now; there, the farmers are healthy, young, and motivated. The clips flash on the screen while Asya reminisces: "On the kolkhoz we worked from dawn till dusk for three rubles. And that was happiness, because there was no money." Money, or the lack thereof, is indeed the source of Asya's unhappiness in the present situation. Asya's son, the baby who in the early film was the main source of her pride, is now an outlaw implicated with the mafia. His father, Stepan, whom at the time Asya refused to marry out of pride, is an alcoholic and a corrupt farm official. The only character who shows compassion and integrity is the "capitalist," Sasha Chirkunov, who has always been in love with Asya since the old days, and whom she has repeatedly rejected. The film ends with a self-destructive act on the part of Sasha, symbolic of self-immolation. And only then, Asya realizes that she loves him.

25 *The Muslim* (1995) directed by Vladimir Khotinenko

When Konchalovsky presented the film at the 1994 Cannes Festival, he mused: "Freedom sometimes brings unexpected fruit. Everyone thought the end of communism was fantastic . . . it provided great hope. Then suddenly it isn't working."[20] The film conveys the director's frustration, and his conviction that democracy, just as Marxism, are Western inventions and therefore alien to the Russian people. *Ryaba* reiterates the nationalist belief that the encroachment of foreign systems on Russian soil is doomed to fail, and that Russia must pursue her own way out of the crisis. The film would have worked better without the quotations from the early film. Those old clips do not enhance it. They only remind us how great a film *Asya's Happiness* was, and how mediocre *Ryaba* is by comparison. Perhaps, it too suffers from the requirements of the market.

Another film that purports to explore Russia's moral state by focusing on the microcosm of the village and its spiritual disintegration is *The Muslim* (1995). Director Vladimir Khotinenko, who had flirted with comedy in the past, with this film moved into the realm of tragedy. The script is by Valery Zolotukha, who collaborated to previous films. The story hinges on the theme of homecoming from the Afghan war that, like Vietnam for Americans, was still a harrowing issue in Russian society. After seven years spent in Afghanistan, partly in captivity, and partly with an Afghan family that lost a son in the war, Kolya (Evgeny Mironov) comes home as a converted Muslim. He is perceived as the Other in his own village. Here, he finds that the collapse of the regime has encouraged all sorts of illegal activities, sometimes for mere survival, more often for greed. This is the case with the director of the kolkhoz, who replaced his party card with a gold Orthodox cross and is engaged in lucrative land deals at the expense of the villagers (Pyotr Zaychenko plays the macho *muzhik*). Kolya is deeply affected by the situation and retreats more and more into his spiritual world. The mother (Nina Usatova) is the commonsense figure, who foresees the tragic outcome of her son's estrangement, because the village regards him as a threat. Kolya, disgusted with the general corruption, his brother's drunkenness, and the fact that his girlfriend became a prostitute, turns extremely judgmental. As a consequence, the conflict moves up to a higher level and becomes the confrontation between human frailty and ideological inflexibility.

The viewers are constantly challenged as to where to place their sympathy—with the sinful but human village folks, or with a religious paragon of morality devoid of compassion. The theme is not new, especially in Russia, where it occupies a large place among the literary classics. Here it is reproposed in a contemporary context. Khotinenko came of age as a director in the perestroika years and established himself as one of the most promising talents of that generation. Like his other films, *Muslim* is a *pritcha* (parable), which carries a symbolic meaning but is deeply rooted in the reality of today's Russia. As such, it captures the current mood, the collective feeling of aggressiveness, alienation, and fear.

The film debut of St. Petersburg stage director Dmitry Astrakhan, *Get Thee Hence!* (1991), looks back at the village of pre-revolutionary Russia, and tells a tale of violence, yet hope, which applies to yesterday as well as today. Perhaps, this was one of the reasons the film won an array of prizes and was nominated for an Oscar. The story unfolds around a Jewish family in a small southern town, where Jews and Orthodox Russians live together as good neighbors, sharing work and fun. The head of the family, Matvei, even supports his daughter's inter-ethnic marriage, as does the whole community. But violence erupts periodically in the surrounding areas. After a horrific pogrom in a nearby village at the hands of the Black Hundreds--a hate group secretly sponsored by the tsarist government--Matvei's family is threatened, and decides to confront the enemy. Standing firm on the road that leads to his house, and backed by his neighbors, Matvei awaits the approaching menace. They watch the blurred silhouette of a huge truck, a monster-machine with yellow eyes, loaded with dark figures carrying scythes and black banners. It is a compelling and symbolic image meant to shift the issue of evil from the realistic to the mythological level. "Get thee hence!" is a biblical devil exorcism; the film is an exorcism against the demon of intolerance.

The Time for Sadness Has Not yet Come (Sergei Selyanov, 1995) is one of the few films that end on a positive note. It offers, if not an answer to Russia's problems, at least a sense of reconciliation of her many contradictions. St. Petersburg film director and head of STV production company, Sergei Selyanov, injects a note of optimism in a generally dismal portrayal of Russia. Starting with the very title, this film suggests that there is still hope. The main theme is that of identity--how to find one's own true identity that was lost in the pursuit of myths. Ivanov, the film protagonist (Valery Premykhov), is a money forger once lured by the consumer market myth and now disillusioned. To escape from the constraints of his life, he boards a plane and, while flying over Russia, abandons himself to daydreaming. A flashback brings him to the village of his childhood, which embodies the Soviet myth—the utopian belief in a geographically and ethnically integrated industrial paradise. The village also breeds the folk myths of fairy tales and magic. Ivanov's third fantasy is the myth of the West, symbolized by Paris as the city of love. The film demystifies these illusory constructions one by one.

The first myth to be debunked is the concept of the Soviet homeland, which was sustained by a well-constructed set of cultural icons. Among the heroes of popular mythology was the border guard with his German shepherd dog, celebrated in thousands of bronze sculptures as the vigilant defender of the frontier. Another such symbol was the railroad network—a connective grid, unifying the country. The tracks that run by Ivanov's childhood village, however, have been truncated. The village is symbolically cut off from the map, and the identification of the villagers with the Soviet fatherland is revealed to be illusory.[21] The second myth, reliance on folk tales and magic, is also proven to be ineffectual, as miracles that were expected to occur do not materialize. The film, however, offers an alternative to these myths: reconciliation with life—the process of existing—which provides the key to one's own true identity.

This alternative is pursued through the figure of Methodius (Pyotr Mamonov), a land surveyor, who appears from nowhere in the village with his "magic" surveying instruments and instantly becomes a spiritual guide among the local folks.[22] Methodius is a Soviet functionary in charge of mapping railroad itineraries. But he is not an ordinary functionary. His technological skills merge with a pantheistic sense of nature, emphasized by both visual and aural elements. The hills and meadows around the village have the essential quality of naïf paintings. Recurrent shots of the sun in the sky look like children drawings, a big orange disk on a brilliant blue background; and the moon looks like a ball of cottage cheese. During a long dark night, mysterious sounds from the fields and the woods fill the soundtrack. They may be just the sounds of animals and birds, and the wind rustling through the trees, but they evoke a portentous atmosphere and conjure up an instinctual feeling for the mystery of nature.

Using his theodolite, Methodius looks for the mystic "center" of the world. There, he drives in his stake, and predicts that "in twenty years a new life will begin." That sentence has an ironic ring, being a propaganda slogan of the day; but at the same time the scene comes across as a magic ritual. Twenty years later, still in his fantasy, Ivanov and his friends come back to visit the spot, and find that a glorious tree grew out of Methodius' stake. In the end this vision helps Ivanov understand that while the "center" may be a myth, life is a reality.

The myth of the West is also demystified. Before consumerism reached Russia together with the McDonald's restaurants and the Gucci boutiques, one focal point of this mythology was Paris, as the land of glamorous romance. In his flight from reality, Ivanov hijacks the plane, pretends to takes the stewardess hostage, and demands to be taken to Paris. The objective is to have a romantic adventure with the complicity of the stewardess. But as they set foot on the ground, the would-be lovers realize that the view of the Eiffel Tower through the plane window was just a makeshift, another illusion. The plane actually landed in Ivanov's home village, where the police were waiting for them. After a first moment of panic, the two highjackers avoid the police and find a love nest amidst the tall grass of a green meadow. This is the last episode of the film, which brings Ivanov's fantasy sequel back to full circle—to the kernel of his self. In this case, paradise is lost and found.

The film also comments on how cinema represents the world. By drawing attention to the use of lenses, selecting frames through the surveying telescope, and creating aerial views of the fields that look like abstract canvases, the film conveys the sense that there is no such thing as objective reality—a myth congealed—but only the experience of space and time. In its existentialist affirmation of life, the film reconciles past and present, and the individual with the homeland.

I never met a Russian who did not have a dacha. The dacha is much more than a country retreat; it is a state of mind. The word comes from the root, *dat'* (to give), and at first referred to the properties given to the state bureaucrats as perks under the tsarist regime. Because of that practice, the dacha became an integral and essential household accessory among the middle class--the gentry, of course, had their own country estates. Families that for some reason did not receive a government dacha would buy one for money. Those who could not afford to buy would rent it. But in all cases, the word stuck. The dacha mania was well captured in a 1903 play by Maxim Gorky, *Dachniki* (Dacha Dwellers), which was more recently made into a film, *Summer Folk* (Ursulyak, 1995). The word's original meaning was then revived in Soviet times, when private property was confiscated, and dachas were routinely handed out to deserving members of the nomenklatura, or taken away from them, according to their political fortunes.

Under the Soviets, privilege by rank was strictly observed. There were top dacha enclaves for the upper echelons of the party, the government, and the military. One such enclave was Zhukovka, on a hill overlooking the Moscow River, where Khrushchev, Brezhnev, and Kosygin had their residences. Those were very secluded places, because the Soviet upper classes did not want to flaunt their privileges. One notch down, were the dacha complexes for scientists, writers, artists, and the intelligentsia at large, clustered in villages such as Peredelkino and Serebriany Bor, a few miles from Moscow. There, famous people lived door to door, in a configuration that had been planned on a bureaucrat's desk. There was none of the luxury we in the West associate with celebrities' extravagant lives. They lived in graceful wooden cottages, in uniform, elegant comfort.[23] The benefit package for workers did not include a dacha, except for special cases. But it included small plots of land—600 square meters—mainly to grow a garden and supplement the family's diet. The plot also came with the permit to build a small house of fifty square meters. In addition, most workers came from peasant families and had parents or relatives in the village, who owned their own little house and plot. For the urban dweller, the dacha was sort of a mythical place, the symbol of a return to nature. On weekends and holidays, people would leave the city in droves, on government Chaikas, middle-class Zhigulis, or the *elektrichka* (local train), headed for a cleansing of the lungs and the soul.[24]

A new kind of dacha owner emerged after privatization, and by 1995 became very conspicuous. I had not been to Peredelkino in a while, and on a Friday afternoon, as we were riding down Rublyovskoe Shosse, the main highway leading to the resort, the new constructions struck me as an eyesore. They did not belong in that landscape--massive brick turreted mansions, mimicking the architecture of medieval fortresses and Florentine palazzos, surrounded by tall iron fences. They mushroomed everywhere, randomly, encroaching on the rural communities that had been preserved on the outskirts of Moscow all around the ring road. The gingerbread houses, once surrounded by meadows, were now being suffocated between the new stone giants. Many had already disappeared, together with the yellow and blue wildflower patches that in springtime used to highlight the landscape. The land was being bought by developers one plot after another.

Last time Tyotya Dunya came to town to deliver her honey and preserves, she complained about construction going on in her backyard. She serviced a pool of customers, whom she acquired over time by word of mouth. I will be forever grateful to the friends who recommended her, because she sweetened my days with her products and the stories about them—her being able to talk to the bees, and how the goat ate a whole gooseberry bush. But last time her story was sad. A redbrick *kottedzh*, four stories high, was being built a few yards from her tiny wooden house. "On that plot there used to be my neighbor's garden," she said. "We would compare crops over the fence. Then the bulldozers came and leveled everything. My cherry trees got sick, and so did the bees that won't talk to me anymore. And the goat stopped eating altogether in protest." She sighed and continued: "The new house has 10 bedrooms, and each has its own bathroom; and there is a pool and a sauna; also a garage for two cars. All our houses in the village have only one floor; not even the party secretary was allowed to build a two-story house for himself. But now, who's gonna stop these people? And who are they, anyway?"

Perhaps the phrase, "new Russians," had not yet entered Tyotya Dunya's vocabulary, but the new Russians had entered her world like a tornado. Money was changing the face of dormant Russian villages in an ugly way, because the multi-billion dollar construction business that sprang up after land privatization was totally unregulated. The existing legislation on land and construction no longer applied to the new situation, and hastily drafted government decrees could not fill the gap. There were no obstacles to the wave of brick and cement that was pouring over the Russian landscape. And the problem was more than aesthetics. The new mansions were being built on farmland with total disregard to infrastructure. Inadequate access roads and lack of sewage facilities created a strain on the communities. Often, raw sewage was simply allowed to flow into the ground and to pollute the land and the water.

Life in the village has always been difficult. Generally, there was no running water, and the population used the village well. Outhouses were the norm, and there were no private telephones. The one pay phone by the grocery store was permanently out of order, and the store itself had only empty shelves to display. Nevertheless, the villagers, most of them pensioners in their seventies, knew how to survive in that environment. But they would not be able to survive the march of the *kottedzhy*.

We turned onto the country road that cuts through the woods to Peredelkino. There, nothing had changed significantly, except that a few dachas were now rented out to corporate expats. Those families, though, were respectful of the local culture and appreciated the privacy and peace the place afforded. The same birch and pine trees along the road, the same little pond with the autumnal golden colors reflected in its mirror-like water, and the perennial fisherman holding his rod as if he were part of the landscape. Years ago, I had taken a picture of the pond and the fisherman; if I were to hold it now against today's scenery, it would produce a seamless fit—a perfect *tromp-l'oeil*, as in Magritte's "La Condition Humaine."

We left the car at the dacha and took a stroll before dinner. We walked down the trail that leads to Pasternak's grave by a little church with azure and golden domes. The simple grave was covered with fresh flowers, as always is all year round, a testimony to the poet and to an epoch in which the struggle between the individual and the state required fortitude. Pasternak lived in his dacha nearby as an internal exile for thirty years. Under the circumstances, many would have compromised, but he did not, and became an example of spiritual strength for the intelligentsia in the stagnating decades of the Brezhnev regime.[25]

A group of teenagers were hanging out on their cross-country bikes—beautiful, healthy kids in designer sportswear, swayed by the rhythms pouring in from their headphones. They were obviously gathering for an outing, oblivious of the poet's grave and the middle-aged folks immersed in meditation. One day, they will inherit Peredelkino's dachas. Let's hope they will not turn them into *kottedzhi*.

Fabricated worlds

The "abroad," fairy tales, aesthetic landscapes.
As noted, one of the myths debunked in *Time for Sadness* is the "abroad" (*zagranitsa*), meaning not just a geographical expression but the culture of the Western world. For three centuries, the Russians have been offered glimpses of the West through the "window" opened by Peter the Great—the reports of the few privileged countrymen who were able to visit it, and the rare contacts with the aliens that crossed the border into Russia. But for the majority of the population the border was sealed. As it is well know, the forbidden fruit is a coveted fruit, which has all the wonderful qualities everyday reality lacks. The West became a sort of promised land for the Russians, an unreachable dream. But when traveling became possible the dream lost its mythical connotations; travels abroad became a matter of fashion, rather than a matter of destiny. Several films of the post-Soviet period treated the "abroad" theme, depicting the disillusionment of those who attained, or were about to attain, the unreachable dream and had to resize their expectations. Often these films sounded a patriotic note, with the protagonists reevaluating their national identity and choosing the homeland over the promised land. Some films on this theme are comedies, and will be discussed later.

Dmitry Astrakhan addresses this topic in his second film, *You Are My Only One* (1993), leaving room for hope at the end. The protagonist, Evgeny Timoshin (Alexander Zbruev), is a St. Petersburg engineer, who in mid life is faced with a tough choice. Suddenly he is offered the possibility of escaping the dull routine of family and professional life and start anew in the world of his dreams—America. This opportunity comes up when the firm he works for enters into a joint venture with an American company. To make the promised land even more tantalizing, the deal includes not only money and glamour, but love as well. The American representative of the joint venture, Anya (Svetlana Ryabova), was only fourteen when she emigrated with her family in the 1970s; at the time she had a crush on Timoshin, and now she comes back with the intention of luring him away. To emphasize the offer's appeal, the film gives us a detailed portrayal of Timoshin's life—his diminutive, cluttered apartment where he, his wife Natasha (Marina Neyolova), and their teenage daughter, must compete for a bit of privacy; and the frustration at work, where he performs uninspiring tasks day after day for a pittance of a salary.

But this environment, humiliating and emasculating as it may be, is also his anchor. This is where Timoshin's emotional and cultural roots are. Notwithstanding the constant bickering with Natasha, who herself has withered under the burden of her job as a doctor coupled with housework chores, there is a strong bond between the two of them. The bond is emphasized by flashbacks to the days of their youth, where they are shown as schoolmates and, later, newlyweds. The reference is to the Brezhnev years known as the "time of stagnation." This label is well deserved in the broad context of the country's sluggish bureaucracy and lagging economy. But many who came of age in that period remember it with nostalgia as a happy one. Stalin's terror was long gone; party control was still present but directed toward specific political targets; the KGB kept a vigilant eye on everybody but clamped down mostly on intellectual dissidents; Khrushchev's cultural reform had left its mark on society; and even after the crackdown that followed his ousting, the young managed to create a counterculture based on Western models—first among them, the rock culture. Finally, heavy government subsidies afforded a modest degree of affluence to the urban population—that was the first generation after the revolution that could afford to have leisure time. The flashbacks show that the young people enjoyed it with relish. They also show the carefree good old days, full of hope and great expectations, as a sort of paradise lost when compared to the current situation. And as such, not as a real time, but one that existed only in Evgeny's and Natasha's imagination—the time of stagnation as myth.

Timoshin is therefore pulled in opposite directions by two magnetic poles, and in the end he chooses to stay right in the middle. He rejects Anya's glamorous offer, and with it the American myth, shouting in her face: "I do not love you." More than an explanation to her, this sounds like an acknowledgement to himself of an obvious truth. In the same way, he abandons the fantasy of the golden past and the emasculating grieving over his lost potential, and recognizes that life has something to offer even in the present situation. Namely, the bond between individuals linked by the same cultural values and, through these values, the bond with the motherland.

In the last scene, Timoshin's birthday party suggests, if not a spiritual rebirth, some kind of awakening. The party is a happening led by Timoshin's father, who lives in the margin with a band of eccentric street musicians. The jolly group puts on a sort of Fellinesque circus performance in the tenement courtyard, and calls on everyone to join--neighbors, friends, and former foes. It is a party of reconciliation and life celebration. Once again, Timoshin comes to the realization of an obvious truth and shouts to his wife, who is still upstairs in the apartment: "Natasha, you are my only one!" It does not matter that she does not hear him, because his words are directed to himself more than to her. This sentence has an important function in the overall structure of the film, as the title suggests, because it refers to a popular song from the counterculture of the 1970s—which is the leit-motif on the film soundtrack. In that final scene, Timoshin extricates the song from the myth, and turns the easy refrain into an affirmation of values. As he ponders his own words, the camera cuts to a picture of Evgeny and Natasha as children in their school uniforms—not a nostalgic fantasy of their youth, but a picture of an enduring bond with each other and their roots.

California, the dreamland of many Russian émigrés, is the backdrop of Karen Shakhnazarov's *American Daughter* (1995), and another attempt to debunk the American myth. At the same time, the film pays homage to Hollywood by adopting one of its classical genres. Filmed in just five weeks in San Francisco, the movie relied on a minimalist budget provided by tycoon Boris Giller of Kazakhstan (who later co-produced the 1997 Oscar nominee *The Prisoner of the Mountain*s). However, *American Daughter* did not fare well either in the United States or at home. All the ingredients for success were there, but the mix did not come out right.

The film combines sentimental Russian themes with Hollywood road movie clichés, telling the story of a Russian father (Vladimir Mashkov) who comes to California in order to kidnap his daughter. The girl lives with her mother, now married to a wealthy American businessman. Father and daughter sympathize and become fugitives, hopping from bus to bus, hitchhiking, being picked up by good-hearted truckers and chased by angry cops along scenic Route No.1, always rescued by the ingenuity of the indomitable American daughter (ten-year-old Allison Whitbeck). Although there are some good moments, the director's treatment of the genre produced a hybrid, where ill-digested Hollywood

Faraway in Space and Time   193

26   *American Daughter* (1995) directed by Karen Shakhnazarov

conventions are supposed to glamorize a Russian script.[26] Shakhnazarov is at his best when he deals with stock characters from the Russian repertoire (such as an émigré taxi driver played by the popular actor Armen Dzhigarkhanyan), or when he digs into his Russian soul and discloses the vulnerability of the male protagonist on alien territory. Mashkov, who on the Russian screen is the hottest sex symbol, in this film had to change his persona and turn into an awkward wanderer in an oversized cowboy outfit.

But there were plans for even bolder adventures involving Russian "space cowboys." By 1999, California was no longer the ultimate exotic cinematic space. Newer frontiers were needed, and director Yuri Kara envisioned sending the lead of his next film, Vladimir Steklov, to the space station Mir. The two cosmonauts accompanying the actor would have doubled as cameramen. The script was based on the novel *Cassandra's Brand*, by Chingiz Aitmatov, and told the story of a cosmonaut, who refuses to abandon a space station slated for destruction. As it turned out, the set was actually destroyed before the film could even get started.[27]

If the West turned out to be disappointing to many film characters, it has always been "an unhappy experience" for Russian filmmakers. As Solovyov put it, "Eisenstein had only sad memories of Hollywood. . . . Tarkovsky [was unhappy in exile], Konchalovsky [too]. . . . I asked him, 'Why did you come back? You were successful there as a director.' He said, 'When I think of the faces of the American producers, the faces of the members of the Politburo look much nicer to me.' And, indeed, we should not look for happiness where we do not belong; happiness is where we belong."[28]

A dreamland of a different kind, which has no reference on the global map, offers an escape to the two protagonists of *Land of the Deaf* (1997). This is yet another successful picture by Valery Todorovsky, based on a short story by Renata Litvinova, "To Possess and to Belong" (*Obladat' i prinadlezhat'*). The film was produced at the Gorky Studio, whose head, Sergei Livnev, had established a program to finance films by young directors on a shoestring budget. But, as Todorovsky said, "This is not small-budget cinema. This is a normal, full-fledged film on a very respectable budget by Russian standards."[29] Indeed, the film is respectable all in all, bringing to the screen creativity and professionalism. At the same time, it retains features of the Gorky Studio new wave, such as unknown, or little known, actors in the main roles and a playful handling of genre.

The narrative shell of *Land of the Deaf* is the American gangster genre adapted to the Moscow scene, with its paraphernalia of mafia rival clans, gambling, drugs, prostitution, and spectacular shoot-outs. Some situations are absurdly stylized, like the scene of the last fierce gunfight that

Faraway in Space and Time 195

27   *Land of the Deaf* (1997) directed by Valery Todorovsky

results in the annihilation of every single man on both sides. The camera does not show the bodies, only chalk silhouettes drawn on the sidewalk by the police, depriving the viewer of any possible emotional reaction. The same technique is applied to the other clichés of the genre, emptying them of emotional content and showing them as such. The emotions are reserved for the two protagonists, Yaya (Dina Korzun) and Rita (Chulpan Khomatova), and their bizarre relationship. To get even an approximate understanding of this relationship, it is necessary to consider the other plot elements.

Rita is in love with Alyosha, a good-looking good-for-nothing, who takes advantage of her unconditional devotion. He is a compulsive gambler, deeply indebted to the owner of a nightclub, to whom he "pawns" Rita as security for his debt. Rita manages to run away with the help of the nightclub strip teaser, who decides to quit her demeaning job. Her name is Yaya—a name that she herself invented and consists of the repetition of the first person pronoun, "*ya*." The name stresses Yaya's fiercely independent nature, bordering on selfishness, and her aversion for the masculine gender— "I hate all men," she declares. The dramatic structure requires the juxtaposition of Yaya's selfishness with Rita's supposed selflessness, in order to build a conflict, which is reconciled in the end with the elimination of the obstacles that hindered their spiritual union—namely, Alyosha and the male element altogether.

The encounter between the two women is fateful, because it changes their lives. "Where is the exit?" asks Rita when she first meets Yaya at the nightclub. And Yaya guides her to the ultimate "exit." After a series of adventures, they are able to free themselves from the male-dominated world of gambling and racketeering, and leave for the "land of the deaf." Yaya, who is deaf, has created a fantasy, which implies that deaf people, isolated by necessity from the real world through the sound barrier of their disability, are protected from the harrowing noises of the technological civilization that affect the human brain and soul. According to Yaya, the "land of the deaf is a big island: sea, palm-trees, white mountains, sun"; there, "people are happy, they are kind and smiling," and "money is always around."[30] Two conditions must be met, however, in order to leave for the "land of the deaf." To qualify, Rita must learn sign language and pretend to be deaf to share in the love culture of the community; and they both should make a lot of money to "buy the ticket," which is very expensive. These two conditions are actually the kernel of the story—love and money.[31]

Yaya loves Rita and wants to snatch her away from the world of the "normal" people, and especially from Alyosha. Rita loves Alyosha and wants to possess him through her passive-aggressive behavior disguised as self-abnegation. Alyosha loves only himself and in the end drops Rita because, as he puts it, her selfless love has become a burden and he can no longer stand her saintly devotion. The question of whether a lesbian relationship between the two girl friends is implied comes naturally, but is actually beyond the point of the film. No erotic scene between them is either shown or suggested, they simply share their temporary home as roommates. However, there are moments of intense emotions between the two young women, which can only be characterized as love and jealousy. To frustrate any kind of prurient expectations on the part of the viewer, the script addresses the question straightforwardly. "Are we lesbians?" the two girls ask themselves giggling, displaying a very naive understanding of what the word means. They reminisce about their children games, when they shared the bed with other girls at the boarding school, and wonder if "this is what it means." The question is, therefore, resolved playfully. Rather, not resolved, but removed altogether.

Money, which is the girls' and everybody else's major concern, is also eliminated in the end, together with the ring of money-grubbers, in a Grand Guignol type of scene. In the final shoot-out that puts an end to the rival clans, Rita becomes deaf for real because of a gunshot that was fired too close to her ear. This circumstance admits her automatically to the "land of the deaf," where money is no longer needed.

Since the story deals with sound, or the lack of it, the film has an interesting sound track. Yaya's deafness affects her speech. Her voice sounds odd, her sentences are fragmented, her pitch a bit too high. It is a mannerism that recalls the speech of a mechanical doll and, therefore, contributes to the perception of Yaya as an eccentric character.[32] She is clearly out of place in the land of the "normal" folks. This is visually underlined, in a kitschy way, by the sculpture an artist made of the multi-armed Indian god Siva, using Yaya as a model. The sculpture is located in the artist's studio, which the two girls use as their temporary home in the absence of the owner. Siva is an odd presence there, among a population of old official statues of the regime. Another oddity is the fact that Yaya can communicate normally with Rita and Alyosha; she seems to "hear" what they say. No explanation is offered for this seeming contradiction. We, therefore, accept it as part of the "fiction," as a necessity of the script, and as still another way of laying bare the rules of the game.

There is another group of "freaks," who are deaf but do not make it to the "land of the deaf." Possibly because they are males and, therefore, do not figure in Yaya's plan. They are the "good" mafiosi. Their boss, Hog, is touched by Rita's innocence and gives her money and a job of sorts. Rita becomes his "ears," with the task of alerting him to the intentions of his enemies. But in the end even this expedient cannot save him and his clan from extermination. Hog is a parody of the Godfather, not so much because he is "good" and has feelings for his family, but mainly because of the way he speaks. His guttural, barely intelligible utterances are a caricature of the Brando character's speech.

Sound is also used to create spaces. While learning sign language, Rita enters the deaf zone. All of a sudden, the traffic noise in the congested urban environment vanishes. The two friends—and the viewer—can hear only the murmur of the sea, as they float in slow motion over the waves of cars and pedestrians. This is repeated in the scene of the final shoot-out, when Rita becomes deaf for real and all worldly noise is cut off.

This film defies any conventional approach. Attempts to identify moral issues (who are the good guys?), sociological issues (women triumph), psychological issues ("land of the deaf" as a Freudian hang-up) dissolve into laughter, because the film "plays" with those issues, casting them outside of logic. The playful tone, together with a touch of the absurd, focuses the attention of the viewer on the foreground, on the very fabric of the cinematic text. Rather than a social commentary, this is a commentary on the state of cinema. It's been noted that the film is not simply a study on genre, but suggests the end of Genre, and even more radically, the end of the myth that inhabited the Russian cinematic space until the 1990s. Both the characters and the spaces in this film are new constructions, not traceable back to any traditional models. These constructions have not replaced the old models yet. But they have been sketched as new archetypes. The retreat to the "land of the deaf" seems to offer a pause for reflection, as a prelude to the period of "new narrative."[33]

Some fabricated spaces do not imply either the "abroad" or a utopian dream, but can be characterized simply as fairy tales. Vladimir Mashkov surprised everyone when he made his debut as a director with a film in this genre, *Sympathy Seeker* (1997). It has been said that the macho image Mashkov creates on the screen does not correspond to his real-life self.[34] *Sympathy Seeker* supports this view. Here he reveals a gentle nature in a comedy of errors with fairy tale elements, reminiscent of Eldar Ryazanov's and Emil Braginsky's early works.[35] The script is more appropriate for the stage than for the camera, as the plot unfolds basically in one room with a cast of five characters. In fact, three famous stage actors play the main male roles (Valentin Gaft, Lev Durov, and Oleg Tabakov). The camera rarely follows the characters outside, keeping a firm footing on the set and recording their comings and goings. But the magic overtones expand the space into a world of fantasy and happiness.

Schoolteacher Nastya (Elena Shevchenko) is known in the village as a "Kazan orphan" (the Russian film title), meaning a person that does not have any relatives in the whole world. Her mother, now dead, told her that she was the result of a summer romance in a resort town on the Black Sea. The fairy tale begins on New Year's Eve in Nastya's little house in the woods, where the snow glitters on every branch rivaling the brilliance of the starry sky. Suddenly, not one but three "fathers" enter the scene. The men come in response to an ad that Nastya placed in the newspaper, and each of them claims her as his own daughter. No one can prove his paternity for sure, although all three can provide details of their seaside romance with Nastya's mother. After the initial shock, and a scuffle, the men realize that it would be better to be friends than foes. Still competing for Nastya's attention, like Snow White dwarfs, they get busy transforming the modest room into the setting of the most fantastic New Year's feast. Father number one was a circus magician, and he applies his art to decorating the tree. Father number two is a retired B-league cosmonaut, and he applies his technical expertise to repairing the TV set. Father number three was a ship's cook, and he applies his skills to the preparation of culinary delights. Outside the window, in the winter night, the silhouette of a sparkling cruiser is seen floating in the black sky. The fifth participant in the banquet is Nastya's fiance, Kolya (Nikolay Fomenko), who announces that the three fathers are soon to be grandfathers. Perhaps, as a glimpse of the future, one of Nastya's schoolchildren makes a brief appearance.[36] Everything ends well, and the group decides to live happily ever after together. The film does not claim to be more than a sentimental tale, but as such it is well crafted and refreshing, full of good humor, good feelings, and a touch of poetry.

Another fairy tale brought a ray of hope in the alienating world of the big city. It would seem that nobody needed yet another version of the Cinderella story, but Georgi Danelia gave it an appealing twist. *Nastya* (1993) is a delicate, sentimental comedy, sustained by a generous dose of folk wisdom and gentle humor—although a much weaker work by comparison to a number of Danelia's previous films. His first film, *A Summer to Remember* (1960, co-directed with Igor Talankin), was the story of a five-year old boy discovering the world, in the vein of late Italian neorealism. It became a staple in all Soviet film anthologies circulating in the West in those years. The second film, *I Walk Around Moscow* (1964), was the portrait of a group of teenagers, enjoying a long, leisurely summer day around the city, hanging out, doing nothing, but carrying the expectation of a bright future awaiting them just around the corner. The film is now a curiosity because it marks the debut of 16-year-old Nikita Mikhalkov in the lead role. About that film, Danelia said: "It is not a slice of life, nor a newsreel. It is a modern fairy tale with noble heroes and beautiful fairies. Indeed, if you look, all my films are to some extent fairy tales."[37] In the films that followed, however, the radiant optimism of the early days gave way to sad humor and bitter irony. This trend reached its peak in 1980, with *Autumn Marathon*, which the director called, "a sad comedy."[38]

With *Nastya*, a bright light goes on again. This post-perestroika fairy tale affirms that all is well in society as long as there are beautiful souls who believe in love and honest work. One of these souls is eighteen-year-old Nastya (Polina Kutepova), working as a salesgirl in a school supplies store and tending her bed-ridden mother at home. Her plain, freckled looks are not popular with the boys, who are after flamboyant beauties in miniskirts. Unexpectedly, she falls in love with Sasha (Valery Nikolaev), a young man she meets by chance on the late night tram. That night, she wishes she could look like the gorgeous ballerina pinned up to her bedroom wall. Because of Nastya's special relationship with a good fairy—a bag lady on a bicycle, whom the girl helped out of a pothole—Nastya is granted her wish, and she wakes up in the morning a stunning beauty. Now, everybody is at her feet. But coming to the moral of the story, Nastya realizes that she is losing the only thing she really cares for—namely, Sasha's love. Reversing the magic, she goes back to her previous looks, previous life, and true love.

In the fantastic part of the story, the sets are stylized to stress the fairy-tale atmosphere, and the characters are flat cutouts. The villains are caricatures—like the womanizing prefect of the local city district (Alexander Abdulov), ready to exchange administrative favors for sexual ones, courtesy of Nastya. Or, like the organizer of a VIP pageant in a metro station, regaling statuesque beauty queens with luscious mink fur coats, while the trains pass by carrying away behind locked doors the haggard faces of ordinary passengers. In the role of the festival organizer, Danelia cast Yuly Gusman, a Moscow celebrity, manager of the Cinema House and a Duma deputy—which adds a touch of self-reflexive humor to the episode. On this two-dimensional background, the real characters, Nastya, her mother, Sasha, and a few minor ones, stand out and captivate the sympathy of the viewers. Danelia and his co-screenwriter, Alexander Volodin, gave the film a retro quality, while dealing with contemporary material relevant to today's society.

A fabricated world may also be conceived as purely aesthetic space. This is the cinematic construction Alexander Sokurov created in *Mother and Son* (1997). Even in those times of economic difficulties for the movie industry, Sokurov remained true to his calling as a film artist and made yet another *film d'auteur* that brought him critical acclaim at home and abroad.[39]

A remote spot on a hilltop, a dilapidated cottage, a dying mother (Gudrun Geyer), and a devoted son (Alexei Ananishnov) constitute the main elements of the film. There is no story, just a situation. As in most of Sokurov's works, the situation reflects the dominant theme of death, treated as an aesthetic category. Sokurov himself made the connection between death and art: "Death is not a theme that is exclusively mine. Death is one of the principal subjects of classical Old World art. . . . For me, Life and Death (more importantly Death) are not quandaries associated with emotional or philosophical attitudes and contexts but are rather questions of art."[40]

In which sense is death a question of art? Even a superficial viewing of Sokurov's films—features as well as documentaries—will convince us that he was not talking about the representation of death as mannerism. Rather, there seems to be a deeper connection in his works, such as the transubstantiation of the human spirit into an aesthetic form. Artistic creation implies death, according to the Apollonian principle. The moment an artistic form is achieved it becomes finite, congealed in its perfection, and ceases to exist as matter in formation. Pier Paolo Pasolini once argued that, in life as in film, it is only with death that one can have a meaningful montage.[41]

In *Mother and Son* the cinematic language conveys the experience of death, aesthetically, as the dissolving of the human body into the pictorial landscape. This is achieved by flattening the image and destroying the illusion of depth; by blurring the edges around the human figures, obliterating the figure-ground effect; and by filming through glass panes at various angles in order to give the subject (nature and humans) the same elongated, undulating shapes (the so called "anamorphic effect").

These techniques are aimed at destroying the realism of the image and creating the artificial environment of oil painting. The scenes when the son carries the mother outside for their last walk, and later when he roams the countryside alone, are memorable visual experiences. Here the lonely figures blend with the fields, trees, hills, and stormy clouds in the glowing sky, all transfigured through the camera eye into a landscape of pure colors and shapes. The sound track emphasizes the aesthetic metamorphosis by mixing human whispers and moans with the sounds of wind, rustling foliage, thunder, and birdcalls.

This is not art for art's sake, though. For both the mother and the son, dying is a most painful experience that affects them, and the viewer, deeply. Neither is there a religious sense, because Sokurov's vision is not a mystical one—"Death is so unjust," the mother says.[42] Rather, the beauty of the image stirs the deepest emotions, and brings the viewer to that higher level of awareness where grief and elation merge into the experience of the sublime. And at that level one can intuitively understand the bond between mother and son not just in terms of human compassion, but as a natural force that links the individual to the whole.

Nightmarish landscapes

Literary settings, the realm of the id, alienation.
Filmmakers with an inclination toward the grotesque did not have to look very far for models. There are some illustrious examples in Russian literature, notably in the works of Gogol and Dostoevsky. The city of St. Petersburg emerged from those works as a spectral landscape, born of an ill-conceived idea that forced Western values on Russian culture—massive granite constructions built on the marshes of the native soil. Even Pushkin, certainly not prone to romantic delusions, introduced St. Petersburg as a nightmarish background in his poem, *The Bronze Horseman*. And the trend continued well into the twentieth century with Bely and Blok. In those literary universes, St. Petersburg acquired surrealist features and became the breeding ground for neurotic people, when not outright freaks and frightening phantoms.

Andrei Eshpai brought to the screen such a place and time encased in the frame of a literary classic. His film version of Dostoevsky's

Faraway in Space and Time 203

28   *Humiliated and Insulted* (1991) directed by Andrei Eshpai

Humiliated and Insulted (1991) succeeded in capturing the spirit of the novel. Eshpai's intent was to connect that time with the present. He saw more than one reason for his choice of Dostoevsky's text. "It was in 1861, the year of the Reform of Alexander II, that Dostoevsky wrote this novel, and it was then that the term 'glasnost' originated," said the director. "I put myself in Dostoevsky's shoes as an artist in the midst of reforms and proceeded from the individual's inner world to the social environment."[43]

Eshpai displays a gift for extracting from his actors the full potential of their dramatic talent. Nastassia Kinski is powerful in the role of the heroine, Natasha, caught in the downward spiral of her pride and voluptuous self-destruction. Nikita Mikhalkov brings to life the grand manner, perverse charm, and cynicism of the devious prince Valkonsky with great acting virtuosity. The rest of the cast creates a gallery of supporting

29   *Humiliated and Insulted* (1991) directed by Andrei Eshpai

characters depicted with unfailing precision—from Valkonsky junior, childish, idealistic, and manipulated by his father, to little orphan Nellie, borrowed by Dostoevsky from the Dickens gallery of characters, to Natasha's devoted friend and unhappy dreamer who narrates the story.

As in most of Dostoevsky's works, the plot has many elements of the potboiler, and the story line is more suggested than enacted. The dramatic strategy relies on the characters' sharp confrontations, intricate relations, and theatrical *coups de scène*. The film successfully reproduces the nightmarish atmosphere, where the St. Petersburg cityscape blends with the characters' psychological set up. The director's best achievement is the translation of Dostoevsky's literary style into a visual medium. Like literary scholar Mikhail Bakhtin, who first noted the "polyphony" of Dostoevsky's prose, Eshpai said that he hears a melody in Dostoevsky's works: "It may be wistful, agonizing, tortured, or, at times, sugary and naive. Still it is a melody. It is the deeply musical structure of the prose which resolves the philosophical contradictions."[44] Once more, I must quote Dostoevsky, and this time more apropos: "It is Beauty which will save the world."

St. Petersburg's spectral landscape is also the setting of Balabanov's

Of Freaks and Men (1999). This is a story populated by monsters. The leader of this ungodly group is a certain Johann (Sergei Makovetsky), of whom little is known besides the fact that he came from the West. It is the turn of the twentieth century; Johann infiltrates the Victorian households of the St. Petersburg bourgeoisie and through deception and blackmail starts a lucrative porno business. He produces piquant photographs of young women being whipped on their bare derrières by a tightlipped *babushka*. Later, he ventures into cinema. Johann is ruthless in his pursuit and does not hesitate to kill in order to protect his business. Little by little the "men" disappear and the scene becomes the domain of the "freaks."

Stylistically the film is a virtuoso tour de force, rendering the atmosphere of the libraries, dining rooms, and boudoirs of a middle class that concealed its Freudian complexes within the walls of apartments smelling of floor wax and eau de cologne. The film's sepia tone parallels the tint of the photographs in Johann's portfolio. Johann found a fertile ground for his business in those secluded abodes, which kept lustful desires under the lid of propriety. Johann's targets are willing victims. Among them is Liza, young and angelic, and fatally given to voyeuristic pleasures. She eventually fulfills her wish to leave for the West when her father disinherits her, and ends up in a brothel in Berlin. Some victims are themselves physical freaks, like the blind wife of a respectful doctor who seeks sexual fulfillment outside of marriage and gets exploited and humiliated; and the Siamese twin brothers, who are linked together in their path to self-destruction.

There are enough elements in the film with the potential for a moral and social critique (the end of an epoch due to the inner weakness of the upper class, which succumbs to an attack from vulgar, proletarian forces), but the critical commentary is deliberately absent. The film does not take a moral stance; it simply presents the facts, maintaining an authorial distance. The intention to focus on the medium, rather than society or psychology, is indicated at the very beginning by a series of period photos of spanking erotica, which run with the credits and are clearly the models for the film's décor and mise en scène. The narrative follows the style of the silent melodrama, with intertitles filling chronological gaps. Balabanov, who briefly returned to cinematic formalism in between two mainstream thrillers, *Brother* and *Brother 2*, makes it a point to avoid moralizing in his works. He shares this trait with the younger generation, which strongly reacted to the imposed code of Soviet morals. But without a moral underpinning, the images that come to the fore are those that Johann creates, without the layer of mediation—sado-masochistic images of human exploitation for the viewer's pleasure; a practice that has always catered to the lower end of the public taste, then as well as now.

In the end, the old world is destroyed and Johann's gang is disbanded. The last shot seems to suggest that Johann is leaving the city after accomplishing his deed (to plant the seed of pornography into filmmaking?). Johann's solitary figure in a long black coat dominates the frame; he is standing on an ice block in the Neva River, floating toward the ocean, while St. Petersburg's cityscape dissolves on the horizon.

Another film dealing with freaks, although in a different key, is Sergei Solovyov's *The House Under the Starry Sky* (1991). The film is a would-be equivalent to David Lynch's postmodernist kitsch, like Solovyov's two previous films (*Assa*, 1988; and *Black Rose Is a Symbol of Sorrow, Red Rose Is a Symbol of Love*, 1989), which together with this one constitute a "perestroika trilogy" in the words of the director.[45] But while Lynch is a master at walking the fine line between the grotesque and the refined, Solovyov disguises a sermon on Holy Russia under a phantasmagoric veneer. The Motherland, under the spell of a Bolshevik Mephistopheles, has produced monsters, freaks, and dwarfs whose only way to salvation is an airplane ticket to New York. The situation is not hopeless, though, as two pure adolescents are able to defeat the demon and float in a balloon over the liberated land. But the lovely couple is just another cliché, which has the same emotional appeal to the viewer as the wooden dolls sold on the Arbat.[46]

While most filmmakers of the old guard were experiencing a creative crisis, Alexander Sokurov kept producing one masterpiece after another at a slow but steady pace. With *Moloch* (1999) he returns once more to the theme of death, but not in the same way as he did in *Mother and Son*. Rather, death is seen here as the corruption of the human spirit—an extreme form of alienation. This film does not fit in the history category, although it purports to present a portrait of Hitler. Its strategy is to involve the viewer in the nightmarish atmosphere surrounding the Fuehrer,

30   *Moloch* (1999) directed by Alexander Sokurov

while exploring the effects of his mind's poisonous emanation. Screenwriter Yuri Arabov said in an interview that he built the character of Hitler from historical documents. For example, the Fuehrer's monologues at the dinner table, which sound like the hallucinations of a madman, come from the notes of Hitler's secretary, Piker, who recorded them word-by-word.[47] But neither screenwriter nor director were interested in history. They were interested in the relationship between Eva Braun (Elena Rufanova) and Hitler (Leonid Mozgovoy), as a study of a victim's submission to the power of evil.

Eva is the leading character and the conceptual focus. Her youthful enthusiasm, exuberant beauty, and athletic body are juxtaposed with the sinister figure of a man who is only the ghost of himself. He is a phantom out of a Gothic horror story, with episodes of grotesque buffoonery. Arabov said that he chose the fortress of Klingsor as a setting to create the atmosphere of the "evil sorcerer's" abode, the realm of "the Antichrist," who in Western European culture is the force that "opposes the Knights of the Round Table," the principle of good. Sokurov creates the Gothic atmosphere that dominated German Expressionist films of the 1920s through the use of vast and empty interiors, dark brownish tones, high-contrast lighting, long shots of the castle emerging from the mist, rumbling thunder behind the clouds, and grand dramatic scores by Beethoven, Mahler and Wagner. In the film, Hitler is the personification of evil, representing its banality rather than its romantic side. As such, he is a mask, not a *dramatis persona*.[48] The drama is Eva's prerogative. In the opening sequence, we are shown the two conflicting forces waging war on the battleground of her soul: an enameled medallion with a swastika on the lid and an image of the Virgin Mary and Baby Jesus inside. She stares at the image, kisses it, then shuts the lid and starts her day with joyous anticipation, and some apprehension, for the arrival of the Fuehrer.

The action covers a one-day span, a brief visit by the Fuehrer to his remote mountain retreat, where he is supposed to find solace from the worries of statesmanship. But neither the surrounding nature nor Eva's company are able to dissipate the dark cloud that seems to accompany him all along, like the shadow of death. He is first seen in a long gray raincoat in which his body disappears. Later, in bed, he's completely covered with a white sheet, projecting the image of a corpse in a shroud. Hitler is obsessed with death, he fears it, and suffers from hypochondria. He wants to exorcise his own death by destroying the lives of others, like an insatiable Moloch devouring his victims. One scene in particular reveals his bent for destruction. Surrounded by his entourage, consisting of Josef Goebbels, Martin Bormann and a couple of SS men, Hitler watches the screening of recent war footage. The camera focuses on his eyes, which gleam in the dark and betray a demented ecstasy at the sight of falling bombs and rolling tanks.

Conversely, Eva is perturbed by that display of violence, steps to another room, and entertains suicidal thoughts, reaching for a small gun that she carries in her purse. Her dilemma is how to reconcile the petty, sadistic nature of the man with her passion for him. Adi, as she calls him, humiliates her intellectually and neglects her physically, being sexually impotent most of the time. In private, he is inept and clumsy; when he sheds his "emperor's clothes," he turns into a comic figure, with socks and garters sticking out of his oversized boxers—an obvious Chaplinesque quotation. Eva sees his true nature, but decides to ignore the evidence. She resolves the dilemma with an act of total submission. She tells him: "Do you know what my dad told me in 1929, when we met? 'This young man is an absolute zero.' Now, we know that he was dead wrong. You got the better not only of him, but also of millions of others. But even if you were a zero, so what? Would this change anything in our relationship, in my feelings for you? I would still love you with all your weaknesses."[49]

In the course of one day, we watch Eva's transition from life to death. Early in the morning, Eva steps out on the fortress walls that dominate the deep valley below. She is naked; she breathes in the chilly air, and starts a gymnastic routine, graceful and vigorous at the same time. The mist from the valley has risen to the level of the terrace, and Eva's figure seems to be dancing on a cloud. Her white, sinuous body stands out against the granite wall, contrasting in color and texture—a live creature against inert matter. Some witnesses from a mountain peak facing the castle enjoy this vision on a less symbolic level. Eva is shown through the viewfinders of the security forces patrolling the zone. The soldiers show their appreciation for her athletic body with lewd comments, to which she responds with a mocking gesture. This scene, at the beginning of the film, establishes Eva as a healthy, natural creature, a corporeal being, as opposed to her ghost-lover. But her gusto for life turns into a death wish at the end of that day with the Fuehrer.

In the wee hours, the guests are about to leave. Eva is close to a nervous breakdown, as she rushes to the lower courtyard to say good-bye. The camera follows her descent; first she runs down the stairs, then she gets into an elevator, which plunges down the shaft. The movement of this scene is opposite to the movement of the opening scene. While at the beginning the vertical dynamism pointed to the sky, at the end it points to the underground. It's a fall into hell.[50] Taking leave, Hitler comes up to Eva, holds her hand, and says: "The most delicate thing on earth—beauty. What can match the power of this delicate thing? As long as you're alive, I'm alive." But the last sequence suggests the opposite—Hitler's deadly emanation has poisoned everything and everybody around as a contagious disease, including Eva. In this case, the Beauty could not save the Beast. And, in the lines that seal the film, Eva tells him so, with sadness and tender condescension: "Adi, how can you say that? Death is death. No one can conquer it."

When the glasnost period began in full swing, around 1987, Kira Muratova made a triumphal return to the studios. Having been ostracized for twenty years because of a couple of unorthodox films she directed in the late sixties, she regained her rightful place in the community of filmmakers, and proceeded with the production of a picture that became an immediate source of controversy, even in the new times. *Asthenic Syndrome* (1990) was a naturalistic collage of disjointed episodes depicting the contemporary Soviet reality as a violent, inhuman society on the brink of a nervous collapse.[51]

After a brief parenthesis of cautious optimism, as shown in the *Sentimental Policeman* (1992), Muratova returned to her early theme with renewed intensity. Two of her films in particular, *Passions* (1994) and *Three Stories* (1997), bring to the screen an unforgiving portrait of human regression back to the instinctual stage. Muratova found the perfect protagonist for her stylized world of brutish relations and refined appearances in the persona of Renata Litvinova, the celebrated diva of the nineteen-nineties Moscow cultural elite. Litvinova was first of all a writer of short stories and a screenwriter, who had enjoyed some success since her student days at VGIK. Her short stories served as the basis for segments of Muratova's films. Litvinova's novellas have been compared to the works of Ludmila Petrushevskaya, who in the late 1980s was considered a feminist writer, although she always rejected that label. Litvinova pushed the theme of woman's empowerment to an absurd degree, turning her heroines into implacable avengers. This played well in the hands of Muratova, who used that hyperbolic element to stress the end of the patriarchal discourse that informed the Soviet world. But the feminist theme was not Muratova's central concern, as we will see. The collaboration with Muratova propelled Litvinova to the status of movie star. However, after her fame reached the peak with *Passions* and *Three Stories*, her star began to decline. The nineties closed with Litvinova out of the picture.[52]

Passions consists of a series of vignettes without logical connections, which include two basic settings: a seaside hospital and the hippodrome. Mise-en-scène and editing break up and rearrange these spaces in a surreal way. Tableaux of emerald green lawns and sunny beaches, where nurses in starched white uniforms wheel around injured jockeys from the racetrack, are intercut with scenes at the races, where the camera lingers with aesthetic enjoyment on the horses, closing up on their sinuous bodies full of energy and grace.

31 *Passions* (1994) directed by Kira Muratova

Two young women provide some unity to the narrative structure, at the same time stressing the tone of mischievous mockery pervasive of the whole film. Violetta (Svetlana Kolenda) is a circus performer with a passion for horses. She seems to be at home at the racetrack, but she looks misplaced on the hospital grounds, where she is visiting a recovering jockey. In both places she wears incongruous clothes — a white tutu at the races, and clownish outfits at the hospital — adding still another absurdist element to a world whose verisimilitude is being severely challenged. Lilia (Renata Litvinova) is a nurse, perfectly at home on the hospital grounds in her immaculate uniform. But when she goes to the races in a black sequined dress, she is a misfit; she does not belong in an environment pulsating with sensuous energy. In fact, Lilia has a passion for corpses, and at the hospital she recites endless monologues filled with a necrophiliac fascination with the morgue. Her morbid fixation with death has an erotic component, indicated by coded signs that contrast with her aseptic uniform, such as a colorful folk shawl, tall black boots, and a front slit up to the crotch.

Although the script is by Muratova, Litvinova wrote those monologues herself.[53] The dissonance between the content of the monologues and the way Litvinova delivers them, in the mannerism of the "dumb blonde" à la Monroe, has the effect of making the audience burst out with laughter. At the end of the film, after delivering one such monologue, Litvinova states that, "Diamonds are a girl's best friends." But the discrepancy here is not just a comedic expedient. It is a distancing device, which brings to the fore the absurdity of life and death. In Muratova's created world without transcendence, death is not only inevitable; it is terminal. To couple it with Eros is an attempt to neutralize it.

This concern, which was expressed in light tones in *Passions*, acquires a sinister coloration in *Three Stories*. The stories in question are: "Boiler Room No. 6," "Ophelia," from a novella by Litvinova, and "The Little Girl and Death."[54] All of them involve a murder—two in the case of "Ophelia"—which is committed for trivial reasons and presented as a matter of fact, without any psychological probing of the killer's motive. In "Boiler Room," the assassin (Sergei Makovetsky) murders his communal apartment neighbor because she got on his nerves; as he explains, she used to walk around naked and, in addition, she would leave her hairs sticking to the soap bar in the bathroom, which he found disgusting. He, therefore, slashed her throat with a blunt object. We do not see the murder, we only see the result: the body of the victim in a makeshift coffin. It is a beautiful woman; her white body, disfigured by a grotesque gash on the neck, looks like a wax museum horror exhibit. "Boiler Room" is shot in the Grand Guignol style, and its black humor is intended to provoke laughter. The viewer laughs. There are, however, deeper implications. The boiler room venue carries connotations of Vulcan's cave, and a homosexual bordello in the back room seems to have been borrowed from Fellini's *Satyricon*. These allusions to a pagan civilization fit the overarching theme of the three stories, as it becomes clear in the course of the film. It should be noted that the boiler room is not a metaphor for hell, because it is devoid of connotations of sin and retribution. The stoker is very upset by the murderer's request to burn the corpse, and states repeatedly that the "technology" is not suitable for that purpose, and that this is not a place for the dead.

At the core of the film's conception is the power of bestial instincts in the human being, which are normally concealed under a veneer of civilization but ready to resurface when the social conditions allow. In the story "Ophelia," a set of motifs alludes to Greek antiquity and the degeneration of the Platonic idea of beauty. The corruption of beauty and the triumph of the beast are expressed through the eponymous heroine. Litvinova again plays the role of a hospital worker, this time an archivist. Like the previous nurse, she too is a necrophiliac, who declares she feels a special attraction to the dead Ophelia in Shakespeare's play. Opha, for short, is a cold-blooded murderess, seeking revenge against her mother who gave her up to the orphanage as an infant. The theme of the degradation of beauty starts with the degradation of her name; the melodious sound of Ophelia is truncated into a dull, disyllabic thump.

Opha has two goals: to reach an orgasm, which she never did in her life, and to kill her mother. In the pursuit of these goals, she has a relationship with a gynecologist from the hospital, which does not produce the desired effect, and she coldly murders a maternity ward patient who gave her baby up for adoption. Opha strangles her with a nylon stocking in an empty hallway. In the end, she achieves both her goals at once. She drowns her old mother in the Black Sea, and as a result she experiences an orgasm.[55]

Throughout the episode, Opha is associated with two sets of signs: signs that connote classical aesthetic perfection, and others that connote a decaying materialistic world. Her facial features seem to be chiseled in alabaster. An Ionic capital pops up here and there out of context to accentuate the classical paradigm, and Opha's finger establishes a connection with it by smoothly tracing its spiral volutes. These images are intercut with cheap abstract art and pseudo-folk pictures stressing materialistic themes, which hang from the walls of an artist's studio where Opha sleeps with the gynecologist. At the hospital, Opha is seen against a background of white sculptures and neoclassical colonnades. But when she goes out on her killing spree, she is surrounded by decaying structures and miserable people. The visual style of "Ophelia" is surrealist, stressing incongruity and alienation. It is intended to provoke an amused, skeptical reaction. The viewer is baffled, and grins skeptically.

The third story, "The Little Girl and Death," is the most disturbing of the three, because of the relationship it establishes with the viewer. The distancing effects Muratova creates and maintains in the first two stories dissipate in the last one. This story is shot in a realistic style, with some gruesome naturalistic details. Perhaps it was intended to repulse the viewer—and in many ways it does. But, in the end, the viewer empathizes with the old man that gets murdered, and at that moment the distancing effect is lost. This happens mainly because of the performance of Oleg Tabakov, a product of the great dramatic tradition of the Russian theater and cinema, who brings to this role the human dimension that was removed from the rest of the film. The episode consists of one scene. An old man confined to his wheelchair is babysitting the six-year-old neighbor's daughter. The girl gets tired of hearing the word, *"nyelzyá"* ("you can't") in response to her wishes—you can't go out, you can't take off your clothes, and so on—and decides to get rid of her guardian. She, very calculatingly, puts rat poison in his drinking water. When he begins to writhe in agony, she cheerfully leaves the house chanting, *"nyelzyá, nyelzyá, nyelzyá . . ."*

The theme of classical antiquity in this episode is not obvious, although the mise en scène conveys the flavor of a Mediterranean house, with a large terrace surrounded by trees. Rather, allusions to a pagan civilization are here related to witchcraft and sorcery. At one point, the girl takes off her clothes and parades in the nude with a string of colored beads around her neck. There is nothing playful in this prank, which is coded to connote her as witch. She is also seen interacting with a black cat, and spinning two tops—magic tools with life and death power. The camera establishes a visual analogy between the girl spinning the tops and the old man peeling an apple in a long, continuous spiral movement, which ends with his death.[56]

These are not casual images. There are no superfluous details in Muratova's rigorous structure. For all its disjointed appearance, the film has an ironclad inner coherence. The references to pre-Christian worlds connote an era of crude human relations and hedonistic pleasures, devoid of the concepts of sin and transcendence—an era of materialist values that has made a come back in most of the contemporary industrialized societies. From here, Muratova's vision is retrospective. She does not see a further stage of development on the Hegelian path of evolution. Rather, she sees devolution, a regression of the human being to the animal status. Being a child of the Soviet era, Muratova reacts to the official utopian ideology that was imposed on society by turning it upside down. But her concerns are broader than ideology, and encompass fundamental humanistic questions.

References to animal instincts and behavior are consistent throughout the film and culminate in the opening shots of "Little Girl." These are extremely gruesome images of a cat savagely gnawing on a chicken carcass. The sequence is very long—4 minutes of cinematic time, with imperceptible cuts between shots. These images, accompanied by the cat's wild cries, generate a physical sense of nausea. We do not feel sorry for the chicken, or angry at the cat, we feel disgusted with the grossness of the natural process. We are repulsed by the mirror that shows us the nature of our reptilian brain. We laughed at the Grand Guignol murder, we skeptically grinned at Opha's provocations, and we gasped in horror at the little girl's callousness. But it is the grim attack on the chicken that brings all those actions together and points to the beast that lies under the veneer of civilization developed through the centuries.

It is not easy to like Muratova's films. After a trip in the absurd and the surreal, the realism/naturalism of the last episode bring us back home, to this day and age. Muratova does not project the terminal stage on the path of regression into the future, but tells us that we are already there. The beast has resurfaced. Even if one does not agree with Muratova's pessimistic view of mankind, one must concede that she makes her case in a compelling way through her mastery of the cinematic medium.

Soviet dystopias

Steel icons, mythmaking, the lower depths.
A film with great potential, which was not fully developed, is *Children of the Iron Gods* (1993). The film marks the debut of director Tomasz Tot, with a script by Pyotr Lutsik and Alexander Samoryadov.[57] The son of a Hungarian diplomat, Tot grew up in Moscow and graduated from the State Film Institute. His film strikes the viewer as a sophisticated work, rooted in cinema history and sustained by a keen understanding of the nature of the moving image; it displays conceptual freshness and a daring approach to filmmaking.

Tot and the two screenwriters are part of a group that can be called "the 1990s new wave." Most of them gravitated around the Gorky Studio, which launched or facilitated their careers through an initiative designed to finance films by young directors.[58] This new wave had two primary objectives, to demystify the cultural stereotypes that constituted the mythology of the Soviet state, and to establish new myths through the creation of new cinematic spaces. The tone of these films may vary, some are overtly ironic, satirizing the idea of Sovietness; others are absurdist with a touch of humor; still others pretend to be serious but undermine their seriousness with hyperbole. Whatever the case may be, the new wave directors appropriated the sacred icons of the Soviet past in order to extricate them from the historical context, neutralize them, and use them anew as the basis for the epos of their time. It was both rejection and recognition of the common heritage.[59]

The pioneers of this approach in the fine arts, Komar and Melamid, amazed audiences abroad some twenty years ago with their works. Their paintings had a Magritte-like quality in a surrealist pictorial Soviet space, and went down in art history as "sotsart." Those paintings were banned in the Soviet Union, but many underground artists practiced the genre, and many people appreciated their humor and admired their courage. One of the first liberating gestures in the new Russia was the installation of a "sotsart" exhibition at the Central Lenin Museum on Revolution Square, in June 1992. There, images such as Lenin declaring that "Coca Cola is the real thing" by A. Kosolapov, now publicly displayed, marked the end of "sotsart" as political opposition and the beginning of its role as historical artifact.

In *Children of the Iron Gods*, the action takes place in a gigantic metallurgical plant in an unnamed town in the Urals, surrounded by the vastness of the steppe. The time is vaguely coded as the late 1930s, and suggests the alienating atmosphere of a dystopian world. The men working at the plant are as massive and tough as the environment; they seem to have been born of the plant's huge belly of iron and fire. The film's aesthetics give the story a mythological dimension. The workers are larger-than-life figures, exiled to a place that stifles their powers. Their energy is not exhausted at the end of the working day, and they look for an outlet to their frustration in fist fights, women, booze, and daredevil ventures into the wilderness of the steppe. Among them, is young Ignat Morozov (Evgeny Sidikhin), a cross between the mythical Slavic hero, the *bogatyr*, and the Stalinist bronze effigy of the idealized worker. He is impressive in his might, and endearing in his child-like innocence. A cinematic model for Ignat is the hero of *The Communist* (Gabrilovich and Raizman, 1957), played by Evgeny Urbansky. That hero displayed the same cast-iron figure as Sidikhin, but in that case his sculptured features were meant to be the true mirror of his inner self, rather than a cultural icon.

From the aesthetic point of view, Tot and cameraman Sergei Kozlov pay homage to the directors of the past, going back to the Golden Age of Soviet cinema. They adopted Eisenstein's grand epic style, Dziga Vertov's glorified imagery of technological structures, and Pudovkin's sweeping charge of Mongol warriors on horseback. At the same time, they criticize the ideology that such a style implied, by giving it a surrealist slant. The film subtitle tells us that this is an "ironic epos," and a commercial advertisement presents the film as a "tragi-farcical story about the mysterious Russian soul, the Russian expanse, and adventure."[60] Memorable is the skirmish in the winter landscape, in which three Russians subjugate a whole Bashkirian tribe. The scene is romantically staged but it is undermined by humor. The confrontation is triggered by a prank, where the Russians steel a couple of sheep from the village and then use a cannon-like contraption to defend their prey.

Inspiration from American cinema is also prominently displayed. A breathtaking train robbery by a pack of Russian horsemen, whom Ignat had joined for the occasion, is a fond acknowledgment of the Hollywood western. But as in the episode with the Bashkirians, there is no material motivation for this action; the men are ready to kill and die for sheer fun and adventure. The camera deflates the heroic theme after the robbery, showing Ignat as he carries home his booty that consists of four pathetic metal chairs. The following shot reinforces the surrealist vein: Ignat pauses, puts down one chair and takes a seat; he rests for a few seconds, his back turned to the camera, dwarfed by the immensity of the snowy expanse, watching the mighty skyline of the factory compound on the misty horizon; then, gets up, picks up the chair and throws it up in the air with a nonchalant gesture; finally, he resumes his walk, leaving behind four metal skeletons that clash incongruously with the solemn landscape.

32 *Children of the Iron Gods* (1993) directed by Tomasz Tot

The soundtrack is remarkable, encumbered by a cacophony of machine-generated noises that suffocate the human voice. Conversations are sparse and haphazard. The machines roar with the visceral voice of primordial beasts. This connotation is reinforced visually through camera movements and angles that animate the metal structures, transforming them into fire-spitting monsters—or gods. Ignat is first seen dangling from a crane, "flying" over the domain of the machine, battling and subduing the elements: iron, fire, and the boiling water where the steel is tempered.

One episode of the film glorifies the steel's superior quality and, by association, Ignat as the man of steel. An unnamed army general visits the plant to conduct a test, consisting of firing a state-of-the-art heavy projectile into a steel slab to verify its piercing capacity. The general maintains that his weapon is able to penetrate the factory's steel. The factory director swears to the resilience of his product. These two characters, perched on a makeshift wooden tower, observe the experiment with binoculars, bickering with each other like Laurel and Hardy,[61] while down on the ground, Ignat gives a daring demonstration of his confidence in the superior quality of the factory steel—and one more proof of his gusto for bravado. He plays a sort of Russian roulette by placing himself behind the steel slab, seconds before the cannon is fired. As expected the steel is bulletproof, having been highly tempered, just as Ignat's character.[62]

And yet, Ignat is also capable of being sweet and tender on a primitive, instinctual level. When he is in a romantic mood, he does not have the words to express his feelings. "*Khochu babu*" ("I want a broad"), he says, and walks down the pier to the shed that hosts the local bordello. His favorite girl comes out, and he engages in a sort of delicate courtship, which the camera records in a discrete way, mainly through long shots softened by the blurring mist that rises from the river. The scene has the natural beauty of a ritual mating game. The analogy with the animal kingdom is then extended throughout the next sequence, when Ignat's mood changes from love to fury. Enraged by the presence of a rival male; he grabs the woman and throws her across his shoulder the way he did the sheep in an early episode; when he gets to the crowded canteen, he throws her to the men as if they were a pack of wolves.

Children of the Iron Gods has no plot; rather it is a series of episodes that ultimately lead nowhere, like the lives of the men who work at the plant. Each episode is an outburst of sort, like a fired bullet; each has its own climax, which is eventually deflated. The last episode is a boxing match between Ignat and a gigantic Bashkirian by the name of Bikbulatka. The factory champion declined to fight in order to put forward the younger contender. It is an initiation for Ignat. Co-workers and challengers seem to attach great importance to the match, but the motives are unclear since there is no reward for the winner. It is a ritual, which they perform periodically. Symbolically, it reiterates the theme of confrontation between East and West, the iron civilization encroaching on the Asian steppe. The two contenders fight brutally and impassively, with bare hands. Ignat wins, although at a disadvantage given his young age and lack of experience. But he almost gets killed in the process. The last shot of his bloody face reminds us of similar battered heroes, such as *Rocky* or *Raging Bull*. But in Ignat's case, the victory offers no closure; rather, the suggestion that this is the end of just another episode and that the next day life will resume as usual. For all their bravado, Ignat and his comrades are not in charge of their lives; they are the puppets of the elusive masters—the army general and the political apparatus behind him—who control the realm of the "iron gods."

In the 1980s, a number of films dealt with the Stalinist period, exposing the dreadful results of the dictator's political folly. The first was *Repentance*, which satirized the tyrant in a carousel of grotesque imagery, and marked the beginning of the era of glasnost.[63] These films focused on the ugly face of the regime. In the new era, *Prorva* (1992) by Ivan Dykhovichny was the first film to focus on its aesthetics.[64] The Russian word *prorva* expresses the horror of nothingness, and has no equivalent in English. It has, therefore, been replaced with the more mundane title, *Moscow Parade*. Seemingly contradictory, the two titles are actually the two faces of the same reality, an illusion of beauty and grandeur covering up an existential chasm.

The "horror of nothingness" is suggested in the film through the compelling cinematography of Vadim Yusov, the choice of props and design, and the acting of a superior cast. One of the protagonists is Moscow herself, her image reproducing the postcard aesthetics of the time. The Kremlin is neatly reflected in the river; metro and railway stations dazzle the passengers with their mosaics and marble bas-reliefs; the gilded fountains of the Exhibition of Economic Achievements, and the pretentious baroque skyscrapers that punctuate the Moscow landscape, testify to the magnificence of the empire. Posters and monuments of the period reinforce the glossy kitsch. The year is 1939, and the atmosphere is decadent, marking the peak of the curve and the beginning of the fall.

"I'm looking for the meaning of the word *prorva*. It's the title of my

33 *Moscow Parade* (1992) directed by Ivan Dykhovichny

new story," says a handsome young writer, who is under NKVD surveillance. "*Prorva* is vague: abyss, chasm, but not quite. The story is about what's going on in Russia. What people fear is nonexistent, it's a nothing. But this nothing sucks in and kills people. Like a *prorva*," he says.[65] Like the writer, most of the characters are young, beautiful, and elegant—secret service officers, military brass, a lawyer, a prima ballerina, and the Commissar of Culture who is a fanatic activist and an expectant mother. They are socialites moving with ease in the refined apartments of the party elite, on exclusive yachts, and in private nightclubs. They know how to put on a public image and how to wear the mask of happiness and success. But the tension in their glances, the forced expression of their *joie de vivre*, the studiousness of their gestures and poses betray to the viewer that this is life as fiction.

Anna, a cabaret performer, played by German actress Ute Lemper with the velvety sensuality of a Marlene Dietrich, renounces the prevailing social pretense. Disgusted with her alcoholic, impotent husband, and with her sadistic lover, both members of the NKVD and part of Stalin's entourage, she takes refuge in the proletarian arms of Gosha, a muscled railroad porter. Evgeny Sidikhin is a perfect Gosha—this young giant does not even have to act, he *is* the role. Love between Anna and Gosha seems possible, but communication is not. Anna gets almost killed during a quarrel that she provoked, and the unfortunate hulk ends up in the Lubyanka dungeons. As expected, most of the members of the fashionable social circle meet their tragic destiny in a final police round up.

The film form itself is a *prorva*. The editing consists of short takes and abrupt jump cuts that deny the viewer the comfort of a logical, sequential narrative. Narrative and characters are subordinated to the picture's stylized aesthetics. The characters convey the feeling of being "on stage" all the time, even in their most intimate, dramatic moments, which deprives the viewer of emotional participation. *Prorva* refers to well-known pictures of the 1930s; first among them, the greatest box-office success of all times, *Circus*. The wondrous Moscow cityscape; the grand piano by the picture window, accompanying the romance of the two lovers; the dazzling street parade of gymnasts, workers, and flag-waving youth are obvious quotations from the old film. But, while in the old picture these images were perceived as substance, in *Prorva* they are exposed as mere simulacra.[66]

The theme of mythmaking concludes the film. A dream sequence shows Anna back in the cabaret. A black eye patch, a result of the beating she received from Gosha, crosses her beautiful face. She sings a song in French; it is a call to her lover: "It is a melody, a souvenir./It is a portrait of you, which I want to keep./Close your eyes, my darling,/let the world be silent./Dance with me one last time, my love." And Gosha appears in a tuxedo, and smiling moves towards her.

Hammer and Sickle (Sergei Livnev, 1994) is also set in the 1930s, at the peak of the Stalinist power, but is not concerned with the upper classes. Its focus is on the workers. Instead of playing with glamour and the illusions it conjures, Livnev's film plays with horror. The imagery has Gothic connotations. Following an order by Stalin to increase the pool of male recruits, a sex-change experiment is performed on an unsuspecting woman. The operation is successful, but because of a change of policy the experiment is abandoned. The young new man, Evdokim Kuznetsov (Alexei Serebryakov), left to his own devices, becomes a construction

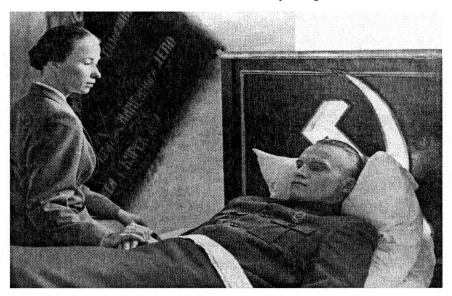

34   *Hammer and Sickle* (1994) directed by Sergei Livnev

worker in one of the grand projects of the regime, the Moscow metro. He distinguishes himself among the Stakhanovite brigades and rises to the top. There, he enjoys the perks of a worker-hero, which include an elegant apartment, fashion clothes, a convertible car, and a wife who matches his celebrity status, being herself a farmer-heroine. In fact, the popular couple is selected to serve as a model for the monumental sculpture by Vera Mukhina, *The Worker and the Collective Farmer*, which greets the visitors to the Exhibition of Economic Achievements.[67] This film is, in a way, the Russian counterpart to Wajda's *Man of Marble* (1976), which deconstructed the myth of the workers' paradise. The celebrity status comes to Evdokim with many strings attached, all summed up in the assumption of a persona that reflects the requirements of the state. When he rebels against this state of affairs, violently confronting Stalin, he is shot. But not killed.

With Evdokim paralyzed from the neck down and unable to speak, the state can continue to spin the myth of the worker-hero now turned writer.[68] Visually, the film switches from the parody of Stakhanovite icons to the parody of the Lenin Mausoleum. Evdokim is shown in his house-museum as a living mummy, lying on a bed decorated with the hammer and sickle logo. Tour guides extol his virtues to groups of schoolchildren and foreign delegations of communist functionaries and fellow writers. Evdokim is now a celebrity in the literary world because, as the legend goes, he wrote an autobiography, *Hammer and Sickle*, that went through 170 editions; there, he described how he saved Stalin from an enemy's bullet, covering the father of the people with his own body. Evdokim suffers these, and other, abuses—such aggressive sex on the part of his wife—with impotent rage, expressed only through the movement of his eyes. In the final chilling scene, he is shot again by a schoolboy, who gets carried away while acting out a scenario on the struggle against the enemies of the people. The last close up shows that Evdokim's eyes remain open and alert, perhaps suggesting that he has passed into the realm of the living dead—the ghosts that keep returning, such as Stalin and Lenin. In any case, *Hammer and Sickle* drives the definitive nail in his coffin.[69]

Scientific Section of Pilots (Andrei I, 1996) is another film that dismantles a prime symbol of the Soviet state, the Moscow metro. To do so, the director chose not to go back to the days in which the metro gleamed in all its glory, but to set the action in the present time, focusing on the decay of the infrastructure. In this thriller, the Moscow metro is being terrorized by a mysterious killer. The police are being put on the alert by warning signs—drops of blood dripping from a chandelier, and an abandoned suitcase full of bloody meat—but they are unable to prevent the murders that follow. Confusing sequences and images suggest the confusion of the police and the special forces assigned to the case. The chief investigators and metro authorities speak and move like automatons, repeating empty sentences, performing routine gestures, with fixed glazed eyes. This mechanic style of acting is reinforced with frequent shots of computer screens showing error warnings, jammed electric circuits, entangled graphs, crisscrossing tunnel maps. At times the frame goes black for a few seconds. Most of the film is shot in the dark tunnels, rather than in the glowing stations. And when the latter are shown, the camera does not linger on the vestige of the original glory, but on the signs of decay.

In Soviet times, the state maintained the Moscow metro like a shrine, celebrating the idea of the workers' paradise. The hallowed icons of workers and farmers, in bronze, marble, and mosaic, testified to the pride of the people. The panoramic landscapes of magnificent crops and mighty factories glorified their achievements. When the myth crumbled, those images lost their gleam—symbolically and literally. An army of *babushki* that used to keep those halls spick-and-span lost their jobs. The friendly *militisia*, who made those places safe to passengers even in the wee hours, were assigned to other duties. The people became concerned with unsafe trains, malfunctioning escalators, and rampant crime. The metro underpasses turned into shady bazaars and a haven for beggars and the homeless. As a Russian film scholar wrote, "the would-be communist paradise turned into post-communist hell."[70] *Scientific Section* conveys the notion that hell had always existed behind the facade.

Notwithstanding the deterioration of the infrastructure, the Moscow metro in the mid 1990s still had trains running every 85 seconds and operated its escalators at the speed of 0.9 meters per second (twice as fast as our American escalators). It also carried about nine million people daily (average daily volume in New York is three million) for a fare of 600 rubles (about $0.12). For 56 years before price liberalization, the fare had been a mere *pyatachok* (5 kopeks). Even with the increase, metro travel was still subsidized by about 90 percent.[71] I used metro on occasions, although not as the main means of transportation, because it was too crowded and I felt claustrophobic. I had reason for that, especially after the accident.

On that day, I inched my way to the up escalator, squeezed in a human cluster. On the steps, people were standing back-to-back and shoulder-to-shoulder. Before me was a big woman, blocking the way completely with two large bags and a heavy bundle. As we got to the top, she tripped and fell, and this caused a domino effect with those behind her piling up on top of each other. I found myself at the bottom of the pile, unable to move. Fortunately, nobody got hurt, and in a matter of seconds all got up and left. Someone helped the big woman to her feet and picked up her stuff. But I could not get up. The escalator had not stopped, and my long coat had been caught in the gears under the top edge. I looked with horror as the coat was slowly getting swallowed, pulling me in that direction—I felt like someone sitting on quicksand. The stream of passengers that kept coming up stepped around me with surprising swiftness. Everybody was shouting to the operator to stop the escalator. It stopped.

A nice gentleman came to my rescue. I was now standing, watching as he was pulling my coat out. It had been badly chewed up, and the lower half looked like spaghetti. I wanted to abandon it, but the nice gentleman insisted on carrying it for me, and taking my arm he appointed himself my escort. We boarded a train. I was thinking of the most efficient way to get rid of both the coat and the nice gentleman, as it became clear that he intended to escort me all the way to my bedroom. He talked non-stop; what he was saying, apart from his gallant advances, actually got my attention. "Such a fine coat, it's a pity. These things did not happen before. I mean, before the democrats ruined our country. I'm ashamed when foreigners, like you, come to Moscow and see this level of degradation. The whole city is a bazaar, speculators all over, they call it free market; and the people are starving. But, believe me, before we were a great country. Then, Gorbachev betrayed us. These scoundrels in the government are bad enough, but Gorbachev started it. He is to be blamed for everything." I heard enough. The train stopped at a station. As the doors were closing, I jumped out, leaving behind the nice gentleman with his bitter thoughts.

I ran the short distance home because it was quite cold, thinking along the way that I should send the bill for my lost coat to Gorbachev.

War theaters

The Afghan theater, the Chechen theater.
War films create two basic types of cinematic spaces, those that glorify the war as an expression of the national power, and those that denounce the war as a destructive adventure. The USSR produced hundreds of films on WW II, which at first reflected the nationalistic approach and later, since the late 1950s, moved toward the humanistic one.[72] The more recent wars—in Afghanistan and in Chechnya—have not inspired many filmmakers in the 1990s. The few, who tackled the subject continued in the humanistic mode.

A few documentaries, denouncing the callous treatment of the Afghan veterans back home appeared in the period of glasnost, even before the

Faraway in Space and Time 227

end of the conflict. Allusions to that war were included in some films—for example, at the end of *Courier* (Shakhnazarov, 1987). Later, the Afghan war was used as background in *The Muslim*. The only full-length feature film on the subject, *Peshawar Waltz*, was released in 1993 and presented at the Moscow Film Festival.[73] At the time, it attracted some attention because of the controversial subject and the entrepreneurial way in which it was produced. However, it did not find a distributor, either in Russia or abroad. The film was the result of the work of three young men, screenwriter and director Timur Bekmambetov, co-director Gennady Kayumov, and Dmitri Yurkov, head of the production company Iskona Film which he founded in 1990. Bekmambetov said that they wanted to make a statement about "a pivotal moment in the life of our generation."[74] The film was shot in Kazakhstan on a shoestring budget provided by a private sponsor. *Peshawar Waltz* was eventually purchased by the American company New Concorde and released on DVD in 2002, with the title *Escape from Afghanistan*. The American release was re-edited and re-dubbed to change the nationality of the two main characters. In the original, the protagonists were a British journalist and a French doctor from the organization *Médecins sans Frontières*; in the U.S. version, they are both American. Considering the fact that the video was released after 9/11, the change seems to be meant to enhance the image of the Americans in their war in Afghanistan.

The film combines special effect battle scenes with realistic elements. Black-and-white documentary footage of Soviet soldiers relating their experiences are incorporated in the script, and veterans of the war play several characters. A non-professional actor (Barry Kushner from Liverpool, who was a social worker in Kazakhstan) plays the role of the protagonist, TV journalist Charlie Palmer. Palmer and his companion, doctor Victor Davis (Viktor Verbitski), bribed their way into a mujahedin camp on the Pakistani border to interview Soviet POWs. Soon they find themselves in the middle of a prisoners' uprising, in which violence erupts mercilessly on both sides. The Americans remain trapped with the Soviet insurgents in the underground, which is eventually transformed in a flaming inferno. Violence and moral outrage climax in the last scene, where Soviet helicopters attack the surviving POWs in order to cover up Pakistan's involvement in the war. One soldier shouts to the choppers: "They betrayed us, goddamit, they betrayed us. You, sonsabitches, why did you do that to us? You knew it the whole time. I can't believe you betrayed us. You, bastards." Palmer is able to escape, while everybody else perishes in the action. But the shock from the tragedy is too much for him, and he ends up shooting himself. His last words: "I collect images, you see. And I try not to let them get to me. But sometimes they do—the destruction of men for convenience's sake. It's universal; I've seen it everywhere I worked. I've seen so much. I don't even want to talk about it anymore." Implicit in these last reflections is the awareness of the reporter's responsibility in gathering images. Where to draw the line between recording reality to provide information and exploiting events for personal gratification and professional gain? But, notwithstanding its good intentions, the film is rather amateurish. Its best part are the action scenes, which are spectacular and gripping.

The first feature on the Chechen war, *Prisoner of the Mountains* (Sergei Bodrov, Sr., 1996), came out one year from the beginning of the conflict.[75] In this film, the war itself remains off screen, but its reality weighs heavily on the people involved and their relationships. A group of rebels attacks a Russian patrolling unit and takes two surviving soldiers into captivity. The two prisoners are kept under lock and key in the barn of Abdul-Murat, the patriarch of a Muslim village. They are to be exchanged for Abdul-Murat's son who is held in a Russian camp. But in the end the plan fails, with tragic consequences for both sides. Sasha Kostylin (Oleg Menshikov), a seasoned officer with a cynical outlook, and Vania Zhilin (Sergei Bodrov, Jr.), a new recruit still innocent of killing, develop a buddy relationship, notwithstanding their disagreement on how to approach the natives. While Kostylin works at gaining their captors' trust in order to plot an escape, Zhilin establishes friendly contacts with the local people and begins to feel a deep affection for Abdul-Murat's daughter. But the endless chain of violence and retaliation prevents any possibility of love. Abdul-Murat's son is killed in a fight with the prison guards, Kostylin is tracked down and killed in revenge, and Zhilin's life is spared only because the old patriarch does not have the heart to raise his hand against him. The last scene is an ominous reminder that the war continues. A squadron of Russian MIG fighters appears on the horizon and gradually expands to fill the screen like a smothering blanket, as it approaches the mountain village.[76]

The film is based on Leo Tolstoy's story *The Prisoner of the Caucasus*

35 *Prisoner of the Mountains* (1996) directed by Sergei Bodrov, Sr.

(*Kavkazskii plennik*) written in the mid 1800s, which portrays an episode of the deeply ingrained enmity between the Russian conquerors and the local population.⁷⁷ Contrary to the official policy of imperialist conquest, Tolstoy showed deep sympathy for the natives. As a veteran the Crimean war, he knew the realities of combat first-hand; he had also traveled extensively in the Caucasus and was fascinated by the local customs and village life. This was just another facet of his belief that civilization corrupts, and that the truth resides in the simple folk. Bodrov's interpretation of the conflict echoes Tolstoy's idealization of the "noble savage," and reflects a post-imperialist sensibility and an approach that recognizes common human values beyond ethnic and cultural diversity. Soviet pictures, even those that favored the individual rather than the state, have never portrayed the enemy with the slightest bit of sympathy. Ideologically, this is a new film. Aesthetically, however, it is not. It remains within the tradition of the Soviet war movie genre, with a solid script, logical motivations, well-defined characters' psychology, clear-cut values, and a cinematography that supports the narrative and stirs the emotions.

The shooting was done on location, in Daghestan, and the director exploited the beauty of the surroundings and the spontaneity of local non-professional actors, extracting from them their natural potential. He also cast his own son in his first film role, and placed him opposite Oleg Menshikov, one of the most prominent stars of the decade. For Sergei Bodrov, Jr. this was a stepping-stone. Eventually, he achieved popular acclaim in his next films, *Brother* and *Brother 2*, before being killed in a tragic accident. It is a bitter irony that in real life he became a "prisoner of the mountain." Sergei Bodrov, Jr. died on September 21, 2002, while he was shooting his first film as director in the mountains of Northern Osetia. A snow avalanche fell on the village where the crew had its headquarters, and most of the crewmembers perished, together with a large number of local people.

At about the same time, another film on the Chechen conflict came out, which tells us a different story, *Purgatory* (1997) by Alexander Nevzorov. While *Prisoner* is meant to stir the "good feelings" and leave the viewer with the comfort that even in terrible times the human spirit survives and wins, *Purgatory* is a punishing experience that involves the viewers directly in the carnage of the battle and deprives them of hope and pride in the outcome. Possibly, no other film of the decade was met with so much outrage by so many viewers. The film was aired on the Russian television channel, ORT (owned by Boris Berezovsky at the time), in March 1998, and therefore seen by millions of people, even though it ran late at night. This triggered an outpour of furious criticism in the press, and in the liberal circles, arguing that to sneak into private homes such an explosive visual device was tantamount to an attack on the population. Besides the merit of their argument, there were well known extracinematic reasons for the Russian democrats to hate Nevzorov. One was the fact that he had become Berezovsky's protégé, and had put his creative talent in the service of his patron's bank and media empire, perceived as being corrupt and predatory.[78] But, even more odious in the eyes of the liberal intelligentsia was Nevzorov's history as an archconservative nationalist agitator.

Nevzorov started his career as an investigative journalist at the Leningrad television station in the late perestroika years, with a program called "600 Seconds." His good looks and naughty-boy image immediately gained him the sympathy of the viewers. His program was revolutionary at the time, his stance being anti-government. Thanks to the policy of glasnost, he was able to champion the cause of the outsider--whoever happened to be in the opposition. At first, it was the democrats. But as the situation evolved and the democrats became the government, Nevzorov moved more and more to the right, defending the ousted Communists, the perpetrators of the 1991 coup, and then the rebellious parliament members defeated in the 1993 military crackdown. Nevzorov himself took part in that uprising and was arrested during the assault on the Ostankino television station. He had been involved for a couple of years with the subversive groups of General Albert Makashov and Colonel Viktor Alknis in the foundation of a political party named, Nashi (Our Guys). The name was the title of one of his television films that glorified the action of the OMON troops, in January 1991. The troops were sent to quell a revolt in Vilnius, Lithuania, and killed a number of civilians, provoking an outcry of protest among the democrats. Nevzorov became obsessed with war and military action, rather than interested in political activity. He dressed in fatigues most of the time and talked about being the head of the Volunteers' Union, an organization of freedom fighters operating in any possible war theater—Bosnia, Abkhazia, Nagorno-Karabakh. This was before the Chechen campaign. A few days after the coup of 1993, "600 Seconds" was taken off the air for persistent bias and provocation and its virulent anti-government rhetoric. By then, Nevzorov had alienated the audience, who now saw him at best as an immature boy searching for a cause to fit his public persona; at worst, as a dangerous advocate of political violence. Only the disaffected, the hardliners, the neo-Nazis, and the warmongers remained in his camp. He vanished from the television screens and faded into the shady maze of the big business network.

Nevzorov resurfaced with *Purgatory*. However, the film does not look like an intermediary station on the way to heaven; if anything, it looks like hell itself. The film, of which Nevzorov was the producer, screenwriter, and director, consists of a fictional episode at the beginning of the first Chechen war. It is January 1995; a detachment of Russian troops has been trapped in a hospital building in Grozny and is under attack by

Chechen forces. The film action is the bloody battle for the possession of the building. Taking advantage of his training as a reporter, Nevzorov had his cameramen, Viktor Mikhalchenko, shoot the film in the style of a documentary, using a hand-held betacam in many battle scenes to place the viewer in the middle of the action. But he also employs sophisticated technology for special effects and displays a savvy use of framing and editing. The film is spectacular from beginning to end, giving the viewer only brief moments of respite between the sustained pyrotechnics of exploding tanks, crushed buildings, and blown up bodies. The overall tint is intensely red and yellow—the colors of fire. Sergei Selyanov, although very far from being one of Nevzorov's sympathizers, had one positive thing to say about the film: "This is cinema."[79] His argument was that, from a strictly aesthetic point of view, one could appreciate the film and Nevzorov's talent. From an ideological and moral point of view, however, no one could find anything positive to say about it. Most of the voices that took part in the general debate pointed out the film's lack of ethics, distortion of facts, and exploitation of gory images to satisfy the populace's taste for the Roman circus show.[80]

The following are only a few examples in the tapestry of atrocities the film weaves. A young Russian recruit has his throat slit and is then decapitated by the Afghan mercenaries fighting with the Chechens; the head is subsequently attached to a shoulder-fired missile and launched into the Russian camp. Russian soldiers are shot in the genitals; in retribution, the Russians shoot in the crotch two volunteer women sharpshooters from the Baltics, who have joined the Chechen side, and then finish them off with a bullet in the head. A Russian tank officer is nailed to a cross (also by the Afghan mujahedins) and let bleed to death; he had lost his legs in combat and the blood is flowing down from the stumps in streams. A vast array of horrible wounds is shown in detail, including the empty eye socket of the Russian commander. A number of mujahedins urinate on the fallen Russians, desecrating the nobility of death.

But the most shocking scene, which remained etched in the memory of the Russian public, involves an action performed by the Russian army against its own men. Actually, the intent was not hostile, but the images are so revolting that the viewers perceived them as a crime. In order to clear the field of the thousands of corpses left after the battle, partly because it was impossible to bury them and partly because it was embarrassing to account for so many casualties, the Russian command orders its tanks to run the dead over and crush them to pulp. In a sequence of unbearably long duration, the camera closes up on the tank tracks that keep rolling, lifting from the ground bloody fragments of human flesh—a leg, a hand, intestines, bones. At every turn, the parts become more indistinct, blending with the earth into a dark-red gooey paste.

At first, the film does not seem to have a logical structure. The action is fragmented to convey the chaos of the battle; the characters are introduced in very short flashes, without establishing their identity. But as the narrative unfolds, characters come more clearly into focus, and three of them emerge as structural points of reference. One is the tank lieutenant Igorka Grigorashchenko (R. Zhilkin), the sacrificial victim nailed to the cross, who rejected the offer of the Chechen commander to switch sides (he was offered a $5,000 Rolex for that) and stuck with "the guys." His motives were not ideological, as he used the cliché of Stalinist war films in an ironic way: "Forward! The Motherland is calling." What motivates him is the bonding with the group. It is a gesture of personal dignity and brotherly solidarity, rather than an abstract sacrifice for a political ideal.

The other two main characters are the Russian commander, colonel Vitaly Suvorov (Viktor Stepanov), and the Chechen field commander, Ichkeri Israpilov (Dmitri Nagiev). The battle on the field is paralleled by a personal confrontation between the two, a verbal duel fought over their cell phones. Suvorov, hunkered down in the hospital basement with a handful of men, waits for the Russian tank unit to come and rescue them. Israpilov, in control of the building, plays cat and mouse with the trapped Russians. He was a surgeon at the hospital before the war, and feels particularly violated on his own turf. The hospital in this context becomes a metaphor for the whole of Chechnya, Israpilov's home. For the good part of the film, Israpilov pours insults and sarcasm on the besieged commander listening on the phone, alienating the viewers that sympathize with the Russian troops. But on one occasion, Nevzorov allows this character to express feelings that are secretly shared by a growing number of Russians. Israpilov jumps on Grigorashchenko's tank and confronts him with angry words: "You have come to our place. Why? This is my home; I live here under this sky, on this land. What are you doing here?"[81] He also tells Grigorashchenko that the Russian government has betrayed its own men by placing them in an impossible situation. Therefore, the theme of "our guys" vs. "the powers" is reiterated, even if it is voiced by the adversarial party. One must also note that, in his perversity, Israpilov is a fascinating figure. Nagiev, who plays the role, is a pop culture star, a DJ and a showman, who applies to this character the slick imaging that made him an idol of the masses. The Israpilov character is a mix of militaristic brutality and natural elegance, endowed with light-green eyes in a tanned, sculpted face, a gold pirate earring, long hair pulled back in a pony tail, and a warrior body in combat attire and sensuous leather boots. The devil, as we know, is charismatic; and Israpilov is intended to be a devil figure. Not even his legitimate claim to territorial sovereignty can change that.

Nevzorov's sympathies are with Colonel Suvorov and his men. This name inevitably brings to mind the great eighteenth-century Russian general, Alexander Vasilevich Suvorov, who battled the Turks under Catherine II, and later the French. And this does not exhaust the historical references to the time of the grandeur of the Russian empire. It is certainly significant that the colonel loses an eye in combat at the very beginning. The camera stresses the eye patch and the missing eye all along. This triggers the analogy with another eighteenth-century military figure, one-eyed General Mikhail Kutuzov, the un-flamboyant hero of the Napoleonic war. Perhaps, this Suvorov is meant to be a blend of the two, an idealized image of valor, endurance, and Russianness.

In the end, these are the values that survive after the carnage. Fresh Russian troops storm the hospital, rescue their comrades, and kill all the "Chichi," including Israpilov. But the final scene does not convey a sense of triumph. A tightly framed shot shows Suvorov and his men surrounding the comrade who died on the cross. The image is solemn and mournful, like a Renaissance canvas of the dead Christ. But unlike that death, which was intended to generate hope, this death is seen as a pointless sacrifice. "Our guys" have gathered to pay homage to the fallen brother and to reiterate their allegiance to the group. This is the end of an episode of courage and solidarity in spite of a faulty war strategy and misguided government policies, with no projection in the future. A title runs across the screen, confirming the futility of the action and condemning the conduct of the war, "Soon after, the hospital was reoccupied by the Chechen forces."

Another film on the Chechen conflict came out one year later, and the press routinely measured it against the two that preceded it. *Checkpoint*

(Rogozhkin, 1998) was rightly rated by the critics as being superior to both Bodrov's sentimental war tale and Nevzorov's demagogic docudrama.[82] The film was praised for capturing the current mood of alienation bordering on the absurd. This mood is conveyed in a somewhat hyperbolic fashion, without ever slipping into farcical situations à la M.A.S.H. Rogozhkin had achieved popularity with his comedy *Peculiarities of the National Hunt in the Fall* (1995), which indeed was full of gags and gross humor. He then repeated the same theme in the same vein in two more films, *Peculiarities of National Fishing* (1998) and *Peculiarities of the National Hunt in the Winter* (2000). None of these comedies, which were quite successful in Russia, had any appeal to foreign audiences, with the possible exception of the Finns. The humor was too unpalatable and, definitely, beyond the grasp of a public unfamiliar with Russian culture. But *Checkpoint* is subtler; the film's strategy is to employ comic elements to conceal the tragic subtext.

A platoon of Russian soldiers is sent to an outpost in rebel territory. The viewer learns their story from a narrator within the group, who goes by the nickname of Pepel (Ashes). Each soldier in the platoon is known only by his combat name, which defines him, like a comedy stock character: Yurist (Lawyer), Krysa (Rat), Mócha,[83] Kaif (High, as on dope), Skelet (Skeleton), Khalyava (Freeloader), Boeing. The platoon's commander is known as Ilich (a reference to Lenin); the general from the local headquarters, Batya (Father).

Their task is to control a road that cuts through a meadow and leads to the cemetery, watching for possible arms smuggling. There is no fighting in the area, and no traffic on the road. Panoramic shots of the surrounding forests and mountains convey a sense of immersion in nature, a sacred pagan territory alien to the urban occupiers from the north. At the outpost, the monotony of the daily chores is broken from time to time by a funeral procession; the natives bury their kin, occasional victims of the war. They pass by silently, meeting the watchful eyes of the soldiers with glimpses full of hatred. At times, a group of young men puts on a demonstration; keeping at a safe distance from the checkpoint, they discharge their guns in the air and wave the green scarves of the Muslim rebels. They know that the platoon has been removed from the frontline and sent to the boonies as a punishment, on the charge of shooting a civilian woman.

One villager, a sniper, plays the part of the avenger and keeps the outpost in the viewfinder. The soldiers are on the alert all the time, especially when they make the short trip to the outhouse, which is a favorite target. But the sniper never hits the mark. The only victim of those first few days at the outpost is a rat that private Krysa used to carry on his shoulder as a pet. Krysa is distraught by the senseless loss of his *"boevoi tovarishch"* (comrade in arms), who had survived several combat actions in his vest pocket, and gives it a military burial; afterwards, he regularly brings roses to its grave.

This is not the only "peculiarity" of the life at the outpost. Yurist sports a foxtail hanging from his helmet. Mócha wears headphones even when he stands at attention. The comic elements are many and sustained, but always mixed with a sense of foreboding and impending death. One soldier is caught with his pants down—literally—when an OSCE convoy visits the outpost; while being on sentry duty, he took off his clothes because of the heat, except for the bulletproof vest and the helmet, and then had to stand at attention completely exposed. The international inspectors, however, do not pay any attention to him; they are on a hunting mission to nail down the soldier suspected of brutality against the civilian population. Among the inspectors are two young women, proud of their humanitarian task, but excited by the presence of such a wild bunch of warriors. One of them hands Khalyava her business card, as if she were on a vacation tour. "If you ever come to Canada, give me a call," she says as the jeep takes off—even more absurd is the reply of the young recruit: *"Ob'iazatel'no budu*! (Absolutely!)"

The Russian lieutenant-prosecutor who investigates the case and accompanies the OSCE delegation is a plump blonde with freckles, whose image would be more suited to the bakery shop than the military. Comic situations build up in her interrogation of the soldiers, who display a semi-respectful/semi-mocking attitude. To make up for her insecurities, she is eager to find a suspect, no matter what, and close the case. The episode that triggered the investigation was in itself "comic." The platoon is searching a village for arms and rebels. Two soldiers enter a house and find a small child pounding a hammer against a landmine. They run for their lives seconds before the house blows up. But the village women hold the Russians responsible for the death of the child, and one of them gets a gun and begins to spray the platoon with fire. A soldier

36 *Checkpoint* (1998) directed by Alexander Rogozhkin

shoots her in the legs in self-defense. No one saw who pulled the trigger; and no one comes forward during the investigation. But now, under pressure from the international community, Batya, the general, in collusion with the prosecutor, picks one of the men randomly. The scapegoat happens to be Krysa, who had already had a brush with death when the sniper killed the pet-rat in his place.

During those few days covered in Pepel's diary, Manimat, a young woman from the village often comes to the outpost to sell her cousin's sexual favors to the soldiers in exchange for rounds of ammo—the cousin is deaf and mute and passively consenting. The soldiers eagerly pay the price, not suspecting that they are contributing to their own destruction. But this detail tips off the viewer to who the sniper is. In the trading process, Manimat meets Yurist, and the two enjoy a short and platonic idyll. The tragic outcome that brings the drama to its inevitable conclusion involves a case of mistaken identity. In a few minutes of cinematic time, all the dramatic elements converge at the checkpoint. Yurist and Pepel, who are on sentry duty, switch helmets for fun; from a distance, Yurist can no longer be identified by his foxtail. A truck from the village comes up the road, drops off a heavy sack, and hurriedly departs. Yurist cautiously inspects the sack, and discovers with horror that it contains Krysa's body—Batya had quietly delivered him to the rebels to appease the locals. At that point, Manimat shoots Yurist in the nape of the neck—her first successful hit. She kills her friend by mistake. Simultaneously, the cousin steps on a landmine and a big explosion resonates through the meadows and valleys. Manimat's shrill and prolonged cry of horror blends with the detonation, disturbing the serenity of the natural habitat. Yurist turns around to stare at the camera; his eyes already glazed, a rivulet of blood coming out of his mouth.

Throughout the film, the narrator, Pepel, senses the irrationality of the situation. His voice-over narration underscores the opening panoramic shot of the forests and mountain peaks: "There is no salvation in the beauty of these mountains, which are foreign to us. . . . Our time is confined to the present day, or even the present moment; and the eternity of the mountains does not belong in this simple scheme." On occasions, he reiterates that theme: "Nobody knows what we're doing here," he says.[84] But there is no attempt on his part to explain their predicament or to look for cause and effect relations. He is an observer, relating the facts in a sad and concerned tone.

It has been suggested that on the symbolic level the Russians are not waging a war against a specific enemy, but against nature—the element opposite to civilization, which here is connoted by the impervious surroundings and the indigenous population.[85] I do not disagree with this suggestion, but I would take it further. In a parodic way, the film suggests that the Russians are actually struggling against Fate. In the Greek tragedy, Fate is the elemental, irrational force that dominates human lives. In the film, narrative and visual devices bring to the fore references to the Greek tragedy model. However, comic situations trivialize the solemnity of the classical paradigm.

In the Caucasian mountains, the ancient Colchis, the locus of the tragic demise of mythological heroes and demigods, these intruders are doomed to perish. They do not know. They are oblivious of their destiny. They go about their chores and activities—cooking, showering, playing cards, playing juvenile pranks on each other, smoking dope—as if they were on a camping trip. They complain, of course, of the inevitable inconveniences, such as the sniper, the prosecutor's investigation, a bad supply of dope laced with pepper, and the like. But those are considered minor contingencies that can be easily fixed—Kaif puts the peppered dope in the soup and everybody enjoys the meal.

Their carefree attitude contrasts sharply with the omniscient point of view of the film's "author," aware that Fate is against them. This overarching presence becomes the consciousness of the viewer, who throughout the film "knows" much more than the characters do. The telling sign of Yurist's imminent death is the losing of the foxtail, a sort of symbol of the "hero's" invulnerability. He is hit exactly in the place where the foxtail was, his "soft spot," like Achilles' heel. Other images echo the mise en scène of a Greek tragedy, like the swarm of black-clad village women furiously attacking the Russians, and claiming a victim. They are the Harpies, performing the role that Fate has assigned to them. And so does Manimat, killing by accident, not by intention—an extended close up on the finger pulling the trigger connotes her as instrument. Accompanying the unfolding events is the sad voice of Pepel; his tone is that of the Chorus, mournful and resigned. "We keep guard over the realm of the dead," he observes. A lone white horse crossing the checkpoint in the direction of the cemetery reinforces the presence of death--a surreal image that lies outside the diegesis and belongs to the tragic subtext.

Narrative and subtext are cleverly interwoven. The slaughtering of Krysa is a narrative expedient to expose the irresponsibility and corruption of the high command in this war. But, ultimately, the film demystifies an ideology that stems from the nineteenth-century notion of Russia's "Eastern roots"—the notion that the ancient Slavs came from the Asian steppes and, therefore, the Russians had a right to reoccupy their ancestral homeland, Caucasus included. Russia has been pursuing her manifest destiny for two hundred years, expecting the population of the occupied areas to fraternize with the Russian "brothers." Instead, the Russians always found a fierce resistance from the natives who fought to preserve their independence. The Russian empire was able to extend its borders, but it could not impose its culture on the rebellious mountain tribes. Many nineteenth-century intellectuals who embraced the idea of the Russians' dual nature—half European and half Asian—and were drawn to the Eastern lands, once there felt like strangers.

The theme of the conquest of the Caucasus emerges in the film when

Yurist finds in the ground an old medal, which supposedly belonged to a fallen soldier. The date is 1864, and the inscription says: "For service in the Caucasus (*Za sluzhbu na Kavkaze*)." Yurist is intrigued and treats it like a quaint treasure. It has no meaning to him, except as a souvenir. Its meaning lies in the authorial discourse addressed to the viewer. It is one of the many signs and premonitions, which point to the Russians' fatal predicament. Another image that connotes a wild force from the East is the raven. Early in the film, Pepel pensively follows the flight of the ominous bird high up in the sky.

The special quality of the Caucasus as the last frontier, the place where the brave meets his nemesis, has been cultivated in the nineteenth-century epos in prose and poetry. This was mainly a romantic notion. But even a skeptic like the hero of Lermontov's short story "The Fatalist" (1840), serving in the Chechnya region as an officer of the Guard, in the end had to agree that, perhaps, in the Caucasus Fate does play a role. The thoughts of the "hero of that time," acknowledging the loss of ideals and purpose, may very well apply to this film of our time:[86]

> We drift through the world, without beliefs, pride, pleasure or fear, except that automatic fear that grips us when we think of the certainty of death. We can no longer make great sacrifices for the good of mankind, or even for our own happiness, because we know they are unattainable. And as our ancestors rushed from illusion to illusion, so we drift indifferently from doubt to doubt. But, unlike them, we have no hope, nor even that indefinable but real sense of pleasure that is felt in any struggle, be it with man or destiny.

And so, this is a tragedy without catharsis, because it is a tragedy without passion. At the end of the film, the subtext comes to the surface and the viewer is confronted with the senseless face of death—Yurist's face, a tragic mask with empty eyes.

5
Laughter through Tears

"Whom are you laughing at?"

The speaker is the mayor of a provincial town, and one of the main characters in the comedy *Inspector General* (*Revizor*, 1836) by Nikolay Gogol. This is the last scene before the final *coup de scène*. The mayor and his entourage of city notables have just learned that they have been duped by the swindler who pretended to be the inspector general from St. Petersburg. To minimize the blow to their ego, everyone points at someone else, laughing at other people's stupidity and isolating themselves from derision. The mayor is the only one who comes to his senses and realizes that each one of them is responsible for what happened. Metaphorically, he holds a mirror in front of each guest as he utters the famous line: "Whom are you laughing at? You're laughing at yourself."

This was a stroke of genius that made *Inspector General* one of the most significant and disturbing comedies in Russian theater. Throughout the nineteenth century, the play was interpreted in the realistic mode with strong satirical elements. Its full significance became evident only later, in the avant-garde theater of the early twentieth century. In the staging by Vsevolod Meyerhold, this line was being addressed to the audience, tearing down the barrier between the stage and the house, and engaging the public in the play directly. This strategy has both literary and moral implications. On the literary level, the plane shifts from satire to the grotesque—from a classical eighteenth-century genre to a modernist, absurdist one. On the moral level, the public is no longer shielded by the conventions of the satire, which is aimed at vices or villains contained in their own fictional world, and therefore affords the spectator a judgemental attitude; rather, in the ambiguous reality of the absurdist theater, the public becomes an actor and, therefore, the object of derisive criticism. The familiar world is turned upside down, as in the "carnival."[1]

One hundred and sixty years from its St. Petersburg debut, *Inspector General* (Sergei Gazarov, 1996) reappeared on the Russian screens. The comedy had been filmed only three times in Russia, once before the revolution (V. Sashin, 1916), and twice in the Soviet period (M. Frich, 1933; V. Petrov, 1952), although it had been regularly performed on stage. This was its first cinematic remake in post-Soviet Russia and was dedicated to Moscow's 850th birthday. In this version, the mayor is brought back to life by the awesome talent of Nikita Mikhalkov. Opposite Mikhalkov is Evgeny Mironov, very effective in the role of the swindler Khlestyakov; he is the perfect incarnation of self-satisfied vulgarity and braggadocio. In the secondary roles is a *pléiade* of major and minor stars from the Russian screen and stage.[2] The dialogue is Gogol's, word by word. The staging is faithful to the original text, preserving the realism of the period decor and costumes, while applying the right degree of hyperbole to turn reality into caricature. The unities of space, time, and action are maintained wherever possible to convey the impression of watching a stage performance, while cinematography and editing are used unobtrusively to liven up the narrative without disturbing the static atmosphere of the dormant provincial setting.

Gogol would have been pleased with this version of the play, because he had taken pains in providing precise instructions for the actors. He actually warned them: "From a disregard of these remarks may result a total loss of effect."[3] He was referring to the frozen tableau at the end, when a messenger announces to the assembled guests that the real inspector general has arrived. "The words just pronounced," Gogol wrote, "strike all like a thunderbolt. . . . The whole group, having suddenly changed its position, remains as if petrified." At the premiere, and all subsequent performances, the audience as well remained petrified for the duration of the dumb scene, a long minute before the curtain falls. The effect was to turn the actors (and the public by extension) into puppets, which become inert the moment the hand of the puppeteer rests.

This device graphically illustrates the underlying nature of the Gogolian universe, populated not by living characters but by objectified bodies. The protagonists of Gogol's stories are people without an awareness of themselves; lacking existential consciousness, they live a vegetative life. This state of non-existence breeds vulgarity and, ultimately, the kind of petty evil that comes from the darkest corners of the underdeveloped human psyche. The Russian word for this mental setup is "*poshlost'*," which can be approximately translated into English as "philistine materialism." Within the framework of his religious belief, Gogol perceived these characters as the devil's emanations. It was not his intention to create such a nightmarish world. In fact, Gogol was profoundly affected by his works; he regarded them as a sin, and plunged into devastating spiritual crises which eventually killed him. His aspiration was to create noble heroes; instead, only petty demons came out of his pen.[4] One such petty demon is Khlestyakov, who is able to take advantage of the whole town only because the town representatives are even pettier than he is in their personal pursuits, corruption, and greed. The women, too, are vapid creatures in Gogol's surrealist world, empty shells adorned with gaudy ribbons and frills. Such are the mayor's wife and daughter, who both fall for Khlestyakov's gross advances. While seeking God, Gogol got entangled in a web of devilish ghosts.

But the mayor is an exception. He is the only character in the whole Gogolian universe to acquire the embryo of a consciousness. Although his vision is a parody of moral awakening, it is nevertheless key to the "carnivalization" of the play, because he sees himself as a character in a comedy. In Mikhalkov's interpretation, the mayor is first astounded at having being duped—"I'm killed. I'm simply killed dead"; then, he becomes self-deprecatory—"How could I, old blockhead that I am! Stupid old ram!" Then, he nostalgically recites his past glories—"Thirty years I've been in the service.... I've fooled swindlers upon swindlers.... I've bamboozled three governors!" Finally, he gives in to despair—"He'll spread the story all over the earth! And I'll not only be a laughingstock, but some quill-driver, some paper-spoiler will be found to put me in a comedy! That's what hurts! ... And they'll all show their teeth in a grin and clap their hands." Here, the mayor sobs so loudly, that the famous line which comes up precisely at this point is almost inaudible. But the guests hear it. The camera pans over their astonished faces; no one laughs anymore.

In the film, the mayor is further singled out with the addition of an element that is not in the original text. In the frozen-frame scene, the guests who are standing still along the banquet table fade out like vanishing ghosts. The mayor remains alone. Suddenly, the stillness of the set is broken by two black rats scurrying along the table in front of him. The viewer intuitively connects the rats with the very first scene, where the mayor receives the letter announcing the inspector general and tells his associates of a bad omen he had the previous night: "I had a sort of presentiment. All last night I kept dreaming about two most extraordinary rats. Honest, I've never seen any like them: black, and awfully big. They came, sniffed about, and went away again." In the end, his subconscious vision becomes a realized metaphor.

Fluttering butterflies

Notwithstanding the surrealist world he created, Gogol was considered in his time an exponent of the Natural School.[5] On more than one occasion, inspiration for his stories came from real life. It is well known that the plots for both *Inspector General* and *Dead Souls* were based on episodes from the provincial chronicle, which Pushkin related to him as possible literary subjects.

What happened in Moscow in the 1990s would be a suitable sequel to *Dead Souls*. Once again, a swindler of far-reaching imagination and financial acumen made billions of rubles trading empty papers. In this case, he did not deal with the dead but with the living. The scam was cruel, and left behind millions of victims—low-income citizens robbed of their life savings. The investment company MMM and its president, Sergei Mavrodi, were the protagonists of a drama, which unfolded over a six-month period and peaked in July 1994 with a catastrophic crash.[6]

MMM began to impose its presence on the Russian market in the fall of 1991 with a spectacular publicity gimmick. It rented the Moscow metro for one day—a Sunday—and offered free rides to the entire population. Conspicuous signs at all metro stations displayed the firm logo, and invited the passengers to have a ride on MMM. At that time the fare was only five kopeks, and the sum the firm paid the city administration for the day was relatively small; but the commercial gain was enormous. From that day on, the three butterfly-shaped Ms remained impressed in the consumers' mind.

I enjoyed the ride and appreciated the ingenious advertising trick. But

I was already familiar with MMM as a "cooperative" for the sale of computers and electronic equipment.[7] When I moved to Moscow, laptops were not a common feature, and I did not want to pack my PC because of the uncertainty of the duration of my stay. But as time went by and my writing projects expanded, I felt in dire need of a computer. Not only a computer; I needed a fax machine, a TV set, and a VCR. It was the summer of 1991. The few Soviet stores by the generic name, Elektronika, had only national brand TVs—huge, boxy cases with small screens. A few imported VCRs from Korea were available at very high prices. Fax machines were nowhere to be found; only a few businesses had them. Most people would go to the post office and wait hours in line to send a fax, because of insufficient phone lines. Before the fiber optic cable age, every international call in and out of the USSR would go through one central switchboard in Moscow. The operator would put it in a queue, and would ring up the caller for the connection within the average time span of 24 hours. If the caller was not by the phone when the operator rang, the call would simply be cancelled. This centralized system was due mainly to technological failure, but it was also a convenient way for the KGB to monitor calls. In the early 1990s, this nightmare was somehow alleviated by international telecommunications companies, which would provide access numbers to their satellites for a subscription fee. Thanks to that technology, it was possible to use a fax machine from one's own apartment. The Internet and e-mail were just beginning to emerge, but were not yet available to ordinary citizens.[8]

Occasional ads began to appear in newspapers by newly formed cooperatives selling imported high-tech equipment. Among them was MMM. I decided to go and check it out. The trip to the desolate suburb took me about an hour from downtown Moscow. I got to a warehouse. There was some movement outside, several cars stood by a dock loading large boxes. Inside, rows of Philips, Sony, and Samsung containers were stacked against the bare walls. The environment was quite modest, and suggested a clearinghouse arrangement with a quick turnover. But the service was good. An army of young salesmen was bustling around, helping customers eagerly and efficiently. Even the payment transaction was smooth and easy. In a country where most stores still used the abacus to add up purchases, MMM's staff had calculators. The prices were in rubles, instead of the usual, and illegal, pricing in hard currency. They even provided me with a receipt—which did not have any value beyond its nice appearance. "We operate the Western way," one rosy-cheeked clerk told me with a broad smile when I congratulated him. I left the warehouse with my precious cargo, and with an appreciation for the Russian burgeoning market.

The MMM butterflies began fluttering on billboards and TV screens. In the new Russia, thanks to the law legitimizing private enterprises, the small cooperative grew into a holding that included a bank, a voucher investment fund, and a joint-stock investment firm. The backbone of MMM's operations was the investment firm, which in February 1994 launched a program promising fantastic weekly returns of up to 10 percent on its securities. In July, MMM counted 60 trading offices in Moscow and 76 branches all over Russia, and claimed 5 million shareholders.[9] Allegedly, MMM's shares accounted for half of all transactions on Russian stock markets. The company's commercial jingles sank into the consciousness of the nation—"*Em-em-é, nas znaiut vsé* (Em-em-em, all know them)," chanted children and adults alike.

One major factor for the company's popularity was a TV commercial conceived as a serial. The same character, Lyonya Golubkov, appeared on screen night after night in a new skit. The narrative progressed not in terms of action, but in terms of moving up the wealth ladder. Lyonya's profile was designed to represent the ordinary Russian worker; in a few months, he became a folk hero. According to the commercial, the little man of modest appearance, an excavator operator married to a woman named Rita, accumulated a fortune trading MMM's shares. Lyonya would stand in front of a chart with an upward line showing the stages of his ascent to the sphere of wealth. At the bottom there was just a pair of designer boots for Rita. But every week Lyonya's pointer moved up a notch—a car, Rita's fur coat, a dacha, a trip to the U.S. At the top of the chart there was an apartment in Paris. Unfortunately, MMM crashed before Lyonya could get to such dizzy heights.[10]

MMM succeeded in duping its massive clientele thanks to two elements: the rags-to-riches dream (the intangible element), and concrete money in the investors' pockets (the tangible element). In all pyramid schemes, as long as the house of cards holds, the players do see a return; the return is the bait that keeps them hooked until the inevitable collapse. MMM's shares rose 70 times in value from February to July. The company would quote the price of its own shares twice-weekly in advance on television. The investors who bought shares on Tuesday for 115,000 rubles a share already knew that MMM would repurchase them on Thursday for 125,000 rubles (this was the last quote before the crash). The company made good on its word for six months, winning the hearts and minds of an army of Lyonyas. Every day, teachers, workers, pensioners, students stood in line, rain or shine, outside MMM's offices to trade their shares and supplement their income. They worshipped the company's president, Sergei Mavrodi, and considered him their benefactor.

The government, although aware of the potential fraud, lacked the instruments to stop it. The Finance Ministry issued several warnings about companies trading false securities, including MMM's shares and "tickets." The tickets were an additional gimmick. They represented one hundredth of a share, and were issued in order to expand the company's charter capital, which amounted to only 991,000 regular shares—not enough to claim 5 million shareholders. Moreover, people who did not have the money to buy one whole share could invest a few rubles on a fraction of it. Over the years, the authorities built several cases against MMM for fiscal violations, but the law regulating business was vague and insufficient to press charges. Mavrodi responded to the Tax Service's attempts to close down the company with the threat of a shareholders uprising. "I personally cannot predict what concrete shape the anger of the people will take: a revolution, a civil war, or something else," he wrote in an open letter published in *Rossiiskaia gazeta*, and warned that 5 million investors were a political force capable of taking down the government.[11] However, rumors of a crackdown prompted many investors to sell rather than buy.

On July 26, the shareholders and ticketholders who made their daily trip to the MMM offices found the door closed. "*U em-em-em; u kotorogo net problem* (At em-em-em's, no probléms)"—the brash commercial slogan now sounded hollow. The company announced that because of a shortage of cash it could not redeem its shares and had to close temporarily. The first reaction was disbelief; then, panic; then, the investors turned their anger on the government, which they blamed for Mavrodi's troubles.

Up to this point, the story had been absurd but not unique. Many people fall victim of similar schemes every day all over the world, although not on such a massive scale. But what followed brought the absurd element to unprecedented levels. Mavrodi was eventually arrested a few weeks later, during a dramatic raid of his penthouse apartment, for large-scale tax evasion and resisting search. These were the only two charges that could be brought against him under the law, and they were not related to the pyramid scam. MMM reopened its doors promptly, and began to redeem its shares at less than 1 percent of their pre-crash value. Mavrodi directed the operation from his cell in the Matroskaya Tishina prison by issuing directives to his lawyers.

Thousands of shareholders rushed to MMM's headquarters on Varshavskoe Shosse, not to sell their worthless papers, but to buy the new "tickets" (MMM did not sell shares anymore). The Finance Ministry issued a statement, warning the public that "buyers of MMM tickets become entitled only to pretty postcards."[12] But the mood among the investors was fiercely anti-government. Since Mavrodi's arrest, the Lyonyas of Russia united, and held daily demonstrations outside the Moscow police headquarters. Many displayed signs demanding: "Hands off Mavrodi!" The unscrupulous financier was seen as a Robin Hood, battling the government to benefit the people. Soon the protestors organized a political movement, called MMM Shareholders Union, whose ultimate goal was to have Mavrodi win the 1996 presidential election. But Mavrodi had a more modest and more practical objective: to be elected as a deputy to the Duma in order to acquire immunity from prosecution. Thanks to popular support, he succeeded. In November 1994, the people of the Moscow suburban district of Mytishchi chose him as their representative.

Mavrodi had promised to pay back the investors who suffered losses as soon as he was elected and free to run the company personally, without interference from law enforcement authorities. Mavrodi's supporters relied on campaign promises, and expected their champion to honor his word. The day after victory, the expectations of the faithful were crushed. Mavrodi's first move was to suspend all buying transactions until further notice. For the first time, the investors standing in the rain outside the company's headquarters, clutching packets of colored papers in their hands, felt betrayed. The crowd began to throw empty bottles and stones at the building, and insults at Mavrodi: "Thief!" "Swindler!"

"We were robbed!" "Throw him out of the Duma and back in jail!" The rain kept pouring, mixing with the tears of anger and frustration that flowed out of thousands of aching living souls.

This would be an appropriate ending for a morality play: the villain is eventually unmasked and the greedy and gullible are left with a handful of paper butterflies and a bitter lesson learned. In real life, this saga had a prolonged and twisted coda.[13] But for our purposes, with this scene, "*E' finita la commedia.*"

The new poor

The Russians' propensity to find the comic in the most distressful situations has been refined through centuries of practice. It is a safety valve for a populace that has felt abused and oppressed in the course of history. But satire was an exception in Soviet times. In a film by Eldar Ryazanov (*Garage*, 1980), one character addresses a scholar doing research in satire, saying: "You have an odd profession. You are studying a subject which does not exist."[14] That film itself was a rare example of satire, which had virtually disappeared in Soviet cinema, suppressed by the official canon of socialist realism. The liberating force of laughter could be a subversive element, and therefore something to be feared in a totalitarian, closed society.[15] In the post-Soviet period, Ryazanov continued the trend of his biting "socio-fantastic" tales, but in the absence of the totalitarian state, they lost some of the edge. In *The Promised Skies* (1991), the context is the uncaring world of incipient capitalism, and reflects the tribulations of those who have the misfortune of being in its way. The dwellers of a shantytown on the outskirts of Moscow are about to lose their cardboard shacks to a big American development company, with which City Hall is eager to make a multi-million dollar deal. This was the time of perestroika, but Ryazanov captured the dawn of the new era of big business rule. The film pits the underdogs against the establishment, with the scales tipped in favor of the former, but avoids the traps of the pretentious moral parable. Ryazanov's "heroes" are grotesque creatures, funny and pathetic in a clownish way, not always endearing, but inspiring respect for their protestation of human dignity. They are at the same time losers and winners. After an unequal battle against mighty bulldozers, they are magically delivered from their predicament. In a surreal final apotheosis—borrowed from De Sica's post-neorealist *Miracle in Milan* (1950)—the ragged bunch is lifted off and carried away toward the promised skies.

Several years went by before Ryazanov returned to the theme of the poor; rather, the "new poor"—working people who were unable to board the free-market train. *Old Nags* (1999) tells the story of four old-time girl friends, who fell from the status of respected workers of an industrial complex to the humiliating position of street vendors. In the old days, they also enjoyed a certain celebrity as performers in the factory amateur musical ensemble. Now, they have to peddle cigarettes in metro underpasses, suffering from the attacks of the neighborhood's juvenile gangs; or, to sell fruit and vegetables for an abusive southern boss.

The narrative is rambling and suffers from an excess of twists and turns, which lead the heroines through still another skit, still another gag.[16] Aesthetically, the film is not one of Ryazanov's best, especially when compared to his achievements in Soviet times. Nevertheless, it is redeemed by the sense of compassion it conveys for the victims of social injustice, combined with hilarious stunts and vaudeville acts. Elements of the musical have often been part of Ryazanov's films, and here they have a self-reflexive function. Ludmila Gurchenko, who plays one of the leading roles, debuted in Ryazanov's first film, *Carnival Night (1957)*, which dealt with the struggle of an amateur musical group against the bureaucracy. *Old Nags* rests on the shoulders of the four lead actresses, old nags themselves in the film world. Thanks to their talent and professional skill, the balance between farce and human drama is sustained throughout.[17]

The central episode unfolds around a con job performed at the expense of Lyuba (Lia Akhedzhanova, who also played a central role in *Promised Skies*). An unscrupulous business baron convinces the woman to sell her apartment—a fine piece of real estate on the Moscow River embankment—for a 100,000 dollar check, which turns out to be fake. She is hastily relocated to a shack on the cemetery grounds. No doubt, the symbolism is intended. But, rather than dying or disappearing, Lyuba, with the help of her friends, becomes the business baron's nemesis. The gags cover a broad span, from the farcical to the fantastic, including a car chase on the metro rail and underwater. At one point, an army general

37   *Old Nags* (1999) directed by Eldar Ryazanov

(Valentin Gaft), who took a fancy to Anna (Irina Kupchenko), has a whole battalion join the action. Liza (Ludmila Gurchenko) resorts to the seduction skills of her youth to entice the business baron into a honey trap. Through clever tricks and a bit of force (the general holds the business baron at gunpoint), Lyuba gets her apartment back. However, the business baron has the four friends arrested.

At the end of the story, Ryazanov makes sure that his personal feelings for the embattled representatives of one of the most victimized classes—older women—are clearly disclosed. He sits on the bench in the garb of the judge presiding at the trial of the four friends, who stand accused of assault and extortion. Under his watch, the trial turns into a musical performance, where reason and the code of laws dissolve into an emotional outpouring of singing and dancing. As the *deus ex machina*, Ryazanov acquits the suspects—the real victims. He accompanies their departure from the courthouse with a gaze full of sadness and appreciation. He is also saying good-bye to old-time companions of his cinematic journey.

The new economy has been harsh especially on older women. Not infrequently, while shopping at the farmers market, I felt compelled to share my bag of groceries with a little *babushka*, who could not afford to buy a jar of pickles at the current prices. But everyone in Russia and the periphery, who did not have resources, felt they were in a desperate situation. This is what a resident of Kharkov, Ukraine, wrote in a letter to *Izvestia*:

> I am a former colonel in the Soviet army, but I have been a homeless pensioner for four years. I am trying to sell both my ordinary and my dress uniforms, two orders and eight medals, and a Moskvich automobile in good condition. Besides, although it is difficult for me to write this, I am selling my father's Order of Lenin, Order of the Red Star, Order of the Red Banner of Labor, and a letter signed by Stalin. . . . I am ashamed, but many of us who retired from the military in 1981-1991 are in the same boat."[18]

That boat was very large and included people from all the respected professions.

In the rearview mirror

A tragicomedy by Nikolay Dostal, *Cloud-Heaven* (1991), captured the widespread feeling of frustration in the country at the end of the Soviet era. The setting is a small provincial town, where life is so dull that people have become lethargic and go through a mechanical routine day after day, as in the Gogolian provinces of a century and a half ago. The story hinges on a cruel trick of fate.

A young fellow named Kolka (pop singer Andrei Zhigalov) decides to put some zest into a long Sunday afternoon by bragging to his friends that he has got a fabulous job offer and is moving to the Russian Far East. A shock wave spreads through the town, waking up long-dormant minds and atrophied bodies. Everyone gets so excited about the news that the lie acquires a life of its own, and becomes Kolka's nemesis. Overzealous neighbors put Kolka's room up for rent and proceed to help themselves to his furniture. His girlfriend is sad but proud about Kolka's departure. When he, desperate, shouts at her that this is all fiction and he wants to stay, she smiles at him and gives him her blessing for the trip. Like the whole town, the young woman does not want to be robbed of her vicarious dream. Kolka's bright opportunity is the only ray of light that has ever flashed through their lives. In the end, accompanied by a procession of friends, city officials, and the local band, Kolka is forced to board a bus to nowhere. The film is a bitter parody of the Soviet new-wave cinema of the 1960s, with its naive optimism, lyrical flights, deep human feelings, and faith in the future. Now, at the end of the era, dreams are just a delusion, and the future is an ephemeral cloud in the sky.

The next film by Nikolay Dostal brings us back decisively into the Soviet past, because of the setting and because of the circumstances surrounding the literary source. When the independent almanac *Metropol* appeared in 1979, it created a scandal. Published outside of the state-controlled printing houses by a group of like-minded writers, poets, and artists, it was immediately seized by the KGB and its contributors were subjected to a campaign of harassment and threats.[19] Among the controversial contents was a short story by Fazil Iskander, "The Little Giant with a Big Sex Drive," also known as "Oh, Marat!" In 1992, Dostal's film version appeared on the screen, with a script by Alexander Borodyansky and Dostal himself. Like the literary text, *Little Giant with a Big Sex Drive* recounts the extraordinary adventures of a provincial Don Juan, with a penchant for absurd imagery and situations. In the opening sequence taking place in our time, an old man in a wheelchair is attended by an attractive nurse. She is wearing a business suit, and looks more like a corporate executive than a caregiver. The nurse takes him for a ride along the deserted boardwalk of a decaying resort town. The film's sepia color, the drab surroundings, the severe nurse's demeanor, and the condition of the old man connote a joyless and lifeless environment. But the erotic tales the old man spins bring back another time and another reality, and restore the screen to its full color palette.

Suddenly, the Black Sea resort of Sukhumi in the early 1950s materializes before our eyes. That same gray boardwalk is transfigured into a scintillating stage—sunshine, rolling waves, white colonnades, palm trees, slender girls in Capri pants, sidewalk cafés, shiny convertibles—and in the midst of it, the protagonist of the old man's tales, the local newspaper photo reporter Marat (stage comedian Gennady Khazanov). He is a diminutive man with a generous heart and an insatiable sex drive. For him, sex is both a physical pleasure and an aesthetic experience, a celebration of life and of woman's beauty. Strolling along the boardwalk with his camera, he chases every pretty woman that crosses his path and captures her on film and, eventually, in his arms. Background music consists exclusively of Italian pop songs of the period, which ironically underline the "dolce vita" atmosphere of the seaside town. Marat himself looks like one of the many mustachioed comic characters brought to the screen by Giancarlo Giannini or Marcello Mastroianni. This set of cinematic codes at the very beginning invites the viewer to watch the film as a comedy, for its entertainment value.

Following his sex drive, Marat runs into a series of disappointing and potentially dangerous situations. He has an affair with the mistress of Lavrenti Beria and becomes impotent when he discovers the identity of the woman's patron; he shares the favors of a circus snake charmer with her inseparable boa constrictor; he is enticed in a sumptuous villa full of statuesque beauties who turn out to be lesbians; he gets involved with a pretty midget and is symbolically captured by the Lilliputians; and finally he disappears with a foreign tourist—American or Yakutian, it is not clear—who takes him away to her land never to be seen again.

The narrator becomes progressively engrossed in his performance, as the action alternates between the two epochs and the two settings. The nurse (Irina Rozanova) gradually mellows to the fire of his erotic tales, her hair gets loose, her jacket comes off, her blouse unbuttons, her beauty is revealed. The sepia tone dissolves and the image turns to color. Like a magician, the old man keeps pulling an endless series of verbal tricks out of his hat, and in the end reveals his true identity as the legendary Marat. The nurse gives in to his seductive power, sits on his lap, and the wheelchair without control begins to roll down the steps (a close up of the bouncing wheel provides an ironical reference to *Battleship Potemkin*) carrying two happy people toward the open sea.

Little Giant is a playful commentary on the creation of narratives, the making of images, and the use of visual codes—in short, it is a commentary on mythmaking. While creating the Marat myth, it debunks the Soviet myth, all the while maintaining a tongue-in-cheek attitude.

Chicha (1992) by Vitaly Melnikov is another commentary in a comic vein on the stifling effects of the Soviet regime. Before glasnost, the life of the eccentric in Soviet society was awkward and even dangerous. Such characters were rarely reflected in cinema or the theater, with the exception of Melnikov's heroes who have always marched to a different drummer.[20] In *Chicha*, the main hero is the latest oddball. Stepan Chichulin, Chicha for short, lives in a small southern town where all aspects of life are dictated by firmly established rules. The milieu is reconstructed in the film with attention to details, creating a microcosm that reflects the ideal socialist model. For years, Chicha has been singing in the Red Army choir as a tenor, hiding his stupendous bass voice. He is aware of the physical and psychological harm of hiding his true nature, but he is too afraid of the choir conductor to ask for a new assignment. To stay out of trouble, the silent majority in those days "sang" submissively with an official voice. One day, Chicha lets his mighty bass roar out in the middle of a performance. This act of rebellion costs him his job and his social position.

But with the new times, and with the emergence of the entrepreneurial spirit that possessed all former Soviet citizens, Chicha is able to turn the situation to his advantage. He accumulates a small fortune impersonating popular stars, and even performs for the local mafia bosses. Fate, however, is going to play an unexpected trick on him. Chicha receives an invitation from Moscow to participate in a gala performance in front of a big audience. This is for Chicha the chance of a lifetime. But on the train to the capital, he realizes with horror that his wonderful voice is gone forever. The apparent moral of the story is that by betraying his true talent, he has squandered a God-given gift. But the film refrains from judgment; instead, it focuses on the bitter irony underlying the predicament of many Russians. Yesterday, there was no opportunity; today, the opportunity is here but they cannot take advantage of it.

Director Vasily Pichul and screenwriter Maria Khmelik, who are husband and wife, have worked as a team since the late 1980s. The young couple acquired instant fame with *Little Vera* (1988) that was perceived as a significant turning point in the cinema of the glasnost wave. Their second film, *Dark Nights in Sochi* (1989), by contrast, was poorly received and quickly forgotten.[21] With the next picture, *Dreams of an Idiot* (1993), the authors abandon the realistic style and the direct approach to contemporary reality, and employ metaphors, satire, and references to another time. Based on the novel *The Golden Calf* (1931) by the satirical writers Ilf and Petrov, the film is set in the NEP period, a brief parenthesis of limited economic freedom in Soviet history. Parallels with the present

256   Imaging Russia 2000

38   *Dreams of an Idiot* (1993) directed by Vasily Pichul

situation are suggested by anachronisms—setting the action in Moscow metro stations, or on the grounds of the Exhibition of Economic Achievements, which did not exist in those days.

The novel hinged on the figure of the charming rogue, Ostap Bender, and the film follows the novel rather closely.[22] Ostap Bender, goes through a series of incredible adventures that take him and his gang of three from sunny resorts on the Black Sea to the torrid deserts of Central Asia. His aim is to make a million rubles and leave for Rio de Janeiro. He therefore decides to rob a "Soviet millionaire," who lives in disguise as a poor clerk. Money, however, is not the real motivation for Bender. Rather, it is a pretext to bring excitement and drama to his life. He is a born actor, and the world is his stage. Most episodes are faithfully reproduced in the film, translating the verbal texture into surreal images; and potentially grotesque situations are handled with a sense of elegance and measure. Where the film sharply departs from the literary text, is in the casting of the hero. The cinematic Ostap Bender (Sergei Krylov) is businesslike, unattractive, and colorless, despite his gaudy clothes. He lacks the light touch of the literary prototype, his bubbling mischievousness and self-irony. Rather, he projects the image of a mafia boss. Perhaps, given the references to the present day, the change was intentional.

The prospectors

Another comedy, *Weirdoes* (1991) by Alla Surikova, was inspired by the wave of foreign "specialists" that invaded Russia as soon as the doors opened. It pokes fun at the foreigner, who arrives with his baggage of Western culture and technical know-how and is flustered by the local "weirdoes." But the film takes its distance from the current events and comments on the present by way of the past. In the early nineteenth century, an Austrian engineer comes to Russia to build the first railroad and is faced with the dismal backwardness of the infrastructure and the primitive mentality of the people. Situations and characters are intended as a parallel between the Russia of Nicholas I and contemporary Russia, suggesting that little progress has been made. In the film the bureaucracy is firmly in charge of all administrative functions, and displays the Gogolian characteristics of pettiness and corruption. Stereotypes abound in the depiction of pompous clerks and greedy peasants. But there are redeeming figures on the side of good and justice, who join the engineer in the pursuit of his goal: a brave army officer, a peasant *bogatyr*, a reformed secret service agent, and—believe it or not—even the Virgin Mary in disguise. Alla Surikova is an old hand at comedies, and this film reveals her professional touch. Nevertheless, it is less sparkling than her previous works, most notably, *The Man from Boulevard des Capucines* (1987).[23]

Moscow has been a magnet for builders and traders since the fifteenth century. Most Westerners who crossed the border into the mysterious land of Muscovy became permanent residents. One compelling reason was that they were not allowed to leave by a decree of Tsar Ivan III. As it is known, after building the Kremlin wall and the Cathedral of the Assumption, architect Aristotele Fioravanti tried to return to his native Italy, but was caught and ended his days in prison. Many foreigners, however, chose to stay, finding life in Moscow rather pleasant. As in the more recent communist past, they lived in separate compounds, under surveillance by the state police, enjoying the privileges that money and status can buy.

The most ancient of these compounds, Nalivka, was established at the time of Ivan the Terrible, on the little island on the Moscow River across from the Kremlin. That was a rough spot because the population consisted mostly of mercenaries, carousing and harassing their neighbors between assignments in Ivan's wars—the next-door neighborhood known as Baltschug (swamp) bustled with markets and shops and was a prestigious residential area. Next came the Anglisky Dvor (English Compound), one block from the Kremlin wall, which hosted mainly English traders and diplomats. Today, we can visit the museum—opened in 1995—and look at the everyday artifacts that testify to a prosperous bourgeois life style. On display are also portraits of representatives of the English Merchant Adventurers' Co., who, in the mid sixteenth century, undertook an expedition by sea to discover new lands and markets. They came ashore in Arkhangelsk in the middle of the winter, risking to be trapped in the frozen waters, and descended onto Moscow on horse-drawn sleds loaded with merchandise. The commander, Richard Chancellor, eventually became an ambassador at the court of Ivan the Terrible. Anglisky Dvor also served as the headquarters of the Triangle Rubber Co., one of the first pre-revolutionary U.S.-Russian joint ventures. The German colony, Nemetskaya Sloboda, in the city's northeast on the Yauza River, had a more romantic tinge and was an attraction to young Moscovites. The inhabitants were soldiers and professionals, who enjoyed the pleasures of the tavern and the bedroom, as well as intellectual life. Peter the Great, who was a frequent visitor in his young years, found there his first love and the seeds of the ideas that later spurred his Westernization of Russia.

The foreigners who left diaries and memoirs concurred that the Russians were "weirdoes" by Western standards. Many readers are familiar with the observations to this effect by the Marquis de Custine, the nineteenth-century French diplomat recently featured in Sokurov's film, *Russian Ark* (2002).[24] In the late fifteenth century, the Venetian ambassador Ambrogio Contarini made similar remarks in his travel diary: "The Russians are very good-looking, both men and women, but they are also generally crude. They are great drunkards and love to boast of it, looking down on teetotalers. . . . Russian life passes in the following way: in the morning they work the markets until about midday, and then make their way to the taverns to eat and drink. After that it's impossible to interest them in any sort of endeavor."[25] The Westerners' superiority complex offended the local population, who wavered between a welcoming and a suspicious attitude. The arrogance of the foreigner was effectively captured in a brief scene in Andrei Tarkovsky's *Andrei Rublev*. Here, Italian master architects, garbed in the latest Florentine fashion, sneer at the attempt of the Russian boy to forge the bell for the cathedral's belfry. In the end, the boy turns out to be the real artist, sustained by passion and inspiration rather than know-how. In *Weirdoes*, the foreigner is portrayed in a good light, as honest though naïve. This approach may have been different if the film were made after 1991.

A major sign that Russia was undergoing a change at the beginning of the 1990s was a foreign invasion. As soon as the curtain was lifted, a swarm of prospectors rushed into the newborn nation. A number of social entrepreneurs had already had some sporadic contacts with Russian counterparts—NGO officials, social workers, charity representatives, and religious groups. They came in with a mission and, as true missionaries, branched out into unknown territory, setting up small offices in outposts such as Novgorod, Pskov, Voronezh, Samara, Ekaterinburg, and as far out as Siberia. But the bulk of the prospectors concentrated in Moscow, which was the center of everything under the previous centralized government—and, therefore, the only Russian city most of them could pinpoint on the map.

They came in droves, like a conquering army. There were generals—top corporate executives; privates—wide-eyed interns barely out of Russian 101; and officers of all ranks in between. The prevalent attitude could be summed up as follows: "We're aware you suffered under a brutal dictatorship which hindered the country's development. But now we're here to help and bring you our civilization. We will provide you with everything the country is lacking, including our culture. Your culture is good, don't get me wrong, we like your folklore—balalaikas, vodka, and those cute churches. You have many things we enjoy. But we're here primarily to make big bucks, and you will benefit in the process." This group did not include diplomats and senior members of the press corps, who, being officially briefed every day, had a better understanding of policies and appropriate behavior. But in the business world, which included Western filmmakers and media people, they made no bones about their motives, and were not too subtle in displaying their approach to the natives.

Moscow became their playground. As early as 1992, the pages of *The Moscow Times* were peppered with dozens of ads catering to the foreign community. The newspaper itself was a foreign product, published locally in English by a Dutch entrepreneur. The change of scene was startling. In Soviet times, there was little nightlife: no bars, clubs, or casinos. Moscow by night consisted of state-run restaurants, which offered basically the same fare—standard Soviet cuisine and a dance floor. Two establishments, Aragvi and Baku, stood out because of their regional specialties from Georgia and Azerbaijan, and an exotic atmosphere. But none of those places needed to advertise, because the demand greatly exceeded the offer. To make reservations one needed connections, status, and money to bribe the staff, including the doorman who was normally besieged by a long line of frustrated patrons and had the power to lock and unlock the door. A *"lysyi"* would do the trick ("baldhead," meaning the pate of Lenin on a ten-ruble bill). In the new Russia, the restaurant Byloe (Bygone Days) on Petrovka Street, exploited the Soviet theme for the nostalgic clientele—hammer and sickle mosaic above the entrance, portraits of venerable leaders on the walls, and reconstituted Soviet dishes—but the prices were definitely capitalist.

In perestroika times, a few coop restaurants were much sought after, as the first swallows of the new entrepreneurial spirit. They were very modest, in improvised facilities and often lacked food supplies. But they were refreshing in the stifling official environment; every green leaf from the farmers market was particularly fragrant, every bite into a ripe tomato was a sensuous experience. In 1992, the coops faded out; the expatriates imported their nightlife style and foreign-owned establishments started competing with each other, highlighting their national features.

The Exchange, in the Radisson-Slavyanskaya Hotel, proudly announced that it was "the city's only American Steak House." TrenMos (Trenton-Moscow joint venture) claimed to be "the first American restaurant in Moscow," at the same time offering "a taste of France." The elaborate menu featured Cassoulet Toulousain with Duck Confit, Escallop of Foie Gras, and Tournedos Périgueux. How did this square with Trenton, NJ!? Nobody bothered to ask that question. Rather, everyone in the corporate hierarchy, from senior officer to young recruit, relished in the good fortune that placed fat dollars in their wallets and Parisian delights on their plates. Les Champs Elysées represented serious competition. Although located on the outskirts of town, in the Hotel Pullman, it was close to the famous Fyodorov's eye clinic, and, at least in name, had a more legitimate claim to French delicacies. Still another French restaurant, Potel & Chabot, was nested on the grounds of the Moscow Commercial Club—the club of the new Russian millionaires, ironically located on Communist Street. Most restaurants had limousine service door to door.

Italian restaurants, as is always the case, offered superior food in a less ostentatious mise-en-scène. Arlecchino was the oldest foreign restaurant in Moscow, which opened already in perestroika days thanks to a deal with the Filmmakers Union. The restaurant rented the 6-floor facilities in the Kinocenter building, and the patrons had to take the elevator to reach the dining room. It was not the best commercial location. But the restaurant was always full, patronized by a choice clientele that appreciated the genuine taste of its Antipasti, Trance di Dentice all'Acqua di Mare, and Rigatoni all'Amatriciana (the menu was in Italian; no translation). The next to open was Pescatore, which rented the facilities of the former Soviet Peace Committee on Prospect Mira (Prospect of Peace). It offered swordfish, lobster, and snapper flown in from Italy several times a week, as well as local salmon. Many more followed, from upper-crust establishments to pizzerias. Pizza lovers loved in particular Patio Pizza, which also featured the best salad bar in town.

An array of restaurants from the four corners of the world mushroomed all over the city in no time. Le Chalet had on its menu much more than cheese fondue and chocolate; it had "a variety of original dishes prepared as only the Swiss can do." Korea House specified that it had "authentic Korean food served by real Korean chefs." Moscow Bombay declared to be "the most delicious Indian restaurant in the center of Moscow." The Greek Restaurant set up shop on a moored ship of the ex-Soviet river fleet, named after the poet Alexander Blok; so, Blok became synonymous with moussaka and baklava. The Sadko Arcade, by the International Expocenter, announced that "Eating out is in!" In its complex, besides the many shops, it hosted the Steak House, Swiss House, Beer House, Pasta House, Pizza Pazza, and Trattoria. A real curiosity was the Starlite Diner, built in Florida and shipped to Moscow. This silver diner was complete with silver stools, a soda fountain, vinyl-upholstered booths, and Formica tabletops; waitresses in pleated skirts and white socks dispensed banana splits and chocolate malteds. There were also fake foreign establishments, like the Russian-owned Santa Fe, with its faux South-West décor and imitations of burritos and refried beans.

Among these international culinary attractions, McDonald's occupied a very special place. It shone like the supreme icon of Western culture. Its universally recognized logo meant much more then fast food to the Muscovites; it meant a way of life. To many teenagers, a lunch at McDonald's was like a voyage to the U.S. Here, the clientele was primarily Russian, except for some occasional Americans who got homesick and felt the urge to stuff themselves with burgers and fries. The prices were affordable to the Russian middle class—the ruble equivalent of $1 for a Big Mac. But the working poor who made a monthly salary of $20 continued to survive on potatoes, cabbage, bread, and milk as they did in pre-McDonald's times.

The first McDonald's opened in 1990, and many more gradually spread all over the country. There were four of them in Moscow; the oldest one, on Pushkin Square, set the tone for all the others. There, everything was different from the typical Soviet café. True Americana décor took the customers on a virtual trip to the Grand Canyon, to Eldorado landscapes of cacti and wild horses. But the biggest difference was the staff's speed, efficiency, and cheer. Accustomed to being harassed by acidic waitresses and indifferent waiters, who were the rule in state-run establishments, McDonald's customers were elated to be tended by clusters of smiling adolescents in impeccable pink/white uniforms. Like a community of benign elves, they fussed around, clearing tables, mopping floors, arranging chairs, directing traffic. At the counters, more elves handed out double cheeseburgers and took the money with lightening speed, and with a smile indelibly painted on their faces.

The fact that this was a non-smoking establishment made it even more of an oddity among the smoke-saturated city restaurants. In Moscow, to smoke was *de rigueur*; the Russians never heard of an anti-smoking campaign, the Europeans contemptuously dismissed it, and the Americans quickly forgot about it and went back into the habit. Nevertheless, no one smoked at McDonald's, and the line to get into the restaurant stretched out several blocks all day long. Bands of street children quickly figured out how to make a few bucks out of the situation: they would offer to stay in line for you, or to deliver your order, or to watch your car. But they wanted to be paid upfront. I learned in a painful way that they meant business. I parked the car and refused to give them money, telling them that they would get a tip afterward. Upon my return, the kids were gone and I could not get in the car; they had stuck a piece of gum in the lock. It took me several weeks and a lot of money to get it fixed.

Notwithstanding the length of the line, the wait was less than half an hour thanks to the capacity of the restaurant. This was one of the largest McDonald's in the world, equal only to its Beijing twin. To ensure supplies and quality, the company moved an entire enterprise to Russia: from a farm to raise cattle and grow potatoes to a food-processing factory. The result was a tremendous improvement over the shabby Soviet-era *stolovye* (cafeterias), which dished out to people on the run two basic foods: *sosiski* (boiled franks tasting like sawdust) and *kotlety* (burger-like patties made of anything but beef). In comparison, McDonald's was fast food de-luxe.

The fast-food mania took hold of the Muscovites. After McDonald's, Burger King and Burger Kveen opened a couple of outlets; so did Pizza Hut, Taco Bell, Just Subs, Sbarro, and others. Besides finding the food rich and tasty, the customers were attracted by the pop American image these labels projected. The irony was that, by then, U.S. consumers had already embarked on the opposite trend, toward organic, fatless, sugarless, low-calories foods. At home, Fresh Fields was in, McDonald's was out. It seemed that what we rejected as being hazardous to our health made for good exports—notably, fast food and cigarettes.

There was more than restaurants to Moscow nightlife which would sweeten the expatriates' after hours. For a couple of years, the foreign community and the Russian youth raved about rave parties, which were advertised primarily by word of mouth. I attended one of the so-called Gagarin and Mobile rave parties, held at the Moscow velodrome, a huge cycling racetrack turned into a trance-dance stage for tens of thousands of ravers. These gigantic parties had everything in scale, deafening sound systems, dazzling lights, bicycle racers whooshing around the track followed by multi-colored spotlights, and a stylish, hip crowd. But they were impractical to manage and, after the novelty wore off, the crowd dispersed, preferring to spend the night at the clubs.

264   Imaging Russia 2000

In downtown Moscow, there were clubs on every corner and for every taste. Many were run by local entrepreneurs, especially those that included casinos. They competed with foreign glitz and attracted mostly a Russian new rich clientele. The most popular were Bunker with four concerts a week, from rock to techno; Hermitage, not just a club but a cult institution; LSDance, favored by musicians and DJs for its radical dance music; Petliura's, the cheapest club in town, which gathered weird characters, from homeless junkies to art celebrities; Pilot/Soho, a duplex club, with aeronautical décor upstairs and a futuristic style downstairs; and many others too numerous to count.[26]

But the expatriates preferred their own. The Shamrock Pub opened in 1991, in the facilities of the first supermarket, the Irish House; it had a very authentic look, having been built in Ireland and moved to Moscow. It offered thick Guinness ale and attracted a mix of junior office workers, journalists, and top executives, who liked to sing drunken songs together. But within a couple of years, it was eclipsed by another pub, Rosie O'Grady's, which became the place to be after hours. The U.S. was well represented with the Manhattan-Express, in the Rossiia Hotel across from St. Basil. It advertised itself as "Moscow's only New York Supper Club," and lured customers with promises such as, "We're not in Kansas. But we'll make you feel at home." In fact, it was as far from Kansas as the Oz land, and in that magic environment the patrons were treated to caviar pizza, rap music, and 6-foot-5 hostesses. TrenMos Bar was an offspring of the restaurant. The atmosphere there was friendly and relaxed, livened up by "Moscow's Meanest Margueritas" under a sparkling disco ceiling. CNN was playing in the background as an added bonus. Arlecchino, the disco, was very exclusive, with an entry fee of up to $100 for performances by Alla Pugacheva and other celebrities. Armadillo offered Tex-Mex food, Tequila, and pool tables. Night Flights, in a privileged location on Tverskaya Street, was run by a Swedish-Russian joint venture, "a company formed to operate nightclubs in Moscow for pleasure-seekers." It claimed to be "the natural rendezvous in Moscow nightlife"; in effect, it had the reputation of catering to transient businessmen and hookers. Club Metelitsa-cum-casino, on Novy Arbat, stood for "Western style and Western standards."

For those who preferred a more sedate and elegant ambience there was the Savoy Club, "an oasis in the middle of Moscow." This club was even more pleasant during the day, because it was located in a green area near Mosfilm Studio, on Dovzhenko Street, and included on its grounds the 19-hole Tumba Golf Course. Golfers from two continents were extremely grateful to Mr. Tumba, an enterprising Swede, who first brought to Moscow their favorite toy. But some of them would later migrate to the Championship Golf Course, located on the grounds of the Moscow Country Club. This Russian-American joint venture opened in the summer of 1993. It was nested in the enclave of the former Glav UPDK (the Soviet agency providing services to the diplomatic community, including housing and recreation), and catered to foreign VIPs and Russian millionaires. Besides the golf course, it offered secluded cottages in the woods and amenities such as restaurants, bars, casino, hotel, swimming pool, tennis courts, fitness center, sauna, a private lake for skating in the winter, cross country skiing, and clay pigeon shooting.

Patriotic comedies

As they did in the past, the Russians reacted to the foreign invader in an ambivalent way. On the one hand, they recognized the potential of reaping some benefits—at all levels, from street vendors to bankers. On the other hand, their pride suffered. While peddling Western goods, they leaned toward patriotism and nostalgia for Russian values and traditions.

A general tendency in the films of this period is to present the Western way of life as a corrupting influence. Vladimir Khotinenko's, *Patriotic Comedy* (1992), is a semi-fantastic story blending everyday life and the supernatural. The protagonists, the beautiful Zinaida (Larisa Guseva) and her brother Mikhail (Sergei Makovetsky), live in a dilapidated wooden house on the outskirts of a big city. They are dispossessed and plagued by misfortune. Unknown to them, there is a third dweller in the attic, a benevolent household spirit by the name of Pinya, who loves his hosts, protects them, and now and then even buys them food. Such a spirit in Slavic folklore is known as *domovoy*. As in all fairy tales, good and evil are polarized here in the figures of Pinya and his archenemy, Max, a *domovoy* who committed the great sin of abandoning his own home. Max is now after the magic box containing the "secret force," which Pinya has stashed away in a safe place. Handsome and fancifully dressed, Max eventually turns out to be not only a renegade *domovoy*, but also a mafia chief wanted by the local police. Notwithstanding this escape into the fantastic, the film reaffirms in no uncertain terms the theme of Russia. Troubled, tormented, deprived, Russia is the only spiritual anchor for those who are born on her soil. After having been offered a magical trip to Paris and New York, Mikhail talks his girlfriend into going back home, "Only in Russia will we be able to live," he tells her.[27]

Karen Shakhnazarov's *Dreams* (1993) is less optimistic about the future of Russia. But the director in an interview played down the film's gloomy implications. "This is a scherzo, an impromptu film, a game for ourselves and the viewers," he said.[28] He may be right; this film is certainly not on the same level of his previous pictures—the slightly iconoclastic *Jazzmen* (1981), the unsurpassed *Courier* (1987), the surrealist *Zero City* (1989), and the psycho-political *Assassin of the Tsar* (1991). One well-deserved point of criticism is that in this film the humor is heavy-handed, and too often vulgar jokes are directed at politically incorrect targets, such as women. Nevertheless, the film provides comic relief while dealing with serious matters.

Dreams pokes fun at all possible aspects of contemporary Russian reality, offering a critical commentary on the present situation. The film is structured on the juxtaposition of two epochs, divided by exactly one century of history. A young aristocrat in St. Petersburg of 1893 (Marina Mordvinova), is haunted by dreams in which she sees herself as Masha, a dishwasher in a 1993 Moscow cafeteria. Neither her loving husband, a count and a court dignitary, nor the family doctor, nor a famous French hypnotist can help the unfortunate woman, who keeps providing periodic and detailed accounts of her visions. Some of the episodes in her dreams are hilarious, thanks to the context and to fireworks of gags. The viewer cannot miss the parody of well-known political figures, the paradoxical situations of everyday life, and the absurdity of most ordinary events. The woman's companion in her dreams is the flipside of her noble husband (both played by Oleg Basilashvili). This one is a conman, who sells porno pictures of Masha on the Arbat mall, promotes her image with government scouts looking for a prosperous girl to appoint as the Minister of Economic Affairs, and later uses her in a "honey trap" to blackmail a gullible representative of the International Monetary Fund.

For this role Shakhnazarov engaged Fred Hiatt, who was at the time *The Washington Post* Moscow bureau chief.[29]

The authors have left nothing out of the picture, saturating the script with every bit of recent Russiana, including the shooting of a "political thriller about the1991 putsch." Masha is hired to play the role of a patriot, who agrees to seduce the commander of the oncoming army division in order to find out the time for the storming of the White House and report to Yeltsin. The film-within-the-film sequence—a parody of the classical war movie—adds still another dimension to the already layered reality of dreams.[30]

As the action moves from one dream to another, the humor becomes more and more vulgar. This is the case with the beauty contest of Miss Bust-93, where topless beauties from the Commonwealth of Independent States (CIS) parade on stage, greeted by the babbling of a Russian Orthodox priest to the accompaniment of an American Evangelist choir. Masha, as Miss Russia, wins the title. The ceremony is followed by a fundraising for the construction of the Cathedral of Christ the Savior, where the donors are awarded the privilege of kissing Miss Bust's breasts.

Back in 1893, the count is horrified by what he perceives as the downfall of Russia. He cannot believe that the price of bread would jump to 45 rubles a kilo, and the most sought after profession for young women would be that of hard-currency prostitute. The state of the ruble is a matter of concern also to the doctor, who asks the countess why the prostitutes would prefer to receive foreign currency. "*A komu nuzhny dereviannye?* (Who needs wooden money?)," the countess replies. Here, contemporary Russia's street jargon clashes with the highly formal setting of a St. Petersburg palace, resulting in explosive laughter on the part of the viewer. This literary device, known as *ostranenie* (making it strange),[31] also informs the count's questioning of his wife about the political order of the future country. "What is CIS?" he asks. "I don't know. And they themselves don't know," answers the countess. The count: "But is there a government?" "There are many governments," she answers. The count: "What does it mean, 'many.' Someone must be ruling the country. Is there a tsar?" "No, they have been without a tsar for a long time. . . . There was some kind of revolution," the countess explains. "I understand. It must be a democratic republic, like the French one," the count concludes with a touch of disdain.[32] As a member of the tsar's cabinet, he feels compelled to advise the monarch about the need for reforms in order to avoid a revolution that will eventually plunge the country into the abyss of degradation reflected in his wife's dreams. His report creates a scandal and the count leaves the government post to retreat with his wife to their country estate.

The prolonged sequence of the trip in an open carriage, through thick woods and green meadows, with long shots of the peaceful countryside, stresses the movement away from urban life, politics, and neuroses. When the patrician mansion appears at the end of the road, the countess joyfully exclaims: "Here is my home!" The couple, holding hands, looks forward to a serene existence, no longer disturbed by bad dreams.

One hundred years later, Masha visits that same estate. The cafeteria's administrator has bought the property and wants to fix it in order to turn it into his own dacha. He invites Masha to see the ancient manor, hoping she would be impressed and fall for him. The trip to the countryside is parallel to that of the noble couple, but with opposite implications in the setting, the mood, and the intention. The administrator's middle-class sedan runs through endless suburbs, noisy and congested, full of new tenements, nuclear power plants, and air polluting factories. The woods are gone; now, the dilapidated mansion sits on devastated land. While wandering through the empty halls, Masha comes face to face with the countess' portrait, her mirror image.

But this is no longer a dream. In this final scene planes are shifting, creating an ambiguity of time and space, of life and delusions. Which is which? The viewer has been set up to consider St. Petersburg's world as real, and Moscow's world as dream. But now, St. Petersburg's world has dissipated, and so has the dream. The only "real" world the viewer is confronted with is the contemporary Moscow world. The question arises: is 1893 more real than 1993, or vice-versa? Analogizing classical literature with a playful movie, one might say with Calderon, *"la vida es sueño."* Perhaps, this is what Shakhnazarov meant by "a game for ourselves and the viewers."

Yuri Mamin, a former student of Eldar Ryazanov and one of the first to revive satire as a genre in the perestroika years, brought to the screen biting comedies with considerable success. "Cinema is my weapon, both for defense and attack," he said.[33] *Window on Paris* (1994), a Russian-

French co-production, was his first post-Soviet attack. Nobody can miss the allusion in the title to Peter the Great's policy of opening a "window on Europe," in order to carry out his high-minded program of reforms. In the film, a window in a St. Petersburg *kommunalka* (communal apartment) literally opens on Paris, by magic, and provides Mamin's contemporaries, caught in a different wave of reforms, with an easy escape into the wonderland of the Western consumer society. Having unleashed his characters, Mamin sits back and watches them getting into a gold-rush frenzy, and disgracing themselves. *Window* expresses the frustration of seeing Russia turn into an Eastern bazaar instead of a civilized democracy.

The Gorokhov family—father, mother, and a pregnant daughter—takes center stage, and serves as the stereotype of narrow-mindedness and petty materialism, attributes best qualified by the Russian word, *poshlost'*. Once in Paris, they stop at nothing in order to make a quick buck, or drag back home any sellable goods they can put their hands on. The sense of urgency is aggravated by the fact that the window of opportunities opens only once every twenty years, and only for a few days. Together with other neo-*kommersanty*, the Gorokhov family performs folk dances in the street, goes rummaging in dumps, sets up a warehouse on the roof of a building, and turns the life of their Paris neighbor, Nicole (Agnes Sorel), into a nightmare. The situations are hilarious, but the implications are sad. The unfortunate Nicole one day enters the wrong door and finds herself in St. Petersburg, where she is first robbed and then thrown in jail; she is able to escape and return to Paris only because of a clever stratagem.

The film does not spare French society either. The world on the other side of the window is driven by materialistic concerns no less than the Gorokhov family. But in Paris materialism is more sophisticated. Here, the grotesque effect is achieved by way of hyperbolic refinement, rather than exaggerated vulgarity. For example, Nicole is a sculptor who sells her talent to customers seeking flattering embalmed effigies of their dead pets. And a philharmonic society of gay males wants to engage two Russian musicians if they agree to perform naked from the waist down. To their credit, the Russians reject the offer together with a good salary. A creepy uneasiness with consumer-society values is revealed in a scene at the restaurant, where two Russians facing each other across a table covered

270 Imaging Russia 2000

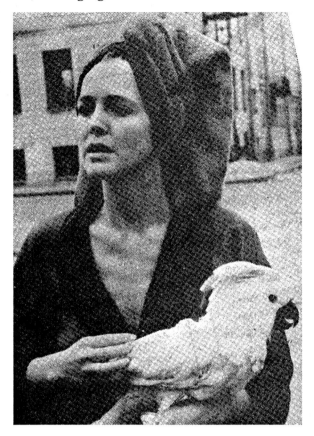

39 *Window on Paris* (1994) directed by Yuri Mamin

with French delicacies, talk about the lack of spirituality, when compared with life at home.

There is one character who is immune from the commercial fever, the gentle music teacher Nikolay Chizhov (Sergei Dontsov-Dreiden), who is the tenant of the magic room. He is a maverick among his colleagues, battling the school administrators who have privatized the institution and turned education into a business. Chizhov decides to use the window on Paris to take his students on a vacation trip, in order acquaint them with Western culture and history. His goal is to take them back home not with a couple of TV sets, but with a richer stock of knowledge which would enable the kids to build a bridge between two worlds. The initiative is risky, because the youngsters at first fall for the trappings of Western pop culture, breaking ranks and happily scattering all over Paris. But, as they begin to get homesick, the teacher pulls them together by the luring melody of his flute and, with a little twist on the Pied Piper model, leads the pack back to Russia.

The film is a good blend of contemporary *byt* (everyday life), fairy-tale fantasy, and patriotic sentiment for an unhappy but beloved Russia. The events are seen through an ironic lens, and the ending sustains the ironic tone, avoiding a moralistic closure. Back home, surrounded by the reality of shock reform and deteriorating living conditions, even Chizhov feels the allure of the Paris wonderland—mostly because he misses Nicole, with whom he had developed a romantic relation. The window is now shut, as the magic period has expired. But Chizhov, with a small group of those who had a taste of the forbidden fruit, keeps looking for a breach in the wall. As the camera pulls back, the wall is shown to be insurmountable—a solid brick barrier that fills the whole screen and dwarfs the men stubbornly pounding at its foundation.

In the beginning was the kiosk

The dwellers of the St. Petersburg *kommunalka* would soon discover that they did not need to go to Paris in order to satisfy their consumer needs. St. Petersburg caught up with the commercial wave with some delay, but in Moscow the consumerist frenzy started in 1992. Abrupt economic reforms and the devaluation of the ruble ushered a new era of street commerce. Moscow resumed the look of the bustling bazaar that was once described in the diary of a seventeenth-century visitor: "People come from all over to take part in a buy and sell market on Red Square that is so busy the pushing and shoving is almost unbearable. They trade everything under the sun, no holds barred."[34]

Markets of all sizes dealing in all sorts of goods covered every inch of every empty lot. The largest open-air market was located in the Lenin Stadium at Luzhniki. On an ordinary day, thousands of traders and shoppers filled the huge arena and spilled over onto the surrounding grounds. A stream of human mules under enormous burdens kept

40 Red Square was the main marketplace from the Middle Ages until the GUM was completed in 1893

coming out of metro station Sportivnaya, moving in the direction of the stadium. The stream clogged the crosswalk on Khamovnichesky Val, blocking the normal traffic flow. When a car pushed its way through the crowd, it looked like the Red Sea waters parting, just enough to let the car by, and immediately closing back up. Traffic cops were powerless and overwhelmed, and the traffic lights were simply ignored as if they were mere decorations. Inside the stadium, the goods were displayed as far as the eye could see, on stalls, tables, chairs, hangers, or simply on the ground. It was an awesome sight. But the expats preferred to shop at another market, located in the Izmailovo Park. This one was for pleasure shopping. While the vendors at the Luzhniki market provided the bare necessities to the Russian population, the Izmailovo traders catered to the foreign clientele looking for antiques and folklore artifacts. This market was open only on weekends; it too was huge, and it was crowded both in summertime and winter sub-zero weather. Like other Westerners, I got the treasure hunting fever, and kept coming back regularly over the first year. As a result, I filled my apartment with Daghestani rugs, vintage amber jewelry, old porcelain cups, lace tablecloths, art nouveau lamps, brass samovars, and carved wooden boxes. Eventually, I got my fill of antiques and would visit the Izmailovo market only when I had guests.

It took some time for the Soviet-era stores to turn into capitalist enterprises. Those stores were a pitiful testimony to the shortcomings of the regime—huge, empty halls, bare shelves punctuated by a few tins of canned fish and jars of pickles, with surly salespeople adding up purchases on the abacus. The first *kommersanty* needed an immediate and practical outlet, one notch above the marketplace. They found it in those rickety metal and glass cubicles known as kiosks. In the Soviet era, the kiosks were state-owned and had specific functions: newsstands (Soyuzpechat), ice cream booths (Morozhenoe), city information service (Mosgorspravka), and shoe repair/shoelace vendors (Remont obuvi). The Gorbachev-era coops expanded the use of the kiosk, adding a few items to their budding business: soft drinks, candy, cigarettes, books. A new line of business that emerged in those days was the flower market on an industrial scale, where the kiosks were supplied by large nurseries in the southern republics that made the flowers available all year round. The infrastructure was still rudimentary; it was not unusual in the middle of the winter to see carnations under plastic tents heated by candles. But the business was aggressively pushed. In the summer, these large enterprises would move onto the turf that had been the prerogative of individual vendors—those who had a stall at the farmers market, and the little *babushki* who stood on street corners with a bouquet of daffodils from their gardens—taking away a good chunk of their business.

Then, with the advent of the free market, the kiosk era began in full. The kiosk turned into a convenience store, filled with imported alcohol and tobacco, Mars bars, Snickers bars, gum, sodas, and snack food. One item in great demand was the videocassette. Pirated videos of national and foreign films sold like hot cakes, fueling a gigantic illegal business. Another illegal business was the money exchange, which at the beginning of the reform was allowed only at banks and exchange points in hotels. But street transactions went on undisturbed; the kiosks would advertise the business by displaying foreign banknotes in their windows—Deutsche marks, Swiss francs, French francs, and the privileged one, the U.S. dollar. They were eager to buy rather then sell. Enterprising young traders would stand right outside bank doors, approaching customers with an offer slightly higher than the official exchange rate. In Soviet times, money exchange was a crime punishable with long prison terms. Nevertheless, it flourished. The *fartsovshchiki* (black marketers) would aggressively buy consumer goods from foreigners, emptying their bags of clothes, shoes, and electric gadgets, and even buy foreign currency at great risk and in great secrecy. In the new Russia, it was still an illegal business, where both buyers and sellers could get 3 to 8 years in prison, but it was endemic and not effectively prosecuted.

The old kiosks suddenly became a most sought after commodity. There were 1,500 Soyuzpechat kiosks in Moscow, renamed Rosspechat after the change. They began to disappear one after the other from the place they had occupied for decades. Some were sold by their operators to the new merchants; many were stolen. The scheme was simple and effective. In broad daylight, the kiosk was secured to a crane, moved to a flatbed, and taken away before anyone had the time to realize what was going on. If the kiosk operator objected, the abductors would produce false papers from City Hall that authorized the move. The operators were left on the sidewalk, divested of their shell, vulnerable like turtles without their armor, speechless and petrified, crushed by this new misfortune which they believed to be still another indignity inflicted on them by the authorities. One hundred kiosks vanished in six months in 1992.[35] They reappeared in different locations under a different guise—a fresh coat of paint, colored light festoons, and a motley display of foreign brands in the windows. However, for a while, they maintained their typical customer-unfriendly way. The customer would walk up to the fortified kiosk walls and bend down to talk to the invisible vendor through a little hole. The vendor would quote a price and take the money, and finally would spit out the requested item. The customer was still being treated as a supplicant, at the mercy of those who owned the goods.

But things were rapidly changing in the main cities. In Moscow, the kiosk itself underwent an ugly-duckling metamorphosis, from unsightly walk-up booth to "pavilion." The transformation was in part spurred by the city's administration, which recognized the need to regulate the unruly phenomenon of street commerce. The authorities were concerned with the clusters of kiosks that cluttered the street, attracting rats and crime—around train stations their number could easily be in the hundreds. Most of all, they were concerned with a form of trade that eluded taxation. City Hall established a new system that favored large entrepreneurs regularly licensed. The first step was for licensed individuals to buy a row of ramshackle kiosks and give them a more attractive, unified look. Gradually, new smart constructions replaced the little kiosks in strategic points downtown. By 1993, kiosks sporting the company logo, "Tisk," stood out by their hexagonal shape in mint green and white. They offered more exclusive and expensive merchandise, such as imported clothes and perfumes. Baskin Robbins' bright pink kiosks displaced the ice cream vendors of old. Even the Orthodox Church had its kiosk, topped with a small onion dome, located outside the renovated church of the Mother of God of Kazan at the Red Square gate. This kiosk sold plastic icons, cheap crosses and pendants, and religious books. The new kiosks had one feature in common: they used the cash register instead of the abacus in order to account for taxes.

The most impressive were the pavilions Slavyansky Ryad, located on Theater Square and Petrovka Street. These superkiosks were large, corrugated metal structures the size of a trailer, endowed with professionally dressed windows, demonstration areas for high-tech electronics, dressing rooms for Western fashion, and air conditioning. The exotic merchandise carried expensive tags, but there was no warranty, and the smart shopper would notice that Pierre Cardin and Armani brands were actually made in Romania. In the pavilions, one would find "French" perfume for 200,000 rubles ($40), "Italian" women's boots for 300,000 rubles ($60), "Swiss" watches for 2 million rubles ($400), and mink coats for 4 million rubles ($800). This setup met the demand of ordinary Russian customers, who would gladly pay the price for such consumer goods, which were unavailable in state stores, or unaffordable in the high-fashion Western shops.

The surviving state-run stores could not keep up with the market because they lacked supplies. The pavilions' suppliers were middlemen operating in the shadow. They preferred not to deal with regular stores in order to avoid registration and taxation. Most of the suppliers at the low end of the chain were "shuttles" (*chelnoki*), who hit the suitcase route at least once a month. They would leave Russia with empty bags by air, train, or boat, and come back loaded with consumer goods. The most traveled routes were to the United Arab Emirates, Istanbul, Poland, South Korea, and China, where they could shop for the cheapest prices.

The shuttles came from all walks of life—housewives, teachers, doctors, and white-collar workers, who found the business paid better than their old jobs. In 1994, the goods they brought back home accounted for 70 percent of cheap clothing and 30 percent of audio-video equipment sold on the market. The shuttles performed an invaluable service to the consumers. A 1993 survey that polled 76 cities showed that half of those cities had no vacuum cleaners and microwaves on sale, and one in three cities had no color TV sets in the stores.[36]

Katya's sister-in-law, Nina, after the brutal murder of her husband became a shuttle. She would leave every month from the bustling port of Novorossiisk to take the Black Sea route to Istanbul. She came to visit one day, her image remade in the latest *chelnoki* fashion—jeans, a Nike T-shirt, purple/green running shoes, and a sequined baseball cap. She looked younger and energized. "I make good money and, in addition, I get out of the house, travel, and make new friends. The trip to Istanbul is long, 32 hours, but there is a lot of people like me on the boat, and we get together and have fun," she told us. On the way back, she said, they did not even have to drag their heavy bags to Moscow; the parking lot at the dock would fill up with trucks at the arrival of a ship, and the truckers would buy every bit of merchandise on the spot and carry it to the four corners of Russia. The Russian shuttles faced some competition by the Chinese, who embarked on the new Silk Road—now on the track of the Trans-Siberian railroad—with bags full of cheap tennis shoes and vinyl parkas. Their main trading center was in Irkutsk, where they did a brisk business. But for those who ventured further West into Russia the business was extremely difficult, as they were often robbed on the train or in their Moscow hotel, and systematically subjected to extortion at every level, from the porters at the train station to the professional racketeers. Even for the Russians, the shuttle business became increasingly more difficult, because the local mafia demanded protection fees and the government imposed customs duties. The shuttles had to confront criminal gangs and customs officials; the situation was dangerous, and often someone would get killed or arrested. But most shuttles found an easy solution: they would pay the racket and bribe the officers, and pass most of the costs over to the consumers. According to Nina, the business was still good, and everybody was happy—shuttles, mafiosi, customs officials, and shoppers.

The kiosk was slowly but inexorably being replaced by the Western-style department store. To the Americans' delight, a hardware store called Global USA opened in early 1994. There, we found all the familiar brands. Finally, we were able to buy shiny sets of pots and pans, coffee makers, steam irons, water filters, self-stick paper for our drawers, steel nails to hang our pictures, and the hundreds of little gadgets that made our life much easier; also, TV sets, washing machines, computers, and electronic equipment. The prices were comparable to those at home, and the store accepted credit cards. The Finnish Kalinka-Stockmann too opened a new hardware store and carried most of the same inventory. Stockmann had been part of the Soviet landscape for many years, as one of the very few grocery stores for foreigners under state control. By the end of 1998, Kalinka-Stockmann became the anchor department store at the newly opened Smolensky Passage, a middle-range shopping center on the Garden Ring.

International designers' boutiques with astronomical prices took over the premium space in the Petrovsky Passage and the GUM, replacing the modest Soviet shops that sold linen, scarves, fur hats, and amber beads for a few rubles. The developers refurbished these art nouveau shrines of pre-revolutionary Russian consumerism, applying fresh coats of creamy and green paint to the walls and restoring skylight domes and wrought-iron banisters. Now they looked again like the Milan "Galleria" as they had when they were first conceived. The shabby TsUM, a nearby Soviet department store, was revamped and turned into an attractive facility for customers of average means. The five-story children's store, Detsky Mir, on Okhotny Ryad (former Marx Prospect), leased the whole ground floor to a dealer of luxury, imported cars. As the demand for commercial space increased, the children's toys and clothes kept moving further away, to the upper levels. Still another luxury complex, the French Galleries, opened in the spring of 1998, in the building that was home to the Panteleevsky Dvor shopping center in the nineteenth century. The new department store displayed shopping arcades on five levels, scintillating with high-profile brand names; but its real attraction was a 21-meter tall steel reproduction of the Eiffel Tower in the middle of the atrium, shooting all the way up to the glass ceiling. A little removed from the center, the Sadko Arcade at the Expo Center on the Krasnopresnenskaya Embankment offered shopping facilities in addtion to restaurants, and a piano bar.

Department stores and shopping malls appeared every day by the dozens, or so it seemed, in the golden district at the heart of the city. But the most ambitious project was the Manezh Shopping Center, sponsored and owned by the city, but managed by foreign companies—like all of the new constructions. For four years—1994 to 1998—the central square, where the main Moscow streets converge from all four cardinal points, was a mess. Through-traffic access was diverted and a tall fence was built around a gigantic excavation pit. Beyond the fence, the construction of the underground shopping mall went on steadily, notwithstanding criticism voicing concerns about possible damage to historical monuments and the use of public money for commercial projects. The projected cost was $330 million, but the management was confident that the complex would become profitable in four to seven years. The reality turned out to be much grimmer; a great amount of retail space could not be leased due to the exorbitant rental prices and difficulties with the city bureaucracy. And when the August '98 financial crisis hit, several shops closed because of a lack of customers. The mall was supposed to be finished for the celebration of Moscow's 850th birthday, in the fall of 1997, but by the end of that year it was still not fully opened; only the ground floor was operational, and the recreational outdoor space. The project consisted of 70,000 square meters of space over four levels, three of them underground, including an array of shops of the most famous international labels, restaurants, a 300-car garage, and an archaeological museum of the artifacts found during the excavation. Aesthetically, it mimicked the theme park idea. The design carried the signature of Zurab Tsereteli, nicknamed the "court artist" for his ties with Mayor Luzhkov. He got most of the prestigious commissions meant to beautify the city, such as the gigantic monument to Peter the Great on the Krimsky Embankment. The descent into the shopping center was supposed to be a voyage through four centuries of history. Each floor reflected the architectural style and the city life of commercial Moscow at different historical times—the 17th, 18th, 19th, and 20th centuries, starting from the bottom up. It, therefore, stressed its native commercial tradition, rather than an imitation of Western models. The fancy Western labels on store doors, the setting suggested, were merely guests.

There was a precedent in Moscow for this kind of patriotic fair-like setup in the park dedicated to the Exhibition of Economic Achievements

(VDNKh), built at the peak of the Stalinist years. There, the emphasis was not on commerce but on the results of socialist labor. The achievements of the Soviet economy were displayed in grandiose or cute pavilions in the architectural styles of the republics of the Union, among scintillating fountains ornate with gigantic corn stalks and dancing maids. An attempt to turn VDNKh into commercial space in the era of the free market economy was not met with success because of the configuration of the pavillions; they were scattered over a very large area, which made it inconvenient to shop. The only result was that the park fell into disrepair and lost its kitchy charm.

The Manezh Shopping Center's troubles culminated at the end of the century in a terrorist blast. In the fall of 1999, a bomb exploded in a video game arcade on the bottom level, appropriately named Dinamit (Dynamite).

Not by bread alone

Parallel to the development of the shopping malls was the emergence of the supermarket. The grocery-shopping field was dotted with brand new outlets of various nationalities.[37] Garden Ring Supermarket, near the zoo, was Irish; Intercar Colognia, in the Pekin Hotel, was German, as was Julius Meinl in the south-west; Irish House on Novy Arbat was, of course, Irish; A-market, on Malaya Bronnaya, was Dutch; Fortcor, also on Malaya Bronnaya, was French; Sadko, on Dorogomilovskaya Street and at Expocenter, was Swiss; Kalinka-Stockmann, near metro Paveletskaya, was Finnish; M. Leader, one of the largest supermarkets in town, was of unknown nationality. This store was located on the airfield formerly known as Khodynka, where during the celebration for the coronation of Nicholas II, in 1896, thousands of people were crushed in a stampede while rushing up to the tables loaded with free food. Shopping at M. Leader was much easier and safer. Most of the customers in these supermarkets were foreigners, but an increasing number of Russians also shopped there. At an American market, known among the expats as "the junk food hall of fame," the vast majority of shoppers were Russian. They were eager to taste exotic delicacies such as peanut butter, Spam, marshmallow, ketchup, and chocolate chip cookies. At first, it was a matter of curiosity for the new food, and a desire to show off their social status—it was cool to drink Kool-Aid. With time, they became more discriminating and took advantage of the great variety of excellent food available in other supermarkets. That is, the very small minority who could afford it. The others might indeed have lived by bread alone.[38] Bread prices rose in 1992 to 10-25 rubles per kilo. In 1993, the government terminated the subsidies on wheat, and the price of bread jumped up to 90-190 rubles per kilo, and the next year to 300-700 rubles. There was little else that pensioners and low-income workers could afford to buy besides bread.

A few supermarkets were direct descendants of the Beriozka stores that existed in the Soviet system. The Beriozkas were created in the mid 1960s to serve the small community of foreign residents and the tourist industry. Some sold groceries; others, books, souvenirs, and antiques. They were operated by the Ministry of Trade and accepted only hard currency. An even more special store was the Diplomatic Gastronom, on Bolshaya Gruzinskaya, established to provide foreign diplomats with tax- and tariff-free products; this store did not accept currency of any kind, only the much-coveted D-coupons issued by the Ministry of Foreign Affairs, and occasionally traded on the black market. There were three Beriozka grocery stores in Moscow; they were stocked with the best of Western and Soviet products, and carried fresh lettuce throughout the winter. The local population was barred not only from shopping there—to own hard currency was a crime—but even from peeping in from the street. The shop windows were blinded with posters or heavy drapes to keep the passersby from seeing what privilege could buy. Foreigners, however, were grudgingly allowed to escort Soviet citizens to the Beriozka stores, as long as they picked up the check.

I took advantage of this concession several times. Although most of our Russian friends were too proud to accept this kind of help, there was one way I was able to assist. A colleague who emigrated to the U.S. and lost the right to go back to the USSR, put me in touch with his parents who were still living in Moscow. Periodically, I would take the elderly couple to the Beriozka store, make sure they got a full cart of good food, and charge it to my credit card. My colleague back home would then deposit a check in my bank account. I was rewarded with a delicious dinner at the couple's cozy apartment, around a table set with a starched linen cloth, fine old china, and crystal glasses. Lev Lvovich was a linguist, and his wife, Ruf Samoylovna, a professor of English. Both lost their university posts when the son emigrated, and were forced into early retirement. They were dignified in their obvious sorrow. "Now, we have a lot of free time to stand in line for food," Ruf would say half-jokingly. They were grateful to their son for the food he sent them, but even more for the messenger. The conversation was mostly about him; they wanted to know every detail of his life, his work, his little daughter. The silk-covered lampshade that hung low over the table magnified the intensity of their gaze. They kept their eyes on me as if they were seeing the son far away, beyond the iron curtain.

The Beriozkas made an easy conversion to capitalism, thanks to the fact that the infrastructure was already in place. A special section of the Ministry of Trade now runs them like a private company; the doors are open to all, and the citizens are welcome as valuable customers. But my two old friends cannot take advantage of it; Lev Lvovich died in the late 1980s after his third heart attack, and Ruf Samoylovna finally moved closer to her son's family, and lives in Florida.

Another resource for food shoppers was the farmers market. The Soviet state granted permission to the collective farm workers to trade produce from their plots, as well as cheese, eggs, honey, and meat from their farmyards. This concession to the collective farmers was actually an economic necessity, because the state could not provide enough food for the population. The trade was regulated by the government, which provided specially built physical facilities and rented out spaces, but the farmers set their prices—much higher than in the state subsidized stores. People resented the "speculators," but bought from them anyway. There were dozens of farmers markets in Moscow, large and small. In post-Soviet Russia, when trade became a prerogative of all citizens and street seller stalls with fruit and vegetables popped up on every corner, the farmers markets were infiltrated by crime and racketing, and fell under the control of organized groups. They became a main target of police raids, seeking illegal immigrants. The Russian farmers complained that they were being squeezed out, as more and more southerners aggressively moved in. The Russians' general attitude toward migration was captured in numerous films, where the produce dealer from the south is an object of parody; he is portrayed as being sleazy and devious, when not openly associated with the mob—as in *Old Nags* and *Ryaba, My Chicken*, to cite only two examples. But the new trend was mainly the result of economic dynamics. While the Russian farmers in the winter could provide only potatoes and cabbage, the southern dealers would bring to the market tomatoes, oranges, and bananas all year round. Not all these products came from the south, though; large wholesale companies would import bananas and oranges from North Africa and the Middle East.[39]

It has always been fun to shop at the farmers market. It was like an immersion in a peculiar culture, with its own language and rituals. Strolling along the aisles, between rows of colorful stalls, I would cause an outburst of calls, summons, appeals, invitations, offers, inducements, entreaties, and proposals from right and left. As my head spun around, the flurry of sounds was matched by a kaleidoscope of colors and shapes—rings of smoked sausage, mounds of cottage cheese, jars of golden honey, cuts of bloody meat, pinky pig heads, apricots and peaches against green watermelons, gleaming strawberry preserves, brownish dried mushrooms stringed together like a necklace. . . Then, my eyes would stop panning, suddenly caught by a particular item—say, a bunch of lilac.

I move up to the flowers and inhale their purple fragrance. I ask the woman: *"Po chom*? (How much?)." She sizes me up with an expert look and quotes a high price. I would be happy to pay it, but I know that I am expected to bargain; it is part of the market culture. I do not want to disappoint the woman, and make a counteroffer for a much lower figure. She pretends to be insulted. A dark-skinned vendor from the neighboring stall shouts at me in his southern accent: "Madàme! Why do you want to buy her lilac when you can buy watermelon from me for much less? Come over here, my prices are lower." The woman reacts swiftly with a barrage of explicit language at his address; then, gives in to my offer and, as if making the ultimate sacrifice, hands me the fragrant clusters of lilac.

Fantastic tales

Remember MMM? Back then, I neglected to say that the company also owned a film studio. The MMM studio produced mainly its own commercials, first and foremost those comprising the Lyonya saga. But before the commercial series, it also produced the full-length feature *Gongofer* (1993). The director of these productions, Bakhyt Kilibaev, also served as MMM's PR department head and spokesperson. Kilibaev started his career with a couple of adventure movies; then, with *Gongofer*, turned to the genre of the Slavic fairy tale, where the supernatural is the dominant component.

Gongofer is made of the stuff of folk storytelling, but there are no good fairies in this movie. Rather, there is a band of demons, witches, werewolves, and other assorted creatures, which rule the earth and sky and control the destinies of the ordinary folk. These are the descendants of the archetypal devilish cohort that populated Gogol's early collections of tales, gathered on summer nights near the village of Dikanka. This menacing background, in traditional folklore, is colored with humor, popular wisdom, and mischievous wit—all attributes of the simpleton-heroes who miraculously triumph over the forces of darkness. In Gogol's tales, however, there is a tendency to replace humor with horror. This is most vividly exemplified in the tale "Viy," from the collection *Mirgorod* (1835), where a horrid ghost takes center stage. This is also the tendency in *Gongofer*, whose plot makes references to "Viy."

Gongofer is hardly a comedy. Except for the narrator's speech, which mimics the storytelling mannerism of the Gogolian narrator in the prologue and the epilogue, and provides a bit of comic relief, the body of the story is a succession of dark and gory episodes.[40] Screenwriters Pyotr Lutsik and Alexei Samoryadov wrote original and provocative screenplays based on the mixing of genres for a number of films.[41] They collaborated on this script with Kilibaev, with the obvious intention of mixing humor and horror and providing a commentary on the nature of the medium. Their screen rendition of the world of superstition, fear, mocking masks from the realm of the dead, hellish dogs, and evil spirits is deliberately deprived of the mystical touch. Instead of a scary infernal saraband, the viewer is confronted with cheap magician tricks and cinematic clichés.

The story hinges on the misadventures of two brave Cossacks who come to Moscow on business from their village. Together with a delegation of fellow farmers, they are in charge of buying a pedigree bull at the agricultural fair hosted at the wondrous VDNKh. The action takes place in the Soviet period at an unspecified time, and does not contain any significant political allusions, except for some ironical references to "party loyalty" (*partiinost'*), which in context come across as comic lines. The whole opening sequence at the fair is shot in the style of a musical, reminiscent of the jolly operetta *Cossacks of Kuban* (Pyriev, 1950). And then, the tone changes. After celebrating their purchase with carousing, accordion music, and gigantic amounts of vodka, Kolka (Ivan Martynov) and his uncle (Viktor Stepanov) miss the train and decide to spend the night on the fairground. That night Kolka is enticed into an erotic affair with a glamorous lady, who later turns out to be a witch (Ekaterina Kmit). The next morning, Kolka finds himself dumped in the woods and with the color of his eyes changed from brown to blue. To Kolka, this is the sign that a demon has entered his soul. In despair he begins to howl like a wild beast, and resolves to get his own brown eyes back at all costs. Kolka and his uncle arm themselves Cossack-style, with an arsenal of sabers, knives, and shotguns, and confront the witch on her turf in her many scary transformations—from dog to old hag. But their bravery and their weapons are powerless against the unclean forces. One deed, which is supposed to eliminate the witch for good, consists of killing the huge boar Gongofer, the pride of the VDNKh agriculture pavilion, and eating its heart raw. While Kolka succeeds in felling the beast—supposedly another incarnation of the witch—he cannot bring himself to swallow its heart. It is simply too disgusting. Failing this test costs him his life; in her final attack, the witch drives a stake into Kolka's heart, turning him into a living dead and taking him into her uncanny realm.

And all this takes place because of a change of eye color. Throughout this series of spooky adventures, the eyes remain the dominant element, both as a narrative device and as a visual paradigm. In Gogol's tale "Viy," the eye is the main power instrument of the dark forces. On one hand, the evil eye projects the deadly beam that hits the victim; and on the other hand, the eyes of the victim are vulnerable entry channels to the soul. In that story, the unfortunate seminarian who is attacked by the witch is conscious all the time that he must avert his eyes, because to make eye contact would be the kiss of death—this is how he dies in the end when the monster Viy raises his floor-sweeping eyelids and looks at him.[42] In *Gongofer*, the witch Ganna picks Kolka as her victim at the fair by making eye contact with him. Later, she seeks him out, arriving in a black limousine whose headlights shine in the night like the yellow eyes of a cat. In the car, Ganna's face is in the shade, while her eyes sparkle like two phosphorescent dots. In the sequence that leads to the erotic climax in Ganna's surreal apartment, she wears a long white gown like the ghost of the tale. After serving Kolka magic potions and soaking him in a hot tub, she becomes sexually aggressive. However, while the two engage in physical activity that connotes sexual intercourse, there is no sex. There is only a metaphor for sex, like the attack of the vampire in Gothic tales. Ganna lies on top of Kolka and works exclusively on his eyes: she voluptuously sucks them out of their sockets. The camera offers us a close-up of one gelatinous bulb after she gently spits it out onto the palm of her hand.

The image is repulsive and memorable—perhaps, an allusion to *Un Chien Andalou*?[43] As such, it may be the key to the film. From this perspective, all the stuff that makes up the plot is sheer nonsense; it is a fantasy, it is make-believe. What is real is the ability to see with our own eyes, to see through the plot, to see the deeper implications of the images created and manipulated through the medium. All good films, one way or another, remind us of this.

Sergei Ovcharov made a couple of films in the 1980s, which were based on folklore and legends, although they were not horror films.[44] Ovcharov's first post-Soviet film, *Drum Roll* (1993), remains rooted in Russian soil, but draws inspiration visually from Chaplin's little tramp and Buster Keaton's surrealist gags. Appropriately, this film is silent, although a full symphonic score sustains the soundtrack that comments ironically on the action.

The drummer of a funeral band inherits a "Stradivarius drum," from a deceased distinguished composer. The drum becomes an inseparable companion to the man, alternately causing him trouble and providing support. The drum is personified and displays human feelings and sensibilities. It serves its master well when it is in a good mood, but displays a temper when it feels unfairly treated. Because the drum makes too much noise, its owner is expelled from the tenement where he lives and becomes a hobo. The two embark on a random journey, and wander

286   Imaging Russia 2000

41   *Drum Roll* (1993) directed by Sergei Ovcharov

about the vast territory of the former Soviet Union now being crisscrossed by a grid of newly established borders. At the crossing of each border, the little tramp is robbed by customs guards of his poor belongings, until he's left with nothing but the drum.

The theme of the nation's fragmentation is echoed by the disintegration of the social fabric. In one episode, the childlike but ingenious little man takes refuge in the subway and joins the dozens of beggars and peddlers crowding the underground space. The scene is hilarious, but the laughter has a bitter aftertaste. Our tramp puts on a show, where he plays a record of Beethoven's Moonlight Sonata with live drum accompaniment. His inspired performance is disturbed by the noise of drunkards vomiting and urinating in one corner. But the passersby are generous, and in no time his tin cup is full of money. Unfortunately, this becomes a magnet for thugs who, one after another, unceremoniously help themselves to the cash. At the end of the day, rival gangs engage in a shootout to get hold of the loot; the tramp is arrested and must pay a bribe with the little money left in order to get released. Another episode worthy of note is the encounter of shantytown dwellers with a foreign delegation of land developers. The drummer meets a French businessman during a Russian-style party, where rivers of vodka and bear hugs turn new acquaintances into sworn friends. As a result he is invited to Paris for a visit. When he comes back, dressed in designer clothes and loaded with cases of electronic equipment, he is promptly robbed at the airport; the Western glitz disappears in a minute upon touching down on the native soil, and the little tramp resumes his miserable looks. The patriotic motif does not resound here.

The film relies on actor Alexander Polovtsev and his remarkable ability to create the innocent but knowing little tramp by miming alone. His stone-faced features bear a resemblance to the protagonist of Buster Keaton's comedies, while his underdog mischievous demeanor has the Chaplin imprimatur. The most Chaplinesque scene takes place in a *stolovaya* (cafeteria). With the drum on his chest, covered with a tablecloth, the drummer stealthily moves around stealing dishes and freezing in place when someone looks at him. The drum cooperates and blends perfectly with the other tables, round and of the same size. While the drummer is gorging himself, unsuspecting customers come up to him with their food to share the table/drum. This is a revolving gallery of social types, and the wide range of facial expressions and exchange of glances between them and the tramp tell us a whole story of human relations and posturing.

Like the Chaplin movies, *Drum Roll* offers a critical social commentary. But its scope is much larger than the specific circumstances affecting post-Soviet Russia. The national reality suggests a universal model. The key to this reading of the film is in the prologue and the epilogue. They are shot in the style of documentaries of the silent period, and purportedly trace the history of drum making. But it becomes clear in the epilog that the drum is a visual metaphor for the world. We see how the cavemen stretch an animal skin across poles placed in a circle. The result is a flat round-shaped kind of tent that becomes the cavemen's habitat. On the outside, the tent serves as a communal dining table and a drum for rituals and dancing. Over the centuries, in a rapid sequence, we see how the tent/drum gets cut up into smaller and smaller pieces; different peoples in different ages become possessive of their own drum, but also oblivious and disrespectful of its nature and value. It is a scene of how mankind destroys its home.

Earlier in the film, there is an episode where the tramp's girl friend uses the drum as a laundry tub, a grill to fry eggs, and a planter. On that occasion, the drummer comes to the drum's rescue and saves it from being abused. However, in the end, in a fit of frustration and despair, the drummer smashes the drum into pieces. He then realizes with dismay that he has destroyed an element of his own existence. The loss of the homeland, and consequently the loss of identity, is a theme that struck a sensitive chord in the heart of the Russian public. For its social relevance, as well as for its artistic value, the film was awarded the Special Jury prize at the 1993 International Moscow Film Festival and the Grand Prix at the Kinotavr Festival.

Three more comedies should be mentioned, which are difficult to place in any specific category, *Peculiarities of the National Hunt in the Fall* (1995), *Peculiarities of National Fishing* (1998), and *Peculiarities of the National Hunt in the Winter* (2000), by Alexander Rogozhkin. They somehow belong among the fantastic tales, because they reflect male fantasies about the great struggle between man and the wild—rather, a parody of it. The three films can be lumped together and discussed as one, because they tell the same story about the "peculiarities of the national drunkenness."

As the story goes, a group of friends periodically gathers for a hunting, or fishing, trip, and turns the expedition into an extended drinking party. Their main preoccupation is to have an abundant supply of vodka wherever they happen to be at all times, day and night. The camera places a great deal of emphasis on the ever-present bottles, or bottle cases. This obsession with alcohol results in all sorts of pranks and gags, which range from gross to silly. The action moves back and forth from the lodge to the woods and the water. The men either sit at the table and drink, or fall into a stupor and sleep. When they venture outdoors in full hunting gear, the only animals they interact with are a cow and a domesticated bear cub; they almost kill the cow and get the bear drunk.

Some characters are recurrent in all three films, such as an army general with a penchant for philosophizing (Alexander Buldakov) and a ranger converted to Buddhism (Victor Bychkov); others appear only in one episode, such as a woman official from the Environment Protection Department, who opposes hunting but enjoys carousing. All of them are notable only for their inanity, ineptitude, and verbosity. Such a character treatment would normally alienate the viewer. With these films, the opposite is true. The fact that these are jolly fellows, gentle and good-natured, having fun in an innocent way, endears them to the Russian public. And what is a scourge threatening public health in Russia—alcoholism—acquires mythical connotations. The hyperbole here does not work like in a morality play to condemn the vice, but raises the level of tolerance to a new height and makes the audience sympathize with the happy bunch.

The films' popularity in Russia was such that they acquired the status of cult movies. But abroad they have been ignored, because the kind of humor they display does not resonate with foreign audiences. The authors anticipated this reaction, and to a certain extent incorporated the point of view of the foreigner in the first two films. In *Peculiarities of the National Hunt in the Fall,* for example, a young Finnish scholar (Ville Haapsalo), who is studying the rituals of the Russian national hunt in the seventeenth century, joins the group to get a hands-on experience. Throughout the film, he has visions of the traditional wolf hunt, with noblemen and their retinues in brightly-colored brocade coats lined with precious furs, servants bringing along food and drinks, beautiful ladies waiting in the rear, bold formations of horse riders, and packs of magnificent hounds tracking down the prey. The Finn has difficulty in reconciling the grotesque contemporary farce with his dream visions. He remains baffled in the end, but with warm feelings towards his weird companions. Many foreigners, I am sure, would sympathize with the Finn.[45]

Invitation to the circus

I do not remember how I found myself at the circus that night. Someone must have sent me an invitation because I was holding a ticket in my hands. From a distance the massive cylinder of the Moscow Circus shone like a reclined crescent moon. But inside it was dark and empty. The doors were wide open. I walked in and looked for my seat. It was the very best, first row and central. A few minutes later, the show began.

I hear the music, a melancholic, drawn out trumpet tune that comes from the depth of the soul. A spotlight goes on and reveals Gelsomina, with her clownish makeup, baggy pants, and all. One foot lightly touches the ground, the other is lifted backward as in a dance, tracing an arc with the curvature of the spine and the neck; her hands are on the trumpet, tilted toward the ceiling. What is she doing in Moscow?—I wonder. Then, I realize that indeed *"la strada"* runs through Moscow, or at least through the films that were made here, many of them. Gelsomina feels at home. Some characters appear, attracted by the melody, and greet her. More enter in a steady stream.[46]

Now the ring is full. I recognize many of the figures in the crowd. There, Khlestyakov and the Mayor dance hand-in-hand, chanting, "em-em-é . . .," and stamping their feet; they have set up a joint venture to deal in mutual funds and are celebrating the windfall.

Ivan Fyodorovich joined the guys at the checkpoint in Chechnya; he recovered his rifle and is engaged in a sniper competition with Manimat. The marksman is no longer needed at home because Katya has moved out. Now she lives with the other Katya, my landlady, in the apartment that I have vacated. She is sitting at the computer, working on a rape case; she has become a public prosecutor.

The drummer, with his drum, decided to leave the new Russia and go back to the USSR. There, he distinguished himself as a top Stakhanovite by overfulfilling the quota of one million and one drum beats per day. A ceremony is going on right now; he is being awarded a medal, together with transsexual Evdokim and his wife. Each holds the insignia of his/her labor—the hammer, the sickle, and the drum.

Historical figures of high rank keep to themselves. Nicholas and his family seek some privacy in the lion cage—the lions are long gone, of course. Alexandra is sitting in a chair, reading a book. Alexei plays with the trainer's whip, chasing his sisters around. Nicholas scans the crowd outside, looking for his assassin. But Yurovsky has moved on; he is now working for a prominent oligarch as a political advisor.

Up on the trapeze, in a dark corner, wrapped in a gray raincoat, Hitler hangs upside-down like a bat. Nearby, Eva Braun performs a balancing act on the tightrope, while the sex-driven little giant from Sukhumi clicks his camera and waits like a cat for her to fall into the safety net.

Stalin is inspecting a gallery of portraits of himself in recent films; he walks by slowly, taking mental notes of the artists who should be sent to the Gulag the next day. The thief, Tolyan, tries to get his attention by pointing to the tattoo on his chest. Stalin is unimpressed, and adds his name to the black list.

Lenin is absent. A government official announces that he could not join the party because, due to the malfunctioning of the Mausoleum's central computer, the coffin could not be opened.

Pugachev no longer wants to be tsar; he decided to become a rock star, encouraged by the success of his great-great-great-grand-niece, pop-queen Alla Pugacheva (actually, everybody knows that there is no relation between the two; he has a habit of usurping names). To conquer the rock scene, he is training a small army of skinheads, who go about smashing the kiosks that sell CDs of successful bands.

Brother 3 has recently rescued Yaya and Rita from a rival gang. The girls fell in love with him and decided to take him to the land of the deaf. "True," Yaya says, "he is not deaf; but he can barely speak, and as a dumb he qualifies."

Ignat lost his job when the metallurgical plant in the Urals was privatized and became part of a giant holding. He brought together a number of disgruntled ex-workers and founded a boxing club. There, in the middle of the ring, he is supervising a tournament between the "Children of the Iron Gods" and the "Thugs of the Steel Moguls."

McCracken has put the Barber of Siberia to rest. Nobody needs the tree-felling machine now because there are no trees left in the region; the local mafia has depleted the forests and exported the timber. But McCracken is still in business; he has successfully sold to a Moscow tycoon a new technology to open a permanent window on Paris. Now the travelers must pay a toll to use the passage. Still, many "shuttles" find it practical. I see Nina in her sequined baseball cap arguing that it is much faster than taking the boat to Istanbul—one step, and . . . *voilà*!

Two swing couples wave at each other from across the ring. The countess from St. Petersburg and Masha, the cafeteria worker, have switched partners. They are having fun. The countess is entertaining the conman of her dreams in her boudoir, while Masha and the count bring food from the cafeteria to the defenders of the White House during the putsch.

The nice gentleman from the metro is no longer carrying my shredded coat. Now he is holding Ryaba the chicken under one arm; the other arm is wrapped around Asya's shoulders. He is escorting them to the market, providing protection against the perils of the post-Gorbachev environment.

Tyotya Dunya and her goat are now homeless. But the champions of the national hunt have hired her as a cook at the lodge. They say that her *samogon* (moonshine) is as good as her cherry preserves. Everybody is happy, including the goat that has fraternized with the cow and the bear cub; together they have started a chapter of the Association for the Protection of Unhunted Animals.

The musical quartet Old Nags has just finished its variety show. The four friends approach Gelsomina and ask her to lead the parade around the ring for the grand finale. Gelsomina's music changes to a jolly marching tune.

One by one, the characters get in line and follow the leader. They step up lively; some perform pirouettes, others turn somersaults, all smile and wave, staring beyond the stage into the dark arena. A spotlight falls on my seat. They see me. They call me. I jump into the ring and join hands with them. I turn to my readers, and bow.

Notes

Introduction

1. Orlando Figes discusses the dichotomy of Russian culture in his compelling book, *Natasha's Dance: A Cultural History of Russia*, (New York: Metropolitan Books, 2002).
2. See James H. Billington, *Russia in Search of Itself* (Washington, DC: The Woodrow Wilson Center Press and Johns Hopkins University Press, 2004); Kathleen E. Smith, *Mythmaking in the New Russia: Politics and Memory During the Yeltsin Years* (Ithaca and London: Cornell University Press, 2002), see in particular the chapter, "Searching for a New Russian Idea": 158-72. Also, James Rupert, "In Search of the Russian Meaning of Life," *WP* (August 4, 1996): A29. The article reports that Yeltsin encouraged his aides to "develop a new national idea to unite all Russians," and the newspaper *Rossiskaya Gazeta* offered its readers 10 million rubles ($2,000) for the best "unifying national idea."
3. See David Hoffman, *The Oligarchs: Wealth and Power in the New Russia* (Washington, DC: Public Affairs, 2002) and Vadim Volkov, *Violent Entrepreneurs: The Use of Force in the Making of Russian Capitalism* (Ithaca: Cornell University Press, 2002). A study by the European Bank for Reconstruction and Development (EBRD), published in 2002, found that Russia's major oligarchic structures were blocking the development of small and medium-size businesses. The report singled out the leading oil and metal companies as still wielding enormous political and economic power at all levels of the state. Reported in *RFE/RL Newsline*, Vol. 6, No. 223, Part I (November 27, 2002). According to an assessment by *The Economist*, more than 70 percent of Russia's $330 billion GDP is controlled by just 20 conglomerates; eight oligarchic clans control Russia's 64 leading companies, including the Yeltsin-era family which still controls more than 20 percent of the GDP. Reported in *RFE/RL Newsline*, Vol. 7, No. 31, Part I (February 18, 2003). Another recent book offers a general overview of post-Soviet Russia, Andrew C. Kuchins, ed., *Russia After the Fall* (Washington,

DC, Carnegie Endowment for International Peace, 2002).

4 By 2002, seven percent of the Russian population could be considered "middle class," according to economist Elena Avraamova, who participated in a nationwide study financed by the Carnegie Foundation. Reported in *RFE/RL Newsline*, Vol. 6, No. 215, Part I (November 15, 2002). An overview of the emerging bourgeoisie is to be found in Harley Balzer, "Routinization of the New Russians?" *The Russian Review*, No. 62 (January 2003): 15-36.

5 In a survey of 1,500 residents of 94 urban and rural areas across Russia in early April 2000, the polling group ROMIR found that only 38.7 percent of respondents agreed to some extent with the view that democracy is the best form of rule despite certain problems it poses. Almost 24 percent of respondents disagreed with the view to some extent, while 24.3 percent were undecided. At the same time, 39.9 percent thought military rule would likely be bad for the country, and 27.5 percent rejected it outright with 27.5 percent undecided. *RFE/RL Newsline* (April 20, 2000). A more recent study shows that the support for democracy has further eroded, with only 22 percent preferring democracy and 53 percent opposing it. See Richard Pipes, "Flight from Freedom: What Russians Think and Want," Foreign Affairs, Vol. 83, No. 3 (May/June 2004), www.foreignaffairs.org.

6 Birgit Beumers, ed., *Russia on Reels: The Russian Idea in Post-Soviet Cinema* (London: I.B. Tauris & Co Ltd., 1999). This is a collection of essays by British, American, and Russian authors, which resulted from a conference on the theme of the "Russian idea." David Gillespie, *Russian Cinema* (Harlow, UK: Pearson Education Ltd., 2003). This is a very good survey of Russian cinema from its early days to the end of the 1990s. However, because it is so rich in content and short on pages (only 200), the films of the 1990s are only touched upon. For articles in English, see in particular, Louis Menashe, "Moscow Believes in Tears: The Problems (and Promise?) of Russian Cinema in the Transition Period," *Cineaste*, Vol. XXVI, No. 3 (Summer 2001): 10-17. Also, visit the websites: ce-review.org/video/video_main.html, kinoeye.org, ntvprofit.ru, kinoart.ru, which offer archival and recent film reviews. They also have a video store.

7 I borrowed the expression from Umberto Eco, "*Lector in Fabula*: Pragmatic Strategy in Metanarrative Text," in *The Role of the Reader: Explorations in the Semiotics of Text* (Bloomington, IN: Indiana University Press, 1979). I am referring only to the title phrase, and not to the content of the article, which focuses on the reader rather than the writer.

Chapter 1

1. A good survey of the beginning of the slump can be found in Daniil Dondurei, "Kino: Zhizn' posle smerti," *NG* (February 6, 1992): 7. See also Louis Menashe, "Requiem for Soviet Cinema 1917-1991," *Cineaste*, Vol. XXI, No. 1-2 (1995): 23-27. My own column in *The Moscow Times* (1992-94) served as a basis for the discussion of several films in this book. On the perestroika period (1985-90), and the previous films of the directors mentioned in this book, see Anna Lawton, *Before the Fall: Soviet Cinema in the Gorbachev Years* (Washington, DC: New Academia Publishing, 2004/original, *Kinoglasnost: Soviet Cinema in Our Time*, Cambridge University Press, 1992). See also Andrew Horton and Michael Brashinsky, *The Zero Hour: Glasnost and Soviet Cinema in Transition* (Princeton, NJ: Princeton University Press, 1992); and Nicholas Galichenko, *Glasnost: Soviet Cinema Responds* (Austin, TX: University of Texas Press, 1991).
2. Alexander Khanzhonkov was a film pioneer, laying the foundation of the national cinema industry. His first venture, in 1906, was a small enterprise for the sale and distribution of foreign movies. The credit for producing the first Russian film (1908), belongs to his competitor, Alexander Drankov. Khanzhonkov, however, started his own production business in the same year. Both were extremely productive and successful until the Bolshevik Revolution. Furthermore, Khanzhonkov organized the first guild of film critics, in 1911, and founded the first movie magazine, *Pegasus*, which included criticism, reviews, scripts, and publicity. He produced 400 films up to 1917, of which 100 are still extant.
3. "A cinema in Altai, Siberia, allowed customers to pay two eggs for a ticket; when eggs ran short locally, the price of entry was payable in empty bottles," as reported in *Transition*, vol. 9, No. 2 (April 1998): 6 (a publication of The World Bank).
4. Three years into the new century, the situation has not improved. Labor Minister Alexander Pochinok, on February 19, 2003, said that 34 million Russians, about one quarter of the population, live below the poverty line, which means they have monthly incomes of less than 1,500 rubles ($48.39), reported in *RFE/RL Newsline*, Vol. 7, No. 33, Part I (February 20, 2003). Moreover, there is a disproportion in the amount of wages among the regions, as the following episode demonstrates. The workers of Norilsk Nickel's trade union were ready to go on strike for an increase in monthly wages from 24,000 rubles ($755) to 28,000 rubles. See *RFE/RL Newsline*, Vol. 7, No. 12, Part I (January 21, 2003).
5. Daniil Dondurei, "Novaia model'," *Kinoatel'e*, No. 3 (1997): 72.
6. Most theaters in 1995 were taxed like ordinary businesses, plus an extra tax

equal to 30 percent of the gross. The manager of a major Moscow film theater complained, "We have to pay about 10 kinds of taxes. We pay to support the pensioners, the poorly organized health sector, the sciences and road construction; and for the municipal police, who don't seem to care if hooligans harass our filmgoers. We're even taxed to support culture. Isn't that amazing?" See Eugene Zykov, "When There's Hope There's Life," *Moving Pictures* (July 17, 1995): 12.

[7] Interview by Viktor Matizen, "Kazhduiu noch' mne snitsia, chto Lenfil'm ob'iavlen bankrotom," *Kino-glaz* (March 1993): 26.

[8] *ibid*: 27.

[9] Here and after, quoted in Anna Lawton, "Tagi-zade The Terrible," *Moscow Magazine* (December 91/January 92): 46-48.

[10] Occasionally he reappeared in the news. In early 2000, his name was on the list of candidates to the presidency of Russia submitted to the Central Election Commission. The Commission rejected the registration of "TISKINO director-general Tagi-zade because he submitted only 482,929 supporting signatures instead of the required 500,000." *RFE/RL Newsline*, Vol. 4, No. 36, Part I (February 2, 2000).

[11] "Sluzhba bezopasnosti ORT," *Kinoatel'e*, No.3 (1997): 29. This practice continued well into the next decade. Lenta.ru reported that the Moscow police confiscated more than 70,000 illegal DVDs worth up to $1 million, in one seizure. Allegedly, the discs were found in a workshop leased by the firm Miriam XXI, on the grounds of the Scientific Research Institute for Precise Instruments, which is part of the Russian Space Agency. See *RFE/RL Newsline*, Vol. 6, No. 215, Part I (November 15, 2002).

[12] "O registratsii kino- i videofil'mov i regulirovanii ikh publichnoi demonstratsii."

[13] Evgeniia Tirdatova, "Antipiratskii zakon priniat," *Kino-glaz* (March 1993): 5.

[14] See Zhanna Vasil'eva, "Dostuchat'sia do Gollivuda," *LG* (August 6, 1997): 8.

[15] In July-August 2000, Kinocenter in Moscow showed *Mission Impossible-2*, 50 times; *Gladiator*, 36 times; *American Beauty*, 20 times; *Matrix*, 20 times; *Magnolia*, 4 times. "Repertuar kinotsentra," *IK* online, No. 8 (2000), www.kinoart.ru.

[16] Other cultural centers and theaters, which offered quality Russian and international programs in Moscow were: the Museum of Cinema, the Cinema House, the Central House of Artists, the movie theater Illuzion, and Khanzhonkov House (the former Elektroteatr Triumfal'nyi, built in 1913 by the movie tycoon).

[17] Anna Lawton, "Bootleggers Beware, These Films Come Legally," *TMT* (October 8, 1993): 7.

18 "Film, TV Join to Fight Russian Video Piracy," *TMT* online (July 8, 1997), www.moscowtimes.ru.
19 In 1994, Dmitri Kholodov was the first journalist to be assassinated, killed by a booby-trap briefcase; he reported on alleged corruption in the Defense Ministry. The people's anger over the slaying of Listyev prompted Yeltsin to fire the Moscow prosecutor and the police chief, citing the fact that they did a poor job in fighting against rampant organized crime. See Margaret Shapiro, "Viewers Demand Government Action," *WP* (March 2, 1995): A26.
20 The Russian press reported stories of contract murders virtually every day. In the years between 1991 and 1995, 26 prominent bankers were murdered. A good summary of the situation in 1997 can be found in David Hoffman, "Banditry Threatens the New Russia," *WP* (May 12, 1997): A1; and Matt Taibbi, "Grim Catalog of Banker Slaying," *TMT* (August 17, 1995):1.
21 About Goskino in Soviet times, see Val S. Golovskoy with John Rimberg, *Behind the Soviet Screen: The Motion Picture Industry in the USSR, 1972-1982* (Ann Arbor, MI: Ardis, 1986).
22 Angela Charlton, "Russian Film Fading from View," *TMT* online (July 28, 1999), www.moscowtimes.ru.
23 Dondurei, "Kino: zhizn' posle smerti."
24 Goskino was a government agency equivalent to the Ministry of Cinema. For a few years after the fall of the USSR the agency was called Roskomkino (Russian Cinema Committee) to differentiate it from the totalitarian institution of old. Starting in 1998, however, the name reverted to Goskino under a sweeping nostalgia wave. It was subsequently incorporated into the Ministry of Culture in May 2000.
25 Reported by Mikhail Shvydkoi, at the time Deputy Minister of Culture of the Russian Federation, at a seminar at the Kennan Institute (Washington, DC, November 7, 1996); and by Alexander Golutva, current Deputy Minister of Culture at a presentation at the Library of Congress (Washington, DC, February 2, 2001).
26 Reported by Voice of America (October 3, 1998).
27 A good survey of the media business situation in 1997 can be found in David Hoffman, "Powerful Few Rule Russian Mass Media," *WP* (March 31, 1997): A1. For a comprehensive study by the same author, see *The Oligarchs: Wealth and Power in the New Russia*.
28 See *Before the Fall*: 204-5.
29 Boris Pinskii, "Kuda idem my s Goskino," *SE* (February 1998): 4.
30 This policy was first conceived and implemented by Stalin's Minister of Cinema Boris Shumyatsky in the 1930s. See Denise Youngblood, *Movies for the*

Masses: Popular Cinema and Soviet Society (NY and Cambridge: Cambridge University Press, 1992).

[31] *LG*, (August 6, 1997): 8.

[32] The phrase is the title of a novel by Yuri Trifonov, *The House on the Embankment* (1976). The author's family lived in the building and he had first-hand knowledge of the themes of corruption and betrayal which he treated in the book. The novel was adapted for the theater and, in the 1980s, became part of the repertoire of the rebellious stage director Yuri Lyubimov at the Taganka Theater.

[33] From a conversation with Ludwig Banyan (November 12, 1991).

[34] She starred in *The Rich Bride* (*Bogataia nevesta*, 1938); *Tractor Drivers* (*Traktoristy*, 1939); *The Swineherd and the Shepherd* (*Svinarka i pastukh*, 1941); *Cossacks of the Kuban* (*Kubanskie kazaki*, 1950), and others.

[35] Literally, VDNKh is the acronym for Exhibition of the Achievements of the National Economy. Built in the 1930s, it was a sort of theme park with spectacular fountains and fairy-tale pavilions that cleverly combined entertainment and ideology. In post-Soviet times, private companies rented the exhibition space and the park turned into a trade center.

[36] One revived feature was the popular contest where the readers vote for the best and the worst films of the year. This had been one of the best indicators of public taste. The winners for 1997 were: *Brother* (Best Film and Best Actor), and *The Thief* (Best Director).

[37] Petr Gladkov (Publisher), *SE* (February 1998): 3.

[38] The Congresses' numbers may cause some confusion, as they reflect two numerical sequences. The Filmmakers Union of the USSR held six congresses over 25 years in the Soviet period, one every four years. The Filmmakers Union of Russia held three congresses between 1991 and 1997. In May 1998, the Filmmakers Union of Russia held the IV Extraordinary Congress.

[39] Pinskii, "Kuda idem my s Goskino."

[40] About the V Congress (1986), see *Before the Fall*: 56-9. Also, George Faraday, *Revolt of the Filmmakers* (University Park, PA: Pennsylvania State University Press, 2000).

[41] Elena Stishova, "S'ezd proigravshikh, ili Nauka pobezhdat'," *IK*, No. 4 (1998): 9-10.

[42] Lev Karakhan, "Um i vlast', sila i mudrost'...," *IK*, No. 8 (1998): 23-24.

[43] *ibid*: 5.

[44] John Varoli, "Famed Film Studio on Brink of Closure," *TMT* online (August 7, 1998), www.moscowtimes.ru.

[45] Interview with Viktor Sergeev, "Spasenie utopaiushchikh," *IK*, No. 5 (1999), www.kinoart.ru.

⁴⁶ Matizen, "Kazhduiu noch' mne snitsia, chto Lenfil'm ob'iavlen bankrotom."
⁴⁷ Nick Holdsworth, "Cash-Strapped Lenfilm Goes to the Car Wash," *TMT* online (April 4, 1997), www.moscowtimes.ru.
⁴⁸ Interview with Karen Shakhnazarov, "Spasenie utopaiushchikh." Not only the studios, but also other film institutions could barely make ends meet. The venerable VNIIK (The State Film Research Institute), nested in an elegant ninenteenth-century mansion, had to rent out one of its suites to a Japanese business.
⁴⁹ Interview with Viktor Sergeev, *ibid.*
⁵⁰ Andrei Zolotov, Jr., "Tax Breaks Herald New Silver Age in Film," *TMT* online (January 14, 1999), www.moscowtimes.ru.
⁵¹ Daniil Dondurei, "Spasenie utopaiushchikh."
⁵² Marina Lapenkova, "TV Stations Wage Battle for Control of Mosfilm," *TMT* online (July 8, 1997), www.moscowtimes.ru.
⁵³ Vladimir Grammatikov had a negative view of the Gorky Studio's shoestring-budget film program that was recently terminated, and declared his intention to go back to restore the studio's reputation as a producer of quality children's films. Interview with Vladislav Chebotarev, "Raboty khvatit vsem," *IK*, No.5 (1999), www.kinoart.ru.
⁵⁴ Irina Rodionova, "Kinozakonotvorchestvo," *Segodnia* online (August 26, 2000), www.segodnia.ru.
⁵⁵ "Kul'tura zaprogrammirovana do 2005-go goda," *SMI.ru* online (August 31, 2000), www.smi.ru.
⁵⁶ *RFE/RL Newsline*, Vol. 6, No. 173, Part I (September 13, 2002).
⁵⁷ *RFE/RL Newsline*, Vol. 7, No. 25, Part I (February 7, 2003).
⁵⁸ *Mythmaking in the New Russia*: 158-72.
⁵⁹ Andrei Razumovskii, "Iskusstvo rasporiazhat'sia svobodoi," *Kinoatel'e*, No. 3 (1997): 39.

Chapter 2

¹ From the Yeltsin government faxes were frantically sent out to Western organizations in Moscow. One said: "8:46 a.m. Monday. We have been xeroxing the decree of BY in hundreds and have been throwing copies into windows. People shouting, 'More, more.' We are waiting, waiting and waiting. . . The Russian government has NO ways to address the people. All radio stations are under control. The following is BY's address to the Army. Forward it to USIA. Broadcast it over the country. Maybe, Voice of America. Do it! Urgent!" See, "Make It Known," *WP* (August 20, 1991): A15.

2 "Yeltsin: 'Country Is Faced with the Threat of Terror'," *WP* (August 21, 1991): A28.
3 Lebed gained some notoriety in the following years as the restless commander of the Russian army in Moldova, opposing the policies and directives from Moscow. Later, he ran against Yeltsin in the presidential elections of 1996, and subsequently held a post in Yeltsin's cabinet for a short period of time; he was eventually elected governor of Krasnoyarsky krai. He died in a helicopter crash in April 2002.
4 Quotations here and later are from my own notes, if not otherwise indicated.
5 He was eventually elected as a deputy to the Duma for Democratic Russia, the party that lifted Yeltsin to power. In November 1993, Gleb Yakunin was defrocked by the Orthodox Church for his attacks against the "Church nomenklatura," and Patriarch Alexi II in particular, whom he accused of having been a collaborator of the KGB. For a profile of Yakunin, see Betsy McKay, "The Outsider's Democrat," *TMT*, (March 1, 1993): 9.
6 In subsequent years, Kalugin moved to the USA. His name resurfaced in the press, when he was tried *in absentia* for treason and received a 15-year sentence (June 25, 2002). The sentence was later upheld by the Supreme Court. Kalugin, from his residence in the USA, said that the case was politically motivated. It was "the result of a letter sent by a group of KGB veterans to President Putin, asking him to settle accounts with the deserter." *RFE/RL Newsline*, Vol. 6, No. 113, Part I (June 18, 2002) and No. 176, Part I (September 18, 2002).
7 At the press conference on August 19, Yanaev delivered the following statement: "I'm addressing you . . . at a crucial moment for the Soviet Union, and for the entire international community. . . . The Soviet Union is facing a deep crisis, which can call into question further reform and bring major upheavals on the international scene. . . . Under the circumstances, we have no other alternative but to take resolute action in order to stop the country from sliding down to disaster." The following exchange with a Russian journalist conveys a measure of the drama--defiance on the part of the press and a defensive attitude on the part of the junta. Q.: "Where is Mikhail Sergeevich [Gorbachev]? What is he sick with? Specifically, concretely, which disease does he have? And those tanks in the streets of Moscow, against whom are they directed?" A.: "Let me say that Mikhail Gorbachev is now on vacation; he's undergoing treatment in the south of our country. He's very tired after these many years and will need some time to get better. . . . As for the state of emergency . . . in order to rule out any dangers and menaces we had to take certain steps to ensure security." See, "Yanaev: 'The Situation Has Gone out of Control in the USSR'," *WP* (August 20, 1991): A21.

8 Quoted in Betsy McKay, "Miner's Memoir," *The Moscow Guardian* (July 26, 1991): 9.
9 The time of the broadcasting coincided with another gesture of protest. Molchanov presented the documentary as the last segment of his popular talk show, "Before and After Midnight," which covered controversial issues and deep-set problems. After that, he left Gosteleradio, denouncing its controlling policies and advocating the establishment of an independent TV channel. At the time, that sounded like an impossible dream.
10 In the course of the decade, Mayor Yuri Luzhkov left his imprint on the Moscow landscape--from the reconstruction of the Cathedral of the Savior to the realization of an underground deluxe shopping center on Manezh Square. A joke was circulating that Metro will soon be named after Luzhkov, rather than after Lenin (*Moskovskii Metropoliten imeni Luzhkova*). But by September 2002, the flamboyant Moscow mayor became nostalgic for old glories and put forward a proposal to restore the monument to Felix Dzerzhinsky, the sinister founder of the Cheka, because "he solved the problem of homeless children and bailed out the railroads in a period of devastation." The liberal forces strongly denounced the proposal and some suggested that "Luzhkov's change of heart could be explained by his desire to fawn on president Putin and the other chekists who have come to power in recent years." On January 21, 2003, a special commission of the Moscow City Duma voted to reject Luzhkov's proposal, ruling that the restoration would mark the reinstallation of "a symbol of terror, concentration camps, and the persecution of the intelligentsia." *RFE/RL Newsline*, Vol. 6, No. 174, Part I (September 16, 2002); No. 175, Part I (September 17, 2002); and Vol. 7, No. 13, Part I (January 22, 2003).
11 Quoted in David Remnick, *Resurrection* (New York: Vintage Books, 1999): 23.
12 Interview with Rustam Ibragimbekov, "Zhizn' posle krizisa," *IK* online (February 1999), www.kinoart.ru. Ten years after the coup, citizens' attitudes had taken a curious turn. According to the director of the polling agency VTsIOM, Yuri Levada, most Russians were not going to celebrate the tenth anniversary of the failed pro-communist coup in August 2001, because in their opinion there were two conspiracies to stage a coup in Russia at that time. The first was organized by older members of the nomenklatura, who were against the reform, and failed. The second conspiracy, which was successful, was orchestrated by Yeltsin and his democratic entourage. Ordinary people felt that they were mere spectators, rather than actors in the historical process. Reported by *RFE/RL Newsline*, Vol. 5, No. 156, Part I (August 17, 2001).
13 On the representation of history, see Michel Foucault, *The Order of Things* (New York: Vintage, Reissue edition, 1994) and *Archaeology of Knowledge* (New York:

Pantheon Books, 1982); Michel de Certeau, *The Writing of History* (New York: Columbia University Press, 1988); Roland Barthes, "The Discourse of History," in *The Rustle of Language* (Oxford: Basil Blackwell, 1986): 127-40; Marc Ferro, *Cinema and History* (Wayne State University Press, 1988); Robert A. Rosenstone, ed. *Revisioning History* (Princeton University Press, 1994); Frank Stern, "Screening Politics: Cinema and Intervention," *Georgetown Journal of International Affairs*, Vol. 1, No. 2 (Summer/Fall, 2000): 65-73.

14 Reported in Jay Leyda, *Kino. A History of the Russian and Soviet Film* (Princeton, NJ: Princeton University Press, 1983): 199.

15 Playwright and historian Edvard Radzinsky discovered and published the Note in *Ogonek* (May 19,1989), and later included it in his book *Nikolai II: zhizn' i smert'* (Moscow: Vagrius, 1998). In 1996, six years after the film was released, Radzinskii wrote a play, called "*Posledniaia noch' poslednego tsaria (Last Night of the Last Tsar)*," based on his history book. The play was staged by Valerii Fokin, and produced by the Bogis Agency; it was first performed at the Meridian Cultural Center and later at the Manezh Exhibition Hall (October-November 1996). It was a theatrical event, thanks to the originality of Fokin's vision. He conceived of the mise-en-scène as a circus, where the audience would actually sit under a tent, and mixed drama, ballet, and music. The highly unorthodox staging worked perfectly, underscoring the philosophy of the play, and without ever sinking to the level of vulgar expedient.

16 The quotations are from the English translation of Radzinskii's book, *The Last Tsar* (New York: Doubleday, 1992): 384-90.

17 We know historically that Yurovsky had an uneventful bureaucratic career as a faithful servant of the regime, and died in 1938 in a Kremlin hospital of a stomach ulcer. In his last letter to his children there is no indication that he suffered any pangs of conscience.

18 From my interview with the director (November 5, 1991).

19 See *Before the Fall*: 160.

20 On the American career of Andrei Konchalovsky, see Denise J. Youngblood, "The Cosmopolitan and the Patriot: the Brothers Mikhalkov-Konchalovsky and Russian Cinema," *Historical Journal of Film, Radio and Television*, Vol. 23, No. 1 (2003): 27-41.

21 See, *Before the Fall*: 221-23.

22 Here and after, quotations are from the film presentation at the Cinema House, Moscow, with Gostev and other members of the crew (March 13, 1993).

23 See *Before the Fall*: 179-83.

24 From the sound track, here and after.

25 The presentation took place on April 28, 1994, at the International Press Center

and Club in Moscow, and consisted of several long segments on video.

26 A bitter change if compared to his still hopeful view of the future after the first film of the trilogy. See interview with Viktor Matizen, "Budushchee u Rossii est', tol'ko nam ego ne dozhdat'sia," *Stolitsa*, No. 13 (April 1991): 36-39.

27 Artemy Troitsky, "Flying Bullets, Surreal Scenes," *TMT* (October 6, 1993): 9.

28 *Chapaev* (Sergei and Georgii Vasil'ev, 1934). The mustachoed protagonist of this film became a popular folk hero.

29 In October 2000, the Duma passed a bill that would extend the pensions and benefits for which current deputies are eligible to those who participated in the armed uprising in 1993. *RFE/RL Newsline*, Vol. 4, No. 209, Part I (October 27, 2000).

30 Which reminds us of Karl Marx's statement: "History repeats itself, first as tragedy, and then as farce" (c.1850).

31 See *Before the Fall*: 29-31.

32 Information on family background also in Youngblood, "The Cosmopolitan and the Patriot."

33 See Ellen Barry, "Mikhalkov Wins Oscar for *Burned by the Sun*," *TMT* (March 29, 1995): 1-2.

34 Nikita Mikhalkov, "Blind Faith," *Sight and Sound* (January 1996): 61.

35 See *Before the Fall*: 153-7. About early Gherman's films, *ibid*: 56-59.

36 He made a cameo appearance in *Slave of Love* (*Raba liubvi*. Mikhalkov, 1976) as an underground Bolshevik leader, but the character was not developed.

37 He especially reminds us of the little protagonist of De Sica's *Bicycle Thieves*. Italian Neorealism had a significant influence on the new wave of Soviet cinema in the 1960s, the period when the director's father, Gregory Chukhrai, made internationally acclaimed films, such as *Ballad of a Soldier* (1959) and *Clear Skies* (1961).

38 Zhanna Vasil'eva, "Nakolka vremen demokratii," *LG* (October 22, 1997): 8.

39 The film received numerous awards. At the Venice Film Festival it received the President of the Italian Senate's Gold Medal, the Prize of the International Youth Jury, the UNICEF Award, and was nominated for the Gold Lion. In Russia it received five Nika awards. It was also nominated for the Golden Globe and the Oscar Best Foreign Film.

40 Sergei Chernov, "Film World Hails *Khrustalyov, My Car!*," *TMT* (September 9, 1999).

41 Petr Zaichenko, "Russkii bunt," *IK* online (June 1999), www.kinoart.ru. Historian Richard Stites identified the phenomenon as "popular utopianism," and argued that the emotional drive of Pugachev, and the other legendary rebel, Stenka Razin, later turned into intellectual aspirations, "passed into the mental

makeup of the socialist intelligentsia," and resurfaced in the revolutions of 1905 and 1917. *Revolutionary Dreams* (New York/Oxford: Oxford University Press, 1989): 12-24. Another scholar reports a comment by a nineteenth-century reviewer of Vereshchagin's paintings of the Turkestan campaign: "We see a violence that could not be French or even from the Balkans: it is half-barbarian and semi-Asiatic—it is a Russian violence." Figes, *Natasha's Dance*: 412.

[42] Here and after, Alexander Proshkin at the film's presentation at the National Gallery of Art in Washington, DC (November 5, 2000).

[43] In Russian folklore, the raven is a bird possessing magic powers. In some villages the peasants believed that the legendary rebels Stenka Razin and Emelian Pugachev flew in the sky as giant ravens. In the film, the raven of the opening scene lands on the windowsill of Catherine's room, as a foreboding of the uprising.

[44] All quotes are from *Seans*, No 17-18 (1999): 77-79.

[45] Interview with Nikita Mikhalkov by Liubov' Arkus, *Seans*, No. 17-18 (1999): 89.

[46] The reception took place on November 10, 1999, at Georgetown University.

[47] Arkus, *Seans*.

[48] The stylization of cultural codes, such as the puppet theater, is nothing new in cinema. It was used successfully in *Alexander Nevsky* (Eisenstein, 1938)— stylization of folk legends and saint *vitae*—at a time when the USSR wanted to emphasize its national roots in the face of the German aggression. In *Barber*, the stylization of popular art forms has an additional cultural justification because in the late nineteenth century there was a trend toward "Russianness" in fashion and in the arts, called "Russian style" or "*moderne.*" During the reign of Alexander III, when censorship made it difficult for the artists to address social and political issues, they turned to legends and the fantasy world of folk tales. Those were the images that dazzled the Parisian audiences at the turn of the century in the form of the *Ballets Russes*, and which contributed to create a stereotyped idea of Russia.

[49] Arkus, *Seans*.

[50] Ravaging the Russian land is also the theme of Andrei Konchalovsky's *Siberiade* and Elem Klimov's *Farewell*. See *Before the Fall*: 32 and 39-40.

[51] Like in Shakhnazarov's film, the scene of the execution is a faithful rendition of the "Yurovsky Note." But here there is no lengthy sequence of the burial, because this film does not focus on the "assassin" but on the family. And therefore it ends with their death.

[52] *RFE/RL Newsline*, Vol. 4, No. 156, Part I (August 15, 2000).

Chapter 3

1. The term was first used in *The Moscow Times*, in a weekly column by Michael Hetzer, to denote the community of expatriates navigating the new map of currency supermarkets and discotheques.
2. Nick Allen, "Tatum Shot Dead by Eleven Bullets," *TMT* online (November 5, 1996), www.moscowtimes.ru.
3. "Slim Chance Police Will Find Killers," *TMT* online (November 13, 1996), www.moscowtimes.ru.
4. Erin Arvedlund, "Police Find Tatum Getaway Car, Few Clues," *TMT* online (November 22, 1996), www.moscowtimes.ru.
5. Christian Lowe, "Questions Linger on Tatum Murder," *TMT* online (November 13, 1996), www.moscowtimes.ru.
6. Sujata Rao and Erin Arvedlund, "No Leads Reported on Tatum Murder," *TMT* online (November 6, 1996), www.moscowtimes.ru.
7. Robert Brown, "Who Was Paul Tatum?" *TMT* online (November 13, 1996), www.moscowtimes.ru.
8. Adam Tanner, "The Battle of the Radisson Goes on, Quietly," *TMT* online (August 12, 1994); and Ellen Barry, "Tatum: One Man's Genius, Another's Villain," *TMT* online (April 28, 1995), www.moscowtimes.ru.
9. Erin Arvedlund "Tatum's Life Headed for Silver Screen?" *TMT* online (February 1, 1997), www.moscowtimes.ru. Tatum's brother-in-law, Rick Furmanek, came to Moscow with his wife and children in 1992, and for 1½ years worked for the joint venture.
10. Gemini Film was founded in 1993 on the initiative of the German movie company Scriba Film Holding, whose partners in film production and distribution included an impressive array of international giants: Warner Brothers, Regency (USA), Alkor Film and TV (Germany), and Canal+ (France). Gemini Film's releases in 1994 included: *JFK, The Fugitive, Unforgiven, Sommersby, Made in America,* and *Falling Down.*
11. Besides Paul Tatum, they included Boris Gryaznov, general director of Sovincenter Hotel (built in the 1970s by Armand Hammer); Evgeny Tsimbalistov, general director of Hotel Rossiya; and Andrei Ilyukhin, vice-president of Mosintour, whose headquarters were in the the Hotel Moskva. All cases were alleged to be contract hits, but none has been solved. See Jeff Grocott, "Hotels, Hulks & Homicide," *TMT* online (February 3, 1998), www.moscowtimes.ru. Other frequent targets were journalists, bankers, and politicians. See note 20, chapter I. The trend continued into the new century. Konstantin Georgiev, the CEO of Hotel Pekin, was gunned down in the center of Moscow in January

2002 by a lone assassin. See *RFE/RL Newsline*, Vol. 6, No. 18, Part I (January 29, 2002). By 2003, Moscow's hotels have become the most expensive in the world, according to data released by the Russian branch of the Thomas Cook Travel Agency. See *RFE/RL Newsline*, Vol. 7, No. 1, Part I, (January 3, 2003).

[12] Sergei Solovyov directed a more traditional screen version of *Three Sisters*, released in 1994. However, he too connected that time with the present by inserting quotations from Alexander Solzhenitsyn's works. The actors were students from Solovyov's workshop at VGIK.

[13] *Circus* (1936) by Grigory Aleksandrov. Music by Isaak Dunaevsky.

[14] The novel, *What Is to Be Done?* (*Chto delat'?*), was written by Nikolay Chernyshevsky in 1862. It advocated socialist ideals as a solution to Russia's problems, and was extremely popular with the younger generation. It was banned by the tsarist government and the author was exiled. Lenin used the title in 1902 for one of his most famous writings.

[15] From the press release (in English).

[16] The Hermitage Theater was the first location of Stanislavsky's Moscow Arts Theater. The facility had previously been used for circus performances.

[17] He was the cinematographer in Pavel Lungin's films, *Taxi Blues* and *Luna Park*.

[18] Kristina Orbakayte is the daughter of pop singing queen, Alla Pugacheva. While still an adolescent, she became famous as the heroine of the film *Scarecrow* (*Chuchelo*, Bykov 1984). See *Before the Fall*: 46-7.

[19] Tom Birchenough, "New Russia--New Film?" *Moscow Revue* (July 1994): 12.

[20] Premykhov wrote the scripts for Dinara Asanova's *Tough Kids* (*Patsany*, 1983) and *Dear, Dearest, Beloved . . .* (*Milyi, dorogoi, liubimyi, edinstvennyi . . .*,1984), and played the lead in both films. See *Before the Fall*: 47-9.

[21] *Is It Easy to Be Young?* (*Legko li byt' molodym*, 1986) by Latvian director Yuris Podnieks. This was the first documentary film to present the picture of alienated youth. It had great resonance abroad, where it was taken as evidence that glasnost was "for real." A feature film followed, *Little Vera* (Pichul, 1988), which created a sensation at home and abroad with the portrait of a dysfunctional working class family. The lead actress, Natalya Negoda, later appeared in a photo session in *Playboy* magazine (May 1989), with the caption: "The Soviets' First Sex Star." The theme of alienated youth was also central to *Sideburns* (Mamin, 1990). See *Before the Fall*: 184, 201-2, and 229-30.

[22] Not to be confused with a group called Russian National Union (*Russkoe Natsional'noe Ob'edinenie*, RNO), headed by Konstantin Kasimovsky, which was smaller, less organized, and more marginal.

[23] There were numerous stories on Neo-Nazis and skinheads in the local press over the decade. Among them, see Julia Solovyova, "Court Outlaws Neo-Nazi

Organization RNE," *TMT* online (April 20, 1999); Dmitry Babich, "The National Socialists," *TMT* online (April 24, 1999); and Nick Allen, "Moscow Skinhead Violence," *TMT* online (May 23, 1998), www.moscowtimes.ru. More recentlyy, *Novaia gazeta* (No. 70) reported that the skinhead group called Rabid Stallions was allegedly linked to the pro-Putin youth movement Walking Together. See *RFE/RL Newsline*, Vol. 6, No. 181, Part I (September 24, 2002). Another scourge of society are the street children, orphans or abandoned by their parents, who go by the name of *bezprizorniki*, like their predecessors in the aftermath of the revolution and WW II. They survive on crime and attack unsuspecting citizens in packs, taking away anything that can be snatched in a few seconds: wallet, handbag, watch, jewelry, etc. Gypsy kids also use this tactic, but they are not orphans; they are part of a well-organized family business.

24 The ominous connotations of Luna Park attractions in Russian film culture derive from the archetypal Ferris wheel in the film by Kozintsev and Trauberg, *The Devil's Wheel* (*Chertovo koleso*, 1926), based on a story by Veniamin Kaverin, "The End of a Thieves' Den." But the nefarious role of the Ferris wheel is well established also in non-Russian film. Possibly, the most famous thriller-coded wheel is the Riesenrad in Vienna's Prater in *The Third Man* (Carol Reed, 1950).

25 Oleg Borisov passed away in the mid 1990s, a few years after the release of *Luna Park*.

26 Khvan was awarded the prizes for Best Debut and Best Director at the Kinoshock Festival in the southern resort of Anapa. The script is by Pyotr Lutsik and Alexei Samoryadov.

27 Menshikov at the time was a promising stage actor. He received the Laurence Olivier award in 1992 for playing opposite Vanessa Redgrave, at the Globe Theater in London, in a drama depicting the romance of Isadora Duncan and the Russian poet Sergei Esenin. Later, he acquired international fame as one of the principals in Mikhalkov's Oscar winner *Burnt by the Sun*. Mikhalkov chose him again for the lead role in *Barber of Siberia*.

28 In Europe, and especially in the UK, some critics have been raving about this film. Roger Clarke of *The Independent* went as far as to call Balabanov "one of the world's great contemporary filmmakers," and "Russia's David Lynch." Quoted in Andrew James Horton, "Lynch Pin? The Imagery of Aleksei Balabanov," *Central Europe Review* online, www.ce-review.org, Vol. 2, No. 18 (May 9, 2000).

29 Daniil Dondurei, "Ne brat ia tebe, gnida . . .," *IK*, No. 2 (1998): 64-67.

30 The majority of Russian viewers thought that Sergei Bodrov "cannot act" but found him "charming and spontaneous." In fact, thousands of teenage girls made him a movie idol on a par with Leonardo Di Caprio. This film in the

mind of the Russian viewer is a sequel to *Prisoner of the Mountains*, where Bodrov, Jr. played a young and still innocent soldier in a war zone. See I. Mantsov, "Strogii iunosha," *IK*, No. 2 (1998): 61-64. *Brother* won the popular contest of the magazine *Sovetskii ekran*, both for best film and for best leading actor, and was nominated for the Nika Award (the Russian Oscar).

[31] The Russian critics in general praised the film because of its "American" style, and the self-reflexive mode that they thought was successfully achieved. See in particular N. Sirivlia, "Bratva," *IK*, No. 8 (2000): 23-29.

[32] Dmitri Savelyev, "Deputy Director," *TMT* online (February 12, 2000), www.moscowtimes.ru.

[33] See Hoffman, *The Oligarchs: Wealth and Power in the New Russia*.

[34] One of the honors received in Soviet times was the title, "Hero of Socialist Labor."

[35] Kliment Voroshilov was the Commissar of War under Stalin and a member of the State Defense Committee during WW II. The marksman in the film had served in a regiment named after Voroshilov.

[36] Dmitrii Bykov, *IK* online (October 1999), www.kinoart.ru; and Elena Stishova, "Strel'ba v tsel'," *IK*, No. 8 (1999): 30.

[37] Stishova, *ibid*.

[38] Interview taken by Liudmila Donets, "Vse my vyshli iz Pushkina," *IK* online, www.kinoart.ru (June 1999). The final scene of Ivan's absolution has a Christian overtone by association with characters from *Brothers Karamazov*. What triggers the association are the characters' names. The main character in the film is known only by name and patronymic: Ivan Fyodorovich, like the older brother in the novel. Alyosha, the cop, has the name of the younger brother who is exposed to Ivan's demon in a dramatic scene and reacts with compassion, eventually setting Ivan free to seek redemption. One central philosophical discussion in the novel is about the rejection of God if he allows violence against children, and even Alyosha agrees that in such a case the attacker must be killed. The reference to *Brothers Karamazov* in the film eluded the critics. The few with whom I discussed it found it pretentious and distasteful. Nevertheless, it is part of the text and should be pointed out.

[39] *Oblomov* (*Neskol'ko dnei v zhizni I. I. Oblomova*, 1980); see *Before the Fall*: 31. The film is based on the novel by Ivan Goncharov, *Oblomov* (1859). The novel raised heated debate among contemporary critics, and its protagonist became the quintessential example of the "superfluous man," a type portrayed in the literature of the period as ineffective and socially worthless. The radical critic, Nikolai Dobroliubov (1836-1861), first used the term "oblomovism" in his well known article, "Chto takoe oblomovshchina?," to denote a disease affecting

the whole gentry. Later, Lenin expanded Dobroliubov's formula to include the working class, implying that "oblomovism" is a national negative trait. In his film, Mikhalkov retells the story with an anti-Soviet twist, stressing the poetic Russian nature of Oblomov vs. the materialistic philosophy of his German foil.

[40] The term is a combination of the words "Khrushchev" and *"trushchoby"* (slums). It denotes the thousands of apartment buildings that, under Khrushchev, were raised in a rush on the outskirts of all major cities to alleviate the housing problem.

[41] Moscow City Council passed legislation, in May 2001, that allowed people who received privatized apartments in the early 1990s to return them to the government. Many citizens who privatized the apartments without a full understanding of the demands of ownership had tried to give them back but until then there was no procedure to do so. See *RFE/RL Newsline*, Vol. 5, No. 99, Part I (May 24, 2001).

[42] See Yuri Belkin, "Apartments to Kill for," *TMT* (April 15, 1995): 8.

[43] Quoted in Anne Barnard, "Mayor Beefs up Guards in Crime War," *TMT* (May 17, 1994): 2.

[44] See Sergey Rybak and Jonas Bernstein, "City Hall Incorporated," *TMT, Business Review* (November 21, 1995): I-II.

[45] *Love* was awarded three main prizes at the Cannes Film Festival--the Public's Prize, the Prize of the Catholic Jury, and the Prize of the European Association of Feature Films.

[46] Films that treated this theme were *Commissar* (Askol'dov, 1967/rel. 1986), *Theme* (Panfilov, 1979/rel. 1986), *Passport* (Daneliia, 1990), *Get Thee Out!* (Astrakhan, 1991), *Luna Park* (Lungin, 1992), and *See Paris and Die* (Proshkin, 1993).

[47] Interview with Valery Rubinchik (June 22, 1992). The script is by Renata Litvinova; see the discussion of Litvinova's literary works and her performance as an actress in Kira Muratova's films in Chapter 4.

[48] Here and after, quoted in Anna Lawton, "Mothers and Sons: A Modern Clash on Film," *TMT* (April 9, 1993): 7.

[49] *The Cold Summer of '53* (*Kholodnoe leto 53-go goda*). The winner of several foreign awards, the film was shown to the U.S. Congress in Washington, in 1988, during a series of special screenings to acquaint the American legislators with the achievements of glasnost. About *Cold Summer*, see *Before the Fall*: 158-9.

[50] Film presentation at the Cinema House, Moscow (May 6, 1993).

[51] Interview by G. Belostotskii, "Staraius' byt' veselym," *Dom Khanzhonkova* (May 1992): 4.

[52] Many may remember Sokolov in a very different role, as the lead in *Little Vera* (1988), which conquered foreign audiences in the late eighties. See *Before the*

Fall: 201-2.
53 From the film sound track.
54 From the film sound track.
55 For a survey of Abdrashitov's and Mindadze's previous films, see *Before the Fall*: 53-4, 169-70, and 190-1.
56 Vadim Abdrashitov (interview by Ella Korsunskaia), "Mesto neuznavaemo. Uznavaema voina," *Kinostsenarii*, No. 5 (1997): 144. Mindadze's script won the contest of the journal *Kinostsenarii*; the prize was Goskino's funding for the film's production.
57 *ibid*: 145.
58 The original version was called *Tret'ia Meshchanskaia*, which is a street address, and can be roughly translated as *Bourgeois Street No. 3*. In a sentence, it condenses the film's main theme—three people (a triangle) in a petty-bourgeois environment. The authorities decided that the title was not appropriate for circulation in the Soviet Union, and changed it to *Love Triangle* (*Liubov' vtroem*). When the film was sent to Berlin for distribution abroad, the German distributors did not like that title, which smacked of the traditional melodrama and did not reflect the film's realism and social significance, and changed it to *Bed and Sofa*. This title has never been used in the Soviet Union. In Russia, today, the film is still known as *Love Triangle*.
59 Interview by Elena Stishova, "Ia ponimal, chto nado delat' svoe kino," *IK*, No. 3 (1998): 5-10. In that interview, Mira Todorovskaya said that the film was completed in just five months, with only forty days of actual shooting. The time constraint was dictated by the shoestring budget, provided entirely by Goskino.
60 Grigory Kozintsev and Leonid Trauberg, in 1922, founded the Factory of the Eccentric Actor (FEKS), a Petrograd group that sought inspiration in popular forms of the performing arts, such as the circus, the music hall, the pantomime, and the sideshow. They also admired the dynamism and the mass appeal of Hollywood comedies and adventure movies. Their first film, *The Adventures of Oktyabrina* (*Pokhozhdeniia Oktyabriny*, 1924), combined politics and buffoonery. This kind of extravagance was not exclusive of FEKS; it was a pervasive avant-garde feature, which infiltrated the works of several film directors, such as Lev Kuleshov (his wife and main star, Alexandra Khokhlova, is an example of eccentric acting) and Sergei Eisenstein, who displayed an eccentric streak in *Strike* (1924).
61 Alexander Timofeevsky, "The Last Romantics," in *Russian Critics on the Cinema of Glasnost*, eds. Michael Brashinsky and Andrew Horton (New York: Cambridge University Press, 1994): 29.

Chapter 4

1. *Ruslan and Ludmila*, 1820.
2. *Russia on Reels*: 59.
3. Most of the new festivals are funded by Goskino, provided that they are devoted to Russian cinema and held in Russia. The following is the list of such festivals funded in 2000, with the awards expressed in thousands of rubles: Open Russian Film Festival "Kinotavr": 3,500 ($120,000 ca.); International Cinema Forum of Slavic and Orthodox Peoples "Golden Knight": 2,500; Open Festival of the Cinema of the CIS and the Baltic countries "Kinoshok": 2,000; Open Festival of Non-fiction Cinema "Russia": 2,000; Festival of Russian Cinema "Window on Europe": 2,000; International Festival of Documentary, Short-length Features, and Animation Films "Message to Man": 1,500; International Festival of Cinema Actors "Constellation": 1,500; Competition of Student Films for the national Prize "St. Anna": 1,200; Open Russian Festival of Animation Films: 1,000; Russian Festival of the Visual Arts: 1,000; Moscow International Festival of Children's Animation Films "Goldfish": 1,000; International Festival of Animation Films "Croc": 1,000; Russian Film Festival "Literature and Film": 700; Russian State Film Festival "Long Live Russian Cinema!": 700; Film Festival of Archival Films "Belye stolby": 500; International Student Festival "VGIK": 500; Festivals taking place at the Khanzhonkov House: Open Russian Festival "Film Women," named after V. Kholodnaya; Film Festival of the Oscar and Nika films-winners and films-nominees; Film Festival "Moscow Pegasus": 300; New-Year Children's Film Festival "Fairy Tale": 200; Cine-club Festival "New Cinema of Russia": 150 (two grants); St. Petersburg International Film Festival "Festival of Festivals": 150 (two grants); International Festival "Children and the Environment—XXI Century": 150; Baikal International Film Festival "Man and Nature," in Irkutsk: 150; Festival "Anigraf –Television Films": 100; Russian Educational Film Festival of the Young Friends of Cinema in Uglich "Cine-Porcupine—2000": 100; Festival of the Arts "Young Nights": 100.
4. "Interview with Konstantin Ernst," *Kinoatel'e*, No. 3 (1997): 22. In 1999, Rudinstein left his post as the festival director to concentrate on production and distribution. His successor was Alexander Atanesyan, a veteran administrator of the Moscow International Film Festival.
5. George Faraday, "Art for Whose Sake?" *TMT, Insight* (July 8, 1995): I. Quoted here is Leonid Yarmolnik, lead and producer of *Moscow Holiday* that was in competition.
6. *ibid*: II. The distributor quoted here is Evgeny Miropolsky.
7. *ibid*: III.

8 Anna Gudkova, "Stariki-razvratniki," *Kino park*, No. 3 (March 2000): 23.
9 Among them, *Peculiarities of the National Hunt*, 1995; *Prisoner of the Mountains*, 1996; *The Thief*, 1997. In 1995 Mikhalkov pulled *Burnt by the Sun* out of the Nika competition, calling it corny and unfair; he has been snubbing the ceremony ever since.
10 For a short history of the festival, see Anna Lawton, "A Long Lens on Movie History," *TMT* (July 2, 1993): III.
11 This atmosphere is recreated in *Moscow Does Not Believe in Tears* (Menshov, 1980), when the three girlfriends watch from the sidelines the parade of celebrities entering the theater Rossiya on the occasion of the 1959 Moscow Festival. In the crowd, they meet the still unknown Innokenti Smoktunovsky, soon to be gaining world renown as the Soviet Hamlet in the eponymous film by Grigori Kozintsev (1964).
12 Zhanna Vasil'eva, "Mnogo ambitsii, malo ammunitsii," *LG* (July 23, 1997): 8.
13 Sergei Solov'ev, "Chto u nas khoroshego," *Kinoatel'e*, No. 3 (1997): 5.
14 Yurii Shumilo, "Kinoproizvodstvo," *ibid*: 2. In this editorial, the author lists the members of various clans. In Solovyov's clan, he puts: Aleksander Abdulov; Renat Davletyarov, president of the "organizers of film production"; show-businessman Stas Namin; Sergei Livnev, head of Gorky Studio; Viktor Sergeev, head of Lenfilm. In Nikita Mikhalkov's clan, screenwriter Rustam Ibragimbekov and film producer Leonid Vereshchagin.
15 See Yulia Solovyova, "Film Festival to Shed Pomp for Quality," *TMT* online (July 16, 1999), www.moscowtimes.ru.
16 See *Before the Fall*: 124-7.
17 The great divide between urban and rural areas in Russia has its roots in the nineteenth-century emancipation of the serfs and industrialization at the turn of the century. Subsequently, Stalinist policies of collectivization and the need for labor in wartime caused a population movement to the cities. To retain agricultural manpower in the villages, the government did not issue internal passports to the peasants until the mid-seventies, keeping them bound to the land. When the ban was lifted, the new generation drifted toward the cities leaving behind only the old.
18 Among them, the Anger Film Festival (France) and the Moscow Film Festival Debut Award.
19 ITAR-TASS reported cases that seem to come straight from Gogol's *Dead Souls*. On October 8, 2002, the agency reported that there were several ghost towns in the Far North and the Far East, which remained on the official register even if their inhabitants had vacated them. Conversely, journalists in Karelia discovered that local officials wanted to remove from the official lists several towns

that were still inhabited by elderly and needy residents. That way, local officials would no longer be responsible for providing for the basics of life such as potable water. See *RFE/RL Newsline*, Vol. 6, No. 191, Part I (October 9, 2002).

[20] "A Full, Divers Plate at Cannes," *The Moscow Tribune* (May 17, 1994): 8. *Ryaba My Chicken* is a Russian/French production with an impressive list of sponsors: Centre national de la cinématographie, Chara Commercial Bank, AO Logovaz, Le Studio, Canal+, ARK Film, Paris Media, Roskomkino, and Russkaya ruletka.

[21] Geography, as a science, was very politicized in Soviet times, with a strong emphasis on the idea of "borders," both as a symbol of national unity and as a national defense concern. This theme is highlighted in John Haynes, *New Soviet Man: Gender and Masculinity in Stalinist Soviet Cinema* (Manchester and New York: Manchester University Press, 2003). See also James von Geldern, "The Center and the Periphery: Cultural and Social Geography in the Mass Culture of the 1930's," in *New Directions in Soviet History*, Stephen White, ed. (Cambridge: Cambridge University Press, 1992): 62-80; and Svetlana Boym, *Common Places: Mythologies of Everyday Life in Russia* (Cambridge, MA, and London: Harvard University Press, 1994).

[22] Pyotr Mamonov is a rock celebrity from the band Zvuki mu. He is a legendary figure of the pre-perestroika Leningrad rock scene and the avant-garde underworld. He played his first major film role in Lungin's *Taxi Blues*. He therefore brings dissonant connotations to the character of a Soviet functionary.

[23] The American Embassy had two dachas: the big dacha in Tarasovka, and the small dacha in Serebriany Bor. Staff could sign up to spend the weekend there. I liked in particular the small dacha in the winter. The nearby river was frozen and covered with snow, and became a wondrous ski trail. Back indoors, a steamy sauna would warm you up before an evening by the fireplace.

[24] For historical details, see Stephen Lovell, *Summerfolk: A History of the Dacha, 1710-2000* (Ithaca, NY, and London: Cornell University Press, 2003).

[25] Boris Pasternak died in his dacha in Peredelkino in 1960. The victim of a vilifying campaign, he was expelled from the Writers Union on party's orders and prevented from publishing his works. He was not allowed to accept the Nobel Prize in 1958, which was awarded to him for *Doctor Zhivago*. The manuscript had been smuggled out of the Soviet Union and published in Italy in 1957. But, notwithstanding ostracism and harassment, he did not lose his dacha, which remained with his family after his death. When I first visited the dacha in 1981, a niece of the poet was living there and had turned the house into a museum. At that time, she was struggling with the authorities that did not like the idea of a private museum and wanted it to be turned over to the state. But, eventually, she prevailed.

26 The most obvious film that comes to mind is *Paper Moon* (Bogdanovich, 1973) with Ryan O'Neal and Tatum O'Neal.
27 Reported in *RFE/RL Newsline*, Vol. 3, No. 125, Part I (June 28, 1999).
28 Interview with Sergei Solovyov by Max Miller, "Sergei Solov'ev idealist v rezko meniaiushcheisia real'nosti," *Kino-glaz*, No. 3 (1995): 23.
29 Interview with V. Todorovsky by Natal'ia Moskal'enova, "Ia ne otkryvaiu zvezd. Ia ikh obsluzhivaiu," *SE*, (February 1998): 12.
30 From the soundtrack.
31 See Mikhail Brashinskii, "Liubov'-2," *IK*, No. 11 (1998): 17-23.
32 About Eccentrism, see chapter III, note 60. The two girls also remind us of the protagonists of the Czech film, *Daisies* (Chytilová, 1966), puppet-like and irreverent, whose pranks were seen as politically subversive. The director was ostracized for years, because of the content and her bold avant-guard style.
33 Mikhail Brashinskii, "Liubov'-2": 23.
34 See Egor Likholetov, "Vladimir Mashkov: ne seks simvol, no muzh," *Kino park*, No. 3 (March 2000): 7.
35 This impression is reinforced by the fact that it is a New Year's Eve story, like *Irony of Fate, or Have a Good Sauna* (1975), which has been aired on TV for 25 years on New Year's Eve and remains one of the most popular films to this day. See *Before the Fall*: 16-17.
36 The child actor is Misha Filipchuk, who then moved on to a major role in *The Thief*.
37 Quoted in Jeanne Vronskaya, *Young Soviet Filmmakers* (London: George Allen & Unwin Ltd., 1972): 78.
38 *Autumn Marathon* (1980). See *Before the Fall*: 22-3.
39 *Mother and Son* was awarded three prizes at the International Moscow Film Festival: the Tarkovsky Prize, Prize of the Film Critics Guild, and Special Prize for the Development of the Language of Cinema. It was also extremely well received at the New York Film Festival. The financing package was secured through collaboration with the German company Zero Film, and included Goskino money. Sokurov is considered by many the heir to Andrei Tarkovsky, stylistically, although not thematically and philosophically. About Sokurov's previous works, see *Before the Fall*: 138-43 and 238-9.
40 Kirill Galetski, "The Foundations of Film Art: An Interview with Alexander Sokurov," *Cineaste*, Vol. 26, No. 3 (Summer 2001): 5.
41 "La paura del naturalismo (osservazioni sul piano-sequenza)," *Nuovi argomenti*, No. 6 (1967): 11-23. Already noted by Ben Lawton, "Boccaccio and Pasolini: A Contemporary Reinterpretation of *The Decameron*," in *The Decameron*, M. Musa and P. Bondanella, eds. (New York: Norton, 1977): 306-22.

[42] Sokurov is often called "Tarkovsky's heir." While it is true that Tarkovsky was his mentor, and that Sokurov shares some of the teacher's stylistic features, there is a fundamental difference between the two in their philosophical worldview. While Tarkovsky had a religious sense of life, rooted in the Russian Orthodox faith, Sokurov's worldview is secular, devoid of mysticism. Rather, his images transcend the material world on the aesthetic level.

[43] Anna Lawton, "Dostoevskii dlia nas i dlia nikh," *Video-Ass*, No. 27 (Winter 1995): 70. Also, from an interview with Eshpai (March 16, 1993).

[44] *ibid*: 71.

[45] About Solovyov's previous films, see *Before the Fall*: 197-9. David Lynch became a great favorite among the intellectual elite. Not so among the average public. Russian TV station Ostankino (Channel 1) aired the *Twin Peak* serial, starting in November 1993, and discovered that the show's weird Americana was lost to the Russian public, while *Santa Barbara* scored the highest rating.

[46] The Arbat is one of Moscow's historical sites, and became the first pedestrian mall in the perestroika years, where vendors were allowed to trade their goods.

[47] See the interview with Iurii Arabov by Natal'ia Riurikova, "Pochemu my vmeste," *Kinostsenarii*, No. 4 (1999): 2-11. Arabov won the Best Screenplay award at the 1999 Cannes Film Festival. He has written all the screenplays for Sokurov's features, up to and including *Taurus* (2001). *Moloch* was awarded the Grand Prix at the Kinotavr Film Festival, but with a polemical gesture Sokurov rejected the award because he disagreed with the jury's other selections.

[48] This is not to detract from the actor's performance, which is superb. Leonid Mozgovoy has an extraordinary ability to assume the physical features of the characters he plays. Before *Moloch*, he played Anton Chekhov in Sokurov's *Stone* (1992), and more recently, Lenin in *Taurus*.

[49] From the screenplay, *Kinostsenarii*, No. 4 (1999): 32.

[50] In the script, Arabov created a different imagery with the same signification. In the morning, Eva rides her bicycle to a nearby lake to take a swim. Both the ride and the swim emphasize her vitality and physical enjoyment. In the evening, as the limos depart, Eva rides her bicycle to the lake again. The water has changed colors, from blue to black; she dives and sinks to the bottom, *ibid*.

[51] See *Before the Fall*: 213-14

[52] Litvinova wrote the screenplays for *Non-Love* (Rubinchik, 1992) and *Tractor Drivers 2* (Aleinikovs Brothers, 1992). *Land of the Deaf* was based on Litvinova's story "To Possess and to Belong" (*Obladat' i prinadlezhat'*). About Litvinova's prose, see Tat'iana Moskvina, "Foemina sapiens," *IK*, No. 4 (1998): 47-57. On the Litvinova phenomenon, besides Tat'iana Moskvina, see also Andrei Plak-

hov, "Maniia stilia, ili toska Renaty Litvinovoi," *SE* (February 1998): 27-29, and Petr Pustota, "Ee ili liubiat ili nenavidiat," *ibid*: 24.

53. The script is by Kira Muratova with Evgeny Golubenko, based on stories by Boris Dedyukhin.
54. Screenplays: "Boiler Room" by Igor Bozhko, "Ophelia" by Renata Litvinova, "The Little Girl and Death" by Vera Storozheva with Kira Muratova.
55. The drowning of the Shakespearian Ophelia obviously serves as an ironical subtext to the story.
56. Apples are conspicuous in this episode and in "Ophelia," and are significant inasmuch as they deny the usual signifier. In the Judeo-Christian iconography, the apple stands for sin, transgression, fall. In this film, there are no such concepts; the apples are part of the mise en scène and nobody is tempted to eat them.
57. These two young screenwriters have stirred some discussion in the film circles because of their style. Andrei Konchalovsky, allegedly, said that their works are not screenplays but a completely new genre. See Dmitrii Bykov, "Chugunii," *Ekran*, No. 8 (1993): 14-15. In 1993 Tot received the Nika award for Best Director; Lutsik and Samoryadov for Best Screenplay.
58. Those discussed in this book are: Valery Todorovsky, Alexander Khvan, Dmitri Meskhiev, Andrei I, Tomas Tot, Ivan Dykhovichny, and Sergei Livnev.
59. A more avant-garde trend has been in existence since the days of perestroika, under the label of Parallel Cinema. The founders of the Leningrad branch were Evgeny Yufit, Andrei Myortvy, and Evgeny Kondratyev; in Moscow the main figures were Gleb and Igor Aleinikov. See *Before the Fall*: 240-4. The trend continued in the Post-Soviet period. The brothers Aleinikov's film *Tractor Drivers 2* (1994), a parody of the homonymous Stalinist movie from the 1930s, had some resonance abroad. Gleb Aleinikov, after the death of his brother in a car accident in the mid-1990s, established the Cine Fantom Club at the Moscow Museum of Cinema, which offers an annual festival of experimental films and serves as the headquarters for independent filmmakers.
60. *Kino-glaz*, No. 3 (1933): 44.
61. Alexander Kalyagin, a popular character actor often cast in comic roles, plays the director.
62. One of the most popular novels in the socialist realist mode was Nikolai Ostrovsky's *How the Steel Was Tempered* (*Kak zakalialas' stal'*, 1934), which earned its author the Order of Lenin.
63. *Repentance* by Tengiz Abuladze (1984/1986); see *Before the Fall*: 162-6. See also Josephine Woll and Denise J. Youngblood, *Repentance: The Film Companion* (London: I. B. Tauris, 2001).

⁶⁴ The film is a Russian/French/German production by Project Camp, Canal +, Paris Media, Mosfilm, and Ritm.
⁶⁵ From the film sound track.
⁶⁶ In semiotic parlance, the sign no longer consists of a "signifier" and a "signified," but of two "signifiers." It's an image, whose referent is just another image, or a copy without the original. Jean Baudrillard in his works used the term "simulacrum" to refer to this concept.
⁶⁷ The monument is real and famous, though the circumstances in the film are fiction. It was originally displayed in the Soviet Pavilion at the Paris World Exhibition in 1936.
⁶⁸ There was a model in real life in the person of writer Nikolai Ostrovsky, mentioned in a previous note.
⁶⁹ See an excellent discussion of this film in Louis Menashe, "Buttons, Buttons, Who's Got the Workers? A Note on the (Missing) Working Class in Late- and Post-Soviet Russian Cinema," *International Labor and Working-Class History*, No. 59 (Spring 2001): 52-59.
⁷⁰ Nina Tsyrkun, "Tinkling Symbols: Fragmented Society - Fragmented Cinema?" in *Russia on Reels*: 61.
⁷¹ See Angela Charlton, "Overflowing Moscow Metro still Inspires Devotion," *The Moscow Tribune* (April 15, 1995): 2. While minor accidents have always been frequent, only a major one has been recorded. In 1983, an escalator at Aviamotornaya station collapsed and the passengers were crushed in the gears, causing the death of twenty-seven people and injuring hundreds. See Ellen Barry, "Escalators: No Stairway to Heaven," *TMT* (April 13, 1995): 24.
⁷² See a recent essay by Denise J. Youngblood, "A War Remembered: Soviet Films of the Great Patriotic War," *The American Historical Review*, Vol. 105, No. 5 (June 2001): 839-56.
⁷³ It won the Best-Director award at the Karlovy Vary International Film Festival. About the documentaries of glasnost, see *Before the Fall*: 175-6.
⁷⁴ Nina Klose, "Tale of the Soviet Union's 'Vietnam'," *TMT* (July 14, 1993): 16.
⁷⁵ The film was financed both privately (by Boris Giller's company, Caravan, and BG Production) and with state funds from Goskino. It was nominated for the 1997 Academy Award as Best Foreign Film and won the Nika award (the Russian Oscar) for Best Actor—co-shared by Bodrov, Jr., and Menshikov—Best Director, and Best Script.
⁷⁶ The scene looks like a cinematic quotation from *Apocalypse Now* (Coppola, 1979), with the difference that Coppola used helicopters.
⁷⁷ Alexander Pushkin and Mikhail Lermontov had also treated this theme in their poems by the same title.

78 The film was produced by A.G.N. Company, allegedly one of Berezovsky's many media enterprises.
79 Sergei Sel'ianov, "Eto - kino," *IK*, Vol. 7 (1998): 58-60.
80 See a series of opinions in "Posleslovie," *IK*, Vol. 7 (1998): 54-70.
81 From the sound track.
82 See Elena Stishova, "Zapiski kavkazskoi voiny," *IK* online (No. 1, 1999), www.kinoart.ru; Dmitrii Bykov, "Identifikatsiia Rogozhkina, ili Ad absurdum," *IK* online (No. 1, 1999), www.kinoart.ru
83 This name could also be read as Mochá (Urine), and its double meaning creates a comical misunderstanding during an interrogation by the prosecutor. At the beginning of the film, the voice over narrator explains that the character has a speech problem and pronounces the word "*mózhno*" ("it is possible") as "*mócha*," and that this is the reason for his nickname.
84 Quotations are from the soundtrack.
85 Bykov, "Identifikatsiia Rogozhkina, ili Ad absurdum."
86 "The Fatalist" was part of a collection of short stories by Mikhail Lermontov, featuring the same protagonist. The collection was considered a novel by the title, *A Hero of Our Time* (*Geroi nashego vremeni*, 1840). The quote is from an English edition, Paul Foote, tr. (Penguin Books, 1966): 180.

Chapter 5

1 The term "carnival" was first used in literary criticism by Soviet scholar Mikhail Bakhtin to describe features of the grotesque prose of Gogol and the polyphonic text of Dostoevsky. He identified "carnival" as a subversive device. See Mikhail Bakhtin, *Rabelais and His World* (Bloomington, IN: Indiana University Press, 1984) and *Problems of Dostoevsky's Poetics* (Ann Arbor, MI: Ardis, 1973). See also M. Keith Booker and Dubravka Juraga, *Bakhtin, Stalin, and Modern Russian Fiction: Carnival, Dialogism, and History* (Westport, CN: Greenwood Press, 1995).
2 Marina Neyolova and Anna Mikhalkova (as the mayor's wife and daughter); Oleg Yankovsky, Aleksei Zharkov, Vladimir Ilin, Zinovi Gerat, Avangard Leontev (in the roles of the city notables); and Armen Dzhigarkhanian (as Khlestiakov's servant).
3 Here and below, from the English translation of the play in George Rapall Noyes, ed., *Masterpieces of the Russian Drama* (New York: Dover Publications, Inc., 1961): 157-232.

⁴ Tormented by guilt, Gogol attempted to write a sequel to his novel *Dead Souls*, in which the swindler/protagonist repents and finds moral salvation. But, artistically, Part II was quite unsatisfactory; it was a dry exercise lacking inspiration. Gogol burnt the manuscript in desperation shortly before his death.

⁵ The Natural School emerged around 1840 and included a few minor writers, besides Gogol. Its most fervent advocate was the literary critic and journalist, Vissarion Belinsky (1811-1848). The Natural School prepared the ground for the appearance of the literary current known as Russian critical realism, which includes major figures such as Dostoyevsky, Tolstoy, and Turgenev.

⁶ I singled out this particular episode because it is best suited for a dramatic plot. But I must note that there were dozens of such swindlers in those years, who eventually ended up in jail or took refuge abroad.

⁷ The term "cooperative" was a perestroika euphemism for a private enterprise. Usually it applied to small businesses in the service sector.

⁸ In later years, the Internet spread rather rapidly among the population. In April 2003, some 10.2 million Russian citizens, or 9.1 percent of the population, were Internet users, according to data provided by the companies SpyLOG and J'ason & Partners. *RFE/RL Newsline*, Vol. 7, No. 86, Part I (May 7, 2003).

⁹ Mikhail Dubik, "Investors Play on in MMM Pyramid," *TMT* (July 26, 1994), www.moscowtimes.ru.

¹⁰ The creator of those commercials was Bakhyt Kilibaev, better known as the director of the film *Gongofer* (1993) that presents strong Gogolian elements.

¹¹ Dubik, "Investors Play on in MMM Pyramid," www.moscowtimes.ru

¹² Quoted in Euan Craik and Mikhail Dubik, "Thousands Buy Shares as MMM Reopens," *TMT* (August 23, 1994), www.moscowtimes.ru

¹³ Mavrodi used his immunity to reorganize the business, open other subsidiaries, and extend branches abroad. Over one year, he showed up at the Duma only once, prompting debate on the floor about the need to reform the immunity law (the Constitutional Court eventually imposed restrictions on the immunity law, in February 1996). In October 1995, the Duma voted overwhelmingly to strip Mavrodi of his seat in the parliament on the charge that he was still the head of a company and this was a violation of the federal law regulating deputies' duties. Mavrodi's next move was to run for president of Russia in 1996. He submitted to the Central Election Commission the required list of more than one million signatures in support of his candidacy. But the Commission disqualified 480,000 signatures and rejected Mavrodi as a contender. At this point, Mavrodi disappeared and an international arrest warrant was issued in 1998. MMM was declared bankrupt by a Moscow court in September 1997 with about $20 million in debts. After five years on the run, on January

31, 2003, Mavrodi was arrested in Moscow. While the police had been looking for him over two continents, allegedly he never left the city, living under a false name and changing apartments and dachas constantly. He was charged with fraud. His brother, co-founder of MMM, was arrested earlier, and sentenced to five years in prison. See, *RFE/RL Newsline*, Vol. 7, No. 21, Part I (February, 3, 2003).

[14] Quoted in Andrei Zorkii, "V ocheredi za garazhi," *SE*, No. 11 (1980): 7. About the films of Ryazanov and screenwriter Emil Braginsky, see *Before the Fall*: 16-19.

[15] See Mikhail Bakhtin, *Rabelais and His World*; Henri Bergson, *Laughter: An Essay on the Meaning of the Comic* (Copenhagen and Los Angeles: Green Integer, 1999); and the thriller whose key is "laughter," *The Name of the Rose* by Umberto Eco.

[16] With the death of Braginsky, Ryazanov lost his best screenwriter. The script for this film is by Vladimir Moiseenko, Iuri Fedorov, and Eldar Ryazanov.

[17] Besides Gurchenko, the cast consists of Lia Akhedzhanova, Svetlana Kryuchkova, and Irina Kupchenko. *Old Nags* contains many references to early films.

[18] Cited in Jean MacKenzie, "Russians Miss Good Old Days of 'Stagnation'," *TMT* (February 26, 1993): 8.

[19] The Soviet edition consisted of only eight copies. Each was handmade and included 124 large cardboard pages on which four typewritten sheets were glued. The volume was tied together by three ribbons. Smuggled copies reached the West and the almanac was eventually published by Ardis (Ann Arbor, MI, 1979) in a thick volume of about 800 pages. *Metropol* was not intended to be an underground venture (like *samizdat* publications), but an open alternative to the monopolistic government press. The contributors included very prominent figures among the independent-minded literary community, such as Bella Akhmadulina, Vasily Aksyonov, Andrei Bitov, Viktor Erofeev, Fazil Iskander, Mark Razovsky, Andrei Voznesensky, and others. All were roughed up by the KGB and reprimanded by the Writers Union's leadership. Films, plays, and novels by the contributors were withdrawn from circulation; and in the most extreme case, Aksyonov was forced into emigration. See Anna Lawton's review of *Metropol* in *Slavic and East European Journal*, Vol. 24, No. 3 (Fall 1980): 302-03.

[20] The hero of Melnikov's *One of a Kind* (1985) was a researcher who had the mental power to transmit his dreams. He, therefore, created a profitable business selling dreams to a sleeping audience.

[21] For both these films, see *Before the Fall*: 201-4.

22 Ostap Bender was already known to the reading public as the hero of a previous book by the same authors, *The Twelve Chairs* (1928). Humor and satire were not easy to handle under the Bolshevik regime. The target of laughter had to be ideologically correct, and any slip of the pen could cost the authors very dearly. That is why the book was published with an introduction by the Commissar of Education, Anatoly Lunacharsky, who warned the reader not to fall for Ostap Bender's roguish charm, but to see through his tricks and to judge him for his lack of class consciousness and social responsibility.

23 See *Before the Fall*: 216-19.

24 This film consists of one single long take. The Steadicam operator, Tilman Büttner, talks in detail about the technical wizardry he performed in an interview by Louis Menashe, "Filming Sokurov's *Russian Ark*," *Cineaste*, Vol. XXVIII, No. 3 (Summer 2003): 21-23.

25 Quoted in Katya Svetova and Chris Klein, "Five Hundred Years of Foreigners in Moscow," *TMT* (May 21, 1994): 19.

26 For a more detailed list, see Artemy Troitsky, "Where the City Doesn't Sleep," *TMT* (April 16, 1994): 8.

27 From the film sound track.

28 Interview with Karen Shakhnazarov by Polina Orynianskaia, "Kino – eto zhizn'. No ochen' zanimatel'naia," *Ekstra M* (January 4, 1994): 27.

29 Hiatt reported on himself: "How I appeared in a Russian movie is a tale that well reflects the possibilities of living in a society where all the rules are being rewritten. Or, as I suspected during most of my Mosfilm career . . . perhaps it was all a gigantic practical joke." Fred Hiatt, "Confessions of a Part-time Movie Star," *TMT, Review* (February 11, 1994): 1.

30 The director's father, Georgy Shakhnazarov, was a close collaborator of Gorbachev's, and at the time of the putsch was the only high government official who was placed under house arrest together with the Gorbachev family in the Crimean resort where they were vacationing.

31 The term *ostranenie* was first formulated by Viktor Shklovsky, one of the members of Opoiaz (Society for the Study of the Poetic Language), which began issuing its own publications in 1916. He described *ostranenie* as a device that would break down automatism in perception, bringing about the "seeing" and not just the "recognizing" of an image or a situation. See Viktor Shklovskii, "Iskusstvo kak priem," *Sborniki po teorii poeticheskogo iazyka*, Vypusk II, 1917.

32 From the soundtrack.

33 Interview by Svetlana Kolomoets, "Okno v Parizh," *Kadr*, No.1 (1993): 3. Mamin's debut as a director was the short, *Neptune Festival* (1986). This film made fun of village folk challenging a group of Swedish tourists to a plunging con-

test into the frozen river—a parody of the famous battle on the ice from Eisenstein's *Alexander Nevsky*. Good-humored farce turned into unsettling grotesque and political surrealism in his next two films, *Fountain* (1988) and *Sideburns* (1990), as Mamin became progressively disillusioned with the results of the new course. See *Before the Fall*: 226-30.

34 Paul Aleppsky, an archdeacon from Poland, writing in the 1650s. Quoted in Svetova and Klein, "Five Hundred Years of Foreigners in Moscow": 17.

35 See David Filipov, "The Great Kiosk Caper," *TMT* (August 25, 1992): 1.

36 Report by the market research group Business Analytica. Quoted in Euan Craik, "Study: Imports Capture 40% of Market," *TMT* (November 23, 1994): 11.

37 According to figures released by the Foreign Trade Ministry in 1993, food amounted to 45 percent of total consumer goods imports, and 70 percent of it was consumed in Moscow and St. Petersburg, *ibid*.

38 This is an allusion to the novel, *Not by Bread Alone* (*Ne khlebom edinym*,1956), by Vladimir Dudintsev. The book was a product of the "thaw" period, and defended the rights of the individual against the system. Notwithstanding Khrushchev's liberal policy, the book stirred a big controversy and was publicly condemned. The title, a Biblical reference, alluded to spiritual values; in the present text, I used it literally.

39 See David Filipov, "Undercover at Tsentralnyi Rynok," *TMT* (March 6, 1992): 11.

40 The peculiar mannerism of the Gogolian narrator was first noted by B. M. Eikhenbaum in his essay "Kak sdelana *Shinel'* Gogolia" ("How Gogol's *Overcoat* Is Made,"1919). In that essay, he used the term *skaz* to denote "a construction based on a narrator's manner of narrating."

41 See *Duba-Duba* and *Children of the Iron Gods*.

42 Gogol's tale was adapted for the screen twice: *Vii* (V. Starevich, 1918; and K. Ershov, 1967). It was considered a horror film.

43 *Un Chien Adalou* (Buñuel, 1929) shocked audiences with the image of a woman's eye being slashed with a razor blade. It became an anthology piece and the most quoted example of cinematic surrealism.

44 *Believe It or Not* (1983), *Lefty* (1987), *It* (1989). See *Before the Fall*: 233-5.

45 These films were enormously popular in Finland, according to Richard Stites. This seems to be the only foreign country that appreciated them.

46 This is a reference to *La Strada* (Fellini, 1954). Characters and films mentioned and alluded to in subsequent paragraphs are listed below in order of appearance. Personages from everyday-life episodes do not need further identification. Khlestyakov and the Mayor (*Inspector General*); Ivan Fyodorovich and Katya (*The Voroshilov Marksman*); the guys at the checkpoint and Manimat (*Check-

point); the drummer (*Drum Roll*); Evdokim (*Hammer and Sickle*); Nicholas and Yurovsky (*Assassin of the Tsar* and *The Romanovs: The Crown Family*); Hitler and Eva Braun (*Moloch*); little giant (*Little Giant with a Big Sex-Drive*); Stalin and Tolyan (*The Thief*); Pugachev (*The Captain's Daughter*); Brother 3 (*Brother* and *Brother 2*); Yaya and Rita (*Land of the Deaf*); Ignat (*Children of the Iron Gods*); McCracken (*The Barber of Siberia* and *Window on Paris*); countess, count, Masha, and conman (*Dreams*); Ryaba and Asya (*Ryaba, My Chicken*); champions of the national hunt (*Peculiarities of the National Hunt in the Fall, Peculiarities of the National Fishing,* and *Peculiarities of the National Hunt in the Winter*); musical quartet (*Old Nags*).

Bibliography

Bakhtin, Mikhail. *Problems of Dostoevsky's Poetics*. Ann Arbor, MI: Ardis, 1973
_____. *Rabelais and His World*. Bloomington, IN: Indiana University Press, 1984
Balzer, Harley. "Routinization of the New Russians?" *The Russian Review*, No. 62 (January 2003): 15-36
Barthes, Roland. *The Rustle of Language*. Oxford: Basil Blackwell, 1986
Bergson, Henri. *Laughter: An Essay on the Meaning of the Comic*. Copenhagen and Los Angeles: Green Integer, 1999
Beumers, Birgit, ed. *Russia on Reels: The Russian Idea in Post-Soviet Cinema*. London: I.B. Tauris & Co Ltd., 1999
Billington, James H. *Russia in Search of Itself*. Washington, DC: The Woodrow Wilson Center Press and Johns Hopkins University Press, 2004
Booker, M. Keith and Dubravka Juraga, *Bakhtin, Stalin, and Modern Russian Fiction: Carnival, Dialogism, and History*. Westport, CN: Greenwood Press, 1995
Boym, Svetlana. *Common Places: Mythologies of Everyday Life in Russia*. Cambridge, MA, and London: Harvard University Press, 1994
_____. "Post Soviet Cinematic Nostalgia: From Elite Cinema to Soap Opera," *Journal for Theoretical Studies in Media and Culture* (Spring 1995): 75-84
Brashinsky, Michael. "Liubov'-2," *Iskusstvo kino*, No. 11 (1998): 17-23
_____ and Andrew Horton eds. *Russian Critics on the Cinema of Glasnost*. New York: Cambridge University Press, 1994
Brown, Archie. *The Gorbachev Factor*. Oxford: Oxford University Press, 1996
Buckley, Mary. *Perestroika and Soviet Women*. Cambridge: Cambridge University Press, 1992
_____. *Redefining Russian Society and Polity*. Boulder, CO: Westview Press, 1993
Bykov, Dmitrii. "Chugunii," *Ekran*, No. 8 (1993): 14-15
Coleman, Fred. *The Decline and Fall of the Soviet Empire*. New York: St. Martin's Press, 1996
Condee, Nancy, ed. *Soviet Hieroglyphics: Visual Culture in Late Twentieth-century Russia*, Bloomington, IN: Indiana University Press, 1995
de Certeau, Michel. *The Writing of History*. New York: Columbia University Press, 1988

Dobbs, Michael. *Down with Big Brother*. New York: Alfred A. Knopf, 1997
Dondurei, Daniil. "Kino: Zhizn' posle smerti," *Nezavisimaia gazeta* (February 6, 1992): 7
_____. "Novaia model'," *Kinoatele*, No. 3 (1997): 72
_____. "Ne brat ia tebe, gnida . . .," *Iskusstvo kino*, No. 2 (1998): 64-67
Ellis, Frank. *From Glasnost to the Internet: Russia's New Infosphere*. New York: St. Martin's Press, 1998
Faraday, George. *Revolt of the Filmmakers*. University Park, PA: Pennsylvania State University Press, 2000
Ferro, Marc. *Cinema and History*. Detroit: Wayne State University Press, 1988
Figes, Orlando. *Natasha's Dance: A Cultural History of Russia*. New York: Metropolitan Books, 2002
Foucault, Michel. *Archaeology of Knowledge*. New York: Pantheon Books, 1982
_____. *The Order of Things*. New York: Vintage, Reissue edition, 1994
Galetski, Kirill. "The Foundations of Film Art: An Interview with Alexander Sokurov," *Cineaste*, Vol. 26, No. 3 (Summer 2001): 5.
Galichenko, Nicholas. *Glasnost: Soviet Cinema Responds*. Austin, TX: University of Texas Press, 1991
Gessen, Masha. *Dead Again: The Russian Intelligentsia After Communism*. London: Verso Books, 1997
Gillespie, David. *Russian Cinema*. Harlow, UK: Pearson Education Ltd., 2003
Golovskoy, Val S. with John Rimberg. *Behind the Soviet Screen: The Motion Picture Industry in the USSR, 1972-1982*. Ann Arbor, MI: Ardis, 1986
Haynes, John. *New Soviet Man: Gender and Masculinity in Stalinist Soviet Cinema*. Manchester and New York: Manchester University Press, 2003
Hoffman, David. *The Oligarchs: Wealth and Power in the New Russia*. Washington, DC: Public Affairs, 2002
Holdsworth, Nick. *Moscow, The Beautiful and the Damned*. London: Andre Deutsch Ltd., 2000
Horton, Andrew and Michael Brashinsky. *The Zero Hour: Glasnost and Soviet Cinema in Transition*. Princeton, NJ: Princeton University Press, 1992
_____, eds. *Inside Soviet Film Satire: Laughter with a Lash*. New York and Cambridge: Cambridge University Press, 1993
Karakhan, Lev. "Um i vlast', sila i mudrost'. . .," *Iskusstvo kino*, No. 8 (1998): 23-24
Kelly, Catriona and David Shepherd, eds. *Russian Cultural Studies*. Oxford: Oxford University Press, 1998
Kenez, Peter. *Cinema and Soviet Society: From the Revolution to the Death of Stalin*. London: I. B. Tauris & Co. Ltd., 2001
Konchalovsky, Andrei and Alexander Lipkov. *The Inner Circle: An Inside View of Soviet Life Under Stalin*, J. Gambrell, ed., tr. New York: Newmarket Press, 1991
Korsunskaia, Ella. "Mesto neuznavaemo. Uznavaema voina," *Kinostsenarii*, No. 5 (1997): 144

Kuchins, Andrew C., ed. *Russia After the Fall*. Washington, DC: Carnegie Endowment for International Peace, 2002

Lahusen, T. *Late Soviet Culture from Perestroika to Novostroika*. Durham, NC: Duke University Press, 1993

Lawton, Anna. *Before the Fall: Soviet Cinema in the Gorbachev Years*. Washington, DC: New Academia Publishing, 2004/original, *Kinoglasnost: Soviet Cinema in Our Time*, Cambridge University Press, 1992

_____, ed. *The Red Screen: Politics, Society, Art in Soviet Cinema*. London: Routledge, 1992

_____. "Dostoevskii dlia nas i dlia nikh," *Video-Ass*, No. 27 (Winter 1995): 70

Leyda, Jay. *Kino. A History of the Russian and Soviet Film*. Princeton, NJ: Princeton University Press, 1983

Lovell, Stephen. *Summerfolk: A History of the Dacha, 1710-2000*. Ithaca, NY, and London: Cornell University Press, 2003

Mantsov, I. "Strogii iunosha," *Iskusstvo kino*, No. 2 (1998): 61-64

Matizen, Viktor. "Budushchee u Rossii est', tol'ko nam ego ne dozhdat'sia," *Stolitsa*, No. 13 (April 1991): 36-39

Matlock, Jack, Jr. *Autopsy of an Empire*. New York: Random House, 1995

Menashe, Louis. "Requiem for Soviet Cinema, 1917-1991," *Cineaste*, Vol. XXI, No. 1-2 (1995), 23-27

_____. "Moscow Believes in Tears: The Problems (and Promise?) of Russian Cinema in the Transition Period," *Cineaste*, Vol. XXVI, No. 3 (Summer 2001): 10-17

_____. "Buttons, Buttons, Who's Got the Workers? A Note on the (Missing) Working Class in Late- and Post-Soviet Russian Cinema," *International Labor and Working-Class History*, No. 59 (Spring 2001): 52-59

_____. "Filming Sokurov's *Russian Ark*," *Cineaste*, Vol. XXVIII, No. 3 (Summer 2003): 21-23

Mickiewicz, Ellen. *Changing Channels: Television and the Struggle for Power in Russia*. Durham, NC: Duke University Press, 1999

Mikhalkov, Nikita. "Blind Faith," *Sight and Sound* (January 1996): 61

Moskvina, Tat'iana. "Foemina sapiens," *Iskusstvo kino*, No. 4 (1998): 47-57

Olcott, Anthony. *Russian Pulp*. Lanham, MD: Rowman & Littlefield, 2001

Pasolini, Pier Paolo. "La paura del naturalismo (osservazioni sul piano-sequenza)," *Nuovi argomenti*, No. 6 (1967): 11-23

Pinskii, Boris. "Kuda idem my s Goskino," *Sovetskii ekran* (February 1998): 4

Pipes, Richard. "Flight from Freedom: What Russians Think and Want," Foreign Affairs, Vol. 83, No. 3 (May/June 2004), www.foreignaffairs.org

Plakhov, Andrei. "Maniia stilia, ili toska Renaty Litvinovoi," *Sovetskii ekran* (February 1998): 27-29

Radzinskii, Edvard. *The Last Tsar*. New York: Doubleday, 1992

_____. *Nikolai II: zhizn' i smert'*. Moscow: Vagrius, 1998
Razumovskii, Andrei. "Iskusstvo rasporiazhat'sia svobodoi," *Kinoatel'e*, No. 3 (1997): 39
Remnick, David. *Lenin's Tomb: The Last Days of the Soviet Empire*. New York: Random House, 1993
_____. *Resurrection*. New York: Vintage Books, 1999
Riurikova, Nataliia. "Pochemu my vmeste," *Kinostsenarii*, No. 4 (1999): 2-11
Rosenstone, Robert A., ed. *Revisioning History*. Princeton, NJ: Princeton University Press, 1994
Rule, Wilma and Norma Noonan, eds. *Russian Women in Politics and Society*. Westport: Greenwood Press, 1996
Sel'ianov, Sergei. "Eto - kino," *Iskusstvo kino*, Vol. 7 (1998): 58-60
Shalin, Dmitri N., ed. *Russian Culture at the Crossroad*. Boulder, CO: Westview Press, 1996
Shlapentok, Dimitri and Vladimir. *Soviet Cinematography 1918-1991: Ideological Conflict and Social Reality*. New York: Aldine de Gruyler, 1993
Shumilo, Yurii. "Kinoproizvodstvo," *Kinoatel'e*, No. 3 (1997): 2-4
Sirivlia, N. "Bratva," *Iskusstvo kino*, No. 8, (2000): 23-29
Smith, Kathleen E. *Mythmaking in the New Russia: Politics and Memory During the Yeltsin Years*. Ithaca and London: Cornell University Press, 2002
Solov'ev, Sergei. "Chto u nas khoroshego," *Kinoatel'e*, No. 3 (1997): 5-7
Stern, Frank. "Screening Politics: Cinema and Intervention," *Georgetown Journal of International Affairs*, Vol. 1, No. 2 (Summer/Fall, 2000): 65-73
Stishova, Elena. "Ia ponimal, chto nado delat' svoe kino," *Iskusstvo kino*, No. 3 (1998): 5-10.
_____. "S'ezd proigravshikh, ili Nauka pobezhdat'," *Iskusstvo kino*, No 4 (1998): 9-10
_____. "Strel'ba v tsel'," *Iskusstvo kino*, No. 8 (1999): 27-30
Stites, Richard. *Revolutionary Dreams*. New York and Oxford: Oxford University Press, 1989
_____. *Russian Popular Culture: Entertainment and Society in Russia Since1900*. Cambridge: Cambridge University Press, 1992
_____, ed. *Culture and Entertainment in Wartime Russia*. Bloomington, IN: Indiana University Press, 1995
Taylor, Richard and Derek Spring, eds. *Stalinism and Soviet Cinema*. London and New York: Routledge, 1993
_____ and Ian Christie, eds. *The Film Factory: Russian and Soviet Cinema in Documents 1896-1939*. London: Routledge, 1994
Timofeevsky, Alexander. "The Last Romantics," in *Russian Critics on the Cinema of Glasnost*, Michael Brashinsky and Andrew Horton, eds. Cambridge and New York: Cambridge University Press, 1994): 24-29
Tirdatova, Evgeniia. "Antipiratskii zakon priniat," *Kino-glaz* (March 1993): 5

Troitsky, Artemy. "Flying Bullets, Surreal Scenes," *The Moscow Times* (October 6, 1993): 9

Tsyrkun, Nina. "Tinkling Symbols: Fragmented Society - Fragmented Cinema?" in *Russia on Reels: The Russian Idea in Post-Soviet Cinema*, Birgit Beumers, ed. London: I.B. Tauris & Co Ltd., 1999: 57-65

Vasil'eva, Zhanna. "Mnogo ambitsii, malo ammunitsii," *Literaturnaia gazeta* (July 23, 1997): 8

_____. "Dostuchat'sia do Gollivuda," *Literaturnaia gazeta* (August 6, 1997): 8

_____. "Nakolka vremen demokratii," *Literaturnaia gazeta* (October 22, 1997): 8

Volkov, Vadim. *Violent Entrepreneurs: The Use of Force in the Making of Russian Capitalism*. Ithaca: Cornell University Press, 2002

Von Geldern, James. "The Center and the Periphery: Cultural and Social Geography in the Mass Culture of the 1930's," in *New Directions in Soviet History*, Stephen White, ed. Cambridege: Cambridge University Press, 1992: 62-80

_____. *Bolshevik Festivals, 1917-1920*. Berkeley, CA: University of California Press, 1993

_____ and Richard Stites, eds. *Mass Culture in Soviet Russia: Tales, Poems, Songs, Movies, Plays, and Foklore, 1917-1953*. Bloomington, IN: Indiana University Press, 1995

Vronskaya, Jeanne. *Young Soviet Filmmakers*. London: George Allen & Unwin Ltd., 1972

Woll, Josephine. *Real Images: Soviet Cinema and the Thaw*. London: I. B. Tauris & Co. Ltd., 2000

_____ and Denise J. Youngblood, *Repentance: The Film Companion*. London: I. B. Tauris, 2001

Youngblood, Denise J. *Soviet Cinema in the Silent Era, 1918-35*. Austin, TX: Unversity of Texas Press, 1991

_____. *Movies for the Masses: Popular Cinema and Soviet Society*. New York and Cambridge: Cambridge University Press, 1992

_____. "A War Remembered: Soviet Films of the Great Patriotic War," *The American Historical Review*, Vol. 105, No. 5 (June 2001): 839-56

_____. "The Cosmopolitan and the Patriot: the Brothers Mikhalkov-Konchalovsky and Russian Cinema," *Historical Journal of Film, Radio and Television*, Vol. 23, No. 1 (2003): 27-41

Zorkii, Andrei. "V ocheredi za garazhi," *Sovetskii ekran*, No. 11 (1980): 7

Journals and newspapers

Business World Weekly
Cahiers du cinema
Central Europe Review, www.ce-review.org
Christian Science Monitor
Cineaste
Dom kino
Ekran
Ekran i stsena (LG supplement)
Foreign Affairs, www.foreignaffairs.org
Gazeta soiuza kinematografistov
Historical Journal of Film Radio and Television
Iskusstvo kino, www.kinoart.ru
Itogi
Izvestiia
Kadr
Kapital
Kino-eye, www.kinoeye.org
Kino-glaz
Kino park
Kinostsenarii
Kinovedcheskie zapiski
Kommersant
Komsomol'skaia pravda
Literaturnaia gazeta
Moscow Guardian
Moscow Magazine
Moscow News
Moscow Revue
Moscow Times, www.moscowtimes.ru
Moscow Tribune
Moskovskie novosti
Moving Pictures
New York Times
Nezavisimaia gazeta
Novoe russkoe slovo
Novyi mir
Ogonek
Panorama

Pravda
RFE/RL Newsline
Rossiiskaia gazeta
Seans
Segodnia, www.segodnia.ru
Sight & Sound
SKIF (*Sputnik kinofestivalia*)
SMI (*Sredva massovoi informatsii*), www.smi.ru
Sovetskii ekran
Stolitsa
Variety
Video-Ass
Washington Post
We/My
Wide Angle

Filmography

American Daughter (*Amerikanskaia doch'*. Karen Shakhnazarov, 1995)
Armavir (*Armavir*. Abdrashitov and Mindadze, 1991)
Assassin of the Tsar, The (*Tsareubiitsa*. Karen Shakhnazarov, 1991)
Autumn Marathon (*Ocennii marafon*. Georgii Daneliia, 1980)
Barber of Siberia, The (*Sibirskii tsiriul'nik*. Nikita Mikhalkov, 1998)
Brother (*Brat*. Alexei Balabanov, 1997)
Brother 2 (*Brat 2*. Alexei Balabanov, 2000)
Burnt by the Sun (*Utomlennye solntsem*. Nikita Mikhalkov, 1994)
Captain's Daughter, The (*Russkii bunt*. Aleksandr Proshkin, 1999)
Carnival Night (*Karnaval'naia noch'*. El'dar Riazanov, 1956)
Checkpoint (*Blokpost*. Aleksandr Rogozhkin, 1998)
Chicha (*Chicha*. Vitalii Mel'nikov, 1992)
Children of the Iron Gods (*Deti chugunnykh bogov*. Tomasz Tot, 1993)
Circus (*Tsirk*. Grigorii Aleksandrov, 1936)
Cloud-Heaven (*Oblako-rai*. Nikolai Dostal', 1991)
Coal Miners (*Zaboi*. Vladimir Molchanov, 1991)
Communist, The (*Kommunist*. Iulii Raizman, 1958)
Dreams (*Sny*. Karen Shakhnazarov, 1993)
Dreams of an Idiot (*Mechty idiota*. Vasilii Pichul, 1993)
Drum Roll (*Barabaniada*. Sergei Ovcharov, 1993)
Duba-duba (*Diuba-diuba*. Aleksandr Khvan, 1993)
Encore, Once More, Encore! (*Ankor, eshche ankor!* Petr Todorovskii, 1992)
Foretelling, The (*Predskazanie*. El'dar Riazanov, 1994)
Get Thee Hence! (*Izydi!* Dmitrii Astrakhan, 1991)
Golden Mountains (*Zlatye gory*. Sergei Iutkevich, 1931)
Gongofer (*Gongofer*. Bakhit Kilibaev, 1993)
Gray Wolves (*Serye volki*. Igor' Gost'ev, 1993)
Great Criminal Revolution, The (*Velikaia kriminal'naia revoliutsiia*. Stanislav Govorukhin, 1994)
Hammer and Sickle (*Serp i molot*. Sergei Livnev, 1994)

House Under the Starry Sky, The (Dom pod zvezdnym nebom. Sergei Solov'ev, 1991)
Heads or Tails (Orel i reshka. Georgii Daneliia, 1995)
Humiliated and Insulted (Unizhennye i oskarblennye. Andrei Eshpai, 1991)
I Walk Around Moscow (Ia shagaiu po Moskve. Georgii Daneliia, 1963)
In That Land (V toi strane. Lidiia Bobrova, 1997)
Inner Circle, The (Kinomekhanik Stalina. Andrei Konchalovskii, 1992)
Inspector General (Revizor. Sergei Gazarov, 1996)
Iron Curtain, The (Zheleznyi zanaves. Savva Kulish, 1997)
Khrustalyov, My Car! (Khrustalev, mashinu! Alexei German, 1998)
Land of the Deaf (Strana glukhikh. Valerii Todorovskii, 1997)
Limita (Limita. Denis Evstigneev, 1994)
Little Giant with a Big Sex Drive (Malen'kii gigant bol'shogo seksa. Nikolai Dostal', 1992)
Love (Liubov'. Valerii Todorovskii, 1992)
Luna Park (Luna Park. Pavel Lungin, 1992)
Makarov (Makarov. Vladimir Khotinenko, 1993)
Migrants (Migranty. Valerii Premykhov, 1992)
Moloch (Molokh. Aleksandr Sokurov, 1999)
Moscow (Moskva. Aleksandr Zel'dovich, 1999)
Moscow Parade (Prorva. Ivan Dykhovichnii, 1992)
Mother and Son (Mat' i syn. Aleksandr Sokurov, 1997)
Muslim, The (Musulmanin. Vladimir Khotinenko, 1995)
Nastya (Nastia. Georgii Daneliia, 1993)
New Babylon (Novyi Vavilon. Grigorii Kozintsev and Leonid Trauberg, 1929)
Non-Love (Neliubov'. Valerii Rubinchik, 1992)
Of Freaks and Men (Pro urodov i liudei. Aleksandr Balabanov, 1999)
Oh, You Geese! (O, vy gusy. Lidiia Bobrova, 1992)
Old Nags (Starye klyachi. El'dar Riazanov, 1999)
Old Young People (Starye molodye liudi. Oleg Shukher, 1992)
Passions (Uvlechen'ia. Kira Muratova, 1994)
Patriotic Comedy (Patrioticheskaia komediia. Vladimir Khotinenko, 1992)
Peculiarities of the National Fishing (Osobennosti natsional'nogo rybalovstva. Aleksandr Rogozhkin, 1998)
Peculiarities of the National Hunt in the Fall (Osobennosti natsional'noi okhoty osen'iu. Aleksandr Rogozhkin, 1995)
Peculiarities of the National Hunt in the Winter (Osobennosti natsional'noi okhoty zimoi. Aleksandr Rogozhkin, 2000)
Peshawar Waltz, or Escape from Afghanistan (Peshavarskii val's. Timur Bekmambetov and Gennadii Kaiumov, 1993)
Piebald Dog Running Along the Sea Shore (Pegii p'es begashchii po beregu moria. Chingiz Aitmatov, 1991)

Play for a Passenger (P'esa dlia passazhira. Abdrashitov and Mindadze, 1995)
Prisoner of the Mountains (Kavkazskii plennik. Sergei Bodrov, Sr., 1996)
Promised Skies, The (Obetovannye nebesa. El'dar Riazanov, 1991)
Purgatory (Chistilishche. Aleksandr Nevzorov, 1997)
Retro Triangle (Retro vtroem. Petr Todorovskii, 1998)
Romanovs: The Crowned Family, The (Romanovy: ventsenosnaia sem'ia. Gleb Panfilov, 2000)
Russia We Lost, The (Rossiia, kotoruiu my poteriali. Stanislav Govorukhin, 1992)
Russian Ark (Russkii kovcheg. Aleksandr Sokurov, 2002)
Russian Uprising (see *Captain's Daughter)*
Ryaba My Chicken (Kurochka Riaba. Andrei Konchalovskii, 1994)
Scientific Section of Pilots (Nauchnaia sektsiia pilotov. Andrei I, 1996)
See Paris and Die (Uvidet' Parizh i umeret'. Aleksandr Proshkin, 1993)
Sentimental Policeman (Chuvstvitel'nyi militsioner. Kira Muratova, 1992)
Summer Folk (Letnie liudi. Sergei Ursuliak, 1995)
Summer to Remember, A (Serezha. Georgii Daneliia and Igor Talankin, 1960)
Sympathy Seeker (Sirota kazanskaia. Vladimir Mashkov, 1997)
Tale of the Unextinguished Moon (Povest' o nepogashennoi lune. Evgenii Tsymbal, 1990)
Thief, The (Vor. Pavel Chukhrai, 1997)
Three Stories (Tri istorii, Kira Muratova, 1997)
Time for Sadness Has Not Yet Come, The (Vremia pechali eshche ne prishlo. Sergei Sel'ianov, 1995)
Time of the Dancer (Vremia tantsora. Abdrashitov and Mindadze, 1997)
Tractor Drivers 2 (Traktoristy 2. Igor and Gleb Aleinikov, 1992)
Urga, Land of Love (Urga, zemlia liubvi. Nikita Mikhalkov, 1991)
Voroshilov Marksman, The (Voroshilovskii strelok. Stanislav Govorukhin, 1999)
You Are My Only One (Ty u menia odna. Dmitrii Astrakhan, 1993)
Weirdoes (Choknutye. Alla Surikova, 1991)
Window on Paris (Okno v Parizh. Yurii Mamin, 1994)

Index

Headings or subheadings in *italic type* are films unless otherwise indicated. Page locators in *italic* indicate the presence of a photograph on that page.

Abdrashitov, Vadim: *Armavir*, 155–56; *Play for a Passenger*, 156; *Time of the Dancer*, 156–60; *Train Stopped, The*, 156
Abdulov, Alexander, 200
abroad: as thematic element, 190
Achalov, Vladislav, 68
Afghan war: films about, 226–28
Africans: intolerance of, 123–24
Aitmatov, Chingiz, 178, 194
Akhedzhanova, Lia, 250
Alexandrov, Grigory, 26
alienation, post-Soviet, 137
Alknis, Viktor, 231
All-Russian Exhibition Center, 142
Amarcord, 155
A-market, 279
American Daughter, 192–93, *193*
American Embassy Press and Culture section, 1, 8
Americom Business Centers, 103. *See also* Tatum, Paul
Americom House of Cinema, 105–6, 109–10

Americom Moscow Art Gallery, 106
Ananishnov, Alexei, 201
Andrei I., 224
Andrei Rublev, 63, 259
And the Ship Sails, 155
Angel Day, 24
Anglisky Dvor, 258
Anninsky, Lev, 91
Anpilov, Viktor, 66, 68
anthem, Soviet national, 27
antiquity: as thematic element, 214
Arabov, Yuri, 207
Arlecchino (restaurant/bar), 261, 264
Armadillo (restaurant/bar), 264
Armavir, 155–56
Asians: intolerance of, 123
Assa, 206
assassinations: entertainment industry, 20–21; Paul Tatum, 102–3
Assassin of the Tsar, The, 53–57, 266
Association of Film and Video Distributors (ASKIN), 16
Asthenic Syndrome, 210
Astrakhan, Dmitry: *Get Thee Hence!*, 184; *You Are My Only One*, 190–92
Asya's Happiness, 179
Autumn Marathon, 200

Bakhtin, Mikhail, 204
Balabanov, Alexei: *Brother*, 128–30;

Brother 2, 24, 130–31; *Of Freaks and Men*, 204–6
Ballad of a Soldier, 173
Baltschug-Kempinsky hotel, 111
Baluev, Alexander, 113
Banyan, Ludwig, 26
Barber of Siberia, The: American perspective, 94–95; criticism of, 90–92; ideology, 95–96; Mikhalkov in, 94; politics behind, 92; production costs, 15; promotion of, 92–94; still photos, *93*
Barkashov, Alexander, 68, 121–22
Basilashvili, Oleg, 154, 266
Batalov, Nikolay, 161
Battleship Potemkin, 52
Bed and Sofa, 160
Bekmambetov, Timur, 227
Bellingham, Lynda, 96
Belopolskaya, Viktoria, 91
Belovezhskaya Pushcha meeting, 50
Belyavsky, Alexander, 62
Berezovsky, Boris, 20, 23, 230
Beriozka stores, 280–81
Bern Convention, 17
Black Rose Is a Symbol of Sorrow, 206
Blok (restaurant), 261
Bobrova, Lidya: *Oh, You Geese!*, 178–80; *In That Land*, 180
Bodrov, Sergei, Jr., 128, 228
Bogomolov, Yuri, 91
Boiler Room (in *Three Stories*), 212
Bondarchuk, Sergei, 34
Bonner, Elena, 45
Borisov, Oleg, 127
Bormann, Martin, 208
Borovoy, Konstantin, 48
Branagh, Kenneth, 109
Braun, Eva, 207–9, 290
Bronze Horseman, The (poem), 202
Brother, 24, 128–30, *129*

Brother 2, 24, 130–31, *131*
Buldakov, Alexander, 288
Bunker (nightclub), 264
Burnt by the Sun: catered to Hollywood, 21; foreign success, 75; themes, 75–77
Bush, George H.W., 17–18
Bychkov, Victor, 288
Bykov, Rolan, 62–63

California: as movie backdrop, 192
Cannes Film Festival: flops, 86; prize winners, 75, 125; Tagi-zade's extravagance at, 15
capitalist democracy: critics of, 5; disillusionment with, 51; Konchalovsky on, 183; unnatural in Russia, 2
Captain's Daughter: cinematography, 88–89; funding for, 88; historical perspective, 89–90; plot, 86–88; Polish leads, 90; produced by NTV-Profit, 23; still photos, *87, 89*
Captain's Daughter (novella), 86
Carnival Night, 250
Cassandra's Brand (novel), 194
Cathedral of Christ the Savior, 143
Catherine the Great, 86
Caucasus: as thematic element, 239–40
censorship: abolished, 179
Central Archive of the October Revolution, 55
Central House of Artists, 66
Central Lenin Museum, 216
Championship Golf Course, 265
Chance distribution company, 18–19
Chancellor, Richard, 258
Chechen conflict, films about: *Checkpoint*, 235–40; *Prisoner of the Mountains*, 228–30, *229*; *Purgatory*, 230–34

Checkpoint: narrative devices, 238–39; plot, 235–38; produced by Selyanov, 24; still photos, *237*; strategy, 235; subtext, 239–40
Chernomyrdin, Viktor, 18, 175
Cherry Orchard (play), 98
Chicha, 254–55
Children of the Iron Gods: aesthetics, 216–17; American inspiration, 217; episodic nature, 219–20; at Moscow International, 175; soundtrack, 218–19; still photos, *218*
Chukhrai, Grigory, 173
Chukrai, Pavel: childhood memories, 79–80; limited success, 13; *Thief, The*, 79–82
Churikova, Inna, 96, 181
cinema. *See* film industry
Cinema House, 165
Cinema Service, 35–36
Circus, 114, 222
classical antiquity: as thematic element, 214
Clear Sky, 173
Clinton, William Jefferson, 108–9
Close to Eden, 177–78
Cloud-Heaven, 252–53
Club Metelitsa (casino), 264
Coal Miners (TV documentary), 46-47
Cold Summer of '53, The, 152
comedies: *Inspector General*, 242–44; *Peculiarities of National Fishing*, 235, 288–89; *Peculiarities of the National Hunt in the Fall*, 235, 288–89; *Peculiarities of the National Hunt in the Winter*, 235, 288–89; *Weirdoes*, 257
Communist, The, 217
Communist Party, 4–5, 121
Congress of People's Deputies, 67–68
Congress of the Filmmakers Union: Mikhalkov elected by, 27–28; at Palace of Congresses, 29–30
consumerism: in Moscow, 271
copyright laws, 17–18
Cossacks of Kuban (operetta), 284
Courier, 227, 266
Crystal Palace, 25
Custine, Marquis de, 258

dachas: privatization, 187–88; Soviet-assigned, 187; as state of mind, 186
Dachniki (play), 187
Damiecki, Mateus, 90
Danelia, Georgi: *Autumn Marathon*, 200; *I Walk Around Moscow*, 199; *Nastya*, 199–201; *Summer to Remember, A*, 199
Daniloff, Nicholas, 166
Dark Nights in Sochi, 255
Davidovich, Lolita, 59
Delon, Alain, 177
democracy, capitalist: critics of, 5; disillusionment with, 51; Konchalovsky on, 183; unnatural in Russia, 2
democracy, managed, 5
De Niro, Robert, 174
Depardieu, Gerard, 174
department stores, Western-style, 277–78
Detsky Mir, 277
diaries, foreign, 258
Dobrotvorskaya, Karina, 91
Dome Cinema, 110
Donbas miners: strike documentary, 46–47
Dondurei, Danil, 14, 172
Dontsov-Dreiden, Sergei, 270
Dostal, Nikolay: *Cloud-Heaven*, 252–53; *Little Giant with a Big Sex Drive*, 253–54
Dostal, Vladimir, 32, 33
Dostoevsky, Fyodor, 54, 202

Dreams, 266–68
Dreams of an Idiot, 255–57, *256*
drive-in theaters, 25–26
Drum Roll: at Moscow International, 175; plot, 285–86; social commentary, 287–88; still photos, *286*; themes, 286–87
Duba-duba, 127–28
Durov, Lev, 198
Dykhovichny, Ivan: limited success, 13; *Moscow Parade*, 220–22, *221*
Dzerzhinsky, Felix, 48–49
Dzhigarkhanyan, Armen, 193
Dziga and His Brothers, 24

Eastman Kodak, 23, 110
Eccentrism, 163
Echo radio station, 24
economy: 1998 regression, 25; film industry and, 12; post-Soviet, 3–4
Egorova, Natalya, 126–27
8 and 1/2, 173
Eisenstein, Sergei, 52–53, 217
embassies, foreign, 1, 8, 166–67
Encore, Once More, Encore!, 60–61
English Merchant Adventurers' Co., 258
Ernst, Konstantin, 171
Eshpai, Andrei: *Humiliated and Insulted*, 202–4, *203*; limited success, 13
Europeanization, 2–3
Evstigneev, Denis, 118–19, 126
Excellence on Reporting on Russia Award, 107
expatriates, in Moscow, 109

Faces of Love festival, 172–73
fairy tales: movies as, 198
Fall of the Romanov Dinasty, The, 53
Far Away, So Close, 175

farmers markets, 281–82
fascist organizations, 121
fast-food restaurants, 262–63
Fatalist, The (story), 240
fate: as thematic element, 238–39
Fathers and Sons, 175
Federal Law for the Support of Cinema, 22
Fedotov, Pavel, 60–61
Fellini, Federico, 173, 174
feminism, in screenplays, 210
Film Art (journal), 14, 22
film festivals: Faces of Love, 172–73; Kinotavr, 170–72; Moscow International. *See* International Moscow Film Festival; Non-Stolen Cinema, 19; as propaganda, 169; Second Premiere, 19
film industry: assassinations, 20–21; financial crisis, 13–14; freedom within, 38; government saves, 22; identity quest, 6; liberalization and, 12–13, 14; mid-1990s decline, 75; Moscow's image in, 111–12; nostalgia in, 27; piracy, 17–20; post-Soviet distress, 12; producers, 21–23; production costs, 14–15; re-emergence of, 5; under Soviet regime, 53
Filmmakers Union of Russia: Congress of, 27–30; Kinocenter and, 19; Solovyov and, 176; sponsors Moscow International, 175; Tagi-zade and, 16
Fogel, Vladimir, 161
folk tales: as film motif, 179
Fomenko, Nikolay, 199
Fora-Film: piracy fought by, 18–19; Razumovsky founds, 37
foreign embassies, 1, 8, 166–67
Foretelling, The, 153–54
Forgotten Melody for Flute, 165

Index

Forman, Milos, 174
Fortcor (supermarket), 279
Foucault, Michel, 51
Freedom Bonds, 105
Freedom of the Press Award, 107
French society: portrayed in film, 269
Frunze, Mikhail, 57. *See also Tale of the Unextinguished Moon*
Fund for the Development of Cinema, 29

Gaft, Valentin, 61, 198, 251
Gagarin, Yuri, 173
Gaidar, Yegor, 3, 71
Galibin, Alexander, 96
Garage, 249
Garbo, Greta, 167
Garden Ring Supermarket, 279
Gazarov, Sergei: *Inspector General*, 242–44
Gemini Film, 110
Georgetown University, 9
Gere, Richard, 176
Get Thee Hence!, 184
Gevorkian, Karen, 178
Geyer, Gudrun, 201
Gherman, Alexei: at Experimental Films, 25; *Khrustalyov, my car!*, 83–86; lengthy projects, 13; *My Friend Ivan Lapshin*, 77
Giller, Boris, 192
Gladilshchikov, Yuri, 91
glasnost: censorship abolished, 179; democratic reforms, 50; film production under, 53; Pamyat and, 122
Goebbels, Josef, 208
Gogol, Nikolay, 241, 243, 244, 283
Golden Calf, The (novel), 255–57
Golden Mountains (film), 26
Golden Ring Entertainment, 23, 110
golf courses, 265
Golubkov, Lyonya, 246
Golutva, Alexander: on ASKIN, 16; deputy minister of culture, 36; heads Goskino, 31; heads Lenfilm, 15
Gongofer, 283–85
Gorbachev, Mikhail: fall of, 49–50; in film cameo, 175; ousted, 11
Gorbushka video market, 17
Gore, Albert, Jr., 108–9
Gorky, Maxim, 187
Gorky Studio: films produced by, 24, 194; Grammatikov heads, 35; new wave filmmakers and, 215–16
Goskino: abolished, 35; films stolen from, 19; funding from, 22, 172; Medvedev resigns, 31
Gostev, Igor: *Gray Wolves*, 61–64
Govorukhin, Stanislav: *Great Criminal Revolution, The*, 65–66; political career, 65; as reactionary, 132; *The Russia We Lost*, 64–65; as screenwriter, 90; *This is No Way to Live*, 64; *Voroshilov Marksman, The*, 131–37
Grachev, Pavel, 43, 70, 71
Grachev, Vladimir, 96
Grammatikov, Vladimir, 35
Grand Prix de Jury winners: *Burnt by the Sun*, 75; *Drum Roll*, 288
Gray Wolves, 61–63, 63
Great Criminal Revolution, The, 65–66
Grebnev, Anatoly, 153
Greek Restaurant, The, 261
grotesque, films of the, 202
Gruszka, Karolina, 90
Gurchenko, Ludmila, 250, 251
Guseva, Larisa, 265
Gusinsky, Vladimir, 34
Gusman, Yuly, 200
Gutin, Andrei, 126, 127

Haapsalo, Ville, 289
Hammer and Sickle, 222–24, 223

Index 339

Hammer and Sickle (metallurgic plant), 147
hardware stores, Western-style, 277
Harris, Richard, 94
Hartman, Arthur, 167
Hermitage Gardens and Theater, 118
Hermitage (nightclub), 264
Heth, Paul, 23, 110
Hiatt, Fred, 267
historical films, 51–53
Hitler, Adolf: film portrayals of, 206–9; neo-Nazis and, 121; at "The Circus", 290
Hotel National, 111, 142
Hotel Pullman, 261
hotels, Soviet: American investment in, 103–5, 111
House of Cinema, Americom, 105–6, 109–10
House Under the Starry Sky, The, 206
Hulce, Tom, 59
Humiliated and Insulted, 202–4, 203, 204

Ibragimbekov, Rustam, 51
identity: role of film in, 6; Russia's quest for, 3; as thematic element, 184
independents (nezavisimye), 164–65
Initsiativa distribution company, 18–19
Inner Circle, The, 19, 59–60
Inspector General, 242–44
Inspector General (play), 241–42
Intellectual Property Agency, 18
intelligentsia: films about, 153; foreign community and, 165–66
Intercar Colognia (supermarket), 279
Intergirl, 61
International Expocenter, 261
International Moscow Film Festival: in decay (1993), 175; funding for, 175–76; Mikhalkov as president, 177; old era (1989), 174–75; origin, 173; ORT events, 20; piracy discussion, 18; prestige lost (1997), 176; prize winners, 173–74, 176, 288; re-emergence of (1999), 177; Solovyov as president, 176–77
International Press Center and Club, 106–7
International Youth Festival, 78
In That Land, 180
Intourist, 103
Irish House (pub), 264
Iron Curtain, The, 78–79
Is It Easy to Be Young?, 120
Iskander, Fazil, 253
Iskona Film, 227
Itogi (magazine), 24
Ivan syndrome, 60
I Walk Around Moscow, 199

Jacob, Irene, 154
Jancso, Miklos, 172
Jazzmen, 266
Jewish film themes, 148–49
Jews for Jesus, 122
joint ventures, with foreign partners: films, 21, 59; hotels, 103–5, 111; Kodak-Kinomir, 23
Julius Meinl (supermarket), 279

Kachalina, Ksenia, 150
Kalinka-Stockmann (supermarket), 279
Kalugin, Oleg, 45
Kalyuta, Vilen, 178
Kantemirov Motorized Division, 69, 71
Kara, Yuri, 194
Karamzin, Nikolay, 133
Katya (landlady), 139, 144–47, 276, 290
Kayumov, Gennady, 227
Kennan Institute for Advanced Russian Studies, 9
Khasbulatov, Ruslan, 68, 69, 74

Khazanov, Gennady, 45–46, 253
Khmelik, Maria, 255
Khokhlova, Alexandra, 163
Khomatova, Chulpan, 195
Khotinenko, Vladimir: *Makarov*, 154–55; *Muslim, The*, 182, 183–84; *Patriotic Comedy*, 265–66
Khrushchev, Nikita, 61–64
Khrustalyov, my car!: narrative device, 83; plot, 85–86; still photos, *84*
Khudozhestvenny: modernization of, 25
Khvan, Alexander: *Duba-duba*, 127–28
Kilibaev, Bakhyt: *Gongofer*, 283–85
Kinoatele (journal), 176
Kinocenter: Filmmakers Union and, 19; modernization, 25; restaurants in, 261
kinodroms (drive-in theaters), 25–26
Kino-MOST, 33
Kinotavr film festival, 170–72, 288
Kinski, Nastassia, 174, 203
kiosks, 273–76
Klimov, Elem, 13, 53
Kmit, Ekaterina, 284
Kodak-Kinomir (Kodak-Cinema World), 23, 110
Kolenda, Svetlana, 211
Komsomol Square, 99
Konchalovsky, Andrei: *Asya's Happiness*, 179; *Inner Circle, The*, 19, 59–60; *Ryaba My Chicken*, 181, 183, 282
Konchalovsky, Pyotr, 76
Korea House, 261
Korzun, Dina, 195
Kozintsev, Grigori, 111
Kozlov, Sergei, 217
Kravchuk, Leonid, 50
Kredo-Aspek distribution company, 18–19
Krylov, Sergei, 256

Kulish, Savva: *Iron Curtain, The*, 78–79; on Russian film industry, 21–22
Kupchenko, Irina, 251
Kushner, Barry, 227
Kutepova, Polina, 200
Kutuzov, Mikhail, 234

Ladynina, Marina, 26
Land of the Deaf, 195, 195–98
Law on Cinema: relief due to, 33; tax breaks under, 24
Lebed, Alexander, 43
Le Chalet (restaurant), 261
Lelouche, Claude, 175
Le Meridien/Forte (hotel), 111
Lemper, Ute, 221
Lenfilm studio: financing, 21; First and Experimental Films, 25; funding problems, 32; Golutva heads, 15; Sergeev heads, 31
Lenin, Vladimir, 49, 56, 65, 111, 216, 260, 291
Lermontov, Mikhail, 240
Lev Lvovich, 281
Liberal Democratic Party, 5, 121
liberalization, 12–14
Limita, 118–19, *119*
Little Giant with a Big Sex Drive, 19, 253–54
Little Girl and Death, The (in *Three Stories*), 213–14
Little Vera, 255
Litvinova, Renata, 150, 194, 210, 211, 213
Livanov, Igor, 156
Livnev, Sergei, 24, 194
Logovaz holdings, 24
Lollobrigida, Gina, 173
Love, 148–49, *149*
Love Triangle, 160
LSDance (nightclub), 264

Index

Lukomore, 169
Luna Park, 125–27, *126*
Lungin, Pavel: *Luna Park*, 125–27
Lutsik, Pyotr, 215, 283
Luzhkov, Yuri: Barkashov clashes with, 121; City Property Committee under, 104; Moscow festival funding, 175; Mosfilm grant, 32; personal power, 142
Lyubshin, Stanislav, 150

Makarov, 154–55
Makashov, Albert, 68, 231
Makovetsky, Sergei, films acted in: *Captain's Daughter*, 90; *Of Freaks and Men*, 205; *Makarov*, 154; *Patriotic Comedy*, 265; *Play for a Passenger*, 156; *Retro Triangle*, 161, 163; *Three Stories*, 212
Malikov, Dmitri, 152
Mamin, Yuri: *Window on Paris*, 21, 268–71, *270*
Mamonov, Pyotr, 185
Manezh Shopping Center, 278–79
Manezh Square rally, 39–47
Man from Boulevard des Capucines, The, 257
Manhattan-Express (lounge), 264
Man of Marble, 223
markets, farmers, 281–82
Markovich, Raymond, 23, 110
Martynov, Ivan, 284
Marvin's Room, 176
Mashkov, Vladimir: in *American Daughter*, 192; in *Captain's Daughter*, 86; directorial debut with *Sympathy Seeker*, 198–99; in *Limita*, 118
Matizen, Viktor, 90
Mavrodi, Sergei, 244, 248
Mayakovsky Square, 11
McDonald's restaurant, 142, 262–63
McDowell, Malcolm, 54

Media-MOST, 23, 24, 34
Medvedev, Armen: on copyright law, 18; heads Goskino, 22; resigns from Goskino, 31
Melnikov, Vitaly: *Chicha*, 254–55
memoirs, foreign, 258
Menshikov, Oleg: in *Barber of Siberia*, 95; in *Burnt by the Sun*, 76; in *Dubaduba*, 127; in *Prisoner of the Mountains*, 228
metro, Moscow, 224–26
Metropol, 111, 142
Metropol (almanac), 253
Meyerhold, Vsevolod, 242
Mezhdunarodnaya Hotel, 111
middle class: emergence of, 4; Moscow population, 110
Migrants, 119–20
Mikhalchenko, Viktor, 232
Mikhalkov, Nikita: Cinema Development fund and, 29; directs *Barber of Siberia*, 90–96; directs *Burnt by the Sun*, 21, 75–78; directs *Oblomov*, 140; directs *Urga, Land of Love*, 177–78; elected by Filmmakers Union, 27–28; family history, 76; in *Humiliated and Insulted*, 203; in *Inspector General*, 242; in *I Walk Around Moscow*, 200; political ambitions, 92; presides at Moscow International, 177; on Union Congresses, 30
Mikhalkov, Sergei, 27, 76
Mikhalkova, Nastya, 77
military coup, attempted: photographs, *40*, *42*, *44*; rally during, 39–47; vengeance after, 48–49
Mindadze, Alexander: *Armavir*, 155–56; *Play for a Passenger*, 156; *Time of the Dancer*, 156–60; *Train Stopped, The*, 156
Ministry of Culture: Goskino absorbed into, 35–36

Mirgorod (book), 283
Mironov, Evgeny, 61, 118, 183, 242
M. Leader (supermarket), 279
MMM investment company: advertising, 244, 246; closure, 247–49; film studio, 283; high-tech cooperative, 245–46; holdings grow, 246; pyramid scheme, 246–47; Shareholders Union, 248
Molchanov, Vladimir, 46–47
Moloch: Lenfilm produces, 32; plot, 208–9; still photos, *207*; themes, 206–7
money exchange, 274
Monicelli, Mario, 177
Monroe, Marilyn, 150
monuments, national, 48–49
Mordvinova, Marina, 266
Mordyukova, Nonna, 127
Mores, Paul, 175
Moscow: business holdings, 142; department stores, 277–78; expatriate population, 109; farmers markets, 281–82; foreigner compounds, 257–58; golf courses, 265; kiosks, 273–75; metro, 224; nightlife, 263–65; open-air markets, 271–73; portrayed in films, 111–12; restaurants, 260–63; smoking in, 262; state of emergency, 71; supermarkets, 279–80; Western community, 174
Moscow: cinematography, 113–14; imagery, 114, 116; plot, 112–13; still photos, *113*, *115*; subtext, 112; surrealism, 116–17
Moscow Anti-Fascist Center, 121
Moscow Bombay, 261
Moscow Central Market, 142
Moscow Circus, 289
Moscow City Property Committee, 104
Moscow Commercial Club, 261
Moscow Country Club, 265
Moscow Directors Guild, 21–22
Moscow Film Distribution Bureau, 15
Moscow Film Festival. *See* International Moscow Film Festival
Moscow Parade, 220–22, *221*
Moscow Times, The (newspaper): ads for foreigners, 260; at Radisson-Slavyanskaya, 107
Mosfilm: logo, 27; Media-MOST bid, 34; privatization, 33–35; Shakhnazarov heads, 32–33; Soyuz division, 21
MosIntour, 104
Most-Media, 18–19
Mother and Son, 201
Motion Picture Export Association of America (MPEA), 17–18
movie magazines, 27
Mozgovoy, Leonid, 207
Much Ado about Nothing, 109
Mukhina, Vera, 27
Muratova, Kira: *Asthenic Syndrome*, 210; Litvinova collaboration, 150; *Passions*, 150, 210–12, *211*; returns to filmmaking, 209; *Sentimental Policeman*, 210; *Three Stories*, 212–15
Muslim, The, 182, 183–84, 227
My Friend Ivan Lapshin, 77
mythmaking: as thematic element, 222

Nagiev, Dmitri, 233
Nalivka compound, 257–58
Nashi, political party, 231
Nastya, 199–201
national anthem, Soviet, 27
national film: tax exemption for, 33
National Gallery of Art, 9
Natural School, 244
Naumov, Vladimir, 21
Nemetskaya Sloboda, 258
neo-Nazi movements, 121–22

Nevzorov, Alexander: career history, 230–31; *Purgatory*, 230–34
New Babylon, 111
new wave filmmakers, 215–16
New World (journal), 57
Neyolova, Marina, 190
Nezavisimaya gazeta (newspaper), 24
nezavisimye (independents), 164–65
Nicholas II. *See* Romanov, Nicholas II
Night Flights (nightclub), 264
nightlife: post-Soviet, 263–65; Soviet-era, 260
Nika Award: established, 173; winners, 155
Nikitin Gates, 165
Nikolaev, Valery, 200
Ninotcha, 167
Non-love, 149–50, *151*
Non-Stolen Cinema festival, 19
Novo-Ogarevo treaty, 50
NTV-Profit, 23

Oblomov, 140
Of Freaks and Men, 24, 204–6
Ogonyok (magazine), 24, 55
Oh, You Geese!, 178–80
Old Nags, 142, 250–51, *251*, 282
Old Young People, 153
oligarchs, 4, 133
OMOM troops, 67, 68–70
open-air markets, 271–73
Ophelia (in *Three Stories*), 213
Orbakayte, Kristina, 118
Ormond, Julia, 94
Orthodox Church: conservatism and, 37; kiosk sponsored by, 275
ORT television network: films produced by, 23; *Purgatory* on, 230
ORT-Video, 19–20
Oscar, Russian (Nika Award): established, 173; winners, 155
Ostankino, 70, 121
Ovcharov, Sergei: *Drum Roll*, 285–88, *286*

Palace of Congresses: *Barber of Siberia* premiere, 92; Union Congresses at, 29–30
Pamyat, 122
Panfilov, Gleb: lengthy projects, 13; *Romanovs, The: The Crowned Family*, 96–99
Panfilov, Ivan, 96
Panteleevsky Dvor, 277
paradise lost: as thematic element, 177
Paris: portrayed in film, 186
Parliament, 67–68
Parsons, Peggy, 9
Passions, 150, 210–12, *211*
Pasternak, Boris, 189
Patio Pizza, 261
Patrice Lumumba University, 123
Patriotic Comedy, 265–66
pavilions. *See* kiosks
Pavlov, Stas, 113
Pavlova, Irina, 91
Peculiarities of National Fishing, 235, 288–89
Peculiarities of the National Hunt in the Fall, 24, 235, 288–89
Peculiarities of the National Hunt in the Winter, 235, 288–89
Penta Renaissance Hotel, 110
People's Vengeance Square, 99
Peredelkino, 187
perestroika: portrayed in film, 181; property rights, 140–43; restaurants and nightlife, 260
Pescatore, 261
Peshawar Waltz, 227–28
Peter the Great, 2–3
Petliura's (nightclub), 264

Petrushevskaya, Ludmila, 210
Pichul, Vasily: *Dark Nights in Sochi*, 255; *Dreams of an Idiot*, 255–57, *256*; limited success, 13; *Little Vera*, 255
Piebald Dog Running Along the Sea Shore, A, 178
Pilnyak, Boris, 57, 59
Pilot/Soho (nightclub), 264
piracy, 17–19, 273
Piramida distribution company, 18–19
Pirozhok, Igor, 122
Pizza Hut, 142
Play for a Passenger, 156
Polovtsev, Alexander, 287
Poor Liza (novella), 133
postmodern scholarship, 7
Potel & Chabot, 261
Premykhov, Valery, 119–20, 184
Press and Culture section, 1, 8
press awards, 107
Prisoner of the Caucasus, The (story), 228–29
Prisoner of the Mountains, 192, 228–30, *229*
Private Vices, Public Virtues, 172
privatization: dachas, 187–88; Mosfilm, 33–35; real estate, 140–43
producers: emergence of, 21–23
production costs, 14–15
Promised Skies, The, 249
Pronin, Viktor, 132
propaganda: film industry and, 51
Prorva, 220–22, *221*
Proshkin, Alexander: *Russian Uprising*, 86–90; *See Paris and Die*, 151–52
prospectors, foreign, 259
Pugachev, Emelyan, 86–89, 291
Pugacheva, Alla, 264, 291
Purgatory: atrocities in, 232–33; characters, 233–34; on ORT, 230; plot, 231–32

Pushkin, Alexander: *Bronze Horseman* (poem), 202; *Captain's Daughter* (novella), 86
Pushkin Movie Theater, 25
Putin, Vladimir, 5, 27
pyramid schemes, 246–47
Pyrev, Ivan, 26

Quiet Days in Clichy, 172

Radisson Hotels International, 103
Radisson-Slavyanskaya Hotel, 105–8
Rasputin, 53
rave parties, 263
Razovsky, Mark, 165
Razumovsky, Andrei, 37
real estate, 140–43
Redgrave, Vanessa, 177
Red Square, *272*
restaurants: fast food, 262–63; foreign-owned, 260–63; smoking in, 262
Resurs Bank, 175
Retro Triangle: characters, 160–61; plot, 160; still photos, *161*; themes, 162–64
Richard, Pierre, 177
Rogozhkin, Alexander: *Checkpoint*, 235–40; *Peculiarities of National Fishing*, 235, 288–89; *Peculiarities of the National Hunt in the Fall*, 235, 288–89; *Peculiarities of the National Hunt in the Winter*, 235, 288–89
Romanov, Nicholas II: assassination movies, 53–57; canonized, 99; film portrayals of, 65, 98; at "The Circus," 290
Romanovs, The: The Crowned Family: Chekhovian motif, 98; Nicholas rehabilitated in, 53–54; overall message, 99; production, 96; still photos, *97*
Room, Abram, 160

Rosie O'Grady's (pub), 264
Rossiia Movie Theater, 25
Rozanova, Irina, 61, 254
Rozhin, Vladimir, 153
Rubinchik, Valery: *Non-love*, 149–50, 151
ruble, devaluation of, 3, 143, 145, 271
Rudinstein, Mark, 170
Rufanova, Elena, 207
Ruf Samoylovna, 281
Russian Anti-Pirate organization, 20
Russian Ark, 258
Russian Commodities Exchange, 48
Russian Culture Fund, 28
Russian National Unity, 121–22
Russian Property Committee, 104
Russian Uprising. *See Captain's Daughter*
Russia We Lost, The, 64–65
Rutskoi, Alexander, 68, 69, 72, 74
Ryaba My Chicken, 181, 183, 282
Ryabova, Svetlana, 190
Ryazan Division paratroops, 43
Ryazanov, Eldar: *Carnival Night*, 250; comedies, 153; disappointments, 13; film themes, 249–50; *Foretelling, The*, 153–54; *Garage*, 249; *Old Nags*, 142, 250–51, 251, 282; *Promised Skies, The*, 249

Sadko Arcade, 261, 277
Sadko (supermarket), 279
Samoryadov, Alexei, 215, 283
Santa Fe (restaurant), 262
satire, Soviet, 249
Saving Private Ryan, 52
Savoy Club, 264–65
Savoy Hotel, 111
Schindler's List, 18, 122
Scientific Section of Pilots, 224
Screen (magazine), 27

Second Premiere festival, 19
See Paris and Die, 151–52
Segodnya (newspaper), 24
Selyanov, Sergei: *Brother*, 128; comments on *Purgatory*, 232; films produced by, 24; *Time for Sadness Has not yet Come, The*, 184–86
Semenova, Ludmila, 160
Sentimental Policeman, 210
Serebriany Bor, 187
Serebryakov, Alexei, 222
Sergeev, Viktor, 31
Serp i molot (*Hammer and Sickle*), 222–24, 223
Serp i molot (metallurgic plant), 147
Shakhnazarov, Karen: *American Daughter*, 192–93; *Assassin of the Tsar, The*, 53, 266; *Courier*, 227, 266; disappointments, 13; *Dreams*, 266–68; heads Mosfilm, 32–33; *Jazzmen*, 266; *Zero City*, 266
Shamrock Pub, 264
Shevardnadze, Eduard, 46
Shevchenko, Elena, 198
Shindo, Kaneto, 177
Shklovsky, Viktor, 160
Shmyrov, Vyacheslav, 19
shopping malls, 277–78
Shostakovich, Dmitri, 26
Shub, Esther, 53
Shukher, Oleg, 153
Shukshin, Vasily, 179
Shushkevich, Stanislav, 50
shuttles (kiosk suppliers), 275–76
Shvydkoi, Mikhail, 36
Sidikhin, Evgeny, 161, 163, 216, 222
Simanovich, Grigory, 20
Sinyakina, Anna, 133
Sirivlya, Natalya, 91
skinheads: Africans hated by, 123–24; film portrayals of, 125–28; neo-Nazis,

121–23; working class advocates, 123–24
Slavyanskaya Hotel, 104, 105–8
soap operas: as film genre, 61
Sokolov, Andrei, 154
Sokurov, Alexander: art films by, 13; *Moloch*, 32, 206–9, *207*; *Mother and Son*, 201; *Russian Ark*, 258
Solovyov, Sergei: disappointments from, 13; films directed by, 206; presides at Moscow International, 176–77
Song of the Motherland, 114
Sorel, Agnes, 269
sotsart, 216
Soviet Screen (magazine), 27
Spaso House, 167
Spielberg, Steven, 18
Square of the Ascension, 99
Stalin, Joseph: film portrayals of, 60; Frunze assassination, 59; Pilnyak story banned by, 57; at "The Circus," 290–91
Stalinist era, films about: *Burnt by the Sun*, 75–78; *Cold Summer of '53, The*, 152; *Hammer and Sickle*, 222–24, *223*; *Iron Curtain, The*, 78–79; *Khrustalyov, my car!*, 83–86; *Prorva*, 220; *Scientific Section of Pilots*, 224; *Thief, The*, 79–82
Starlite Diner, 261
Star Wars: The Phantom Menace, 18
State Extraordinary Committee, 41, 45
Steklov, Vladimir, 59, 194
Stepanov, Viktor, 233, 284
Stepashin, Sergei, 177
St. Petersburg: as film setting, 151, 202, 204
Studio of First and Experimental Films, 25
stukachi, 166
STV company, 24

Summer Folk, 187
Summer to Remember, A, 199
summit, Clinton-Yeltsin 1994, 108–9
supermarkets, 279–80
Supreme Soviet of the Russian Republic, 47–48
Surikova, Alla, 257
Suvorov, Alexander Vasilevich, 234
Sympathy Seeker, 198–99

Tabakov, Oleg, 198, 214
Tagi-zade, Izmail Suleimanovich, 15–17
Talankin, Igor, 199
Tale of the Unextinguished Moon, 57–59, *58*
Taman 2nd Motorized Rifle Division, 69, 71
Tarkovsky, Andrei: *Andrei Rublev*, 63, 174, 259; *Ivan's Childhood*, 174
Tasbulatova, Dilyara, 91
Tatum, Paul: American hotel venture, 103–5; assassination of, 102–3; film industry connections, 105–6; legal representation for, 110
Taxi Blues, 125
Terekhov, Stanislav, 68
Thief, The: historical perspective, 81–82; produced by NTV-Profit, 23; still photos, *80*, *81*; themes, 79–80; variant endings, 82
This is No Way to Live, 64
Three Stories, 212–15
Time for Sadness Has not yet Come, The, 24, 184–86
Time of the Dancer: characters, 158–59; director speaks about, 156–58; still photos, *157*
Timofeevsky, Alexander, 164
TISKINO studio, 16
Todorovsky, Mira, 162

Todorovsky, Pyotr: *Encore, Once More, Encore!*, 60–61; *Intergirl*, 61; *Retro Triangle*, 160–64; *Wartime Romance*, 61
Todorovsky, Valery: *Land of the Deaf*, 194–98; *Love*, 148–49; successes, 13
Tolstoy, Leo, 228–29
Tolstunov, Igor, 23
Topadze, Tomaz, 20–21
Torsen, Jens, 172
Tot, Tomasz: *Children of the Iron Gods*, 215–20; limited success, 13
Tractor Drivers 2, 150
Train Stopped, The, 156
Trauberg, Leonid, 111
travel restrictions, 152
TrenMos Bar, 264
Tretyakovka distribution company, 18–19
Triangle Rubber Co., 258
TriTe studio, 28
Trofimenko, Mikhail, 91
Troshin, Alexander, 91
Tsar Ivan the Terrible, 15
Tsereteli, Zurab, 278
Tsymbal, Evgeny: *Defense Counsel Sedov*, 59; *Dziga and His Brothers*, 24; limited success, 13; *Tale of the Unextinguished Moon*, 57
Tumba Golf Course, 265

Udarnik theater, 25–26
Ulyanov, Mikhail, 132, 133
Union of Officers Party, 68
Urbansky, Evgeny, 217
Urga, Land of Love, 177–78
Usatova, Nina, 183

Valenti, Jack, 18
Variety Theater, 26
Varus Video, 20
Vasileva, Tatyana, 152

Verbitsky, Viktor, 227
Vertov, Dziga, 217
vigilantism: in *Voroshilov Marksman*, 136–37
Viktoria Club, 122
village: as thematic element, 178–79, 180
Vlasov, Yuri, 45
Volodin, Alexander, 201
Voroshilov Marksman, The, 23; conservative ideology, 131–32; moral message, 136–37; plot, 133–36; still photos, *134*

Wartime Romance, 61
Wednesday Women, The (novel), 131
Weirdoes, 257
Wenders, Wim, 175
Werewolf Legion, 122–23
Western lifestyle: film reactions to, 265; as promised land, 190
Whitbeck, Allison, 192
White House: battle for, 72–75; images of, *40*, *42*, *44*; rebels trapped in, 67–68; tanks fire at, *72*, *72*
Window on Paris, 21, 268–71, *270*
Winter Theatre, 170
Woodrow Wilson International Center for Scholars, 9
Workers Party, 66–67

Yakovleva, Elena, 160, 163
Yakunin, Gleb, 45
Yanaev, Gennady, 46
Yankovsky, Oleg, 54
Yekaterinburg-ART distribution company, 18–19
Yeltsin, Boris: address during coup attempt, 43, 47; Belovezhskaya Pushcha meeting, 50; economic reform attempts, 3; image stained,

75; media support for, 24; orders troops to capital, 70, 74; Parliament dissolved by, 67–68; popularity, 50–51
Yevtushenko, Evgeny, 45
York, Michael, 177
You Are My Only One, 190–92
Yurkov, Dmitri, 227
Yurovsky, Yakov, 53, 290
Yurovsky Note, 55–56
Yusov, Vadim, 220
Yutkevich, Sergei, 26

Zaks, Jerry, 176
Zaychenko, Pyotr, 88, 177, 183
Zbruev, Alexander, 190
Zeldovich, Alexander: *Moscow*, 112–18
Zero City, 266
Zhemchuzhina (Pearl) hotel, 170
Zhigalov, Andrei, 252
Zhilkin, R., 233
Zhukovka enclave, 187
ZIS (*Zavod imeni Stalina*), 85
Zolotukha, Valery, 154, 183
Zyuganov, Gennady, 5

Printed in the United States
25789LVS00004B/34-36